Complete American Presidents Sourcebook

Complete American Presidents Sourcebook

Volume 2
William Henry Harrison through Andrew Johnson
1841–1869

Roger Matuz
Lawrence W. Baker, Editor

AN IMPRINT OF THE GALE GROUP

DETROIT · NEW YORK · SAN FRANCISCO
LONDON · BOSTON · WOODBRIDGE, CT

Complete American Presidents Sourcebook

Roger Matuz

Staff

Lawrence W. Baker, *U•X•L Senior Editor*
Gerda-Ann Raffaelle, *U•X•L Contributing Editor*
Carol DeKane Nagel, *U•X•L Managing Editor*
Thomas L. Romig, *U•X•L Publisher*

Rita Wimberley, *Senior Buyer*
Dorothy Maki, *Manufacturing Manager*
Evi Seoud, *Assistant Manager, Composition Purchasing and Electronic Prepress*
Mary Beth Trimper, *Manager, Composition Purchasing and Electronic Prepress*

Cynthia Baldwin, *Senior Art Director*
Michelle DiMercurio, *Senior Art Director*
Kenn Zorn, *Product Design Manager*

Shalice Shah-Caldwell, *Permissions Associate (text and pictures)*
Maria L. Franklin, *Permissions Manager*
Kelly A. Quin, *Editor, Imaging and Multimedia Content*
Pamela A. Reed, *Imaging Coordinator*
Leitha Etheridge-Sims, *Image Cataloger*
Mary Grimes, *Image Cataloger*
Robert Duncan, *Imaging Specialist*
Dan Newell, *Imaging Specialist*
Randy A. Bassett, *Image Supervisor*
Barbara J. Yarrow, *Imaging and Multimedia Content Manager*

Marco Di Vita, Graphix Group, *Typesetting*

Library of Congress Cataloging-in-Publication Data

Matuz, Roger.
    Complete American presidents sourcebook / Roger Matuz ; Lawrence W. Baker, editor.
        p. cm.
    Includes bibliographical references and indexes.
    ISBN 0-7876-4837-X (set) — ISBN 0-7876-4838-8 (v. 1) — ISBN 0-7876-4839-6 (v. 2) — ISBN 0-7876-4840-X (v. 3) — ISBN 0-7876-4841-8 (v. 4) — ISBN 0-7876-4842-6 (v. 5)
        1. Presidents—United States—Biography—Juvenile literature. 2. Presidents' spouses—United States—Biography—Juvenile literature. 3. United States—Politics and government—Sources—Juvenile literature. I. Baker, Lawrence W. II. Title.

E176.1 .M387 2001
973'.09'9—dc21
[B]
                                                            00-056794

Cover illustration of Abraham Lincoln is reproduced courtesy of the Library of Congress; Franklin and Eleanor Roosevelt, reproduced by permission of the Corbis Corporation; George W. Bush, reproduced by permission of Archive Photos; Thomas Jefferson, reproduced by permission of the National Portrait Gallery, Smithsonian Institution; Washington Monument, reproduced by permission of PhotoDisc, Inc.; Clintons, Bushes, Reagans, Carters, and Fords, reproduced by permission of Archive Photos; Theodore Roosevelt, reproduced by permission of Archive Photos.

Printed in the United States of America

10 9 8 7 6 5 4 3 2 1

Contents

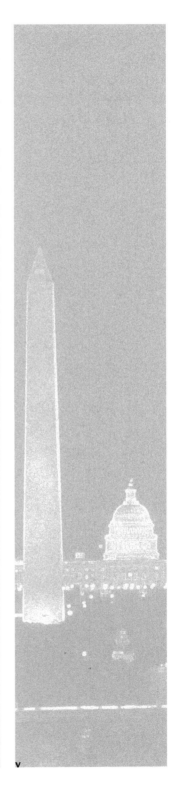

Volume 2

Volume 3

Volume 5

Reader's Guide

An "embarrassed pause" fell on the gathering of delegates at the Constitutional Convention of 1787 when James Wilson of Pennsylvania suggested the idea of a chief executive. Wanting "no semblance of a monarch," as Edmund Randolph of Virginia put it, delegates moved on to other matters.

So went the first real "discussion" about the office of president, according to Virginia delegate James Madison. Madison, later nicknamed "the Father of the Constitution," took lengthy notes on the proceedings. They were published in 1840 in a book, *Journal of the Federal Convention*.

The Convention was called to address the weakness of the American government formed under the Articles of Confederation that was approved in 1781. By the end of the Convention of 1787, delegates had cautiously agreed on a new system. They had debated ideas of government ranging in history from ancient Greece and Rome to the "Age of Enlightenment" (eighteenth century) in Europe; they considered the workings of the Iroquois confederacy of Native American tribes as well as the state governments in America; and they held to their ideals of liberty and their dislike of monarchy, a system in which one person rules a country for life. The delegates eventually returned to Wilson's suggestion and debated it. The new system of government they cautiously agreed to in the end did indeed include an elected chief executive—the president.

"President" was a title used for the position of governor in three states—Delaware, Pennsylvania, and New Hampshire. They were among the first nine states to ratify the Constitution, helping provide the majority (nine of thirteen states) needed for the Constitution to become legally binding.

The process of ratification was not easy. In Virginia, for example, which finally approved the Constitution in 1788 by a slim majority (89-79), there were significant concerns about the powers of the president. Former Continental congressman and former Virginia governor Patrick Henry called it "a squint toward monarchy."

The delegates of Virginia, however, had an example of the kind of leader envisioned when the office of president was created. George Washington had presided over the Constitutional Convention. He introduced no ideas and seldom participated in debates, but he kept delegates focused on the cause of improving the system of government. Washington was known for his honesty and for not being overly ambitious. Americans had turned to him to lead their military struggle in the Revolutionary War (1775–81). After the Constitution was ratified (approved), delegates turned to him to lead the new nation as its first president.

Washington's example as president reveals the realities of political leadership. He was voted unanimously into office, and left office in the same high regard, but he had faced resistance in between. Some viewed his version of the federal government as being too powerful: he had called on state militias to put down a rebellion in Pennsylvania against taxes; and for economic reasons, he sided in foreign relations with Great Britain—still a hated enemy to some Americans—over France, the nation that had assisted Americans in winning independence.

Washington was among those presidents who made firm decisions, then awaited the consequences. Some had viewed the presidency as being more impartial. Such are the perils of the presidency. John Adams, the second president, followed the more forceful actions of members of his party and became so unpopular that he had no real hope for reelection. Thomas Jefferson, whose ideals shaped the Declaration of Independence, lost much popularity by the time he left office as the third president. Jefferson had ordered foreign trade restrictions to assert America's strength and to demand respect from Great Britain and France, but the action ended up hurting the American economy.

Like the Constitution, the office of the president was never intended to be perfect. The Constitution is flexible, meant to be used and adapted to form "a more perfect union." The presidency has ranged at times from being a near monarchy to having little real strength. President Andrew Jackson was dubbed "King Andrew" by his opponents, who felt he overstepped his power in several instances. Franklin D. Roosevelt was given tremendous powers and support, first in 1933 to combat the effects of the Great Depression (1929–41), and later to direct the nation's economy during World War II (1939–45). But when Roosevelt tried to change the Supreme Court, he was met with swift criticism. Roosevelt was the only president elected to office four times, the last time being 1944. (In 1945, he died only three months into his fourth term.) By 1951, a constitutional amendment was passed to limit presidents to two terms in office.

Other presidents were far less powerful or effective. Prior to the Civil War, two presidents from the North (Franklin Pierce and James Buchanan) supported the rights for states to decide whether to permit slavery. Abraham Lincoln was elected to challenge that notion, and the Civil War (1861–65) followed. Lincoln took a more aggressive approach than his two predecessors, and he emerged in history as among the greatest presidents.

After Lincoln's assassination in 1865, the presidency was dominated by Congress. In 1885, future president Woodrow Wilson criticized that situation in a book he wrote, *Congressional Government,* while he was a graduate student at Johns Hopkins University. By the time Wilson was elected president in 1912, a series of strong presidents—Grover Cleveland, William McKinley, and Theodore Roosevelt—had reasserted the president's power to lead.

The presidency, then, has passed through various stages of effectiveness. The dynamics of change, growth, and frustration make it fascinating to study. Different ideas of leadership, power, and the role of government have been pursued by presidents. Chief executives have come from various backgrounds: some were born in poverty, like Andrew Johnson and Abraham Lincoln, and others had the advantages of wealth, like the Roosevelts and Bushes; some were war heroes, like Ulysses S. Grant and Dwight D. Eisenhower, others were more studious, like Thomas Jefferson and Woodrow Wilson. Some came to the presidency by accident, like John Tyler and Gerald R. Ford, others campaigned long and hard for the position, like Martin Van Buren and Richard Nixon.

There are various ways to present information on the presidency. In 2000, a Public Broadcasting System (PBS) television series called *The American President* divided presidents into ten categories (such as presidents related to each other, those who were prominent military men, and chief executives who became compromise choices of their parties). The same year, a group of presidential scholars also used ten categories (such as crisis leadership, administrative skills, and relations with Congress) to rank presidents in order of effectiveness

Complete American Presidents Sourcebook uses a chronological approach, beginning with George Washington in 1789, and ending with George W. Bush in 2001. Each president's section contains three types of entries.

Biography of the president

Each of the forty-two men who have served in the nation's top political office is featured in *Complete American Presidents Sourcebook.*

- Each entry begins with a general overview of the president's term(s) in office, then follows his life from birth, through his service as president, to his post-presidency (if applicable).

- Outstanding events and issues during each presidential administration are described, as are the president's responses in his role as the nation's highest elected official.

- Sidebar boxes provide instant facts on the president's personal life; a timeline of key events in his life; a "Words to

Know" box that defines key terms related to the president; results of the president's winning election(s); a list of Cabinet members for each administration; and a selection of homes, museums, and other presidential landmarks.

- A final summary describes the president's legacy—how his actions and the events during his administration influenced the historical period and the future.

Biography of the first lady

Forty-four first ladies are featured in *Complete American Presidents Sourcebook*. Though some of the women died before their husbands became president, all had an important influence on the men who would serve as president. The profiles provide biographical information and insight into the ways in which the women lived their lives and defined their public roles. Like the presidents, first ladies have responded in different ways to their highly public position.

Primary source entry

Another important feature of interest to students is a selection of forty-eight primary source documents—speeches, writings, executive orders, and proclamations of the presidents. At least one primary source is featured with each president.

In the presidents' own words, the documents outline the visions and plans of newly elected presidents, the reasons for certain actions, and the responses to major world events. Students can learn more about key documents (such as the Declaration of Independence and the Monroe Doctrine); famous speeches (such as George Washington's Farewell Address and Abraham Lincoln's Gettysburg Address); presidential orders (the Emancipation Proclamation issued by Abraham Lincoln in 1863 and Harry S. Truman's executive order on military desegregation in 1946); responses to ongoing issues, from tariffs (William McKinley) to relations between the government and Native Americans (Chester A. Arthur); different views on the role of the federal government (from extensive programs advocated by Franklin D. Roosevelt and Lyndon B. Johnson, to reducing the influence of government by Warren G. Harding and Ronald Reagan); and many inaugural addresses, including the memorable speeches of Abraham Lincoln and John F. Kennedy.

Each document (or excerpt) presented in *Complete American Presidents Sourcebook* includes the following additional material:

- **Introduction** places the document and its author in a historical context.

- **Things to remember** offers readers important background information and directs them to central ideas in the text.

- **What happened next** provides an account of subsequent events, both during the presidential administration and in future years.

- **Did you know** provides significant and interesting facts about the excerpted document, the president, or the subjects discussed in the excerpt.

- **For further reading** lists sources for more information on the president, the document, or the subject of the excerpt.

Complete American Presidents Sourcebook also features sidebars containing interesting facts and short biographies of people who were in some way connected with the president or his era. Within each entry, boldfaced cross-references direct readers to other presidents, first ladies, primary sources, and sidebar boxes in the five-volume set. Finally, each volume includes approximately 70 photographs and illustrations (for a total of 350), a "Timeline of the American Presidents" that lists significant dates and events related to presidential administrations, a general "Words to Know" section, research and activity ideas, sources for further reading, and a cumulative index.

This wealth of material presents the student with a variety of well-researched information. It is intended to reflect the dynamic situation of serving as the leader of a nation founded on high ideals, ever struggling to realize those ideals.

Acknowledgments from the author

Many individuals, many institutions, and many sources were consulted in preparing *Complete American Presidents Sourcebook*. A good portion of them are represented in bibliographies and illustration and textual credits sprinkled throughout the five volumes. The many excellent sources and the ability to access them ensured a dynamic process that made the project lively and thought-provoking, qualities reflected in the presentation.

Compilation efforts were organized through Manitou Wordworks, Inc., headed by Roger Matuz with contributions from Carol Brennan, Anne-Jeanette Johnson, Allison Jones, Mel Koler, and Gary Peters. On the Gale/U•X•L side, special recognition goes to U•X•L publisher Tom Romig for his conceptualization of the project. Thanks, too, to Gerda-Ann Raffaelle for filling in some editorial holes; Pam Reed, Kelly A. Quin, and the rest of the folks on the Imaging team for their efficient work; and Cindy Baldwin for another dynamite cover.

The author benefited greatly through his association and friendship with editor Larry Baker and his personal library, tremendous patience, and great enthusiasm for and knowledge of the subject matter.

Finally, with love to Mary Claire for her support, interest (I'll miss having you ask me the question, "So what new thing did you learn about a president today?"), and understanding from the beginning of the project around the time we were married through my frequent checking of the latest news before and after the election of 2000.

Acknowledgments from the editor

The editor wishes to thank Roger Matuz for a year and a half of presidential puns, for putting up with endless Calvin Coolidge tidbits, and—above all—for producing a tremendously solid body of work. You've got my vote when Josiah Bartlet's time in office is up. Thank you, Mr. Author.

Thanks also to typesetter Marco Di Vita of The Graphix Group who always turns in top-quality work and is just a lot of fun to work with; Terry Murray, who, in spite of her excellent-as-usual copyediting and indexing, still couldn't resist suggesting a sidebar for Zachary Taylor's horse, Old Whitey (um, no . . . maybe if we do *Complete American Presidents' Pets Sourcebook);* and proofer Amy Marcaccio Keyzer, whose sharp eye kept the manuscript clean and whose election e-mails kept me laughing.

In addition, the editor would be remiss if he didn't acknowledge his first family. Decades of thanks go to Mom & Dad, for starting it all by first taking me to the McKinley Memorial in Canton, Ohio, all those years ago. Love and appreciation go to editorial first lady Beth Baker, for putting up with all of the presidential homes and museums and grave markers and books, but who admits that touring FDR's Campobello during a nor'easter storm is pretty cool. And to Charlie & Dane—please don't fight over who gets to be president first!

Finally, a nod to Al Gore and George W. Bush for adding some real-life drama to the never-ending completion of this book . . . and who *did* fight over who got to be president first!

Comments and suggestions

We welcome your comments on the *Complete American Presidents Sourcebook* and suggestions for other topics in history to consider. Please write: Editors, *Complete American Presidents Sourcebook,* U•X•L, 27500 Drake Rd., Farmington Hills, Michigan 48331-3535; call toll-free: 800-877-4253; fax to 248-414-5043; or send e-mail via http://www.galegroup.com.

Timeline of the American Presidents

1776 The Declaration of Independence is written, approved, and officially issued.

1781 The Articles of Confederation are approved, basing American government on cooperation between the states. Congress is empowered to negotiate treaties, but has few other responsibilities.

1787 A national convention called to strengthen the Articles of Confederation develops the U.S. Constitution instead, defining a new system of American government. The powers of Congress are broadened. Congress forms the legislative branch of the new government, and the Supreme Court forms the judicial

1773 Boston Tea Party takes place.

1783 Beethoven's first works are published.

1787 The first hydrogen balloon is launched.

1770 1775 1785 1787

branch. An executive branch is introduced and will be led by an elected official, the president. The president and vice president are to be inaugurated on March 4 of the year following their election (a date that remains in practice until 1933, when the Twentieth Amendment is ratified, changing inauguration day to January 20).

1787   Three of the original thirteen colonies—Delaware, Pennsylvania, and New Jersey—ratify the Constitution, thereby becoming the first three states of the Union.

1788   Eight of the original thirteen colonies—Georgia, Connecticut, Massachusetts, Maryland, South Carolina, New Hampshire, Virginia, and New York—ratify the Constitution, thereby becoming the fourth through eleventh states of the Union. The Constitution becomes law when New Hampshire is the ninth state to ratify it (two-thirds majority of the thirteen states had to approve the Constitution for it to become legally binding).

1789   One of the original thirteen colonies—North Carolina—ratifies the Constitution, thereby becoming the twelfth state of the Union.

1789   The first presidential election is held. Voting is done by electors appointed by each state, and the number of electors are based on the state's population. Each elector votes for two candidates. Whomever finishes with the most votes becomes president, and whomever finishes second becomes vice president.

1789   Revolutionary War hero George Washington is elected president, receiving votes from each elector.

1789   The French Revolution begins.

1787
Dollar currency is introduced in the United States.

1788
New York City becomes the temporary U.S. capital.

1789
U.S. Army is established.

1787   1788   1789

1789   George Washington is inaugurated in New York City. A site for the national capital is selected along the Potomac River in Washington, D.C., and the federal government will be situated in Philadelphia, Pennsylvania, until the new capital is completed.

1789   One of the original thirteen colonies—Rhode Island—ratifies the Constitution, thereby becoming the thirteenth state of the Union.

1789   Political factions solidify. Federalists, who support a strong federal government, are led by Secretary of the Treasury Alexander Hamilton, and Anti-Federalists, who support limited federal power and strong states' rights, are led by Secretary of State Thomas Jefferson.

1791   Vermont becomes the fourteenth state of the Union.

1792   President George Washington is reelected unanimously.

1792   Kentucky becomes the fifteenth state of the Union.

1794   American forces defeat a confederacy of Native American tribes at the Battle of Fallen Timbers in Ohio, opening up the midwest for settlement.

1796   When Vice President John Adams finishes first and former Secretary of State Thomas Jefferson finishes second in the presidential election, two men with conflicting political views and affiliations serve as president and vice president. Political parties—the Federalists and the Democratic-Republicans—become established.

1796   Tennessee becomes the sixteenth state of the Union.

1798   The United States engages in an undeclared naval war with France.

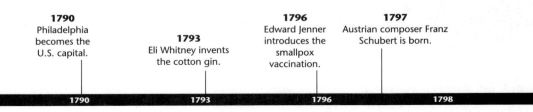

1790
Philadelphia becomes the U.S. capital.

1793
Eli Whitney invents the cotton gin.

1796
Edward Jenner introduces the smallpox vaccination.

1797
Austrian composer Franz Schubert is born.

1790   1793   1796   1798

1798 Federalists in Congress pass and President John Adams signs into law the Alien and Sedition Acts. The laws, which expand the powers of the federal government, prove unpopular and bolster the prospects of anti-Federalists.

1800 The seat of government moves from Philadelphia, Pennsylvania, to Washington, D.C.; President John Adams and first lady Abigail Adams move into the White House (officially called The Executive Mansion until 1900).

1800 In the presidential election, Vice President Thomas Jefferson and former New York senator Aaron Burr (both of the Democratic-Republican Party) finish tied with the most electoral votes. The election is decided in the House of Representatives, where Jefferson prevails after thirty-six rounds of voting.

1803 The historic *Marbury v. Madison* decision strengthens the role of the U.S. Supreme Court to decide constitutional issues.

1803 The Louisiana Purchase more than doubles the size of the United States.

1803 Ohio becomes the seventeenth state of the Union.

1804 The Twelfth Amendment to the Constitution mandates that electors must distinguish between whom they vote for president and vice president (to avoid repeating the problem of the 1800 election, where most voters selected both Jefferson and Burr with their two votes).

1804 President Thomas Jefferson wins reelection. He selects a new running mate, New York governor George Clinton, to replace Vice President Aaron Burr.

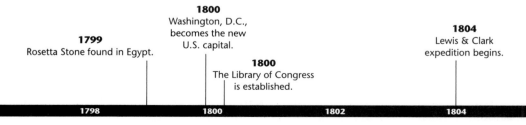

1799
Rosetta Stone found in Egypt.

1800
Washington, D.C., becomes the new U.S. capital.

1800
The Library of Congress is established.

1804
Lewis & Clark expedition begins.

1798   1800   1802   1804

1804 After losing an election for governor of New York, outgoing vice president Aaron Burr kills former U.S. secretary of the treasury Alexander Hamilton in a duel. Hamilton had influenced voters against Burr in the presidential campaign of 1800 and during Burr's campaign to be governor of New York in 1804.

1806 The Lewis and Clark expedition, commissioned by President Thomas Jefferson, is completed when explorers Meriwether Lewis and William Clark return to St. Louis, Missouri, after having traveled northwest to the Pacific Ocean.

1807 President Thomas Jefferson institutes an embargo on shipping to England and France, attempting to pressure the nations to respect American rights at sea. The embargo is unsuccessful and unpopular.

1807 Former vice president Aaron Burr is tried and acquitted on charges of treason.

1808 Secretary of State James Madison, the "Father of the Constitution," is elected president. Vice President George Clinton campaigns and places third as a member of the Independent Republican Party after having accepted Madison's offer to continue in his role as vice president.

1811 At the Battle of Tippecanoe, American forces (led by future president William Henry Harrison) overwhelm a Native American confederacy led by Shawnee chief Tecumseh.

1811 Vice President George Clinton casts the tie-breaking vote in the U.S. Senate (a responsibility of the vice president under the U.S. Constitution) against rechartering the National Bank, and against President James Madison's wishes.

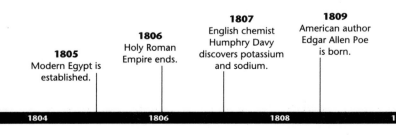

1805
Modern Egypt is established.

1806
Holy Roman Empire ends.

1807
English chemist Humphry Davy discovers potassium and sodium.

1809
American author Edgar Allen Poe is born.

| 1804 | 1806 | 1808 | 1811 |

1812	War of 1812 (1812–15) begins.
1812	President James Madison is reelected.
1812	Louisiana becomes the eighteenth state of the Union.
1813	After having suffered military defeats in Canada, U.S. naval forces win control of the Great Lakes.
1814	British military forces burn the White House and the Capitol during the War of 1812.
1815	The Battle of New Orleans, where American forces (led by future president Andrew Jackson) rout a superior British force, occurs after an armistice was agreed on, but news had not yet reached Louisiana. The War of 1812 officially ends a month later.
1816	Secretary of State James Monroe is elected president. The "Era of Good Feelings" begins: the war is over, America is expanding, and Monroe is a popular president.
1816	Indiana becomes the nineteenth state of the Union.
1817	President James Monroe moves into an incompletely reconstructed White House.
1816	Mississippi becomes the twentieth state of the Union.
1818	Illinois becomes the twenty-first state of the Union.
1819	Alabama becomes the twenty-second state of the Union.
1819	Bank Panic slows economic growth.
1820	President James Monroe is reelected by winning every state. One elector casts a vote for John Quincy Adams as a symbolic gesture to ensure that George Washington remains the only president to win all electoral votes in an election.

1812
The Brothers Grimm publish their book of fairy tales.

1814
Francis Scott Key writes the "Star Spangled Banner."

1818
Mary Shelley writes *Frankenstein.*

1818
Congress adopts a U.S. flag.

| 1812 | 1815 | 1818 | 1820 |

1820 The Missouri Compromise sets a boundary (the southern border of present-day Missouri): slavery is not permitted north of that boundary for any prospective territory hoping to enter the Union.

1820 Maine, formerly part of Massachusetts, becomes the twenty-third state of the Union.

1821 Missouri becomes the twenty-fourth state of the Union.

1823 In his annual message to Congress, President James Monroe introduces what will become known as the Monroe Doctrine. Although not very significant at the time, the Doctrine, which warns European nations against expansionist activities in the Americas, sets a foreign policy precedent several later presidents will invoke.

1824 Electoral votes are based on the popular vote for the first time. Tennessee senator Andrew Jackson bests Secretary of State John Quincy Adams with over 45,000 more popular votes and a 99-84 Electoral College lead, but does not win a majority of electoral votes, split among four candidates. The election is decided in Adams's favor by the House of Representatives. The support of powerful Speaker of the House Henry Clay, who finished fourth in the election, helps sway the House in favor of Adams. When Adams names Clay his secretary of state, Jackson supporters claim a "corrupt bargain" had been forged between Adams and Clay.

1824 John Quincy Adams is the fourth straight and last president from the Democratic-Republican Party, which held the White House from 1800 to 1829. The party splits into factions around Adams and his elec-

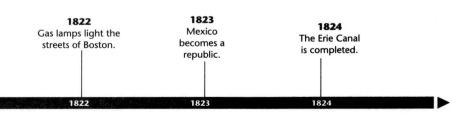

1822
Gas lamps light the
streets of Boston.

1823
Mexico
becomes a
republic.

1824
The Erie Canal
is completed.

1820   1822   1823   1824

tion opponent, Andrew Jackson (called Jacksonian Democrats), respectively.

1826   Former presidents John Adams and Thomas Jefferson die on the same day, July 4—fifty years to the day after the Declaration of Independence was officially issued.

1828   Former Tennessee senator Andrew Jackson defeats President John Quincy Adams. Modern-day political parties are established: Jackson leads the Democratic Party, and Adams leads the National Republican Party. The National Republicans are also represented in the 1832 presidential election, but most party members are joined by anti-Jackson Democrats to form the Whig Party in 1834.

1832   President Andrew Jackson is reelected. Candidates from the Nullifier Party (based on the proposition that states have the right to nullify federal laws) and the Anti-Masonic Party receive electoral votes. Future president Millard Fillmore was elected to the U.S. House of Representatives in 1831 as a member of the Anti-Masonic Party (a pro-labor group against social clubs and secret societies).

1832   The Black Hawk War leads to the taking of Native American land west to the Mississippi River. Future president Abraham Lincoln is among those fighting.

1832   President Andrew Jackson vetoes the charter for the Second National Bank (the federal banking system), creating great controversy between Democrats (favoring states' rights) and proponents for a strong federal government, who gradually unite to form the Whig Party in 1834.

1833   Running water is installed in the White House.

1826
James Fenimore Cooper writes *The Last of the Mohicans.*

1827
Contact lenses are invented.

1831
Nat Turner leads slave rebellion.

1833
The Whig Party is formed.

1826   1828   1830   1833

1834   Congress censures (publicly rebukes) President Andrew Jackson for having taken funds from the federal bank and depositing them in various state banks.

1836   Vice President Martin Van Buren is elected president after defeating three Whig candidates. Whigs hoped that their three regional candidates would win enough electoral votes to deny Van Buren a majority and throw the election to the House of Representatives, where Whigs held the majority.

1836   The last surviving founding father, James Madison, dies the same year the first president born after the American Revolution (Martin Van Buren) is elected.

1836   Arkansas becomes the twenty-fifth state of the Union.

1837   The Panic of 1837 initiates a period of economic hard times that lasts throughout President Martin Van Buren's administration.

1837   Michigan becomes the twenty-sixth state of the Union.

1840   Military hero and Ohio politician William Henry Harrision (known as "Old Tippecanoe") defeats President Martin Van Buren.

1841   President William Henry Harrison dies thirty-one days after being inaugurated president. A constitutional issue arises because the document is unclear as to whether Vice President John Tyler should complete Harrison's term or serve as an interim president until Congress selects a new president. Tyler has himself sworn in as president. Controversy follows, but Tyler sets a precedent on presidential succession.

1841   The President's Cabinet, except for Secretary of State Daniel Webster, resigns, and some congressmen con-

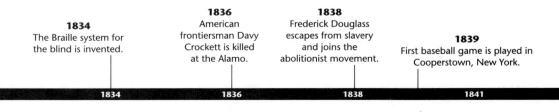

1834
The Braille system for the blind is invented.

1836
American frontiersman Davy Crockett is killed at the Alamo.

1838
Frederick Douglass escapes from slavery and joins the abolitionist movement.

1839
First baseball game is played in Cooperstown, New York.

1834   1836   1838   1841

sider impeachment proceedings against President John Tyler (but the impeachment fails to materialize). Though a member of the Whig Party, Tyler opposes the Whig program for expanding federal powers. He is kicked out of the Whig Party.

1842 The Webster-Ashburton Treaty settles a border dispute between Maine and Quebec, Canada, and averts war between the United States and Great Britain.

1844 Congress approves a resolution annexing Texas.

1844 Tennessee politician James K. Polk, strongly associated with former president Andrew Jackson, is elected president. The years beginning with Jackson's presidency in 1829 and ending with Polk's in March 1849 are often referred to historically as The Age of Jackson.

1845 Congress passes and President James K. Polk signs legislation to have presidential elections held simultaneously throughout the country on the Tuesday following the first Monday in November.

1845 Florida becomes the twenty-seventh and Texas the twenty-eighth states of the Union.

1845 The U.S. Naval Academy opens.

1846 The Mexican War begins.

1846 Iowa and Wisconsin expand the Union to thirty states.

1848 Gas lamps are installed in the White House to replace candles and oil lamps.

1848 The Mexican War ends. The United States takes possession of the southwest area from Texas to California.

1848 General Zachary Taylor, a Mexican War hero, is elected president in a close race. He had joined the Whig

1846
The Smithsonian
Institution is founded.

1844
The YMCA
is founded.

1848
First gold rush in
California begins.

| 1842 | 1844 | 1846 | 1848 |

Party but promised to remain above partisan causes and announced that he was against the expansion of slavery into new territories. Ex-president Martin Van Buren finishes a distant third as a candidate for the Free-Soil Party that also opposes the expansion of slavery into new territories. Van Buren likely drew enough votes from the Democratic candidate, former Michigan senator Lewis Cass, to tip the election to Taylor.

1849   The California Gold Rush brings thousands of people into the new American territory.

1850   President Zachary Taylor dies in office, and Vice President Millard Fillmore becomes president.

1850   President Millard Fillmore supports and signs into law the series of bills called the Compromise of 1850 that the late president Zachary Taylor had opposed. The Fugitive Slave Act, which forces northern states to return runaway slaves, becomes law.

1850   California becomes the thirty-first state of the Union.

1850   The Pony Express begins operation, providing mail service to the far west.

1852   Former New Hampshire senator Franklin Pierce is elected president.

1852   *Uncle Tom's Cabin,* by Harriet Beecher Stowe, is published and further fuels growing support in the North for complete abolition of slavery.

1853   The Gadsden Purchase adds southern areas of present-day New Mexico and Arizona as American territory.

1854   The Republican Party is formed by those against the expansion of slavery and by abolitionists wanting to outlaw the institution, drawing from the Whig Party

1851
The New York Times begins publication.

1853
Steinway pianos begin manufacturing.

1854
The Kansas-Nebraska Act returns slavery decisions to states.

1849   1850   1852   1854

(which becomes defunct) and Democrats opposed to slavery.

1854   Diplomatic and trade relations begin between the United States and Japan.

1856   Civil war breaks out in Kansas Territory between pro- and anti-slavery proponents.

1856   Former secretary of state James Buchanan, a states' rights advocate, is elected president. Former California senator John Frémont finishes second as the Republican Party's first presidential candidate. Former president Millard Fillmore finishes third with about twenty percent of the popular vote and eight electoral votes, as the nominee of the American Party (also nicknamed the Know-Nothing Party).

1857   The *Dred Scott* decision by the U.S. Supreme Court limits the power of Congress to decide on slavery issues in American territories petitioning to become states.

1858   The Lincoln-Douglas debates in Illinois, between U.S. Senate candidates Abraham Lincoln and incumbent Stephen Douglas, receive national press coverage.

1858   Minnesota becomes the thirty-second state of the Union.

1859   Abolitionist John Brown leads a raid on a federal arsenal in Harper's Ferry, Virginia (now West Virginia), hoping to spark and arm a slave rebellion.

1859   Oregon becomes the thirty-third state of the Union.

1860   Former Illinois congressman Abraham Lincoln is elected president despite winning less than forty percent of the popular vote. Democratic votes are split among three candidates. One of the party's candidates, Illi-

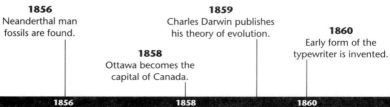

1856
Neanderthal man fossils are found.

1859
Charles Darwin publishes his theory of evolution.

1860
Early form of the typewriter is invented.

1858
Ottawa becomes the capital of Canada.

1854   1856   1858   1860

nois senator Stephen Douglas, finishes second in the popular vote but places fourth in electoral votes.

1860   South Carolina secedes from the Union.

1861   Confederate States of America formed; Civil War begins.

1861   Kansas becomes the thirty-fourth state of the Union.

1863   President Abraham Lincoln, sitting in what is now called the Lincoln Bedroom in the White House, signs the Emancipation Proclamation, freeing slaves in the states in rebellion.

1863   West Virginia becomes the thirty-fifth state of the Union.

1863   President Abraham Lincoln proposes a policy for admitting seceded states back into the Union on moderate terms.

1864   Pro-Union Republicans and Democrats unite as the National Union Party under President Abraham Lincoln (Republican) and Tennessee senator Andrew Johnson, who had remained in Congress after his southern colleagues walked out. The Lincoln-Johnson ticket wins 212 of 233 electoral votes.

1864   Nevada becomes the thirty-sixth state of the Union.

1865   The Civil War ends.

1865   President Abraham Lincoln is assassinated, and Vice President Andrew Johnson succeeds him as president.

1865   The Thirteenth Amendment to the Constitution, outlawing slavery, is ratified.

1867   Over objections and vetoes by President Andrew Johnson, Congress passes harsher Reconstruction

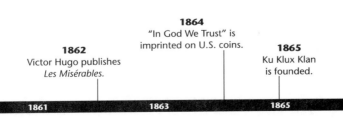

1862
Victor Hugo publishes
Les Misérables.

1864
"In God We Trust" is
imprinted on U.S. coins.

1865
Ku Klux Klan
is founded.

1861   1863   1865   1867

policies (terms under which former Confederate states can operate) than the Johnson (and Lincoln) plans.

1867 Nebraska becomes the thirty-seventh state of the Union.

1867 The United States purchases Alaska (a deal called "Seward's Folly" after Secretary of State William H. Seward, who negotiated the acquisition) from Russia.

1868 President Andrew Johnson becomes the first president to be impeached by the House of Representatives. He is acquitted by one vote in a trial in the U.S. Senate.

1868 Civil War hero Ulysses S. Grant is elected president.

1869 The Transcontinental railroad is completed.

1869 President Ulysses S. Grant fails in attempts to annex the Dominican Republic.

1872 President Ulysses S. Grant is reelected. His opponent, newspaper publisher Horace Greeley, dies shortly after the election, and his electoral votes are dispersed among several other Democrats.

1873 The Crédit Mobilier scandal reflects widespread corruption among some officials in the Ulysses S. Grant administration and some congressmen.

1876 Colorado becomes the thirty-eighth state of the Union.

1876 In the hotly contested presidential election, the Democratic candidate, New York governor Samuel J. Tilden, outpolls the Republican nominee, Ohio governor Rutherford B. Hayes, by over two hundred thousand votes, but falls one electoral vote short of a majority when twenty electoral votes (from the states of Florida, South Carolina, Louisiana, and Oregon) are contested with claims of fraud. The House of Representatives fails to resolve the issue.

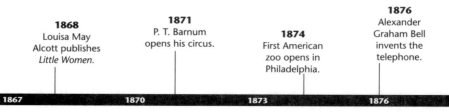

1868
Louisa May Alcott publishes *Little Women.*

1871
P. T. Barnum opens his circus.

1874
First American zoo opens in Philadelphia.

1876
Alexander Graham Bell invents the telephone.

1867   1870   1873   1876

1877   A special Electoral Commission is established to re-solve the 1876 presidential election controversy. Days before the scheduled inauguration of the new president in March, the Commission awards the 20 disputed votes to Republican Rutherford B. Hayes, who edges Democrat Samuel J. Tilden, 185-184, in the Electoral College. Some historians refer to the decision as the Compromise of 1877, believing that Republicans and southern Democrats struck a deal: Hayes would be president, and Reconstruction (federal supervision of former Confederate states) would end.

1877   Federal troops are withdrawn from South Carolina and Louisiana, where troops had been stationed since the end of the Civil War to enforce national laws. Reconstruction ends, and southern states regain the same rights as all other states.

1878   Attempting to reform the civil service (where jobs were often provided by the party in power to party members), President Rutherford B. Hayes suspends fellow Republican Chester A. Arthur (a future U.S. president) as the powerful head of the New York Custom's House (which collects import taxes).

1879   The first telephone is installed in the White House. The phone number: 1.

1879   Thomas Edison invents the incandescent light bulb.

1880   Ohio congressman James A. Garfield is elected president.

1881   President James A. Garfield is assassinated by an extremist who lost his job under civil service reform. Chester A. Arthur becomes the fourth vice president to assume the presidency upon the death of the chief executive. Like the previous three (John Tyler, Millard

1877
The first Wimbledon tennis championship is played.

1879
British Zulu War takes place.

1880
Gilbert and Sullivan compose "The Pirates of Penzance."

1877   1878   1880   1881

Fillmore, and Andrew Johnson), Arthur is not selected by his party to run for the presidency after completing the elected president's term.

1883   The Pendleton Act, mandating major civil service reform, is signed into law by President Chester A. Arthur.

1884   New York governor Grover Cleveland is elected as the first Democrat to win the presidency since 1856. Tariffs (taxes on imported goods) and tariff reform become major issues during his presidency and the following three elections.

1885   The Statue of Liberty is dedicated.

1886   President Grover Cleveland marries Frances Folsom, becoming the only president to marry at the White House.

1888   Former Indiana senator Benjamin Harrison is elected president despite receiving 90,000 fewer popular votes than President Grover Cleveland. Harrison wins most of the more populated states for a 233-168 Electoral College advantage.

1889   North Dakota, South Dakota, Montana, and Washington enter the Union, expanding the United States to forty-two states.

1890   Idaho and Wyoming become the forty-third and forty-fourth states of the Union.

1891   Electric wiring is installed in the White House.

1892   Former president Grover Cleveland becomes the first person to win non-consecutive presidential terms by defeating incumbent president Benjamin Harrison (in the popular vote *and* the Electoral College). Iowa politician James B. Weaver of the People's Party (also

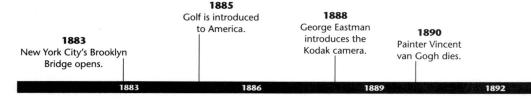

1883
New York City's Brooklyn Bridge opens.

1885
Golf is introduced to America.

1888
George Eastman introduces the Kodak camera.

1890
Painter Vincent van Gogh dies.

1883   1886   1889   1892

known as the Populists) finishes a distant third in the popular vote but garners twenty-two electoral votes.

1893 Lame duck (an official completing an elected term after having failed to be reelected) President Benjamin Harrison presents a treaty to annex Hawaii to the U.S. Congress.

1893 President Grover Cleveland rescinds former president Benjamin Harrison's treaty for the annexation of Hawaii and calls for an investigation of the American-led rebellion that overthrew the Hawaiian native monarchy.

1894 An economic downturn and numerous strikes paralyze the American economy.

1895 With gold reserves (used to back the value of currency) running low, President Grover Cleveland arranges a gold purchase through financier J. P. Morgan.

1896 Ohio governor William McKinley, the Republican Party nominee, is elected president over the Democratic candidate, former Nebraska congressman William Jennings Bryan.

1896 Utah becomes the forty-fifth state of the Union.

1898 The Spanish-American War takes place. The United States wins quickly and takes possession of overseas territories (the former Spanish colonies of Cuba, Puerto Rico, and the Philippines).

1898 President William McKinley reintroduces the Hawaii annexation issue and Congress approves it.

1899 President William McKinley expands U.S. trade with China and other nations through his Open Door Policy.

1900 President William McKinley is reelected by defeating William Jennings Bryan a second time.

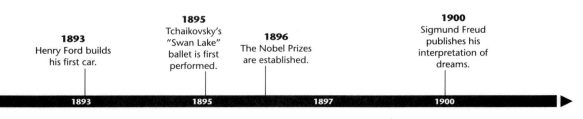

1893 Henry Ford builds his first car.

1895 Tchaikovsky's "Swan Lake" ballet is first performed.

1896 The Nobel Prizes are established.

1900 Sigmund Freud publishes his interpretation of dreams.

1893   1895   1897   1900

1900 Chinese nationalists take arms against growing foreign influences in their country, an uprising called the Boxer Rebellion. American military forces join those of other foreign nations to put down the uprising. American military forces are also stationed in the Philippines to combat revolts.

1901 President William McKinley is assassinated; Vice President Theodore Roosevelt assumes the presidency and, at age 42, becomes the youngest man to become president.

1902 To combat the growing influence of trusts (business combinations intended to stifle competition), President Theodore Roosevelt orders vigorous enforcement of antitrust laws, and an era of business and social reform gains momentum.

1903 The United States quickly recognizes and supports a rebellion in the nation of Colombia through which Panama becomes an independent nation. Through the Panama Canal treaty, which provides a strip of land to be developed by the United States, President Theodore Roosevelt spearheads plans to build a canal across Panama, linking the Atlantic and Pacific oceans.

1904 Theodore Roosevelt becomes the first president who assumed office upon the death of the elected president to win election for a full term.

1905 President Theodore Roosevelt serves as mediator during the Russo-Japanese War. His success at helping end the conflict earns him a Nobel Peace Prize.

1907 Oklahoma becomes the forty-sixth state.

1908 William Howard Taft, who served in the William McKinley and Theodore Roosevelt administrations, is

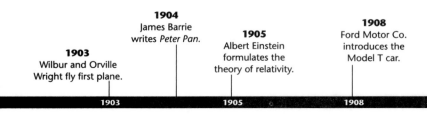

1904
James Barrie
writes *Peter Pan*.

1903
Wilbur and Orville
Wright fly first plane.

1905
Albert Einstein
formulates the
theory of relativity.

1908
Ford Motor Co.
introduces the
Model T car.

1901   1903   1905   1908

elected president. William Jennings Bryan loses in his third presidential bid.

1909 In a sign of the times, President William Howard Taft purchases official automobiles and has the White House stable converted into a garage.

1909 The North Pole is reached.

1912 New Jersey governor Woodrow Wilson is elected president. Former president Theodore Roosevelt, running as the Progressive Party candidate (nicknamed "the Bull Moose Party"), finishes second. Roosevelt outpolls his successor, President William Howard Taft, by about seven hundred thousand popular votes and wins eighty more electoral votes.

1912 New Mexico and Arizona enter the Union, expanding the United States to forty-eight states.

1912 The Sixteenth Amendment, authorizing the collection of income taxes, is ratified.

1912 The Federal Reserve, which regulates the nation's money supply and financial institutions, is established.

1913 The Seventeenth Amendment changes the system for electing U.S. senators. The popular vote replaces the system where most senators were elected by state legislatures.

1914 World War I begins.

1914 U.S. military forces begin having skirmishes with Mexican rebels in a series of incidents that last until 1916.

1914 The Panama Canal is opened.

1916 President Woodrow Wilson is reelected by a slim Electoral College margin, 277-254. He defeats the Repub-

1910
First Father's Day is celebrated.

1912
The *Titanic* hits an iceberg and sinks.

1913
The first Charlie Chaplin silent movie is released.

1915
The U.S. Coast Guard is established.

1910   1912   1914   1916

lican candidate, former U.S. Supreme Court justice Charles Evans Hughes.

1916 President Woodrow Wilson acts as mediator for the nations in conflict in World War I.

1917 Citing acts of German aggression, President Woodrow Wilson asks Congress to declare war. The United States enters World War I. The Selective Service (a system through which young men are called on for military duty) is established.

1918 World War I ends.

1919 Congress rejects the Treaty of Versailles negotiated by President Woodrow Wilson and other leaders representing the nations involved in World War I. Congress also rejects American participation in the League of Nations that Wilson had envisioned.

1919 Attempting to rally support of the Treaty of Versailles and the League of Nations during a long speaking tour, President Woodrow Wilson collapses with a debilitating stroke. The public is not made aware of the severity of the affliction that leaves Wilson bedridden.

1919 The Eighteenth Amendment, outlawing the manufacture and sale of alcohol, is ratified.

1920 Women are able to participate in national elections for the first time.

1920 Ohio senator Warren G. Harding is elected president.

1922 Illegal deals are made by some officials of the Warren G. Harding administration. Two years later, they are implicated in the Teapot Dome scandal.

1923 President Warren G. Harding dies in San Francisco, California; Vice President Calvin Coolidge assumes the presidency.

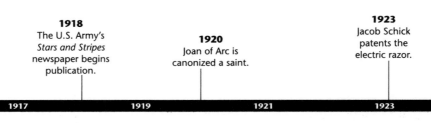

1918
The U.S. Army's *Stars and Stripes* newspaper begins publication.

1920
Joan of Arc is canonized a saint.

1923
Jacob Schick patents the electric razor.

1917   1919   1921   1923

1924 Calvin Coolidge is elected president in a landslide, defeating West Virginia politician John W. Davis, the Democratic candidate. Progressive Party candidate Robert M. LaFollette, a future Wisconsin senator, garners over thirteen percent of the popular vote and wins thirteen electoral votes.

1925 The Scopes Trial is held in Dayton, Tennessee, after a public school teacher instructs his class on the theory of evolution in defiance of a state law.

1927 Charles Lindbergh becomes the first pilot to fly solo across the Atlantic Ocean.

1928 Former secretary of commerce Herbert Hoover, who also supervised international relief efforts during World War I, wins his first election attempt in a landslide (by over six million popular votes and a 444-87 Electoral College triumph).

1929 The stock market crashes.

1930 President Herbert Hoover assures the nation that "the economy is on the mend," but continued crises become the Great Depression that lasts the entire decade.

1932 The Bonus March, in which World War I veterans gather in Washington, D.C., to demand benefits promised to them, ends in disaster and death when military officials forcibly remove them and destroy their campsites.

1932 New York governor Franklin D. Roosevelt defeats President Herbert Hoover by over seven million popular votes and a 472-59 margin in the Electoral College.

1933 President Franklin D. Roosevelt calls a special session of Congress to enact major pieces of legislation to combat the Great Depression. Over a span called The

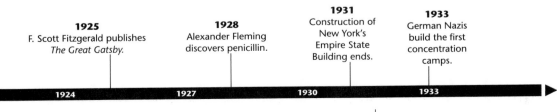

1925
F. Scott Fitzgerald publishes *The Great Gatsby.*

1928
Alexander Fleming discovers penicillin.

1931
Construction of New York's Empire State Building ends.

1933
German Nazis build the first concentration camps.

1924   1927   1930   1933

Hundred Days, much of Roosevelt's New Deal program of social and economic relief, recovery, and reform is approved.

1933 As part of the Twentieth Amendment to the Constitution, the inauguration date of the president is changed to January 20 of the year following the election.

1933 The Twenty-first Amendment repeals prohibition.

1936 President Franklin D. Roosevelt is reelected by a popular vote margin of eleven million and wins the Electoral College vote, 523-8.

1937 Frustrated when the U.S. Supreme Court declares several New Deal programs unconstitutional, President Franklin D. Roosevelt initiates legislation to add more justices to the court and to set term limits. His attempt to "stack the court" receives little support.

1939 World War II begins.

1939 Physicist Albert Einstein informs President Franklin D. Roosevelt about the possibility for creating nuclear weapons and warns him that Nazi scientists are already pursuing experiments to unleash atomic power.

1940 President Franklin D. Roosevelt wins an unprecedented third term by slightly less than five million popular votes and a 449-82 win in the Electoral College.

1941 Pearl Harbor, Hawaii, is attacked; the United States enters World War II.

1942 The success of the first nuclear chain reaction is communicated to President Franklin D. Roosevelt through the code words, "The eagle has landed." A secret program for manufacturing and testing atomic bombs begins.

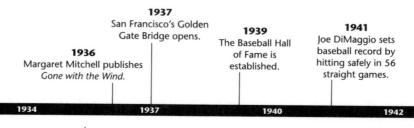

1937
San Francisco's Golden Gate Bridge opens.

1939
The Baseball Hall of Fame is established.

1941
Joe DiMaggio sets baseball record by hitting safely in 56 straight games.

1936
Margaret Mitchell publishes *Gone with the Wind.*

1934   1937   1940   1942

1944 President Franklin D. Roosevelt is elected to a fourth term by over five million popular votes and a 432-99 Electoral College triumph.

1945 President Franklin D. Roosevelt attends the Yalta Conference and meets with British prime minister Winston Churchill and Soviet leader Joseph Stalin to discuss war issues and the postwar world.

1945 President Franklin D. Roosevelt dies; Vice President Harry S. Truman becomes president. It is only then that Truman learns about development and successful testing of the atomic bomb.

1945 World War II ends in Europe.

1945 The United States drops atomic bombs on Japan. Japan surrenders, and World War II ends.

1946 The U.S. government seizes coal mines and railroads to avoid labor strikes and business practices that might contribute to inflation.

1947 An economic aid package called the Marshall Plan, named after its architect, Secretary of State George C. Marshall, helps revive war-torn Europe.

1947 The Cold War, a period of strained relations and the threat of nuclear war between the United States and the Soviet Union, and their respective allies, settles in and continues for more than forty years.

1948 Renovation of the White House begins. Four years later, the project has completely reconstructed the interior and added two underground levels.

1948 Despite the *Chicago Daily Tribune* headline "DEWEY DEFEATS TRUMAN" on the morning after election day, President Harry S. Truman wins the presidency,

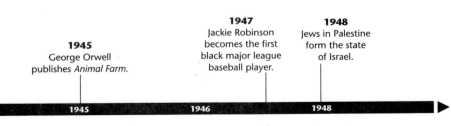

1945
George Orwell
publishes *Animal Farm.*

1947
Jackie Robinson
becomes the first
black major league
baseball player.

1948
Jews in Palestine
form the state
of Israel.

1944   1945   1946   1948

taking over two million more popular votes and winning 303-189 in the Electoral College. The State's Rights Party candidate, South Carolina governor J. Strom Thurmond, places third, slightly outpolling the Progressive Party candidate, former vice president Henry Wallace, and winning thirty-nine electoral votes. Thurmond led a contingent of Southern politicians away from the Democratic Party in protest of Truman's support for civil rights legislation.

1949   The North Atlantic Treaty Organization (NATO) is formed by the United States and its European allies to monitor and check acts of aggression in Europe.

1950   The United States becomes involved in a police action to protect South Korea from invasion by communist North Korea. The police action intensifies into the Korean War.

1951   The Twenty-second Amendment to the Constitution is ratified, limiting presidents to two elected terms and no more than two years of a term to which someone else was elected.

1952   Dwight D. "Ike" Eisenhower, famous as the Supreme Commander of Allied Forces during World War II, is elected president.

1953   An armistice is signed in Korea.

1954   The Army-McCarthy hearings are held. Wisconsin senator Joseph McCarthy presents accusations that the U.S. military and Department of State are deeply infiltrated by communists. McCarthy is eventually disgraced when most of his accusations prove groundless.

1954   In *Brown v. Board of Education,* the U.S. Supreme Court rules that racially segregated public schools are un-

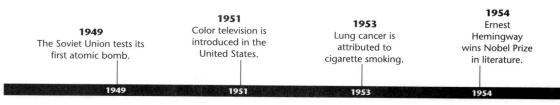

1949
The Soviet Union tests its first atomic bomb.

1951
Color television is introduced in the United States.

1953
Lung cancer is attributed to cigarette smoking.

1954
Ernest Hemingway wins Nobel Prize in literature.

1949   1951   1953   1954

constitutional. In 1957, President Dwight D. Eisenhower sends troops to Little Rock, Arkansas, to enforce desegregation of schools.

1956 An uprising in Hungary against Soviet domination is quickly crushed.

1956 President Dwight D. Eisenhower wins reelection, his second straight triumph over his Democratic challenger, former Illinois governor Adlai Stevenson.

1957 The Soviet Union launches the first space satellite, *Sputnik I.*

1958 The United States launches its first space satellite, *Explorer I,* and the National Aeronautics and Space Agency (NASA) is created.

1959 Alaska and Hawaii enter the Union as the forty-ninth and fiftieth states.

1960 The Cold War deepens over the *U2* incident, where a U.S. spy plane is shot down inside the Soviet Union.

1960 Massachusetts senator John F. Kennedy outpolls Vice President Richard Nixon by slightly more than 100,000 votes while winning 303-219 in the Electoral College. Kennedy, at age 43, is the youngest elected president. A dispute over nine thousand votes in Illinois, that might have resulted in Nixon winning that state instead of Kennedy, is stopped by Nixon. A change of electoral votes in Illinois would not have affected the overall electoral majority won by Kennedy.

1961 The District of Columbia is allowed three electoral votes.

1961 An invasion of Cuba by American-supported rebels at the Bay of Pigs fails when an internal rebellion does

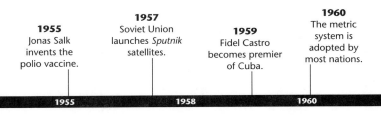

1955
Jonas Salk invents the polio vaccine.

1957
Soviet Union launches *Sputnik* satellites.

1959
Fidel Castro becomes premier of Cuba.

1960
The metric system is adopted by most nations.

1955   1958   1960   1961

not materialize and President John F. Kennedy refuses to provide military backing.

1962   The Cuban Missile Crisis puts the United States and the Soviet Union on the brink of nuclear war after the Soviets are discovered building missile launch sites in Cuba. After a tense, ten-day standoff, the missiles are removed.

1963   A military coup overthrows the political leader of South Vietnam, where American military advisors are assisting South Vietnamese to repel a communist takeover.

1963   A large civil rights march on Washington, D.C., culminates with the famous "I Have a Dream" speech by Rev. Martin Luther King Jr.

1963   President John F. Kennedy is assassinated; Vice President Lyndon B. Johnson assumes the presidency.

1964   President Lyndon B. Johnson steers major civil rights legislation through Congress in memory of the late president John F. Kennedy. The Twenty-fourth Amendment to the Constitution is ratified and ensures the right of citizens of the United States to vote shall not be denied "by reason of failure to pay any poll tax or other tax."

1964   President Lyndon B. Johnson is elected in a landslide, winning almost sixteen million more popular votes than Arizona senator Barry Goldwater.

1965   The Vietnam conflict escalates. President Lyndon B. Johnson is given emergency powers by Congress. Massive bombing missions begin, and U.S. military troops begin engaging in combat, although the U.S. Congress never officially declares war.

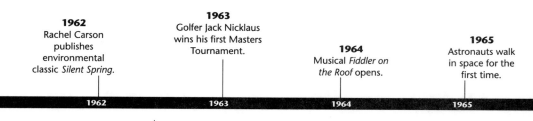

1962
Rachel Carson publishes environmental classic *Silent Spring.*

1963
Golfer Jack Nicklaus wins his first Masters Tournament.

1964
Musical *Fiddler on the Roof* opens.

1965
Astronauts walk in space for the first time.

1962   1963   1964   1965

1966 An unmanned American spacecraft lands on the moon.

1967 Protests, including a march on Washington, D.C., escalate against American involvement in the Vietnam War.

1967 Thurgood Marshall becomes the first African American Supreme Court justice.

1967 The Twenty-fifth Amendment to the Constitution is ratified and provides clear lines of succession to the presidency: "Section 1. In case of the removal of the President from office or of his death or resignation, the Vice President shall become President. Section 2. Whenever there is a vacancy in the office of the Vice President, the President shall nominate a Vice President who shall take office upon confirmation by a majority vote of both Houses of Congress."

1968 Civil rights leader Rev. Martin Luther King Jr. is assassinated in April, and leading Democratic presidential candidate Robert F. Kennedy is assassinated in June.

1968 Former vice president Richard Nixon is elected president, winning with 500,000 more popular votes than incumbent vice president Hubert H. Humphrey and a 301-191 Electoral College edge. Former Alabama governor George C. Wallace of the American Independent Party (for state's rights and against racial desegregation) nets over nine million popular votes and wins forty-six electoral votes.

1969 American troop withdrawals from South Vietnam begin.

1969 U.S. astronaut Neil Armstrong becomes the first man to walk on the moon.

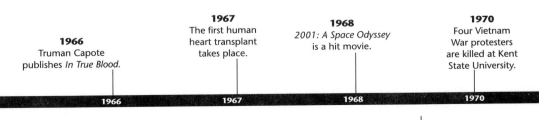

1966
Truman Capote publishes *In True Blood*.

1967
The first human heart transplant takes place.

1968
2001: A Space Odyssey is a hit movie.

1970
Four Vietnam War protesters are killed at Kent State University.

1966   1967   1968   1970

1972 President Richard Nixon reestablishes U.S. relations with the People's Republic of China that were ended after a communist takeover in China in 1949. He visits China and the Soviet Union, where he initiates a policy of détente (a relaxing of tensions between rival nations).

1972 An investigation of a burglary of Democratic National Headquarters at the Watergate Hotel and Office Complex in Washington, D.C., begins and leads to connections with officials in the Richard Nixon administration.

1972 President Richard Nixon is reelected in a landslide.

1973 The Paris Peace Agreement, between the United States and North Vietnam, ends American military involvement in the Vietnam War.

1973 Vice President Spiro T. Agnew resigns over income tax evasion; he is replaced by Michigan congressman Gerald R. Ford.

1974 Nationally televised U.S. Senate hearings on the Watergate scandal confirm connections between the 1972 burglary and officials of the Richard Nixon administration as well as abuses of power.

1974 The House Judiciary Committee begins impeachment hearings and plans to recommend to the House the impeachment of President Richard Nixon.

1974 President Richard Nixon resigns from office over the Watergate scandal. Vice President Gerald R. Ford assumes office.

1974 President Gerald R. Ford issues a pardon, protecting former president Richard Nixon from prosecution in an attempt to end "our national nightmare."

1972
Longtime FBI director J. Edgar Hoover dies.

1973
Skylab space missions take place.

1974
Hank Aaron passes Babe Ruth as baseball's all-time home run hitter.

1972   1973   1974   1975

1976   In a close election, former Georgia governor Jimmy Carter defeats President Gerald R. Ford.

1977   Beset by rising fuel costs and a continued sluggish economy, President Jimmy Carter calls an energy shortage "the moral equivalent of war" and attempts to rally conservation efforts.

1979   The Camp David Accords, the result of negotiations spearheaded by President Jimmy Carter, is signed by the leaders of Egyptian president Anwar Sadat and Israeli prime minister Menachem Begin in Washington, D.C.

1979   Fifty-two Americans are taken hostage in Iran following a religious revolution in that nation in which the American-supported leader was overthrown. The hostage crisis lasts 444 days, with the hostages released on the day President Jimmy Carter leaves office.

1980   Former California governor Ronald Reagan wins a landslide (489-49 in the Electoral College) over President Jimmy Carter. Independent candidate John Anderson, a longtime Republican congressman from Illinois, polls over five million votes. Reagan becomes the oldest president.

1981   Sandra Day O'Connor becomes the first female U.S. Supreme Court justice.

1982   Economic growth begins after a decade of sluggish performance.

1984   President Ronald Reagan is reelected in another landslide, drawing the most popular votes ever (54,455,075) and romping in the Electoral College, 525-13.

1987   A sudden stock market crash and growing federal deficits threaten economic growth.

1976 The United States celebrates its bicentennial.

1978 Pope John Paul II begins reign as leader of the Catholic Church.

1985 Microsoft releases Windows.

1986 The space shuttle *Challenger* explodes.

1976   1980   1984   1987

1988   George Bush becomes the first sitting vice president since Martin Van Buren in 1836 to be elected president.

1989   Several East European nations become independent from domination by the U.S.S.R. Reforms in the U.S.S.R. eventually lead to the breakup of the Soviet Union; the former Soviet states become independent nations in 1991, and the Cold War ends.

1991   After the Iraqi government fails to comply with a United Nations resolution to abandon Kuwait, which its military invaded in August of 1990, the Gulf War begins. Within a month, Kuwait is liberated by an international military force. President George Bush's popularity soars over his leadership in rallying U.N. members to stop Iraqi aggression.

1992   An economic downturn and a huge budget deficit erode President George Bush's popularity. Arkansas governor Bill Clinton defeats Bush for the presidency. The Reform Party candidate, Texas businessman H. Ross Perot, draws 19,221,433 votes, the most ever for a third-party candidate, but wins no electoral votes. Clinton and running mate Al Gore are the youngest president–vice president tandem in history.

1994   An upturn in the economy begins the longest sustained growth period in American history.

1996   President Bill Clinton is reelected.

1998   President Bill Clinton is implicated in perjury (false testimony under oath in a court case) and an extra-marital affair. The House Judiciary Committee votes, strictly on party lines, to recommend impeachment of the president, and the House impeaches the president for perjury and abuse of power.

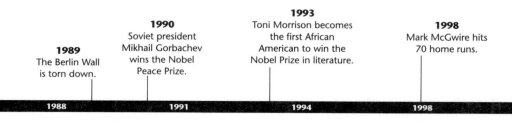

1989
The Berlin Wall is torn down.

1990
Soviet president Mikhail Gorbachev wins the Nobel Peace Prize.

1993
Toni Morrison becomes the first African American to win the Nobel Prize in literature.

1998
Mark McGwire hits 70 home runs.

1988   1991   1994   1998

1999   President Bill Clinton remains in office after being acquitted in a Senate trial.

2000   In the closest and most hotly contested election since 1876, Texas governor George W. Bush narrowly defeats Vice President Al Gore in the Electoral College, 271-266. Gore wins the popular vote by some three hundred thousand votes. The final victor cannot be declared until after a recount in Florida (with its twenty-five electoral votes at stake) takes place. Five weeks of legal battles ensue and Gore officially contests the results before Bush is able to claim victory in the state and, therefore, in the national election.

2000   Hillary Rodham Clinton becomes the first first lady to be elected to public office when she is elected U.S. senator from New York.

2000   In one of his last functions as president, Bill Clinton attends an international economic summit in Asia and visits Vietnam, twenty-five years after the end of the conflict that deeply divided Americans.

2001   George W. Bush is inaugurated the nation's forty-third president and becomes the second son of a president to become president himself.

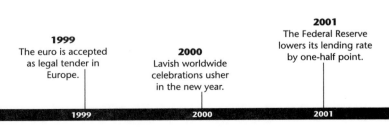

1999
The euro is accepted as legal tender in Europe.

2000
Lavish worldwide celebrations usher in the new year.

2001
The Federal Reserve lowers its lending rate by one-half point.

1999   2000   2001

Words to Know

A

Abolitionists: People who worked to end slavery.

Agrarian: One who believes in and supports issues beneficial to agriculture.

Alien and Sedition Acts: Four bills—the Naturalization Act, Alien Act, Alien Enemies Act, and Sedition Act—passed by Congress in 1798 and signed into law by President John Adams. The Naturalization Act extended from five to fourteen years the waiting period before citizenship—and with it, the right to vote—could be obtained by new immigrants. The two Alien acts gave the president the right to deport or jail foreign citizens he deemed a threat to the nation's stability, especially during wartime. The Sedition Act criminalized criticism of the government. To write or publish views that disparaged the administration was punishable by harsh fines and jail terms.

Allied forces (allies): Alliances of countries in military opposition to another group of nations. Twenty-eight nations made up the Allied and Associated powers in World War I. In World War II, the Allied powers included Great Britain, the United States, and the Soviet Union.

Anarchist: One against any form of government.

Annexing: Adding a new state or possession to the existing United States of America.

Annual Message to Congress: A speech the president delivers before Congress each year. Originally called the Annual Message to Congress and delivered each November, the speech became known as the State of the Union Address and is delivered each January.

Anti-Federalists: A group who wanted a limited federal government and more power for individual states.

Antitrust: Government action against businesses that dominate a certain industry or market and that are alleged to have stifled competing businesses.

Appropriations: Funds authorized for a particular project.

Armistice: An agreement to cease fire while warring parties negotiate a peace settlement.

Articles of Confederation: From March 1, 1781, to June 21, 1788, the Articles served as the equivalent of the Constitution (1787). The Constitution replaced the Articles, which had failed to produce a strong central government, and the present-day United States was formed.

Axis: The countries that fought together against the Allies in World War II. Germany, Italy, and Japan formed the first coalition; eventually, they were joined by Hungary, Romania, Slovakia, Finland, and Bulgaria.

B

Bar: A term that encompasses all certified lawyers—those who have passed all official requirements (the bar exam) to be certified as lawyers.

Bar exam: A test that lawyers must pass in order to become legally certified to practice law.

Battle of the Bulge: Battles surrounding the last German offensive (1944–45) during World War II. Allied forces moving toward Germany from France following the D-Day invasion were stalled by bad weather along the German border. Germans launched a counteroffensive to divide American and British forces. Germans created a "bulge" in the Allied lines, but they were halted and then withdrew.

Bay of Pigs invasion: Failed U.S.-backed invasion of Cuba at the Bay of Pigs by fifteen hundred Cuban exiles opposed to Fidel Castro, on April 17, 1961.

"Big stick" foreign policy: Theodore Roosevelt's theory that in diplomatic efforts, it was wise to "speak softly and carry a big stick," meaning that one should attempt peaceful solutions while at the same time being prepared to back up the talk with action when necessary.

Bill of Rights: The first ten amendments to the American Constitution of rights and privileges guaranteed to the people of the United States.

Black Codes: Laws and provisions that limited civil rights and placed economic restrictions on African Americans.

"Bleeding Kansas": The conflict in Kansas in 1854 between slavery advocates and abolitionists—in the form of both residents and transients, and two different governments—that led to bloodshed. It was the first indication that the issue of slavery would not be settled diplomatically.

Bloc: A unified group able to wield power through its size and numbers.

Boston Tea Party: An event in 1773 in which colonists spilled shipments of tea into Boston harbor to protest taxes imposed on various products.

Bull market: A stock market term that describes a period of aggressive buying and selling of stock that proves profitable for most investors; in contrast, "bear market" is used to describe a more sluggish trading period.

Bureaucracy: A government or big business set up to be run by bureaus, or departments, that strictly follow rules and regulations and a chain of authority.

C

Camp David Accords: An agreement of peace following negotiations led by President Jimmy Carter and signed by Israeli prime minister Menachem Begin and Egyptian president Anwar Sadat on March 26, 1979.

Capitol Hill: A nickname for Congress, since the Capitol building where Congress holds sessions is located on a small hill.

Carpetbaggers: A term of contempt used by Southerners about agents, humanitarians, politicians, and businessmen who came to the South to assist or to exploit Reconstruction policies. The term suggests that Northerners could stuff everything they owned into a bag made from carpet.

Caucus: An organized vote by registered and designated members of a political party to determine the amount of support within a state for the party's presidential candidates.

Censure: To publicly condemn an individual; in Congress, the act of censure expresses Congress's condemnation of an individual's actions and is entered into the *Congressional Record.*

Central Intelligence Agency (CIA): A U.S. government agency charged with accumulating information on foreign countries.

Checks and balances: The system in which the three branches of the U.S. government can review and dismiss acts passed by one of the other branches.

Civil service: Positions under the authority of the federal government.

Civil War: Conflict that took place from 1861 to 1865 between the Northern states (Union) and the Southern seceded states (Confederacy); also known in the South as the War between the States and in the North as the War of the Rebellion.

Coalitions: Groups of people supporting a political issue or cause.

Cold War: A term that describes a period from 1945 to the late 1980s characterized by tense conflicts and failed diplomacy between the Soviet Union and the United States and their respective allies.

Communism: A system in which the government controls the distribution of goods and services and limits individual freedom.

Compromise of 1850: Legislation passed by Congress and signed into law by President Millard Fillmore consisting of five bills: (1) California was admitted as a free state; (2) Texas was compensated for the loss of territory in a boundary dispute with New Mexico; (3) New Mexico was granted territorial status; (4) the slave trade—but not slavery itself—was abolished in Washington, D.C; (5) and most controversially, the Fugitive Slave Law was enacted, allowing slaveowners to pursue fleeing slaves and recapture them in free states.

Confederate States of America (Confederacy): The eleven Southern states that seceded (separated) from the United States during the 1860s and fought the Union during the American Civil War.

Congressional Record: A document that records all speeches and votes made in Congress.

Conservative: A political philosophy of limited government influence and support for conventional social values.

Constitutional Convention: The 1787 convention attended by delegates to strengthen the Articles of Confederation. Instead, delegates adopted the American Constitution that formed the United States.

Constructionist: One who bases decisions on literal readings of the Constitution.

Consul: A diplomat stationed in a foreign country who advises people from his or her own country on legal matters.

Continental Army: The American army during the Revolutionary War against Great Britain.

Continental Congress: The group of representatives who met to establish the United States.

Coup: A sudden overthrow of a government, often by the country's military.

Covert operations: Secret, undercover acts used to help influence the outcome of events.

Cuban missile crisis: A showdown in October 1962 that brought the Soviet Union and the United States close to war over the existence of Soviet nuclear missiles in Cuba.

D

D-Day: A military term that describes the day when an event can be scheduled. D-Day in World War II was June 6, 1944, when Allied forces landed in Normandy, France.

Dark horse: A little-known candidate with modest chances for success who might emerge surprisingly strong.

Delegate: A member of a party or organization who has a vote that represents a larger group and helps determine the leader of that party or organization.

Democratic Party: One of the oldest political parties in the United States, developed out of the Democratic-Republican Party of the late eighteenth century. Andrew Jackson was one of its first leaders. In the years before the Civil War (1861–65), Democrats became increasingly associated with the South and slavery. Following the war, the party gradually transformed and became associated with urban voters and liberal policies. In the twentieth and twenty-first centuries, Democrats have generally favored freer trade, more international commitments, greater government regulations, and social programs.

Democratic-Republican Party: One of the first political parties in the United States, led by Thomas Jefferson and James Madison in the 1790s to oppose the Federalist Party and close ties with Great Britain. It was also called the Republican Party and the Jeffersonian Republican Party at the time, but the term Democratic-Republican helps distinguish that early political group from the Democratic and Republican parties that were formed later. The Democratic-Republican Party dissolved in the 1820s. Many former members began supporting the formation of the Democratic Party led by Andrew Jackson, who was elected president in 1828 and 1832. The modern-day Republican Party was formed in 1854.

Depression: *See* **Great Depression.**

Deregulation: Removal of guidelines and laws governing a business or financial institution.

Détente: A relaxing of tensions between rival nations, marked by increased diplomatic, commercial, and cultural contact.

Draft cards: From the mid-1960s through the mid-1970s, all males had to register for the draft upon turning eighteen. After registering, an individual received a draft card that contained a draft number. A lottery system was used to determine which available males would be "drafted"—required to serve in the military.

E

Election board: A group authorized to operate elections and count votes.

Electoral College: A body officially responsible for electing the president of the United States. In presidential elections, the candidate who receives the most popular votes in a particular state wins all of that state's electoral votes. Votes are distributed among states in ratios based on population. A candidate must win a majority of electoral votes (over fifty percent) in order to win the presidency.

Electoral votes: The votes a presidential candidate receives for having won a majority of the popular vote in a state. In presidential elections, the candidate who receives the most popular votes in a particular state wins all of that states' electoral votes. Votes are distributed among states in ratios based on population. A candidate must win a majority of electoral votes (over fifty percent) in order to win the presidency.

Emancipation: The act of freeing people from slavery.

Enfranchisement: Voting rights.

Expansionism: The policy of a nation that plans to enlarge its size or gain possession of other lands.

Exploratory committee: A group established by a potential political candidate to examine whether enough party, public, and financial support exists for the potential candidate to officially announce that he or she is running for an elected position.

F

Federal budget: The list of all planned expenditures the federal government expects to make over a year.

Federal budget deficit: When government spending exceeds income (from taxes and other revenue).

Federal Reserve System: The central banking system of the United States, which serves as the banker to the financial sector and the government, issues the national currency, and supervises banking practices.

Federalist: A proponent for a strong national (federal) government.

Federalist Party: An American political party of the late eighteenth century that began losing influence around 1820. Federalists supported a strong national government. Growing sentiments for states' rights and rural regions led to the demise of the party. Many Federalists became Democratic-Republicans until that party was split into factions in the mid-1820s. Those favoring states' rights became Jackson Democrats and formed the Democratic Party in 1832.

First Continental Congress: A group of representatives from the thirteen colonies who met in Philadelphia in 1774 to list grievances (complaints) against England.

Fiscal: Relating to financial matters.

Fourteen Points: Famous speech given by Woodrow Wilson that includes reasons for American involvement in war, terms for peace, and his vision of a League of Nations.

Freedmen's Bureau: An agency that provided federal help for freed slaves.

Fugitive Slave Law: The provision in the Compromise of 1850 that allowed Southern slaveowners to pursue and capture runaway slaves into Northern states.

G

General assembly: A state congressional system made up only of representatives from districts within that particular state.

Gerrymandering: A practice whereby the political party in power changes boundaries in a voting area to include more people likely to support the party in power. This can occur when Congressional districts are rezoned (marked off into different sections) following the national census that occurs every ten years.

Gold standard: The economic practice whereby all of the money printed and minted in a nation is based on the amount of gold the nation has stored. (Paper money is printed; coins are minted, or stamped.)

GOP: Short for "Grand Old Party," a nickname of the Republican Party.

Grand jury: A group empowered to decide whether a government investigation can provide enough evidence to make criminal charges against a citizen.

Grass roots: A term that describes political activity that begins with small groups of people acting without the influence of large and powerful groups.

Great Depression: The worst financial crisis in American history. Usually dated from 1929, when many investors lost money during a stock market crash, to 1941, when the last Depression-related relief effort to help impoverished and unemployed people was passed by the government. When America entered World War II (1939–45) in 1941, many more employment opportunities became available in war-related industries.

Great Society: A set of social programs proposed by President Lyndon B. Johnson designed to end segregation and reduce poverty in the United States.

Gross national product (GNP): An economic measurement of a nation's total value of goods and services produced over a certain period (usually a year); the GNP became an official economic statistic in 1947.

H

House of Burgesses: A representative body made up of Virginia colonists but under the authority of British rule.

Human rights: Principles based on the belief that human beings are born free and equal; governments must respect those rights or they can be accused of human rights violations.

I

Immunity: Protection from prosecution; usually extended to someone who can help the prosecution win its case.

Impeachment: A legislative proceeding charging a public official with misconduct. Impeachment consists of the formal accusation of such an official and the trial that follows. It does not refer to removal from office of the accused.

Imperialism: The process of expanding the authority of one government over other nations and groups of people.

Incumbent: The person currently holding an elected office during an election period.

Independent counsel: A federal position established during the 1970s to investigate federal officials accused of crimes. The Independent Counsel Act, intended to perform in a nonpartisan manner in rare occasions, was not renewed in 1999.

Indictment: An official charge of having committed a crime.

Industrialization: The use of machinery for manufacturing goods.

Inflation: An economic term that describes a situation in which money loses some of its value, usually because the cost of goods is more expensive.

Infrastructure: The system of public works—the physical resources constructed for public use, such as bridges and roads—of a state or country.

Injunction: A legal maneuver that suspends a certain practice until a legal decision can be reached.

Insurrections: Armed rebellions against a recognized authority.

Integration: The bringing together of people of all races and ethnic backgrounds without restrictions; desegregation.

Interest rates: The percentage of a loan that a person agrees to pay for borrowing money.

Internationalism: Interest and participation in events involving other countries.

Iran-Contra scandal: A scandal during the Ronald Reagan administration during which government officials made illegal sales of weapons to Iran. Money made from those sales were diverted to secret funds provided to the Contras in the civil war in El Salvador. This was illegal, since Congress must authorize foreign aid.

Iran hostage crisis: A 444-day period from November 4, 1979, to Inauguration Day 1981 when Iran held 52 American embassy officials hostage following the toppling of the American-backed Shah of Iran.

Iron Curtain: A term describing Eastern European nations dominated by the Soviet Union.

Isolationism: A national policy of avoiding pacts, treaties, and other official agreements with other nations in order to remain neutral.

K

Kansas-Nebraska Act: A U.S. law authorizing the creation of the states of Kansas and Nebraska and specifying that the inhabitants of the territories should decide whether or not to allow slaveholding.

Keynote address: The most important speech during opening ceremonies of an organized meeting.

Korean War: A war from 1950 to 1953 fought between communist North Korea and non-communist South Korea; China backed North Korea and the United Nations backed South Korea.

L

Laissez faire: A French term (roughly translated as "allow to do") commonly used to describe noninterference by government in the affairs of business and the economy.

Lame duck: An official who has lost an election and is filling out the remainder of his or her term.

League of Nations: An organization of nations, as proposed by President Woodrow Wilson, that would exert moral leadership and help nations avoid future wars.

Legal tender: Bills or coin that have designated value.

Lobbyist: A person hired to represent the interests of a particular group to elected officials.

Louisiana Purchase: A vast region in North America purchased by the United States from France in 1803 for $15 million.

Loyalists: Americans who remained loyal to Great Britain during the Revolutionary War (1775–83).

M

Manifest Destiny: The belief that American expansionism is inevitable and divinely ordained.

Marshall Plan: A post–World War II program led by Secretary of State George C. Marshall that helped rebuild European economies (also benefiting U.S. trade) and strengthened democratic governments.

Martial law: A state of emergency during which a military group becomes the sole authority in an area and civil laws are set aside.

Medicare: A government program that provides financial assistance to poor people to help cover medical costs.

Mercenaries: Soldiers hired to serve a foreign country.

Merchant marine: Professional sailors and boat workers involved with commercial marine trade and maintenance (as opposed to branches of the military such as the navy and the coast guard).

Midterm elections: Congressional elections that occur halfway through a presidential term. These elections can affect the president's dealings with Congress. A president is elected every four years; representatives (members of the House of Representatives), every two years; and senators, every six years.

Military dictatorships: States in which military leaders have absolute power.

Military draft: A mandatory program that requires that all males register for possible military service. Those who pass a medical test receive a draft number. A lottery system is used to determine which available males must serve in the military. Those whose numbers are drawn are "drafted" into military service.

Military governments: Governments supervised or run by a military force.

Military tribunal: A court presided over by military officials to try cases in an area under a state of war.

Militia: A small military group, not affiliated with the federal government, organized for emergency service.

Missing in action: A term that describes military personnel unaccounted for. They might have been captured by the enemy, in which case they become prisoners of war; they might be hiding out and attempting to return to safety; or they might have been killed.

Missouri Compromise: Legislation passed in 1820 that designated which areas could enter the Union as free states and which could enter as slave states. It was repealed in 1854.

Monarchy: A form of government in which a single person (usually a king or queen) has absolute power.

Monroe Doctrine: A policy statement issued during the presidency of James Monroe (1817–25) that explained the position of the United States on the activities of European powers in the western hemisphere; of major significance was the stand of the United States against European intervention in the affairs of the Americas.

Muckrakers: A circle of investigative reporters during Theodore Roosevelt's term in office who exposed the seamier (unwholesome) side of American life. These reporters thoroughly researched their stories and based their reports on provable facts.

N

National Security Council: A group of military advisors assisting the president.

Nationalism: Loyalty to a nation that exalts that quality above all other nations.

Nazi: The abbreviated name for the National Socialist German Workers' Party, the political party led by Adolf Hitler, who became dictator of Germany. Hitler's Nazi Party controlled Germany from 1933 to 1945. The Nazis promoted racist and anti-Semitic (anti-Jewish) ideas and enforced complete obedience to Hitler and the party.

Neutrality: A position in which a nation is not engaged with others and does not take sides in disputes.

New Deal: A series of programs initiated by the administration of President Franklin D. Roosevelt to create jobs and stimulate the economy during the Great Depression (1929–41).

North Atlantic Treaty Organization (NATO): An alliance for collective security created by the North Atlantic Treaty in 1949 and originally involving Belgium, Canada, Denmark, France, Great Britain, Iceland, Italy, Luxembourg, the Netherlands, Norway, Portugal, and the United States.

Nuclear test ban treaty: An agreement to stop testing nuclear weapons.

Complete American Presidents Sourcebook

Nullification: Negatation; the Theory of Nullification was proposed by John C. Calhoun, a South Carolina congressman who later served as vice president to Andrew Jackson. In Calhoun's theory, a state has the right to nullify federal laws that it deems harmful to the state's interests.

O

Open Door Policy: A program introduced by President William McKinley to extend trade and relations with China, opening up a vast new market.

Oppression: Abuse of power by one party against another.

P

Pacifist: A person opposed to conflict.

Panic of 1837: An economic slump that hit the United States in 1837.

Pardon: A power that allows the president to free an individual or a group from prosecution for a crime.

Parliamentary government: A system of government in which executive power resides with Cabinet-level officials responsible to the nation's legislature. The highest-ranking member of the political party with a majority in such a system of government is usually made the nation's chief executive.

Partisan: Placing the concerns of one's group or political party above all other considerations.

Patronage system: Also called spoils system; a system in which elected officials appoint their supporters to civil service (government) jobs.

Peace Corps: A government-sponsored program that trains volunteers for social and humanitarian service in underdeveloped areas of the world.

Peacekeeping force: A military force sponsored by the United Nations that polices areas that have been attacked by another group clearly defined as aggressors.

Pearl Harbor: An American naval station in Hawaii attacked without warning by Japanese forces in December 1941.

Pendleton Civil Service Reform Act: A congressional act signed into law by President Chester A. Arthur that established the Civil Service Commission, an organization that oversees federal appointments and ensures that appointees do not actively participate in party politics while holding a federal job.

Perjury: The voluntary violation of an oath or a vow; answering falsely while under oath (having previously sworn to tell the truth).

Platform: A declaration of policies that a candidate or political party intends to follow if the party's candidate is elected.

Political boss: A politically powerful person who can direct a group of voters to support a particular candidate.

Political dynasty: A succession of government leaders from the same political party.

Political machine: An organized political group whose members are generally under the control of the leader of the group.

Populism: An agricultural movement of rural areas between the Mississippi River and the Rocky Mountains of the late nineteenth century that united the interests of farmers and laborers. In 1891, the movement formed a national political party, the People's Party, whose members were called Populists. Populist ideals remained popular even when the party faded early in the twentieth century.

Presidential primaries: Elections held in states to help determine the nominees of political parties for the general election. Each party disperses a certain number of delegates to each state. A candidate must win support of a majority of those delegates to win the party's presidential nomination. In states that hold primary elections, delegates are generally awarded to candidates based on the percentage of votes they accumulate; in some states, the leading vote-getter wins all of those state's delegates.

Presidential veto: When a president declines to sign into law a bill passed by Congress.

Primaries: *See* **Presidential primaries.**

Progressive "Bull Moose" Party: Party in which Theodore Roosevelt ran as a third-party candidate in 1912. He came in second to incumbent president William Howard Taft, but lost to New Jersey governor Woodrow Wilson.

Progressivism: A movement that began late in the nineteenth century whose followers pursued social, economic, and government reform. Generally located in urban areas, Progressivists ranged from individuals seeking to improve local living conditions to radicals who pursued sweeping changes in the American political and economic system.

Prohibition: The constitutional ban on the manufacture and sale of alcohol and alcoholic beverages from 1920 to 1933.

Prosecuting attorney: The attorney who represents the government in a law case.

Protectorate: A relationship in which an independent nation comes under the protection and power of another nation.

Proviso: A clause in a document making a qualification, condition, or restriction.

R

Racial desegregation: A policy meant to ensure that people of all racial origins are treated equal.

Rapprochement: Reestablishment of relations with a country after it has undergone a dramatic change in government.

Ratification: A vote of acceptance. A majority of the representatives from each of the thirteen colonies had to vote for the U.S. Constitution (1787) in order for the document to become legally binding.

Recession: A situation of increasing unemployment and decreasing value of money.

Recharter: To renew a law or an act.

Reciprocal trade agreements: When participating nations promise to trade in a way that will benefit each nation equally.

Reconstruction: A federal policy from 1865 to 1877 through which the national government took an active part in assisting and policing the former Confederate states.

Reconstruction Act of 1867: An act that placed military governments (governments supervised by a military force) in command of states of the South until the Fourteenth Amendment was ratified in 1868.

Regulation: Monitoring business with an established set of guidelines.

Reparations: Payments for damage caused by acts of hostility.

Republican government: A form of government in which supreme power resides with citizens who elect their leaders and have the power to change their leaders.

Republican Party: Founded in 1854 by a coalition (an alliance) of former members of the Whig, Free-Soil, and Know-Nothing parties and of northern Democrats dissatisfied with their party's proslavery stands. The party quickly rose to become one of the most important parties in the United States, and the major opposition to the Democratic Party. Republicans are generally associated with conservative fiscal and social policies. The Republican Party is not related to the older Democratic-Republican Party, although that party was often called the Republicans before the 1830s.

Riders: Measures added on to legislation. Riders are usually items that might not pass through Congress or will be vetoed by the president if presented alone. Congressmen attempt to attach such items to popular bills, hoping they will "ride" along with the more popular legislation.

S

Sanctions: Punishment against a nation involved in activities considered illegal under international law; such punishment usually denies trade, supplies, or access to other forms of international assistance to the nation.

Satellite nations: Countries politically and economically dominated by a larger, more powerful nation.

Secession: Formal withdrawal from an existing organization. In 1860–61, eleven Southern states seceded from the Union to form the Confederate States of America.

Second Continental Congress: A group of representatives from the thirteen colonies who began meeting in Philadelphia in 1775 and effectively served as the American government until the Constitution was adopted in 1787.

Sectionalism: The emphasis that people place on policies that would directly benefit their area of the country.

Segregation: The policy of keeping groups of people from different races, religions, or ethnic backgrounds separated.

Social Security: A government program that provides pensions (a regular sum of money) to American workers after they reach age sixty-five.

Social welfare: A term that encompasses government programs that provide assistance, training, and jobs to people.

Solicitor: An attorney who represents a government agency.

Solicitor general: An attorney appointed by the president to argue legal matters on behalf of the government.

South East Asia Treaty Organization: An alliance of nations founded in 1954 to prevent the spread of communism in Asian and Pacific island nations. Original members included Australia, France, Great Britain, New Zealand, Pakistan, the Philippines, Thailand, and the United States. The alliance disbanded in 1977.

Speaker of the House: The person in charge of supervising activity in the House of Representatives. The Speaker is elected by colleagues of the party with a majority in Congress.

Spin doctoring: A late twentieth-century term that describes the practice of having political aides offer the best possible interpretation of a political statement or the effects of an event on their political boss.

State militia: An organized military unit maintained by states in case of emergency; often called the National Guard.

Stock market crash: A sudden decline in the value of stocks that severely affects investors.

Strategic Arms Limitation Treaty (SALT): Missile reduction program between the United States and the Soviet Union.

Strategic Defense Initiative (SDI): A proposed—but never approved—technological system (nicknamed "Star Wars," after the popular movie) that combined several advanced technology systems that could, in theory, detect and intercept missiles fired by enemies of the United States.

Subpoena: A formal legal document that commands a certain action or requires a person to appear in court.

T

Taft-Hartley Act: Act that outlawed union-only workplaces, prohibited certain union activities, forbade unions to contribute to political campaigns, established loyalty oaths for union leaders, and allowed court orders to halt strikes that could affect national health or safety.

Tariff: A protective tax placed on imported goods to raise their price and make them less attractive than goods produced by the nation importing them.

Teapot Dome scandal: Incident that became public following the death of President Warren G. Harding that revealed that Navy secretary Edwin Denby transfered control of oil reserves in Teapot Dome, Wyoming, and Elk Hill, California, to the Department of the Interior, whose secretary, Albert Fall, secretly leased the reserve to two private oil operators, who paid Fall $400,000.

Tenure of Office Act: A law passed by Congress to limit the powers of the presidency.

Terrorist: A person who uses acts of violence in an attempt to coerce by terror.

Theater: A large area where military operations are occurring.

Thirteenth Amendment: An amendment to the U.S. Constitution that outlawed slavery.

Tonkin Gulf Resolution: Passed by Congress after U.S. Navy ships supposedly came under attack in the Gulf of Tonkin, this resolution gave President Lyndon B. Johnson the authority to wage war against North Vietnam.

Tribunal: A court of law.

Truman Doctrine: A Cold War–era program designed by President Harry S. Truman that sent aid to anticommunist forces in Turkey and Greece. The Union of Soviet Socialist Republics (U.S.S.R.) had naval stations in Turkey, and nearby Greece was fighting a civil war with communist-dominated rebels.

U

Underground railroad: A term that describes a series of routes through which escaped slaves could pass through free Northern states and into Canada. The escaped slaves were assisted by abolitionists and free African Americans in the North.

Union: Northern states that remained loyal to the United States during the Civil War.

V

Veto: The power of one branch of government—for example, the executive—to reject a bill passed by a legislative body and thus prevent it from becoming law.

Vietcong: Vietnamese communists engaged in warfare against the government and people of South Vietnam.

W

War of 1812: A war fought from 1812 to 1815 between the United States and Great Britain. The United States wanted to protect its maritime rights as a neutral nation during a conflict between Great Britain and France.

Warren Commission: A commission chaired by Earl Warren, chief justice of the Supreme Court, that investigated President John F. Kennedy's assassination. The commission concluded that the assassination was the act of one gunman, not part of a larger conspiracy. That conclusion remains debated.

Watergate scandal: A scandal that began on June 17, 1972, when five men were caught burglarizing the offices of the Democratic National Committee in the Watergate complex in Washington, D.C. This led to a cover-up, political convictions, and, eventually, the resignation of President Richard Nixon.

Welfare: Government assistance to impoverished people.

Whig Party: A political party that existed roughly from 1836 to 1852, composed of different factions of the former Democratic-Republican Party. These factions refused to join the group that formed the Democratic Party led by President Andrew Jackson.

Y

Yalta Conference: A 1944 meeting between Allied leaders Joseph Stalin, Winston Churchill, and Franklin D. Roosevelt in anticipation of an Allied victory in Europe over the Nazis. The leaders discussed how to manage lands conquered by Germany, and Roosevelt and Churchill urged Stalin to enter the Soviet Union in the war against Japan.

Research and Activity Ideas

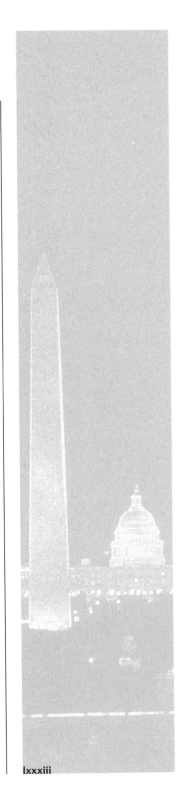

The following research and activity ideas are intended to offer suggestions for complementing social studies and history curricula, to trigger additional ideas for enhancing learning, and to suggest cross-disciplinary projects for library and classroom use.

- The aftermath of the 2000 race between George W. Bush and Al Gore renewed debate over whether the Electoral College system should be abandoned in favor of the popular vote. Research the reasons why the Founding Fathers instituted the Electoral College. Write a paper on arguments for and against the Electoral College, or take one side and have a partner take the other side.

- Several Web sites on presidents are listed in the "Where to Learn More" section. Additional Web sites, linked to presidential libraries and historical sites, are listed at the end of many individual president entries. Using a president of particular interest to you, compare the descriptions of his life and his presidency on the various Web sites. The comparison will show how presidents are appraised by different sources. Pretend you are a media critic. Write a review of the various sites, comparing their different features, the ways they treat the president, and what you find interesting and not useful in each site.

• Plan a debate or a series of debates on important issues in American history. One issue could be the powers of the federal government in relation to the states. That issue can be explored and debated by contrasting the views of a president who took a different view of federal power from the president who preceded him. Such contrasting pairs include John Adams and Thomas Jefferson; James Buchanan and Abraham Lincoln; Herbert Hoover and Franklin D. Roosevelt; and George Bush and Bill Clinton.

• In contemporary times, when a president makes his State of the Union address each year, television networks provide equal time for a member of the opposing party to present his or her party's views. After reading and making notes on one of the speeches in the primary documents section, prepare a response—a speech that takes an opposite view on issues presented by the president.

• Create a timeline of a fifty-year period to parallel the "Timeline of the American Presidents," found on pages xxix–lix. Your timeline might list important inventions, world events, or developments in science and technology. Placing the timelines side by side, consider ways in which the events on your timeline might be connected with events in the presidential timeline.

• Using the resources of your local library, find magazines and newspapers that were published near the time you were born, or pick a date earlier in time. What were some of the big national news stories back then? How did the press view the performance of the president concerning those issues?

• Pretend you are a reporter preparing to interview one of the presidents. Just before your interview is to begin, the president is informed about a major event (select one from the president's entry). You are allowed to follow the president as he plans a course of action. Write an article providing an "insider's view" of the president in action.

• The Congressional cable network C-Span commissioned presidential scholars to rate presidents in ten categories (see http://www.americanpresidents.org/survey/historians/overall.asp). Compare that ranking with other sources that rank presidents in terms of effectiveness. How are the rankings similar and different? What criteria do they use for judging presidents? Consider whether or not you feel the rankings are fair, and write an essay supporting your view.

- Visit a historical site or Web sites devoted to a particular president. Listings for both can often be found in each president's entry. Using biographical information about the president's childhood, his schooling, and his career as president, write a short play in which the president is surrounded by loved ones and aides at a crucial moment during his presidency.

- There were many different kinds of first ladies. Some were politically active (such as Sarah Polk and Eleanor Roosevelt), others believed they should not participate in politics because they were not the one elected to office (such as Bess Truman and Pat Nixon). Compare and contrast those different approaches by profiling several first ladies.

- Research more about a leading opponent of a particular president, perhaps someone he faced in an election. Imagine that the opponent was able to convince voters that he or she should be elected. Write about how history would have been different if the opponent had become president. The focus could be on an election that was very close (such as Rutherford B. Hayes over Samuel Tilden in 1876 or George W. Bush over Al Gore in 2000) or one in which the victor won by a large margin (such as Franklin D. Roosevelt over Alfred Landon in 1936 or Ronald Reagan over Walter Mondale in 1984).

Complete American Presidents Sourcebook

William Henry Harrison

Ninth president (1841)

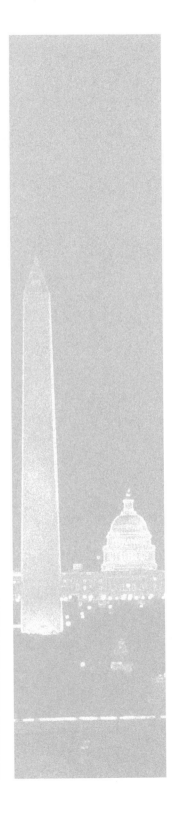

William Henry Harrison

Born February 9, 1773
Charles City County, Virginia
Died April 4, 1841
Washington, D.C.

Ninth president of the United States (1841)

Attained fame as a soldier and was the first Whig to become president

William Henry Harrison served as president for one month before dying of pneumonia on April 4, 1841. There were indications that he might have become a more independent president than expected. However, his inaugural address (his first speech at the formal ceremony installing him as president) suggested that he would allow Congress to lead the nation forward, a scenario (a view of possible future events) for which members of his Whig Party had planned. The Whig Party was a political party made up of different groups within the former Democratic-Republican Party.

Harrison is associated with a presidential campaign that reflects a more manipulative side of politics. In this kind of shrewdly managed political campaign, appearance counts for more than reality, songs and slogans overwhelm discussion on issues, and powerful figures behind the scenes hold the real power. Harrison was the Tippecanoe half of the famous political slogan, "Tippecanoe and Tyler Too!" He earned the nickname for his victory over Native American forces at the Battle of Tippecanoe in 1811.

"See to the government. See that the government does not acquire too much power. Keep a check on your rulers. Do this, and liberty is safe."

William Henry Harrison

William Henry Harrison.
Reproduced by permission of the National Portrait Gallery, Smithsonian Institution.

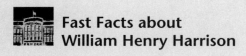

Fast Facts about William Henry Harrison

Full name: William Henry Harrison

Born: February 9, 1773

Died: April 4, 1841

Burial site: William Henry Harrison Memorial State Park, North Bend, Ohio

Parents: Benjamin and Elizabeth Bassett Harrison

Spouse: Anna Tuthill Symmes (1775–1864; m. 1795)

Children: Elizabeth Bassett (1796–1846); John Cleves Symmes (1798–1830); Lucy Singleton (1800–1826); William Henry Jr. (1802–1838); John Scott (1804–1878); Benjamin (1806–1840); Mary Symmes (1809–1842); Carter Bassett (1811–1839); Anna Tuthill (1813–1865); James Findlay (1814–1819)

Religion: Episcopalian

Education: Attended Hampden-Sydney College and University of Pennsylvania Medical School

Occupation: Soldier

Government positions: Secretary of the Northwest Territory; territorial delegate to U.S. Congress; territorial governor of Indiana; governor of Louisiana Territory; state senator from Ohio; U.S. congressman and senator from Ohio; minister to Colombia

Political party: Whig

Dates as president: March 4, 1841–April 4, 1841

Age upon taking office: 68

Harrison came from a wealthier background than his opponent, incumbent (current office holder) **Martin Van Buren** (1782–1862; see entry in volume 1). But Harrison was presented differently to the voters. Harrison was portrayed during the presidential campaign of 1840 as a small farmer who lived in a log cabin and preferred hard cider (fermented apple juice) to Van Buren's taste for fine wines and champagne. Hard cider was served at Harrison campaign rallies. Campaign helpers distributed coonskin (raccoon skin) caps as a symbol of Harrison's life on the frontier. Bands played noisy and high-spirited music. Harrison was urged by fellow Whig leaders to keep his proslavery and high-tariff views to himself. Meanwhile, those same Whig leaders carefully planned legislation that would be enacted by a president who pledged to follow Congress.

The strategy of style over substance worked. Over fifty percent more eligible voters went to the polls in 1840 than had voted in 1836. They favored Harrison, who won in a landslide in the Electoral College (a body officially responsible for electing the president of the United States). (For more information on the Electoral College, see boxes in **George W. Bush** entry in volume 5.)

In frigid (extremely cold) March weather, he delivered the longest-ever inaugural address. All the big plans he represented for the Whig Party were suddenly halted, however. Harrison fell gravely ill late in March and died on April 4.

William Henry Harrison Timeline

1773: Born in Virginia

1791: Drops his studies in medicine in favor of becoming a soldier; leads group of eighty men from Philadelphia to protect settlers in the Northwest Territory (present-day Ohio)

1794: Cited for bravery in the Battle of Fallen Timbers, where Native American forces are defeated by General Anthony Wayne

1798–1801: Serves as secretary of the Northwest Territory, and then territorial delegate to Congress

1801–12: Serves as territorial governor of Indiana

1811: Breaks Indian confederacy led by Shawnee Chief Tecumseh in the Battle of Tippecanoe in present-day Indiana

1813: After retaking Fort Detroit, which had been surrendered to the British in 1812, Brigadier General Harrison defeats an alliance of British and Native American forces in the Battle of Thames in present-day Ontario, Canada

1816–19: Serves as U.S. congressman from Ohio

1819–21: Serves as Ohio state senator

1825–28: Serves as U.S. senator

1828: Named minister to Colombia by President John Quincy Adams; recalled in 1829 by President Andrew Jackson

1836: As one of four regional Whig candidates, Harrison wins seven states and seventy-three electoral votes in the presidential election but loses to Martin Van Buren

1841: Elected ninth U.S. president; one month later, becomes the first president to die in office

Frontiersman with an aristocratic past

William Henry Harrison was born on February 9, 1773, at his family estate, Berkeley Plantation, along the James River in Charles County, Virginia. Three years later, his father, Benjamin Harrison (c. 1726–1791), was among those who signed the Declaration of Independence in 1776. Benjamin Harrison would later become governor of Virginia.

Harrison was privately tutored while growing up. He entered Virginia's Hampden-Sydney College and studied classical literature and history. Following his father's wishes, Harrison began studying medicine in Richmond, Virginia. He continued his studies at the University of Pennsylvania under

William Henry Harrison attained his fame in the military.

Courtesy of the Library of Congress.

noted physician Benjamin Rush (1745–1813). When his father died in 1791, eighteen-year-old Harrison decided to pursue his own path in life. Assisted by Senator Richard Henry Lee (1732–1794) of Virginia, Harrison was assigned to the First Infantry of the Regular Army (a small national army during the early years of the nation).

Harrison recruited a group of eighty men and set out for what was then the Northwest frontier—lands bordered by the Ohio River on the south and the Mississippi River on the west. From Philadelphia, the group hiked to Fort Pitt (now Pittsburgh). Then they traveled by boat to Fort Washington (now Cincinnati). The recruits were paid $2 per month to help defend settlers from Indian attacks.

Harrison and his troops came under the command of General Anthony Wayne (1745–1796) to participate in the Battle of Fallen Timbers (1794) near present-day Toledo, Ohio. Their victory against a coalition (a united group) of Native American tribes made it safe for more settlers to come to the region. Harrison was cited for bravery.

Shortly after the battle, Harrison was named commander of Fort Washington. There he met Anna Symmes (1775–1864; see entry on **Anna Harrison** in volume 2). Anna was the daughter of a judge who owned great tracts (stretches) of land in present-day Ohio and Indiana. Anna's father was not impressed with Harrison. He wanted his daughter to marry a preacher or a farmer instead of a soldier, a profession considered dangerous and low-paying. While Anna's father was away, the couple eloped (ran away secretly to be married) on November 22, 1795. After a few weeks, Anna's father reluctantly accepted the newlyweds. The Harrisons would have ten children. Their fifth child, John Scott, would eventually become the father of **Benjamin Harrison** (1833–1901; see entry in volume 3), the twenty-third U.S. president.

Words to Know

Abolitionists: Those who wanted to abolish slavery.

Delegate in Congress: A person who attends Congressional sessions as a representative of an American territory but who has no voting rights. Only representatives from states that have been admitted into the Union can participate in enacting federal legislation.

Electoral College: A body officially responsible for electing the president of the United States. In presidential elections, the candidate who receives the most popular votes in a particular state wins all of that state's electoral votes. Votes are distributed among states in ratios based on population. A candidate must win a majority of electoral votes (over fifty percent) in order to win the presidency.

Grass roots: A term that describes political activity that begins with small groups of people acting without the influence of large and powerful groups.

Incumbent: The person currently holding an elected office during an election period.

Platform: A declaration of policies that a candidate or a political party intends to follow if elected.

War of 1812: A war fought from 1812 to 1815 between the United States and Great Britain. The United States wanted to protect its maritime rights as a neutral nation during a conflict between Great Britain and France.

Whig Party: A political party that existed roughly from 1836 to 1852. Made up of different groups within the former Democratic-Republican Party, Whigs refused to join the faction that formed the Democratic Party led by President Andrew Jackson.

A few miles southwest of Cincinnati, along the Ohio River, Harrison established a large farm he called Grouseland and built a mill. The house of Grouseland was a replica of the estate on which Harrison was raised. Some people in the area were concerned that he was bringing a plantation society (and possibly slaves) to the territory.

In 1798, Harrison served as secretary of the Northwest Territory. He also represented the area as a delegate in Congress; that is, he attended sessions of Congress as a representative of his territory, but he did not have voting rights. He advised Congress to divide government land in the territory into small homestead lots that settlers could purchase

A painting shows General William Henry Harrison fighting Shawnee chief Tecumseh in the Battle of Tippecanoe.
Courtesy of the Library of Congress.

cheaply. Congress agreed. They also voted to split a section of the Northwest Territory to form the Indiana Territory in 1801. Harrison became the first governor of that territory. The Indiana Territory consisted of present-day Indiana, Illinois, and Wisconsin, as well as parts of present-day Minnesota and Michigan.

As governor, Harrison had orders from President **Thomas Jefferson** (1743–1826; see entry in volume 1) to acquire land from Native Americans through treaties and to defend settlers as they passed through the territory. Harrison served as governor until 1812.

"Indian fighter"

Harrison steadily acquired land for the federal government, sometimes through negotiation (discussion for the purpose of reaching agreement) and sometimes through battle. In the Treaty of Fort Wayne (1809), several tribes turned over a total of three million acres of land for annual payments that ranged from $200 to $5000. Meanwhile, Harrison was not successful in negotiating with the powerful Shawnee chief Tecumseh (1768–1813; see box) and his brother Tenskwatawa (c. 1768–1834), also known as the Prophet. Tecumseh refused to give up land. When Tecumseh went away to meet with other tribes that had allied with the Shawnees, Harrison moved in. He placed his troops at Tecumseh's stronghold at the confluence (meeting point) of the Tippecanoe and Wabash rivers. He invited the Prophet to a meeting.

Harrison's force of one thousand men was attacked before dawn on November 7, 1811. Although the group suffered losses, they managed to raze (demolish; level to the ground) the Prophet's nearby village and effectively broke the confederation led by Tecumseh and his brother. Native American raids continued on occasion, but reports of the Battle of

Tippecanoe made Harrison a national hero and encouraged more settlers to the region. Later in life, he was nicknamed Old Tippecanoe.

During the War of 1812 (1812–15) between the United States and Britain, Harrison's legend grew larger. He welcomed the war, believing that British forces in Canada had provided munitions (weapons and ammunition) to the Shawnees. Following the surrender of Fort Detroit by General William Hull (1753–1825), Brigadier General Harrison led his troops to the Maumee River, near the site of the Battle of Fallen Timbers. They moved north to recapture Detroit after American naval forces took control of Lake Erie. Harrison's troops pursued fleeing British soldiers and Native Americans into Canada. His chase culminated (concluded) with the Battle of the Thames, a river in the southwestern part of present-day Ontario. There, Harrison's soldiers defeated the combined force on October 5, 1813. The defeat closed off the west to the British and effectively ended Native American power in the region. Tecumseh died in the battle.

Tenskwatawa (above), also known as The Prophet, joined forces with his brother Tecumseh to fight the American white man. *Reproduced by permission of Archive Photos.*

Political aspirations

The following year, Harrison resigned from his military commission at age forty-one. He returned to his family farm in North Bend, Ohio, a town established by Harrison's father-in-law. Harrison became a member of Christ Episcopal Church and a trustee (a member of a board appointed to direct the affairs of an institution) of Cincinnati College. He aspired to (hoped for) a political career, but Harrison achieved mixed results over the next twenty years.

He served as a congressman from 1816 to 1819 during the administration of **James Monroe** (1758–1831; see entry in volume 1), whom Harrison lobbied unsuccessfully for such

Tecumseh

The great Shawnee warrior Tecumseh was born around 1768. He participated in his first battle during his mid-teens. Tecumseh often fought to protect the Shawnee boundary on the Ohio River. He played an important role during an attack in present-day Kentucky, in which Indians killed all but one settler. Watching the lone survivor being tortured, Tecumseh denounced his tribesmen, saying that such practices dishonored a warrior. The incident led the Shawnee to abandon the practice, and Tecumseh learned that his speechmaking could be as effective as any weapon. He soon emerged as a tribal leader.

In the early 1790s, Tecumseh followed the Miami tribe's call to unite against the white men. On August 20, 1794, U.S. Army general-in-chief "Mad Anthony" Wayne launched a devastating surprise attack against Native Americans at Fallen Timbers on Ohio's Maumee River. The Americans lost only thirty-eight men, while Native American casualties were several hundred, including one of Tecumseh's brothers. The following spring, Wayne met with representatives from twelve different tribes. The chiefs signed the Greenville Treaty, ceding to the United States the majority of Ohio, part of Indiana, and Fort Detroit (in present-day Michigan) for a $10,000 annuity.

Tecumseh had not attended the council and was furious with the chiefs for signing away the land. Refusing to acknowledge the treaty, Tecumseh headed west to the Wabash River in Indiana with a group of warriors and became the leading hostile chief. Tecumseh's vision for the future of the Indians soon began to materialize. His people had always lived without boundaries, fences, or border guards. Indian land had belonged to all Indians, each tribe respecting another's right to occupancy. Consequently, he reasoned, no tribe had the right to dispose of another's land by signing it away.

In 1805, Tecumseh's brother Laulewasika reportedly fell into a trance, then claimed that he had spoken with the supreme deity (god) and knew which path his Indian brothers must follow. Changing his name to Tenskwatawa ("the open door"), he deemed himself The Prophet and preached a return to many prominent features of Shawnee culture. He told his followers to renounce the white man's ways and give up the tools, clothes, weapons, and alcohol on which they had become dependent. Tecumseh found his brother's preaching in accordance with his own ideals and saw an opportunity to increase his warriors.

In 1808, the brothers established a settlement known as Prophet's Town on the west bank of the Tippecanoe River in present-day Indiana. Visiting tribes from Missouri to Florida, Tecumseh called Native Americans to arms with his powerful oratory. Tecumseh's talk of an Indian confederacy impressed the warriors. He gained the support of the Sauk, Winnebago, Creek, Cherokee, and Seminole tribes. Two years after the founding of Prophet's Town, one thousand warriors were gathered at the settlement.

By the time Tecumseh returned from his journey, the governor of the Northwest Territory and superintendent of Indian Affairs, General William Henry Harrison, had persuaded the chiefs of the Delaware, Miami, and Potawatomi tribes to sign the Treaty of Fort Wayne, ceding to the United States three million acres of land. Word of The Prophet's growing influence among the previously divided tribes had reached Harrison. He invited The Prophet to Vincennes, the territorial capital, to discuss the treaty.

Instead, Tecumseh pulled into Vincennes in August 1810, heading a party of four hundred warriors and alarming the Americans. On August 12, Tecumseh, forty warriors, and Harrison held a meeting at which the chief explained that no Indian had the authority to sell land that had always belonged to all Indians. Harrison's reply was unenthusiastic, and with Tecumseh's anger escalating—and his warriors reaching for their clubs—American guards were summoned and Tecumseh sent back to his camp. Even so, Harrison recognized Tecumseh's talents: "The implicit obedience and respect which the followers of Tecumseh pay him is really astonishing and . . . bespeaks him as one of those uncommon geniuses, which spring up occasionally to produce revolutions."

Believing that war was imminent, Tecumseh set off in 1811 with twenty-four warriors to summon the southern tribes to battle. Instructed to avoid conflict with the Americans, Tenskwatawa was responsible for holding down Prophet's Town in his brother's absence. Taking advantage of Tecumseh's absence, Harrison and his militia of a thousand men crossed the Fort Wayne Treaty line toward Prophet's Town. Tenskwatawa hastily ordered an immediate attack on Harrison's camp three miles away. But Harrison's men drove the Indians off in an historic defensive that became known as the Battle of Tippecanoe. On November 8, 1811, the Americans reached Prophet's Town, found it deserted, and set it afire. Tecumseh returned in early 1812 to find a discredited brother, a diminished group of followers, and rubble.

Tecumseh soon joined forces with the British, as they fought the Americans in the War of 1812 (1812–15). The chief was given a regular commission as a brigadier general, an unusually high rank for a tribal leader. Tecumseh and the British captured Fort Detroit on August 16, 1812, an event that helped save Upper Canada for the British. But an American naval victory on Lake Erie opened up a passage to Fort Detroit, eventually causing the British to retreat. Tecumseh had little choice but to follow the British into Canada. Along the Thames River in present-day Ontario, Tecumseh was killed by a stray gunshot just prior to a crucial battle. Later that day, Harrison forces won the Battle of the Thames, effectively ending both Indian and British power in the Great Lakes region.

"Keep the ball rolling" was a popular slogan during the 1840 campaign. Balls over ten feet in diameter and covered with slogans were often rolled from town to town. *Reproduced by permission of Archive Photos.*

positions as secretary of state and minister to Russia. Harrison was elected to the state senate of Ohio in 1819. He then failed in bids for governor, representative, and senator before being elected to the U.S. Senate in 1825.

Harrison was one of the few supporters of President **John Quincy Adams** (1767–1848; see entry in volume 1), whose administration was largely ineffective due to political forces that favored **Andrew Jackson** (1767–1845; see entry in volume 1). Harrison was named minister to Columbia in 1828, but Adams had his reservations. He noted in his diary that Harrison had an "absolutely rabid" (fanatical) thirst for higher office.

By the time Harrison reached Columbia, however, Adams had lost the 1828 election to Andrew Jackson. Harrison was greeted with news in February of 1829 that he would be recalled. He stayed on until the end of the Adams administration in March. In the meantime, he managed to agitate Simon Bolívar (1783–1830), a revolutionary leader of the region. Harrison was under strict orders to remain neutral, but he openly sided with Bolívar's opponents. His recall by Jackson probably saved Harrison from being expelled from Colombia.

Harrison returned to Indiana with little money. He accepted a position as a courtroom clerk. Meanwhile, he started a grass-roots political campaign (a campaign beginning with local small groups) in Indiana and Illinois. His political campaign began to blossom when he attended anniversary celebrations of the Battle of Tippecanoe. He was widely interviewed and championed for his heroic deeds at the battles of Tippecanoe and Thames. Harrison became part of a loosely organized political party, the Whigs. They were attempting to defeat Martin Van Buren, Andrew Jackson's handpicked successor for the presidency, in the 1836 election.

The Whigs decided to run four regional candidates, hoping that no candidate in the election, including Van Buren, would receive the necessary number of electoral votes.

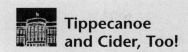

Tippecanoe and Cider, Too!

A newspaper that supported the Democratic Party provided Whigs with campaign material when it stated, "Give (Harrison) a barrel of hard cider and settle a pension of two thousand a year on him, and my word for it, he will sit . . . by the side of a 'sea coal' fire, and study moral philosophy." Harrison's campaign leaders began serving cider at rallies and portrayed their candidate as a man of the people content with simple pleasures (like sitting by the fire in his log cabin) as opposed to the more luxurious lifestyle of President Martin Van Buren.

Hard cider was also the subject of "The Hard Cider Quick Step," one of more than one hundred songs that were played and sung at political rallies for Harrison. Many songs compared the lavish tastes of Van Buren with the down home goodness of Harrison:

Let Van from his coolers of silver drink wine

And lounge on his cushioned settee,

Our man on a buckeye bench can recline,

Content with hard cider is he.

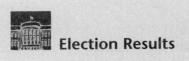

Election Results

1840

Presidential / Vice presidential candidates	Popular votes	Presidential electoral votes
William Henry Harrison / John Tyler (Whig)	1,275,016	234
Martin Van Buren / Richard M. Johnson (Democratic)	1,129,102	60

In such an event, the Constitution mandates (commands) that the election should be decided in the House of Representatives. Whigs felt they had a better chance with that scenario than with a general election. The Whig candidates were Harrison of Ohio; U.S. representative Willie Person Mangum (1792–1861) of North Carolina; U.S. senator Daniel Webster (1782–1852; see box in **John Tyler** entry in volume 2) of Massachusetts; and U.S. senator Hugh Lawson White (1773–1840) of Tennessee. The strategy failed, as Van Buren won 170 electoral votes to 124 for the Whig candidates (Harrison, 73; White, 26; Webster, 14; Mangum, 11). Harrison did well enough in winning seven states to impress Whigs as a viable national candidate (a candidate capable of success).

Old Tippecanoe

Harrison kept campaigning after the election, building a strong base of support among war veterans and increasing his standing in the Whig Party. At the 1839 Whig convention, Harrison won the nomination to run against Van Buren. He was presented as a westerner, a war hero, and an Indian fighter. Virginia speaker of the house **John Tyler** (1790–1862; see entry in volume 2) was named his running mate to appeal to southern voters. Actually, Harrison and Tyler had both been raised in aristocratic (wealthy landholding) families in the same county of Virginia.

The Whig Party did not present a platform (positions and policies). Instead, their campaign featured songs and colorful slogans, the most famous of which was "Tippecanoe and Tyler Too!" In response to an article that suggested Harrison should return to the frontier, Whigs began portraying Harrison as a small farmer who lived in a log cabin. They described Van Buren as a drinker of champagne and fine wines, while Harrison was said to enjoy a glass of homemade hard cider. This beverage was served at his campaign rallies. Coonskin hats symbolic of his life on the frontier were distributed to voters. While bands played loud and long, Harrison, as advised by Whig leaders, kept his speeches short and did not express his proslavery views. He won in a landslide in the Electoral College, taking 19 states and 234 votes to Van Buren's 7 states and 60 electoral votes.

A falling off of Whigs

Harrison arranged a large party to accompany him to Washington, D.C. On the frigid day he took the oath of office, he gave the longest inauguration speech ever made. Henry Clay (1777–1852; see box in **John Quincy Adams** entry in volume 1), one of the Whig power brokers (influential politicians), had edited the speech. He bragged that he had removed many references to Roman history and literature. Clay and Daniel Webster had directed Harrison to emphasize (highlight) his intention to follow the lead of Congress. They planned to enact policies they had long been fighting for without success during the administrations of Jackson and Van Buren.

Later that March, however, Harrison fell gravely ill. When he died on April 4, 1841, he was the first president to perish while in office. After a hastily arranged state funeral, Harrison's body was returned to Ohio. He was buried there in North Bend.

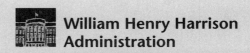

William Henry Harrison Administration

Administration Dates
March 4, 1841–April 4, 1841

Vice President
John Tyler (1841)

Cabinet

Secretary of State
Daniel Webster (1841)

Secretary of the Treasury
Thomas Ewing (1841)

Secretary of War
John Bell (1841)

Attorney General
John J. Crittenden (1841)

Secretary of the Navy
George E. Badger (1841)

Postmaster General
Francis Granger (1841)

A Selection of Harrison Landmarks

Berkeley Plantation. 12602 Harrison Landing Rd., Charles City, VA 23030. (804) 829-6018. Birthplace of President William Henry Harrison, as well as his father, Benjamin Harrison V, a signer of the Declaration of Independence. First official Thanksgiving was also observed on the plantation grounds in early seventeenth century. House has been restored to pre-Revolutionary architecture. See http://www.berkeleyplantation.com/ (accessed on June 26, 2000).

Grouseland. 3 West Scott St., Vincennes, IN 47591. (812) 882-2096. Home of William Henry Harrison from 1803 to 1812. Site reportedly got its name from the grouse (a kind of game bird) that Harrison liked to hunt. See http://www.vincennes.com/ Historical/Grouseland/grouseland.html (accessed on June 26, 2000).

Harrison Tomb State Memorial. Cliff Rd., North Bend, OH. Final resting place of William Henry and Anna Harrison. See http://www.ohiohistory.org/places/harrison/ (accessed on June 28, 2000).

Tippecanoe Battlefield. State Rd. 43, Lafayette, IN 47901. (765) 567-2147. Historic site of the Battle of Tippecanoe in 1811. Ninety acres includes a museum and an eighty-five-foot obelisk that commemorates Harrison and the battle. See http://www.tcha.mus.in.us/battlefield.htm (accessed on June 26, 2000).

Legacy

William Henry Harrison's death touched off a Constitutional crisis. The Constitution had not specifically addressed a mode of succession, that is, a standard method for determining who would be the next president should a president be unable to fulfill his duties. Vice President Tyler was expected to serve as an interim (temporary) president until Congress could decide on a course of action and a successor. Instead, Tyler had himself sworn into office and began performing presidential duties.

Tyler surprised Whigs by challenging the legislation they expected to breeze through the Harrison White House. Instead of a president who could be influenced by Clay and Webster to approve without personally considering legislation passed by Congress, they met resistance from Tyler. The relationship between Congress and the presidency quickly deteriorated, making both Tyler and the Whigs ineffective.

It was the beginning of the end of the Whig Party. They would win another election with another military hero, **Zachary Taylor** (1784–1850; see entry in volume 2), as their candidate in 1848. But Taylor, like Tyler, proved to be his own man. And like Harrison—Tippecanoe—Taylor, too, died shortly after taking office. His vice president, **Millard Fillmore** (1800–1874; see entry in volume 2), was not an effective leader. The Whig Party dissolved shortly after Fillmore left office. Abolitionists (those who wanted to abolish—get rid of—slavery) among the Whigs turned to the Republican Party, which was formed in 1854.

It is impossible to determine how Harrison would have fared as president. Shortly after election, he indicated to Henry Clay that Clay would not dominate the Harrison administration. Daniel Webster was named secretary of state. Other Cabinet posts went to respected and independent Whig politicians representing various sections of the nation. Harrison had been nominated as a man Whig leaders believed they could easily manipulate, but he still had some fight left in him when he died.

Where to Learn More

Cleaves, Freeman. *Old Tippecanoe; William Henry Harrison and His Time.* New York: C. Scribner's Sons, 1939. Reprint, Newtown, CT: American Political Biography Press, 1990.

Gunderson, Robert G. *The Log-Cabin Campaign.* Lexington: University of Kentucky, 1957. Reprint, Westport, CT: Greenwood Press, 1977.

Peterson, Norma Lois. *The Presidencies of William Henry Harrison and John Tyler.* Lawrence: University Press of Kansas, 1989.

Stefoff, Rebecca. *William Henry Harrison, 9th President of the United States.* Ada, OK: Garrett Educational Corp., 1990.

Young, Stanley. *Tippecanoe and Tyler, Too!* New York: Random House, 1957.

Harrison and John Tyler are the only president and vice president team born in the same county.

Anna Harrison

Born July 25, 1775
Flatbrook, New Jersey
Died February 25, 1864
North Bend, Ohio

Brief first lady had not yet joined her husband in Washington, D.C., when he died

Like her husband, Anna Harrison grew up in genteel (well-bred, refined), aristocratic surroundings but lived most of her life on the Northwest frontier in what is now the state of Ohio. She liked pretty clothes and shopping in New York City at the time her father decided to move west to the frontier, where he had purchased large tracts of land. Anna accompanied him.

Not long after arriving near Fort Washington (present-day Cincinnati), Anna met and eloped with **William Henry Harrison** (1773–1841; see entry in volume 2). She became a strong frontier woman, bearing ten children. She often served as a teacher for them and for other local children. Few teachers had made their way that far west.

Anna Harrison was sixty-five at the time her husband was elected president. She was not pleased about his new job: "I wish that my husband's friends had left him where he is, happy and contented in retirement." Anna was ill for one of the few times in her life when the time came to set out to Washington, D.C., for the inauguration (formal ceremony at which the elected official takes office) in early March of 1841.

"I wish that my husband's friends had left him where he is, happy and contented in retirement."

Anna Harrison

Anna Harrison.
Courtesy of the Library of Congress.

On the advice of her doctor, she did not make the trip. She planned instead to join her husband in May, when the weather was warmer.

Anna never made the trip. Shortly after his March 4 inauguration, William Henry Harrison fell ill. A cold turned quickly to pneumonia, and he died on April 4, 1841. Instead of going to Washington, D.C., Anna Harrison waited at home for her husband's body to be returned for burial to the area they had called home for almost fifty years.

Snuck through enemy lines

Anna Tuthill Symmes was born in Flatbrook, New Jersey, in 1775. Her father, John Cleve Symmes (1742–1814), was a judge who was involved in the American Revolution as a colonel in the Continental Army. Anna was four when her mother died. Her father wanted to take her to Long Island to be cared for by her grandparents while he continued fighting. Unfortunately, he had to cross through British-occupied territory in order to reach them. He disguised himself as a British Redcoat (soldier) and managed to pass through with his daughter in his arms to deliver her safely to her grandparents. Then, he went back to war.

Anna received a fine education growing up in New York. At nineteen, she was getting used to the pleasures of city living when her father decided to move west. Anna went with him across the Allegheny Mountains of Pennsylvania and into the Northwest Territory. They reached Fort Washington. Then they continued on a few more miles southwest along the Ohio River to establish an estate and a town her father named North Bend.

Anna soon encountered William Henry Harrison. He had recently returned to Fort Washington as commander after having left to serve with General Anthony Wayne (1745–1796) at the Battle of Fallen Timbers (1794). Harrison was cited (commended) for bravery in that decisive battle, in which American forces defeated an alliance of Native American tribes. Only three years earlier, Harrison had been studying medicine in Philadelphia. He decided on a military career on the wild frontier instead.

Anna and William soon began a romance, but her father disapproved of Anna dating a military man. Soldiering was a dangerous profession with little pay. While her father was away on a November day in 1795, however, William and Anna Harrison eloped (ran away in secret to be married). They were married by a justice of the peace and settled first in Fort Washington. Soon after, the newlyweds established a farm near her father's estate. By that time, John Symmes accepted that his daughter had married a soldier instead of a farmer or a preacher.

Anna would remain at North Bend for most of her life, except for occasional trips. The couple once traveled to Virginia, where Harrison showed her the plantation where he was raised. It must have looked familiar to her, since Harrison modeled their home on the one he grew up in.

Often on her own

For the first twenty years of their marriage, Anna was often at home in North Bend without her husband for extended periods. He traveled to Philadelphia, where Congress assembled in those days, to represent the Northwest Territory from 1799 to 1801. Harrison was also often away on military excursions, including his famous victories in the Battle of Tippecanoe in 1811 and the Battle of Thames in 1813.

Anna, meanwhile, was busy raising her family. She often served as their teacher. She taught children from the surrounding area as well. Harrison resigned from the army in 1815 and returned home. The couple often invited all the members of their church to barbecues at their farm. A steady stream of visitors stayed at their home as well.

But Harrison left home again, this time as a politician. From 1816 through 1819, he served as a congressman. After returning home for about five years, he was elected to the U.S. Senate in 1825. He served until 1828, when he was named minister to Colombia. He made the long journey to Colombia only to be recalled in 1829 by newly elected president **Andrew Jackson** (1767–1845; see entry in volume 1).

Finally, when Harrison returned home in 1830 at age fifty-seven, the couple could look forward to retiring together. Though Harrison took a minor court job to help earn extra money, the couple was able to be together on their farm. Only two of their ten children, however, had lived to adulthood. It had been a long and often difficult life on the frontier, but the Harrisons had each proved to have the hardiness needed to survive.

Politically active again

Harrison had remained a popular figure in the area for his military exploits. He attended anniversaries of his famous battle at Tippecanoe and was a celebrity in the ever-growing number of small towns dotting the former frontier. The appearances he made that celebrated his past gradually turned to opportunities for pursuing high office. He was such a beloved figure that Whig Party members placed him on the ballot (voting ticket) in western states as a candidate for president in 1836. He performed so well that he was nominated as the national Whig candidate in 1840.

Anna grudgingly supported her sixty-six-year-old husband on his last campaign. She thought it would be better for him to enjoy a quiet retirement, but "Pah," as she called him, was swept into office on a wave of popularity.

When Harrison left for Washington, D.C., Anna remained at home nursing an ailment. It was the last time she saw him alive. Harrison died from pneumonia less than a month after taking office. Daughter-in-law Jane Irwin Harrison, widow of the Harrison's son William, accompanied the new president to act as hostess until Anna arrived in May. Instead, Anna received word of his death about the time she had started packing for her journey to the nation's capital. She waited at home for his body to arrive, then saw to his burial on the land where they had lived for almost fifty years.

Anna remained at her home in North Bend until the house burned down in 1858. She was eighty-three years old then. She moved to the nearby farm of her last surviving child, John Scott Harrison. She had helped deliver one of John's sons into the world, and the boy was one of many who received part of his education from Anna Harrison, frontier woman. That boy, **Benjamin Harrison** (1833–1901; see entry in volume 3), was fighting in the Civil War when she died in February of 1864 at the age of eighty-eight. He would later become president of the United States.

Where to Learn More

Anthony, Carl Sferrazza. *America's Most Influential First Ladies.* Minneapolis: Oliver Press, 1992.

Melick, Arden Davis. *Wives of the Presidents.* Maplewood, NJ: Hammond, 1985.

Stefoff, Rebecca. *William Henry Harrison, 9th President of the United States.* Ada, OK: Garrett Educational Corp., 1990.

Harrison's Inaugural Address

Delivered on March 4, 1841; excerpted from
A Chronology of US Historical Documents **(Web site)**

*"Old Tippecanoe" promises a presidency
that follows the lead of Congress*

William Henry Harrison (1773–1841; see entry in volume 2) rode into the presidency on a wave of popularity over his legendary military background and a colorful campaign. Aged sixty-eight at his inaugural, he was the nation's oldest president until **Ronald Reagan** (1911– ; see entry in volume 5) took office 140 years later. Harrison gave his inaugural address—the longest of any president—on a terribly cold day. Showing his hardiness, Harrison dressed lightly for the occasion. Within a month, he caught a cold that soon killed him.

Though he had very little time to act on what he stated in his address, the speech remains significant as a statement on limited presidential authority. Harrison indicated that he generally planned to follow the lead of Congress. Two powerful congressmen of his Whig Party—Daniel Webster (1782–1852; see box in **John Tyler** entry in volume 2) and Henry Clay (1777–1852; see box in **John Quincy Adams** entry in volume 1)—edited and contributed to the speech, doubtlessly influencing the president's modest approach to office. While Harrison may well have gone on to act in a more independent and forceful manner than he indicated in

"It is preposterous to suppose that . . . the President, placed at the capital, in the center of the country, could better understand the wants and wishes of the people than their own immediate representatives, who spend a part of every year among them, living with them, often laboring with them, and bound to them by the triple tie of interest, duty, and affection."

William Henry Harrison

William Henry Harrison. *Painting by James R. Lambdin; engraving by J. Sartain. Courtesy of the Library of Congress.*

the speech, his inaugural address stands as a statement on limited presidential authority.

Things to remember while reading an excerpt from President Harrison's inaugural address:

- The excerpt begins with the new president suggesting that the role of the chief executive has become too powerful. Harrison's administration followed twelve years of forceful leadership by presidents **Andrew Jackson** (1767–1845; see entry in volume 1) and **Martin Van Buren** (1782–1862; see entry in volume 1). Jackson had acted with such independence that his detractors dubbed him King Andrew. Van Buren's authority was undermined by poor economic times, but he remained a powerful politician. Harrison did not name either president directly, but they served as examples of the type of dominating chief executive of which he disapproved.

- Harrison cited two key examples of how his presidency would be modest and, thus, in keeping with what he believed was the true role of a president. He pledged to serve only one term. That, he claimed, would ensure that his decisions would not be influenced by concern for reelection. And Harrison promised to use his veto power sparingly, if at all. He noted that the first six presidents rarely used their veto power—an obvious reference to Andrew Jackson, the nation's seventh president, who used his veto power more often than the first six presidents combined.

Excerpt from
President Harrison's inaugural address

*When the Constitution of the United States first came from the hands of the Convention which formed it, many of the **sternest republicans** of the day were alarmed at the extent of the power which had been granted to the Federal Government, and more particularly of that portion which had been assigned to the executive branch. There*

Sternest republicans: Those who believed most strongly in a representative form of government.

were in it features which appeared not to be in harmony with their ideas of a simple representative democracy or republic, and knowing the tendency of power to increase itself, particularly when exercised by a single individual, predictions were made that at no very remote period the Government would terminate in virtual monarchy. It would not become me to say that the fears of these patriots have been already realized; but as I sincerely believe that the tendency of measures and of men's opinions for some years past has been in that direction, it is, I conceive, strictly proper that I should take this occasion to repeat the assurances I have heretofore given of my determination to arrest the progress of that tendency if it really exists and restore the Government to its **pristine** health and vigor, as far as this can be effected by any legitimate exercise of the power placed in my hands.

I proceed to state in as summary a manner as I can my opinion of the sources of the evils which have been so extensively complained of and the correctives which may be applied. Some of the former are unquestionably to be found in the defects of the Constitution; others, in my judgment, are attributable to a **misconstruction** of some of its provisions. Of the former is the eligibility of the same individual to a second term of the Presidency. The **sagacious** mind of [former president] Mr. [Thomas] Jefferson early saw and lamented this error, and attempts have been made, hitherto without success, to apply the **amendatory** power of the States to its correction. As, however, one mode of correction is in the power of every President, and consequently in mine, it would be useless, and perhaps **invidious**, to enumerate the evils of which, in the opinion of many of our fellow-citizens, this error of the sages who framed the Constitution may have been the source and the bitter fruits which we are still to gather from it if it continues to disfigure our system. It may be observed, however, as a general remark, that republics can commit no greater error than to adopt or continue any feature in their systems of government which may be calculated to create or increase the lover of power in the bosoms of those to whom necessity obliges them to commit the management of their affairs; and surely nothing is more likely to produce such a state of mind than the long continuance of an office of high trust. Nothing can be more corrupting, nothing more destructive of all those noble feelings which belong to the character of a devoted republican patriot. When this corrupting passion once takes possession of the human mind, like the love of gold it becomes **insatiable**. It is the never-dying worm in his bosom, grows with his growth and strengthens with the declining years of its victim. If this is true, it is the part of wisdom for a republic to limit the

Pristine: Unspoiled, natural.

Misconstruction: Misunderstanding. Harrison is making a pun (play on words): since a constructionist applies the Constitution literally, a misconstruction can be a wrong application of the Constitution.

Sagacious: Wise.

Amendatory: Capable of change.

Invidious: Uncomfortable.

Insatiable: Unable to be satisfied.

Complete American Presidents Sourcebook

service of that officer at least to whom she has intrusted the management of her foreign relations, the execution of her laws, and the command of her armies and navies to a period so short as to prevent his forgetting that he is the accountable agent, not the principal; the servant, not the master. Until an amendment of the Constitution can be effected public opinion may secure the desired object. I give my aid to it by renewing the pledge heretofore given that under no circumstances will I consent to serve a second term. . . .

It may be said, indeed, that the Constitution has given to the Executive the power to **annul** the acts of the legislative body by refusing to them his assent. So a similar power has necessarily resulted from that instrument to the judiciary, and yet the judiciary forms no part of the Legislature. There is, it is true, this difference between these grants of power: The Executive can put his negative upon the acts of the Legislature for other cause than that of want of conformity to the Constitution, whilst the judiciary can only declare void those which violate that instrument. But the decision of the judiciary is final in such a case, whereas in every instance where the veto of the Executive is applied it may be overcome by a vote of two-thirds of both Houses of Congress. The negative upon the acts of the legislative by the executive authority, and that in the hands of one individual, would seem to be an **incongruity** in our system. Like some others of a similar character, however, it appears to be highly expedient, and if used only with the forbearance and in the spirit which was intended by its authors it may be productive of great good and be found one of the best safeguards to the Union. At the period of the formation of the Constitution the principle does not appear to have enjoyed much favor in the State governments. It existed but in two, and in one of these there was a **plural executive.** If we would search for the motives which operated upon the purely patriotic and enlightened assembly which framed the Constitution for the adoption of a provision so apparently repugnant to the leading democratic principle that the majority should govern, we must reject the idea that they anticipated from it any benefit to the ordinary course of legislation. They knew too well the high degree of intelligence which existed among the people and the enlightened character of the State legislatures not to have the fullest confidence that the two bodies elected by them would be worthy representatives of such constituents, and, of course, that they would require no aid in conceiving and maturing the measures which the circumstances of the country might require. And it is preposterous to suppose that a thought could for a moment have been entertained that the Presi-

Annul: Undo an action, in this case by presidential veto.

Incongruity: Incompatibility, inconsistency.

Plural executive: More than one leader.

dent, placed at the capital, in the center of the country, could better understand the wants and wishes of the people than their own immediate representatives, who spend a part of every year among them, living with them, often laboring with them, and bound to them by the triple tie of interest, duty, and affection. To assist or control Congress, then, in its ordinary legislation could not, I conceive, have been the motive for conferring the veto power on the President. This argument acquires additional force from the fact of its never having been thus used by the first six Presidents—and two of them were members of the Convention, one presiding over its deliberations and the other bearing a larger share in consummating the labors of that **august** body than any other person. But if bills were never returned to Congress by either of the Presidents above referred to upon the ground of their being inexpedient or not as well adapted as they might be to the wants of the people, the veto was applied upon that of want of conformity to the Constitution or because errors had been committed from a too hasty enactment.

There is another ground for the adoption of the veto principle, which had probably more influence in recommending it to the Convention than any other. I refer to the security which it gives to the just and equitable action of the Legislature upon all parts of the Union. It could not but have occurred to the Convention that in a country so extensive, embracing so great a variety of soil and climate, and consequently of products, and which from the same causes must ever exhibit a great difference in the amount of the population of its various sections, calling for a great diversity in the employments of the people, that the legislation of the majority might not always justly regard the rights and interests of the minority, and that acts of this character might be passed under an express grant by the words of the Constitution, and therefore not within the competency of the judiciary to declare void; that however enlightened and patriotic they might suppose from past experience the members of Congress might be, and however largely partaking, in the general, of the liberal feelings of the people, it was impossible to expect that bodies so constituted should not sometimes be controlled by local interests and sectional feelings. It was proper, therefore, to provide some **umpire** from whose situation and mode of appointment more independence and freedom from such influences might be expected. Such a one was afforded by the executive department constituted by the Constitution. A person elected to that high office, having his constituents in every section, State, and subdivision of the Union, must consider himself bound by the most

August: Dignified.

Umpire: Third-party arbitration.

*solemn sanctions to guard, protect, and defend the rights of all and of every portion, great or small, from the injustice and oppression of the rest. I consider the veto power, therefore, given by the Constitution to the Executive of the United States solely as a conservative power, to be used only first, to protect the Constitution from violation; secondly, the people from the effects of hasty legislation where their will has been probably disregarded or not well understood, and, thirdly, to prevent the effects of combinations **violative** of the rights of minorities. In reference to the second of these objects I may observe that I consider it the right and privilege of the people to decide disputed points of the Constitution arising from the general grant of power to Congress to carry into effect the powers expressly given; and I believe with [former president] Mr. [James] Madison that "repeated recognitions under varied circumstances in acts of the legislative, executive, and judicial branches of the Government, accompanied by indications in different modes of the concurrence of the general will of the nation," as affording to the President sufficient authority for his considering such disputed points as settled. (A Chronology of US Historical Documents [Web site])*

What happened next . . .

Harrison died within a month, becoming the first president who did not serve an entire term. Vice President **John Tyler** (1790–1862; see entry in volume 2) of Virginia had been chosen as Harrison's running mate primarily for regional balance, since Harrison was best known in the western part (the present-day Midwest) of the United States. Tyler proved to be a much more independent leader. Plans that Daniel Webster and Henry Clay had for running their programs quickly through the Harrison administration were soon halted by Tyler. Upsetting the leaders of his own party was one of many factors that made Tyler an ineffective president. He served only the remainder of Harrison's term.

The history of the United States during the 1840s would have been different had Harrison lived. The Whig Party may have come to dominate American politics the way that Jacksonian Democrats had from 1828 to 1840. Instead, a

Violative: In violation.

Democrat, **James K. Polk** (1795–1849; see entry in volume 2), was elected president in 1844, and the Whig Party faded by the early 1850s. Webster served as Tyler's secretary of state but resigned before the end of Tyler's term, and Clay was defeated by Polk in the presidential election of 1844. With the exception of **Abraham Lincoln** (1809–1865; see entry in volume 2), who served from 1861 to 1865, a series of presidents from 1852 through 1884 were generally dominated by Congress. If Andrew Jackson had been powerful to the point of being dangerous, as Harrison implied in his inaugural address, so, too, history shows, it is equally dangerous when Congress dominates the Executive branch.

Did you know . . .

• The presidential election of 1840 featured the first modern presidential campaign. Political rallies, where bands played and slogans were chanted, first became common during that campaign. Harrison often traveled to attend rallies where he could shake hands and wave to the crowds. Meanwhile, political party members continually urged voters to go to the polls. The fanfare and encouragement worked: over 50 percent more people voted in 1840 than in the presidential election of 1836. Harrison's "coattails" (a term that describes the positive effect of a political party leader—suggesting that others can ride on his coattails) were long: along with Harrison becoming the first Whig Party member elected president, Whigs won majorities in both the House and Senate, each of which had been strongholds of Democrats.

Where to Learn More

Esarey, Logan, ed. *Messages and Letters of William Henry Harrison*. New York: Arno Press, 1975.

Green, James A. *William Henry Harrison: His Life and Times*. Richmond, VA: Garrett and Massie, 1941.

Peterson, Norma Lois. *The Presidencies of William Henry Harrison and John Tyler*. Lawrence: University Press of Kansas, 1989.

University of Oklahoma Law Center. "Inaugural Address of President William Henry Harrison." *A Chronology of US Historical Documents*. [Online] http://www.law.ou.edu/hist/harrison.html (accessed on July 19, 2000).

John Tyler
Tenth president (1841–1845)

John Tyler

Born March 29, 1790
Greenway, Virginia
Died January 18, 1862
Richmond, Virginia

Tenth president of the United States
(1841–1845)

"His Accidency" set the precedent for the
mode of presidential succession

The two most notable events of John Tyler's presidency happened at the very beginning and the very end of his term. In between, the Tyler administration was rendered (made) largely ineffective by a hostile Congress and lack of popular support. Indeed, during his presidency Tyler was ostracized from (shut out of) his own party, endured the resignation of his Cabinet, and faced a vote of impeachment (charged with misconduct while in office). Tyler weathered those troubles with the dignity and good humor he displayed throughout his stormy political career.

Tyler had always been a strict constructionist (one who bases decisions on literal readings of the Constitution). But the constructionist approach does not work if the Constitution is unclear about a certain issue. Regarding the two major events of his presidency that had lasting significance, Tyler did not respond as a constructionist. Instead, he applied his own interpretation to matters the Constitution had not specifically addressed.

"I represent the executive authority of the people of the United States and it is in their name . . . that I protest against every attempt to break down the undoubted constitutional power of this department without a solemn amendment of that fundamental law."

John Tyler

John Tyler.
Courtesy of the Library of Congress.

Fast Facts about John Tyler

Full name: John Tyler

Born: March 29, 1790

Died: January 18, 1862

Burial site: Hollywood Cemetery, Richmond, Virginia

Parents: John and Mary Marot Armistead Tyler

Spouse: Letitia Christian (1790–1842; m. 1813); Julia Gardiner (1820–1889; m. 1844)

Children: Mary (1815–1848); Robert (1816–1877); John (1819–1896); Letitia (1821–1907); Elizabeth (1823–1850); Ann Contesse (1825–1825); Alice (1827–1854); Tazewell (1830–1874); David Gardiner (1846–1927); John Alexander (1848–1883); Julia Gardiner (1849–1871); Lachlan (1851–1902); Lyon Gardiner (1853–1935); Robert Fitzwalter (1856–1927); Pearl (1860–1947)

Religion: Episcopalian

Education: College of William and Mary (1807)

Occupation: Lawyer

Government positions: Virginia house delegate; U.S. representative and senator from Virginia; Virginia governor; vice president under William Henry Harrison; elected as Confederate States congressman (died before term began)

Political party: Whig

Dates as president: April 4, 1841–March 4, 1845

Age upon taking office: 51

The first event involved the manner in which Tyler became president. Tyler was the first vice president to assume the nation's highest office following the death of the president. **William Henry Harrison** (1773–1841; see entry in volume 2) died from pneumonia just thirty-one days into his presidency. Vice President Tyler became acting president. The Constitution was unclear about such a circumstance. It stated only that if the president is removed from office, dies, resigns, or is unable to discharge his duties, the office "will devolve on (pass on to) the vice president." It does not specifically state that the vice president will complete the full term of the elected president or serve as an interim (temporary) administrator until a new election can be held.

Most legislators assumed that Congress would convene (meet formally) to debate the matter while Tyler served as interim president. Tyler, however, had himself sworn in as the new president and began carrying out the duties of the executive branch. Many congressmen and a fair portion of the public were outraged by this act. Tyler did not satisfy them. As president, he immediately followed his constructionist principles by challenging major pieces of legislation proposed and passed by his own Whig Party. The remainder of his term was acrimonious (full of bitter resentment).

Tyler's last official act as president was to sign a bill annexing Texas (adding Texas as a state). The Republic of Texas had ceded (separated) from Mexico, but many congressmen were unwilling to admit the territory because it would add another slave state to the Union. Annexation twice failed to be ratified by the Senate.

Tyler responded by sidestepping the normal treaty procedure, which calls for a two-thirds majority in the Senate. Instead of presenting the act as a treaty, he introduced the annexation of Texas as a joint resolution of Congress, which requires only a simple majority of votes in both houses to be accepted. The resolution passed the House easily and squeaked through the Senate by the slimmest of margins—27 votes to 25. Once again, many were outraged, but the lame duck Tyler simply went about serving the final two days of his administration and then retired to his Virginia plantation. (Lame duck describes an official who has lost an election and is simply serving the remainder of his term of office.)

 John Tyler Timeline

1790: Born in Virginia

1807: Graduates from the College of William and Mary

1811–16: Serves in Virginia House of Delegates

1817–21: Serves in U.S. House of Representatives

1823: Elected to Virginia state legislature

1825–26: Serves as governor of Virginia

1827–36: Serves in U.S. Senate

1839: Loses Virginia gubernatorial election

1841: Serves as vice president under William Henry Harrison for thirty-one days; becomes president following Harrison's death

1841–45: Serves as tenth U.S. president

1845: Signs the Congressional Resolution annexing Texas

1861: Elected to Confederate States Congress

1862: Dies in Virginia

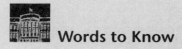 **Words to Know**

Annex: To add on to an existing thing.

Bar exam: A test that lawyers must pass in order to become legally certified to practice law.

Ceded: Separated.

Congressional Record: A document that records all speeches and votes made in Congress.

Constructionist: One who bases decisions on literal readings of the Constitution.

Impeach: Charge with misconduct in office.

Infrastructure: The physical resources constructed for public use, such as bridges and roads.

Interim: A period in between.

Lame duck: An official who has lost an election and is filling out the remainder of his or her term.

Missouri Compromise: Legislation passed in 1820 that designated which states could enter the Union as free states and which as slave states.

Monroe Doctrine: A policy statement issued during the presidency of James Monroe (1817–25). The doctrine explained the position of the United States on the activities of European powers in the western hemisphere. Of major significance was the stand of the United States against European intervention in the affairs of the Americas.

Nationalism: Loyalty to a nation that exalts that quality above all others.

Platform: A declaration of policies that a candidate or political party intends to follow if elected.

Secede: To formally withdraw from an existing organization.

Second Bank of the United States: A banking institution responsible for federal finances.

Tariffs: Taxes on imported goods.

Aristocratic background

John Tyler was born on March 29, 1790, on his family's Greenway Plantation along the James River in the Charles City County area of Virginia. His father, John, was a judge. Tyler attended local schools until age twelve, when he entered the preparatory school of the College of William and Mary. He moved on to the college after completing preparatory school and graduated in 1807. Tyler returned home to study law in Charles City County, first with his father, then with a cousin, Samuel Tyler. These men and Tyler's grandfather influenced Tyler's agrarian (farming; agricultural) and constructionist values. So too did the philosophy of fellow Virginian **Thomas Jefferson** (1743–1826; see entry in volume 1), then president.

In 1809, Tyler passed the bar exam, a test that lawyers must pass in order to become legally certified to practice law. In the same year, his father was elected governor of Virginia. He moved with his father to the state capital in Richmond and began practicing law there with Edmund Jennings Randolph (1753–1813; see box), an eminent statesman who was a former Virginia governor, U.S. attorney general, and U.S. secretary of state. Randolph's support helped elect Tyler to the Virginia legislature in 1811. The following year, Tyler joined the Virginia militia (emergency civilian military force) during the War of 1812 (1812–15), but he saw no action. In 1813, he married Letitia Christian (1790–1842; see entry on **Letitia Tyler** in volume 2), who came from a wealthy Virginia family. They would have eight children.

Tyler was elected to the U.S. House of Representatives in 1816. Although he distinguished himself as a constructionist, Tyler's time in the House was not very successful. He resigned in frustration in 1821. He was associated with the landed aristocracy (the wealthy landowners) that traditionally ran the American government, but times had changed toward a greater concern for and participation of the common people. The War of 1812 had helped inspire a wave of nationalism (loyalty to the nation above all other considerations) and desire for a strong federal government. Tyler, however, still maintained his belief in limiting federal power in favor of states' rights. He was not successful in opposing what he felt were federal intrusions on states, specifically in three major measures: protective national tariffs (taxes on imported goods), the rechartering of the federal bank (the Second Bank of the United States), and the Missouri Compromise of 1820 (legislation passed in 1820 that designated which states could enter the Union as free states and which as slave states).

After returning to Virginia, Tyler quickly restarted his political career. He was elected to the Virginia legislature in 1823, as governor in 1825, and to the U.S. Senate in 1826. In the Senate, he immediately became an outspoken opponent

Edmund Jennings Randolph

Edmund Jennings Randolph was raised in a British household in Virginia, but grew up to become a prominent figure in the American Revolution (1775–83) and the new Constitutional government. Randolph's father came from a prominent Virginia family. He was an attorney for the king of England and returned to England before the American Revolution. Edmund, meanwhile, graduated from the College of William and Mary. Influenced by his uncle, patriot Peyton Randolph (1721–1775), Edmund broke with his father and joined the Continental Army when the American Revolution was underway. When Peyton Randolph (president of the first Continental Congress) died a few months later, Edmund returned to Virginia. He served in the Virginia Convention of 1776, was mayor of Williamsburg, and was attorney general of Virginia before his twenty-fifth birthday. In 1776, he married Elizabeth Nicholas.

In 1781, Randolph began serving as a delegate to the Continental Congress. There and in the Virginia Legislature he worked with **James Madison** (1751–1836; see entry in volume 1) to strengthen the union of the states. At the same time, Randolph became one of Virginia's leading attorneys. He was elected governor of Virginia in 1786. In 1787, he became a Virginia delegate to the Federal Constitutional Convention. His reservations about "energetic government," a concern for the special interests of Virginia, and a kind of indecisiveness caused him to refuse to vote for ratifying the Constitution. Responding to Madison's tactful persuasion, though, he finally supported the Constitution and played a key role at Virginia's ratifying convention.

As the country's first attorney general, Randolph offered balance among the quarrels between fellow Cabinet members of the nationalist policies of President **John Quincy Adams** (1767–1848; see entry in volume 1). He actively opposed bills that mandated federal spending for improving the nation's infrastructure (public structures such as bridges and roads). He also opposed national laws that regulated commerce and agriculture. He found a like-minded advocate for states' rights in **Andrew Jackson** (1767–1845; see entry in volume 1) and backed Jackson for president in 1828.

Although Tyler shared Jackson's philosophical views, he was troubled by what he believed were Jackson's excessive uses of federal powers as president. After helping Jackson forces deny the rechartering of the Second National Bank,

Edmund Jennings Randolph.
Painting by Constantino Brumidi. Courtesy of the Library of Congress.

Alexander Hamilton (1755–1804; see box in **George Washington** entry in volume 1) and Thomas Jefferson. As secretary of state (1794), replacing Jefferson during Washington's second term, he sought to maintain friendly relations with both England and France. Randolph resumed his large law practice following the completion of Washington's administration. In 1807, he was senior counsel for former vice president **Aaron Burr** (1756–1836; see box in **Thomas Jefferson** entry in volume 1) in his treason trial. Randolph spent his last years writing a valuable history of the Revolution in Virginia and mentoring young men, including future president John Tyler. He helped Tyler to establish himself as a lawyer and provided valuable political advice based on his great experience. Randolph's support for Tyler helped the twenty-one year-old to win election to the Virginia legislature, the beginning of Tyler's own long and eventful political career. Randolph died on September 12, 1813.

Tyler broke his alliance with the president when Jackson removed government funds from that bank. He viewed Jackson's act as unconstitutional.

Another break occurred as a result of a tariff that adversely affected the economy of the South. The state of South Carolina threatened to secede (separate) from the Union because of the tariff. Jackson threatened to respond with federal force. Tyler held to his principles regarding states' rights and defended the actions of South Carolina.

By 1836, when Jackson was reelected, Tyler had become a member of the newly formed Whig Party, a diverse

Tyler Becomes President

John Tyler became president of the United States following the death of William Henry Harrison. (See Harrison entry for election results from the Harrison/Tyler campaign.) This marked the first time in U.S. history that a vice president became president following the death of his predecessor. Tyler did not seek reelection.

collection of politicians loosely linked by their support for states' rights and anti-Jackson sentiments. He even appeared as a vice presidential candidate on the ballots (voting tickets) of two states in the 1836 presidential election. Tyler's dislike of Jackson ran deep. Jackson had become the first (and still the only) president censured (officially criticized) by Congress, a result of his seizing the funds of the Second National Bank. Congress began debating whether or not to erase the censure from the Congressional Record, the record of all speeches and votes made in Congress. Tyler was ordered by proclamation of the Virginia legislature to vote for removal of censure. He resigned his seat rather than obey the proclamation.

Tyler too!

Tyler again found himself at home after a frustrating tenure (period of holding office) in Washington, D.C. He was faced with personal and political troubles. Letitia Tyler suffered a stroke that left her in need of constant care. In 1839, Tyler was defeated in a bid to reclaim his Senate seat. The following year, however, he was again on the national scene. The Whig Party nominated sixty-seven-year-old William Henry Harrison for the 1840 presidential election. Harrison had long been popular in the North and the West, dating back thirty years. As a general, he had led American troops to victory over Native Americans in the Battle of Tippecanoe. To round out national support for the Whig candidate, the party chose Tyler, who continued to have political recognition in the South. The ticket (presidential and vice presidential candidates) inspired the famous slogan, "Tippecanoe and Tyler Too!"

The colorful slogan reflected the substance of the Whig candidates. Songs, slogans, parades, and other forms of fanfare were emphasized over discussion on the issues of the day. In fact, the Whig Party did not even present a political platform (a declaration of political policies). Harrison was a popular grandfatherly figure; Tyler was handsome and statesmanlike. The candidates had rarely met before they were paired on the ticket. They formed a front behind which leading (and more controversial) Whig figures planned to pursue their programs. For example, following Harrison's victory, Whig leaders Henry Clay (1777–1852; see box in **John Quincy Adams** entry in volume 1) and Daniel Webster (1782–1852; see box) selected almost all of the members of the new Cabinet. They also edited portions of the new president's first speech, his inaugural address—specifically those passages in which the president announced his plans to follow the lead of Congress. However, everything changed when Harrison died thirty-one days after he took office.

John Tyler became president following the death of William Henry Harrison (above).

Reproduced by permission of Archive Photos.

"His Accidency"

Tyler was not even in Washington, D.C., at the time of Harrison's death. Shortly after, he arrived and began to perform the duties of president even before Congress could begin serious debate on how to proceed in naming a new president. The Constitution was not clear on the exact manner of succession. On April 6, Tyler decided and had himself, as vice president, sworn into office. At the time, the action met with much political and some public outcry. It would eventually set the precedent (the example for future occurrences) for the mode of succession (see box).

Tyler was popular among voters, but not with politicians. He had been an outspoken opponent of the Democratic Party through the 1830s. He joined the Whig Party to oppose Democrats, but he did not share the Whig Party's views on the role of the federal government. Tyler favored states'

Presidential Succession

The original wording of the Constitution on who should succeed a president unable to complete his term was vague enough to spur controversy in 1841. Reprinted below is an excerpt from Article II of the Constitution that describes what should happen if a president is unable to complete his term.

In 1967, the Constitution was amended to clarify the line of succession should a president be unable to complete his term. An excerpt from that amendment follows the passage taken from Article II. The term "pro tempore" that appears in the amendment, refers to the "temporary" leader of the Senate—the Senator (usually from the majority party) who runs day-to-day operations in that legislative body.

From Article II of the Constitution:

In Case of the Removal of the President from Office, or of his Death, Resignation, or Inability to discharge the Powers and Duties of the said Office, the Same shall devolve on the Vice President, and the Congress may by Law provide for the Case of Removal, Death, Resignation or Inability, both of the President and Vice President, declaring what Officer shall then act as President, and such Officer shall act accordingly, until the Disability be removed, or a President shall be elected.

Amendment 25

(Ratified Feb. 10, 1967)

Section 1. In case of the removal of the President from office or of his death or resignation, the Vice President shall become President.

Section 2. Whenever there is a vacancy in the office of the Vice President, the President shall nominate a Vice President who shall take office upon confirmation by a majority vote of both Houses of Congress.

Section 3. Whenever the President transmits to the President pro tempore of the Senate and the Speaker of the House of Representatives his written declaration that he

rights, while Whigs generally wanted to expand the role of the federal government. A good portion of the opposition, then, to Tyler completing the entire term of William Henry Harrison, came from within his own Whig Party.

Tyler's action met with much disapproval from Congress, the Cabinet, the press, and the populace (people). He was dubbed "His Accidency" and "Vice President Acting President Tyler." The situation would grow worse as Tyler made unpopular decisions. Protests occurred regularly around the White House. Tyler was burned in effigy; that is, a dummy (an effigy) was made to represent Tyler and was then burned.

is unable to discharge the powers and duties of his office, and until he transmits to them a written declaration to the contrary, such powers and duties shall be discharged by the Vice President as Acting President.

Section 4. Whenever the Vice President and a majority of either the principal officers of the executive departments or of such other body as Congress may by law provide, transmit to the President pro tempore of the Senate and the Speaker of the House of Representatives their written declaration that the President is unable to discharge the powers and duties of his office, the Vice President shall immediately assume the powers and duties of the office as Acting President.

Thereafter, when the President transmits to the President pro tempore of the Senate and the Speaker of the House of Representatives his written declaration that no inability exists, he shall resume the powers and duties of his office unless the Vice President and a majority of either the principal officers of the executive department or of such other body as Congress may by law provide,

transmit within four days to the President pro tempore of the Senate and the Speaker of the House of Representatives their written declaration that the President is unable to discharge the powers and duties of his office. Thereupon Congress shall decide the issue, assembling within forty-eight hours for that purpose if not in session. If the Congress, within twenty-one days after receipt of the latter written declaration, or, if Congress is not in session, within twenty-one days after Congress is required to assemble, determines by two-thirds vote of both Houses that the President is unable to discharge the powers and duties of his office, the Vice President shall continue to discharge the same as Acting President; otherwise, the President shall resume the powers and duties of his office.

Whigs, who held a majority in Congress, remained confident that they could push their programs through the Whig-dominated administration and they began passing major legislation. One of the first bills called for rechartering the Second National Bank of the United States. The Second Bank was to become the federal banking system. The bank would have offices in several states to regulate the flow of currency and oversee the nation's money supply. Tyler believed the bill impinged (encroached; trespassed) on the rights of states to decide whether or not to have bank branches in their state. He vetoed the measure. Many in Congress were outraged and immediately passed a second

John Tyler Administration

Administration Dates
April 4, 1841–March 4, 1845

Vice President
None

Cabinet

Secretary of State
Daniel Webster (1841–43)
Abel P. Upshur (1843–44)
John C. Calhoun (1844–45)

Secretary of the Treasury
Thomas Ewing (1841)
Walter Forward (1841–43)
John C. Spencer (1843–44)
George M. Bibb (1844–45)

Secretary of War
John Bell (1841)
John C. Spencer (1841–43)
James M. Porter (1843–44)
William Wilkins (1844–45)

Attorney General
John J. Crittenden (1841)
Hugh S. Legaré (1841–43)
John Nelson (1843–45)

Secretary of the Navy
George E. Badger (1841)
Abel P. Upshur (1841–43)
David Henshaw (1843–44)
Thomas Walker Gilmer (1844)
John Y. Mason (1844–45)

Postmaster General
Francis Granger (1841)
Charles A. Wickliffe (1841–45)

bill on the bank. Tyler promptly vetoed it as well.

Following the second veto, Tyler's entire Cabinet resigned in protest, except for Secretary of State Daniel Webster. Tyler named their successors within two days. Tyler was then kicked out of the Whig Party. The situation grew worse in 1842 after Tyler vetoed a series of tariff bills. He believed the tariffs represented federal policies that held power over self-determination by states. The House swiftly called for a resolution to impeach Tyler (charge him with misconduct in office). Public demonstrations outside the White House against the president grew larger and louder. However, fewer than half of the Congressmen voted to impeach the president. The measure failed 127 to 83. A new tariff, more modest and carefully worded, was later passed and signed into law by the president.

That same year, Tyler's wife died. Letitia Tyler had been ill since her stroke in 1839. A few months after her death, Tyler met Julia Gardiner (1820–1889; see entry on **Julia Tyler** in volume 2), a member of a wealthy New York family and some thirty years younger than the president. They were married in June of 1844. The occasion marked the first time that a president had wed while in office. They would have seven children.

The Constitutional sidestep

Tyler's administration did enjoy some successes. The Webster-

Ashburton Treaty of 1842 ended a dispute between the United States and England over the border between the state of Maine and the Canadian province of New Brunswick. The treaty also brought U.S. participation in policing the coast of Africa to stop illegal slave-trading activities. The United States expanded its presence in the Pacific ocean under President Tyler. He invoked the Monroe Doctrine (see **James Monroe** primary source entry in volume 1) to ensure that the Hawaiian islands would not become a colony of any European or Asian nation, and his administration negotiated a trade treaty with China, opening up vast new markets for both nations. Bitterness continued to linger against the president without a party, but Tyler continued to stick to his constructionist principles. He set his sights on annexing Texas, which had ceded (separated) from Mexico in 1836.

The United States, Great Britain, and France all recognized the Republic of Texas as an independent state. Only Mexico continued to lay claim to the territory. By considering the annexation of Texas, the United States was risking war with Mexico. Beyond that, many Americans, particularly northerners, were concerned about admitting a new and huge slave state into the Union.

When Tyler began pursuing annexation, Secretary of State Webster resisted because of the slave issue. As Tyler continued to move ahead on annexation, Webster resigned from the Cabinet. Tyler immediately replaced him with John C. Calhoun (1782–1850; see box in **Andrew Jackson** entry in volume 1), a respected southern politician. Calhoun was a former vice president. He had become the first man to resign from that post when Andrew Jackson showed intentions of using federal troops to enforce tariffs in Calhoun's native South Carolina. Calhoun had also engaged in an historic debate on slavery in 1833 with Daniel Webster, the man he replaced. Negotiations between Tyler and Sam Houston (1793–1863), the president of the Republic of Texas, intensified. A treaty was signed by both men in April of 1844.

All treaties negotiated by the president must be ratified (formally approved) by a two-thirds majority in the Senate. The slavery issue dominated Senate debate on the treaty and proved irreconcilable (incapable of being agreed on). The Senate failed to ratify the treaty. Debate about annexing Texas

Daniel Webster

Daniel Webster was born on January 18, 1782, in Salisbury, New Hampshire. His father, Ebenezer, helped found Salisbury, commanded a militia company during the American Revolution (1775–83), and served in the New Hampshire legislature. He was also a member of the state convention called to ratify the U.S. Constitution. Young Daniel attended village schools, then at age 14 briefly enrolled in Phillips Exeter Academy. Too poor to continue, he started teaching in a country school close to home. After receiving private tutoring, he attended Dartmouth College and graduated in 1801. He studied and practiced law in New Hampshire.

Like his father, Webster was a staunch Federalist, believing in a strong central government for the United States. A champion of New England's shipping interests, Webster disagreed with President Thomas Jefferson's Embargo of 1807, which stopped U.S. trade with Britain and France. Ongoing tensions between the United States and England led to the War of 1812 (1812–15). Elected to the U.S. House of Representatives in 1813, Webster opposed revenue measures that would help finance the American war effort.

Webster moved to Boston, Massachusetts, in 1816. He left Congress to become one of the highest paid lawyers in America. A skilled speaker, Webster became known for his arguments before the Supreme Court in which he defended the power of the federal government over states' rights. While serving in the Massachusetts legislature in the spring of 1822, Webster was chosen to represent the Boston area in the U.S. House of Representatives that fall. In June 1827, Webster was elected U.S. senator from Massachusetts.

In January 1832, a Senate debate on the sale of public lands turned into an exchange over the nature of the Union, allowing Webster to express his firm belief in the Union. South Carolina had been threatening to secede over federally imposed tariffs (taxes on imported goods) that hurt the state. In 1834, Webster, Henry Clay, and John Calhoun established the Whig Party. Andrew Jackson was president at the time and was very popular, but these three powerful senators disliked the president's policies. The Whigs supported a strong central government and believed that the United States would grow by developing technology and strong public programs. They began gathering supporters of their new party in hopes of defeating Jackson in the 1836 presidential election.

In 1836 and 1840, Webster ran for the Whig presidential nomination, but lost both times. In his second bid, William Henry Harrison defeated him, but Webster was chosen as the new secretary of state. In April 1841, Harrison died of pneumonia, but his successor, John Tyler, kept Webster in the post. Webster's main achievement in the position, the Webster-Ashburton Treaty

Daniel Webster.
Courtesy of the Library of Congress.

of 1842, established a permanent border between Maine and New Brunswick, Canada, and avoided a possible war. He left office in 1843.

In 1844, Webster opposed the annexation (the adding of a territory to an existing country) of Texas. He feared that it would lead to war with Mexico and the expansion of slavery. The United States did annex Texas and by 1845 war with Mexico seemed inevitable. Returning to the Senate, Webster called the Mexican War (1846–48) unconstitutional, unnecessary, and unjust. Webster ran again for president in 1848, but lost the nomination to **Zachary Taylor** (1784–1850; see entry in volume 2), a hero of the Mexican War who went on to win the election.

In 1849, Congress became deadlocked over Taylor's proposal to admit California to the Union as a free state (a state where slavery was outlawed). This would tip the balance of power between free (northern) states and slave (southern) states in favor of the free states. Southerners felt this was unfair and threatened secession (separation) and civil war. Webster gave a famous speech on March 7, 1850, in which he supported Henry Clay's proposal for a major compromise that would include California's entry as a free state, organization of other territories gained from Mexico with no restriction on slavery, noninterference with slavery in the District of Columbia, and a declaration that Congress had no authority to interfere with the interstate slave trade. Particularly controversial to the North was a provision calling for the return of fugitive slaves. Webster was enthusiastically received throughout the nation, but antislavery circles—and fellow Whigs—opposed the compromise. In July, however, when Taylor died and **Millard Fillmore** (1800–1874; see entry in volume 2) assumed office, the bill's chances dramatically improved. Congress passed the Compromise of 1850, and Webster defended all its provisions, including the Fugitive Slave Law. Fillmore appointed Webster secretary of state.

In 1852, Webster again sought his party's presidential nomination, but lost to another Whig military hero, Winfield Scott (1786–1866). Webster died later that year, on October 24.

The Whig party failed to support President John Tyler (above) for a second term. He formed a new party—the National Democratic Party—but it gathered little interest and he soon dropped out of the race.

Reproduced by permission of the Corbis Corporation.

moved from the Senate to the electorate as the major campaign issue for the 1844 presidential election.

Tyler formed the small National Democratic Party, consisting principally of officials from his administration. They met in Baltimore, Maryland, and nominated Tyler as their presidential candidate. The Whig Party nominated Henry Clay, a two-time presidential candidate and a widely respected politician known as the Great Pacifier for his ability to find winning compromises on controversial issues. The Democrats nominated **James K. Polk** (1795–1849; see entry in volume 2). Polk was a former U.S. congressman and Tennessee governor strongly associated with Jacksonian ideals still popular in the South.

Polk maneuvered quickly by announcing his support for the annexation of Texas. With his major issue gone, the unpopular Tyler soon left the race. Clay, meanwhile, failed to take a firm stand on the Texas issue. Tyler threw his support to Polk and continued pressing the issue through his role as president. Polk ended up winning a close election and, thus, received a mandate (authorization from the people) for annexing Texas.

Polk's victory encouraged Tyler to try to have the treaty on annexation of Texas passed once again. However, when it became clear that he could not win the two-thirds majority needed for ratification, Tyler came up with a scheme. Confident that he was carrying out the people's will and putting his constructionist philosophy aside, Tyler proposed that Congress vote on annexation by joint resolution. A joint resolution requires only a simple majority of both houses of Congress. When the measure squeaked through in the Senate by two votes, after having passed easily through the House, Tyler signed the Texas resolution annexing the state into law—three days before leaving office.

A Selection of Tyler Landmarks

Hollywood Cemetery. 412 South Cherry St., Richmond, VA 23220. (804) 648-8501. Burial site of President Tyler. See http://www.hollywoodcemetery.org/ (accessed on June 13, 2000).

Sherwood Forest. State Rte. 5, 14501 John Tyler Memorial Highway, Charles City, VA 23030. (804) 829-5377. Plantation and home of John Tyler from 1842 until his death in 1862. The three-hundred-foot-long home is the longest frame house in America. The site is still owned by the Tyler family. See http://www.sherwoodforest.org/ (accessed on July 6, 2000).

Following his presidency, Tyler retired to his Virginia plantation, Sherwood Forest, with his new wife, Julia. The couple would have seven children. The unpopular president gradually won back respect. Through all the turmoil and resentment of his administration, he had remained calm and gracious and had gone about his job with integrity.

The slavery issue that had threatened his hopes for annexing Texas continued to divide the Union. Still faithful to his ideas about states' rights and limited federal powers, Tyler sided with his southern brethren. Now over seventy years of age, he reentered the political arena in 1861. He had become alarmed by the inaugural address of **Abraham Lincoln** (1809–1865; see entry in volume 2). The address stated that federal powers would be used to maintain the Union. Tyler became active in helping Virginia secede from the Union in May of 1861. He attended the provisional Confederate Congress and was elected to the Confederate House of Representatives. However, before he could begin serving in that body, Tyler's health failed and he died early in 1862. He was buried in Richmond next to the grave of **James Monroe** (1758–1831; see entry in volume 1), a fellow president and Virginian.

Legacy

John Tyler set the precedent for succession to the presidency in case the elected chief executive cannot complete his term. The Constitution was later amended to clarify the exact mode of succession. The mode of succession begins with the vice president.

The annexation of Texas proved to be contentious (argument causing), as expected, over the slavery issue. The addition of other territories during Polk's administration, which followed Tyler's, further complicated the issue, resulting in legislation—the Compromise of 1850—that continued to support states' rights to determine whether or not to allow slavery. The issue was far from settled, however, and Tyler continued to participate in the debate. Tyler died as the issue was about to erupt into the Civil War (1861–65).

Where to Learn More

Fraser, Hugh Russell. *Democracy in the Making: The Jackson-Tyler Era*. Indianapolis: Bobbs-Merrill Co., 1938.

Morgan, Robert J. *A Whig Embattled: The Presidency Under John Tyler*. Lincoln: University of Nebraska Press, 1954. Reprint, Hamden, CT: Archon Books, 1974.

Peterson, Norma Lois. *The Presidencies of William Henry Harrison and John Tyler*. Lawrence: University Press of Kansas, 1989.

Seager, Robert. *And Tyler Too*. New York: McGraw-Hill Book Co., 1963.

Letitia Tyler

Born November 12, 1790
Cedar Grove, Virginia
Died September 10, 1842
Washington, D.C.

**Managed family plantation;
died in White House**

etitia Tyler's time as first lady was brief—from June of 1841 to September 1842—and difficult. A stroke had left her incapacitated since 1839. She was accustomed to planning and managing events. She had overseen many of the operations of the Tyler plantation and raised seven children while her husband held various elected positions. Despite her illness, she presided over her responsibilities as first lady from her second-story bedroom in the White House. Only once did she make a public appearance as first lady—at the wedding of her daughter Elizabeth.

Born Letitia Christian on November 12, 1790, on a plantation near Tidewater, Virginia, she was raised to learn domestic responsibilities, from family care to plantation management. Her father was a wealthy merchant involved in Virginia politics.

John Tyler's father (also named John; 1747–1813) was elected governor of Virginia in 1809. **John Tyler** (1790–1862; see entry in volume 2) accompanied his father to the state capital in Richmond. He became acquainted with powerful men, including well-known and respected American states-

"[Letitia Tyler is] the most entirely unselfish person you can imagine. . . . Mother attends to and regulates all the household affairs and all so quietly that you can't tell when she does it."

Daughter-in-law Priscilla Cooper Tyler

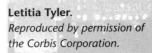

Letitia Tyler.
Reproduced by permission of the Corbis Corporation.

man Edmund Jennings Randolph (1753–1813) and Letitia's father, Robert Christian. Tyler became acquainted with Letitia through these aristocratic leaders. (American aristocrats owned large tracts of land and had social status and political power.) Tyler and Letitia became engaged. After Tyler served briefly during the War of 1812 (1812–15) without seeing action, the couple was married on February 29, 1813.

Tyler's association with Randolph helped Tyler's political career. Tyler pursued politics while Letitia raised their family and presided over the Tylers' plantation. She bore eight children, seven of whom survived.

Tyler's political career took him back and forth between Washington, D.C., and Richmond, while Letitia remained home on the plantation. Tyler was a U.S. representative from 1816 to 1821, served in the Virginia legislature in 1823, and was elected governor in 1825. He then became a U.S. senator in 1826, a position he held until 1836. He was defeated in a bid to reclaim his Senate seat in 1839. Tyler then found himself as a Whig vice presidential candidate and southern counterpart to northerner **William Henry Harrison** (1773–1841; see entry in volume 2), who was nominated for president in 1840. Although the two candidates barely knew each other and had differing political views, they became linked through the famous campaign slogan, "Tippecanoe and Tyler Too!"

Letitia Tyler was unable to share in her husband's return to the national political scene. She suffered a stroke in 1839 and lost much of her physical strength. Following the victory of Harrison and Tyler, her husband remained with her at the plantation. Since vice presidents traditionally had little say in presidential administrations, Tyler could easily hold the position at home. However, Harrison died of pneumonia just thirty-one days after he was inaugurated. There was no established precedent (example for future events) or clear Constitutional guideline for replacing a president. Tyler had himself sworn in as president and assumed full responsibilities. The family soon followed him to Washington, D.C.

Letitia Tyler was unable to perform in a public role as first lady. That responsibility fell to her daughters and, especially, her daughter-in-law, Priscilla Cooper Tyler (1816–1889), who had married the Tylers' son Robert in 1839.

Priscilla was accustomed to public events, having been an actress and the daughter of a noted actor, Thomas Cooper, famous for his leading roles in Shakespearian tragedies. At age seventeen, Priscilla had played the role of Desdemona to her father's Othello in a touring production of the Shakespeare play.

Former first lady and Washington, D.C., socialite (a person prominent in fashionable society) **Dolley Madison** (1768–1849; see entry in volume 1) was still on the scene. With her guidance, Priscilla became known as a charming and popular hostess, arranging lavish state parties and entertaining many guests, including the famous author Charles Dickens (1812–1870). Dolley Madison had also guided Priscilla's predecessor as surrogate (substitute) first lady—Angelica Singleton Van Buren (1816–1878; see entry on **Hannah Van Buren** in volume 1), who assumed the role after marrying Martin Van Buren's son Abraham. **Martin Van Buren** (1782–1862; see entry in volume 1) was a longtime widower when he was elected president.

Priscilla and Letitia helped arrange the White House wedding of the Tyler's daughter Elizabeth, herself a spirited hostess, to William N. Waller on January 31, 1842. Letitia made her only public appearance at this White House wedding, greeting guests and enjoying the festivities from her seat. She died on September 10, 1842, and was buried at the plantation where she was raised.

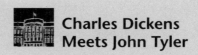 **Charles Dickens Meets John Tyler**

The following passage is an excerpt from *American Notes,* a travel journal by British writer Charles Dickens (1812–1870), author of such works as *David Copperfield* and *A Tale of Two Cities.* Dickens recounts his visit to the White House in 1841.

> We entered a large hall, and having twice or thrice rung a bell which nobody answered, walked without further ceremony through the rooms on the ground floor, as divers other gentlemen (mostly with their hats on, and their hands in their pockets) were doing very leisurely. . . . A few were closely eyeing the movables, as if to make quite sure that the President (who was far from popular) had not made away with any of the furniture, or sold the fixtures for his private benefit. . . . At a business-like table covered with papers, sat the President himself. He looked somewhat worn and anxious, and well he might; being at war with everybody—but the expression of his face was mild and pleasant, and his manner was remarkably unaffected, gentlemanly, and agreeable.

(From Dickens, Charles. *American Notes.* Originally published in 1883.)

Where to Learn More

Boller, Paul F. *Presidential Wives.* New York: Oxford University Press, 1998.

Diller, Daniel C. *The Presidents, First Ladies, and Vice Presidents: White House Biographies, 1789–1997*. Washington, DC: Congressional Quarterly, 1997.

Gould, Lewis L. *American First Ladies: Their Lives and Their Legacy*. New York: Garland, 1996.

Julia Tyler

Born May 4, 1820
Gardiner's Island, New York
Died July 10, 1889
Richmond, Virginia

"Reigned" as first lady despite the controversy her marriage to the much-older President Tyler caused

Julia Tyler was among the most lively, spirited, and public of all the first ladies. She clearly enjoyed her role as hostess at numerous White House parties during her brief period in the White House, from late June 1844 until March the following year. Accustomed to the life of a debutante (a young woman entering social circles) in New York, Julia made White House social occasions formal affairs. Guests were announced and received, orchestras played, and dancing—particularly waltzes—was encouraged. She also actively defended the political positions she shared with her husband, **John Tyler** (1790–1862; see entry in volume 2).

Julia Gardiner Tyler was born to a prominent New York family on May 4, 1820. Her father, David Gardiner, was a lawyer and state senator, and her mother, Juliana McLachlan, was an heiress to the fortune of a Scottish brewer. The Gardiners owned an island home in Long Island Sound that had been in the family since 1639, when adventurer Lion Gardiner purchased it from Native Americans of the Algonquin tribe.

Julia was raised primarily at her family's estate in East Hampton, where she received private tutoring. She later at-

"Nothing appears to delight the president more than . . . to hear people sing my praises."

Julia Tyler

Julia Tyler.
Photoprint by C. M. Bell of painting by Francisco Anelli. Courtesy of the Library of Congress.

tended a private school in Manhattan. As a pretty and wealthy young debutante, she had a coming-out party and joined the New York social circle. Within that circle of people, Julia was known as "the Rose of Long Island."

Julia accompanied her parents on a European tour that included study, sightseeing, and meetings and dinners with various heads of state. Her family arranged the tour, according to some sources, after Julia had appeared as a model in a newspaper advertisement for a department store. Such public displays were considered unbecoming in upperclass New York social circles of the time.

In 1842, the twenty-two-year-old Julia accompanied her parents to Washington, D.C., where they made the social rounds and hoped to find a suitably wealthy or powerful beau (boyfriend) for their daughter. She was quite popular and apparently received several marriage proposals. It was during that time that she first met President Tyler, who had recently become a widower following the death of **Letitia Tyler** (1790–1842; see entry in volume 2). Julia and the president met again during the winter of 1843, when the Gardiners were among special guests invited to ride on a new steam frigate (warship), *The Princeton,* with members of the Tyler administration. The journey turned tragic when a large navy gun exploded on the frigate and resulted in several casualties, among them Julia's father and Secretary of State Abel Upshur (1790–1844).

While President Tyler was consoling Julia on the death of her father, the two fell in love. They became engaged secretly and took wedding vows in New York on June 26, 1844. The marriage—the first time a president had wed while in office—was announced publicly the next day and created some controversy, particularly over their thirty-year age difference.

Julia thoroughly enjoyed her role as first lady, throwing several formal balls. On these occasions, guests were presented to the president and first lady, and couples waltzed the night away. She introduced the custom of having a band play "Hail to the Chief" whenever the president entered a formal occasion. She used her influence to obtain choice positions for friends. She often defended her husband, whose administration was widely unpopular among the press and political opponents. To some, her lavish parties were examples of aristocratic extravagance, but to others she represented youthful

"Hail to the Chief"

There are many stories associated with the playing of the song "Hail to the Chief" for a U.S. president. The first time the song was played to honor a president was in Boston, Massachusetts, on February 22, 1815, to celebrate what would have been George Washington's eighty-third birthday. On July 4, 1828, with President John Quincy Adams in attendance, the Marine Band performed the song at the ground-breaking ceremony for the excavation of the Chesapeake and Ohio Canal. During the Tyler administration, first lady Julia Tyler asked the Marine Band to announce the arrival of President John Tyler by playing "Hail to the Chief." The next first lady, **Sarah Polk** (1803–1891; see entry in volume 2), requested that the band play the tune as a way of making guests aware that President James K. Polk was entering a room. Polk was a short man and often went unnoticed upon his arrival.

The tradition of playing "Hail to the Chief" caught on over the years, though President **Chester A. Arthur** (1830–1886; see entry in volume 3) disliked the song and asked band director John Philip Sousa (1854–1932) to write a new song. His "Presidential Polonaise" never caught on; "Hail to the Chief" became the official musical tribute to the president in 1954.

"Hail to the Chief" was written by English composer James Sanderson. He penned the tune for a stage adaptation of the poem "The Lady of the Lake," written by Scottish poet Sir Walter Scott (1771–1832). It is said that the melody was borrowed from an old Scottish song.

United States Marine Band. "Hail to the Chief." "The President's Own" United States Marine Band: Celebrating 200 Years. [Online] http://www.marineband.usmc.mil/abt_tl_1828_more .html (accessed on July 6, 2000).

---

vigor during a period when American popular culture was embracing new things.

Julia's time in the White House, however, was brief. President Tyler soon stopped his reelection campaign in 1844 after it was obvious that he had no chance to win. After his term was over, the couple retired to Tyler's estate, Sherwood Forest, in Virginia, and raised seven children. The Tylers remained outspoken on such political issues as states' rights and the institution of slavery.

Julia disagreed with a statement signed by several prominent women from the United States and Great Britain in support of abolition (ending slavery). In response, she wrote a defense of slavery that was published in the January 28, 1853, edition of the *Richmond Enquirer* and was later reprinted in the popular magazine *Southern Literary Messenger*. The piece was called "A Letter to the Duchess of Sutherland and Ladies of England in Reply to Their 'Christian Address' on the Subject of Slavery in the Southern States." It argued that black slaves of the South were better off than poor laborers of the North and of Great Britain. Julia Tyler suggested that the proabolitionist women she was addressing should put their efforts toward improving the downtrodden in their own parts of the world.

Former president Tyler became increasingly involved in the slavery issue as well. He supported Virginia's secession (separation) from the Union in 1861 and was elected as a representative to the Confederate Congress. However, he died shortly before taking office. Julia, left to tend to the large plantation and her large family, fell on ill-fortune when the Civil War (1861–65) broke out. Her Virginia home was no longer safe. Julia planned to move her family to her mother's home on Staten Island, New York, but the move north required her to sign an oath of allegiance (loyalty to one's country) to the Union. Since she refused, she was not allowed into the North.

Julia arranged passage on a boat that could avert (avoid) the maritime blockade (blocking of boats at sea) imposed on the South by the North. Her family traveled by boat from North Carolina to Bermuda and then, illegally, to New York. Later, when the boat captain who had smuggled her was arrested for avoiding the blockade, she lobbied—unsuccessfully—to have him pardoned.

While in New York, Julia worked as a volunteer for the Confederate cause. The defeat of the South left her poor. Her support for the South in the war left her at odds with her brother. The family conflict led to disputes over the family inheritance. She received some compensation through her husband's military pension from when he served in the War of 1812. But it was not until 1870 that presidential widows began receiving federal pensions.

Julia returned to live in Richmond after the war. In 1872, she converted to Roman Catholicism and remained devout the rest of her life. She paid a respectful visit to President

Ulysses S. Grant (1822–1885; see entry in volume 3), a gesture meant to help heal the wounds of the Civil War. She died in Richmond on July 10, 1889, and was buried in the state capital, next to her husband.

Where to Learn More

Seager, Robert. *And Tyler Too: A Biography of John & Julia Gardiner Tyler.* New York: McGraw-Hill, 1963.

Tyler, Lyon Gardiner. *The Letters and Times of the Tylers.* Richmond, VA: Whittet & Shepperson, 1884–96. Reprint, New York: Da Capo Press, 1970.

Tyler's Final Annual Address to Congress

December 3, 1844; excerpted from *The American Presidency: Selected Resources, An Informal Reference Guide* (Web site)

An unpopular president attempts to rally support for the annexation of Texas

During the administration of **John Tyler** (1790–1862; see entry in volume 2), the Republic of Texas (established in 1836) sought to become a state. Texas had been a province of Mexico after that nation won independence from Spain in 1821. Between 1821 and 1835, the population of Texas expanded greatly; most of the new settlers were Americans. Tensions rose in the 1830s as American settlers rebelled against actions by the Mexican government. The rebellion seemed to end with the fall of American rebels in the battle of the Alamo in March of 1836, but a month later the Texas army under Sam Houston (1793–1863) won a major battle at San Jacinto (east of present-day Houston). The army rallied under the battle cry "Remember the Alamo, remember Goliad!"—references to two earlier defeats. Following the victory at San Jacinto, Americans in Texas formed an independent republic.

Facing debts and a border dispute with Mexico, representatives of Texas negotiated for statehood with the Tyler administration. Many Northerners were against annexation of Texas, fearing that slavery would expand to the new state. Believing that Texas had vast economic potential, Tyler ap-

"It is the will of both the people and the States that Texas shall be annexed to the Union promptly and immediately."

President John Tyler

proved of annexation. His administration negotiated a treaty of annexation with representatives of Texas.

Under the Constitution, the president has the power to negotiate treaties, but all treaties must be ratified by the Senate. Twice the treaty annexing Texas failed to receive the necessary two-thirds approval in the Senate. Tyler used the occasion of his final annual address to Congress to rally support for annexation. He suggested a sly solution: instead of having the treaty subject to ratification by two-thirds of the Senate, Tyler proposed that annexation of Texas should be handled as a joint resolution of Congress, which requires only a simple majority vote in both Houses to pass.

Things to remember while reading an excerpt from President Tyler's final annual address to Congress:

- In the address, the president went to great lengths to describe hostilities between Mexico and Texas that would likely lead to Mexicans invading Texas to reclaim their former province. By concentrating on that threat, Tyler hoped to rally support for annexation.

- At the time of this speech, Tyler was a "lame duck": he was completing his term until **James K. Polk** (1795–1849; see entry in volume 2), who had recently won election, would officially take over as president in March of 1845. Polk strongly supported annexation of Texas, while his opponent, Henry Clay (1777–1852; see box in **John Quincy Adams** entry in volume 1), was concerned about the expansion of slavery and expressed only mild support for annexation. In the address, Tyler argued that Polk's victory showed that a majority of Americans favored the annexation of Texas.

- Tyler noted that the treaty of annexation had already been approved by the executives of the United States and the Republic of Texas. He proposed that the treaty should be presented as a joint resolution to Congress, which required only a simple majority vote for approval. Thus, Tyler wanted to sidestep the Constitution, which required that all treaties must be ratified by a two-thirds majority in the Senate.

Excerpt from President Tyler's final annual address to Congress

*In my last annual message I felt it to be my duty to make known to Congress, in terms both plain and emphatic, my opinion in regard to the war which has so long existed between Mexico and Texas, which since the **battle of San Jacinto** has consisted altogether of **predatory incursions**, attended by circumstances revolting to humanity. I repeat now what I then said, that after eight years of feeble and ineffectual efforts to reconquer Texas it was time that the war should have ceased. The United States have a direct interest in the question. The **contiguity** of the two nations to our territory was but too well calculated to involve our peace. Unjust suspicions were **engendered** in the mind of one or the other of the **belligerents** against us, and as a necessary consequence American interests were made to suffer and our peace became daily endangered; in addition to which it must have been obvious to all that the exhaustion produced by the war subjected both Mexico and Texas to the interference of other powers, which, without the interposition of this Government, might eventuate in the most serious injury to the United States. This Government from time to time exerted its friendly offices to bring about a termination of hostilities upon terms honorable alike to both the belligerents. Its efforts in this behalf proved unavailing. Mexico seemed almost without an object to persevere in the war, and no other alternative was left the Executive but to take advantage of the well-known dispositions of Texas and to invite her to enter into a treaty for annexing her territory to that of the United States.*

*Since your last session Mexico has threatened to renew the war, and has either made or proposes to make formidable preparations for invading Texas. She has issued decrees and proclamations, preparatory to the commencement of hostilities, full of threats revolting to humanity, and which if carried into effect would arouse the attention of all Christendom. This new demonstration of feeling, there is too much reason to believe, has been produced in consequence of the negotiation of the late treaty of annexation with Texas. **The Executive**, therefore, could not be indifferent to such proceedings, and it felt it to be due as well to itself as to the honor of the country that a strong representation should be made to the*

Battle of San Jacinto: A pivotal battle in 1836 near present-day Houston, Texas, where the Army of Texas defeated a Mexican force and seized control of the area.

Predatory incursions: Raids with an intent to injure. A predator is an animal that preys on others, and an incursion is a raid.

Contiguity: Proximity, geographical closeness; the Republic of Texas bordered on American territory.

Engendered: Developed.

Belligerents: Hostilities.

The Executive: The president—one of several instances where Tyler refers to himself in the third-person.

Mexican Government upon the subject. This was accordingly done, as will be seen by the copy of the accompanying dispatch from the Secretary of State to the United States envoy at Mexico. Mexico has no right to **jeopard** the peace of the world by urging any longer a useless and fruitless contest. Such a condition of things would lot be tolerated on the European continent. Why should it be on this? A war of desolation, such as is now threatened by Mexico, can not be waged without involving our peace and tranquillity. It is idle to believe that such a war could be looked upon with indifference by our own citizens inhabiting adjoining States; and our neutrality would be violated in despite of all efforts on the part of the Government to prevent it. The country is settled by emigrants; from the United States under invitations held out to them by Spain and Mexico. Those emigrants have left behind them friends and relatives, who would not fail to sympathize with them in their difficulties, and who would be led by those sympathies to participate in their struggles, however energetic the action of the Government to prevent it. Nor would the numerous and formidable bands of Indians—the most warlike to be found in any land—which occupy the extensive regions contiguous to the States of Arkansas and Missouri, and who are in possession of large tracts of country within the limits of Texas, be likely to remain passive. The inclinations of those numerous tribes lead them invariably to war whenever pretexts exist.

Mexico had no just ground of displeasure against this Government or people for negotiating the treaty. What interest of hers was affected by the treaty? She was **despoiled** of nothing, since Texas was forever lost to her. The independence of Texas was recognized by several of the leading powers of the earth. She was free to treat, free to adopt her own line of policy, free to take the course which she believed was best calculated to secure her happiness.

Her Government and people decided on annexation to the United States, and the Executive saw in the acquisition of such a territory the means of advancing their permanent happiness and glory. What principle of good faith, then, was violated? What rule of political morals trampled under foot? So far as Mexico herself was concerned, the measure should have been regarded by her as highly beneficial. Her inability to reconquer Texas had been exhibited, I repeat, by eight (now nine) years of fruitless and ruinous contest. In the meantime Texas has been growing in population and resources. . . .

Upon the ratification of the treaty the Executive was prepared to treat with her on the most liberal basis. Hence the boundaries of

Jeopard: Place in danger or jeopardy.

Despoiled: Ruined.

Texas were left undefined by the treaty. The Executive proposed to settle these upon terms that all the world should have pronounced just and reasonable. No negotiation upon that point could have been undertaken between the United States and Mexico in advance of the ratification of the treaty. We should have tried no right, no power, no authority, to have conducted such a negotiation, and to have undertaken it would have been an assumption equally revolting to the pride of Mexico and Texas and subjecting us to the charge of arrogance, while to have proposed in advance of annexation to satisfy Mexico for any contingent interest she might have in Texas would have been to have treated Texas not as an independent power, but as a mere dependency of Mexico. This assumption could not have been acted on by the Executive without setting at defiance your own solemn declaration that that Republic was an independent State. Mexico had, it is true, threatened war against the United States in the event the treaty of annexation was ratified. The Executive could not permit itself to be influenced by this threat. It represented in this the spirit of our people, who are ready to sacrifice much for peace, but nothing to intimidation. A war under any circumstances is greatly to be deplored, and the United States is the last nation to desire it; but if, as the condition of peace, it be required of us to forego the unquestionable right of treating with an independent power of our own continent upon matters highly interesting to both, and that upon a naked and unsustained pretension of claim by a third power to control the free will of the power with whom we treat, devoted as we may be to peace and anxious to cultivate friendly relations with the whole world, the Executive does not hesitate to say that the people of the United States would be ready to brave all consequences sooner than submit to such condition. But no apprehension of war was entertained by the Executive, and I must express frankly the opinion that had the treaty been ratified by the Senate it would have been followed by a prompt settlement, to the entire satisfaction of Mexico, of every matter in difference between the two countries. Seeing, then, that new preparations for hostile invasion of Texas were about to be adopted by Mexico, and that these were brought about because Texas had adopted the suggestions of the Executive upon the subject of annexation, it could not passively have folded its arms and permitted a war, threatened to be accompanied by every act that could mark a barbarous age, to be waged against her because she had done so.

Other considerations of a controlling character influenced the course of the Executive. The treaty which had thus been negotiated had failed to receive the ratification of the Senate. One of the chief objections which was urged against it was found to consist in the fact that the question of annexation had not been submitted to the ordeal of public opinion in the United States. However **untenable** such an objection was esteemed to be, in view of the unquestionable power of the Executive to negotiate the treaty and the great and lasting interests involved in the question, I felt it to be my duty to submit the whole subject to Congress as the best **expounders** of popular sentiment. No definitive action having been taken on the subject by Congress, the question referred itself directly to the decision of the States and people. The great popular election which has just **terminated** afforded the best opportunity of ascertaining the will of the States and the people upon it. Pending that issue it became the imperative duty of the Executive to inform Mexico that the question of annexation was still before the American people, and that until their decision was pronounced any serious invasion of Texas would be regarded as an attempt to forestall their judgment and could not be looked upon with indifference. I am most happy to inform you that no such invasion has taken place; and I trust that whatever your action may be upon it Mexico will see the importance of deciding the matter by a resort to peaceful expedients in preference to those of arms. The decision of the people and the States on this great and interesting subject has been decisively **manifested**. The question of annexation has been presented **nakedly** to their consideration. By the treaty itself all collateral and incidental issues which were calculated to divide and distract the public councils were carefully avoided. These were left to the wisdom of the future to determine. It presented, I repeat, the isolated question of annexation, and in that form it has been submitted to the ordeal of public sentiment. A controlling majority of the people and a large majority of the States have declared in favor of immediate annexation. Instructions have thus come up to both branches of Congress from their respective constituents in terms the most emphatic. It is the will of both the people and the States that Texas shall be annexed to the Union promptly and immediately. It may be hoped that in carrying into execution the public will thus declared all collateral issues may be avoided. . . . Free and independent herself, she asks to be received into our Union. It is a question for our own decision whether she shall be received or not. The two Governments having already agreed through their respective organs on the terms of annexation, I would recommend their adoption by Congress in the form of a joint resolution or act to be perfected and made binding on the two countries when adopted in like manner by the Government of Texas.

Untenable: Unable to be defended.

Expounders: Explainers.

Terminated: Ended. Tyler is referring to the presidential election of 1844, which was won by James K. Polk, a supporter of the annexation of Texas.

Manifested: Shown.

Nakedly: Openly.

Complete American Presidents Sourcebook

(The American Presidency: Selected Resources, An Informal Reference Guide *[Web site]*.

What happened next . . .

The joint resolution idea proposed by Tyler was tried and proved successful. Just a few days before leaving office, President Tyler offered Texas statehood.

In his final annual address, Tyler noted that a dispute concerning the southern border of Texas was still not resolved. Texas claimed the Rio Grande River as its border, while Mexico claimed the border was further north. In 1846, armies from both nations were camped along the Rio Grande. When a scuffle ensued, President Polk asked Congress to declare war on Mexico. The Mexican War (1846–48) that followed was controversial. Nevertheless, an American victory settled the Texas border at the Rio Grande, and the United States negotiated a treaty to take possession of other Mexican territories (most of present-day New Mexico, Arizona, and California) it won in the war.

The issue of slavery expanding into Texas was another problem. A compromise was reached whereby Texas became a slave state and California was admitted as a free state. Nevertheless, the expansion of slavery proved to be an issue that could be resolved only by war. Texas was among the states that seceded from the Union to form the Confederate States of America in 1861. Texas fought on the side of the South in the Civil War (1861–65).

Did you know . . .

- John Tyler was a grand-uncle of **Harry S. Truman** (1884–1972; see entry in volume 4). Truman, like Tyler, was a vice president who became the chief executive upon the death of the president. Unlike Tyler, Truman was later elected president.

Where to Learn More

"Annual Message: December 3, 1844." *The American Presidency: Selected Resources, An Informal Reference Guide* (Web site). [Online] http://www.interlink-cafe.com/uspresidents/1844.htm (accessed on July 19, 2000).

Chitwood, Oliver Perry. *John Tyler: Champion of the Old South.* New York: D. Appleton-Century, 1939. Reprint, Newtown, CT: American Political Biography Press, 1990.

Lambert, Oscar Doane. *Presidential Politics in the United States, 1841–1844.* Durham, NC: Duke University Press, 1936.

Peterson, Norma Lois. *The Presidencies of William Henry Harrison and John Tyler.* Lawrence: University Press of Kansas, 1989.

James K. Polk

Eleventh president (1845–1849)

James K. Polk

Born November 2, 1795
Pineville, North Carolina
Died June 15, 1849
Nashville, Tennessee

Eleventh president of the United States
(1845–1849)

Presided over one of the most successful legislative agendas of the nineteenth century but was hampered by the unpopular Mexican War

In his inaugural address, James K. Polk outlined four major economic and geographic goals for his administration. He achieved those goals by stabilizing the economy and overseeing the largest expansion of U.S. territory of any president. Those accomplishments alone should rank Polk among the most successful of presidents. Instead, a controversial war and regional divisiveness lessened the impact and recognition of his successes.

Polk kept his word that he would serve only one term. His promise was meant to unify political factions within his own Democratic Party and to calm the nation as a whole. But the hardworking president was not able to bridge differences, particularly over the issue of slavery. He left office exhausted and dispirited. He died just over three months after his term ended, at the age of fifty-three.

Overcame physical hardships

James Knox Polk was born in a log cabin in Pineville, North Carolina, on November 2, 1795. He was the eldest of

"Though I occupy a very high position, I am the hardest-working man in this country."

James K. Polk

James K. Polk.
Courtesy of the Library of Congress.

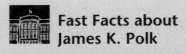

Fast Facts about James K. Polk

Full name: James Knox Polk

Born: November 2, 1795

Died: June 15, 1849

Burial site: State Capitol Grounds, Nashville, Tennessee

Parents: Samuel and Jane Knox Polk

Spouse: Sarah Childress (1803–1891; m. 1824)

Children: None

Religion: Presbyterian; Methodist

Education: University of North Carolina (B.A., 1818)

Occupation: Lawyer

Government positions: Tennessee state representative and governor; U.S. representative from Tennessee; Speaker of the House

Political party: Democratic

Dates as president: March 4, 1845–March 4, 1849

Age upon taking office: 49

ten children of Samuel and Jane Knox Polk. Samuel became a prosperous farmer after moving his family in 1806 to a rural area near the town of Columbia in the Duck River Valley of Tennessee. Samuel Polk's father, Ezekiel, had settled there and was successful as a land speculator (a person who buys land in order to resell it for a larger amount of money). Polk's mother, Jane, was deeply religious and a descendant of John Knox (1513–1572), the founder of the Presbyterian church of Scotland.

Polk was small and thin as a youth and plagued with stomach ailments. He did not have the physical strength to become a farmer. When he was seventeen, Polk's stomach problem was diagnosed as gallstones (small, stonelike mineral deposits that form in the gallbladder). He was operated on by noted physician Ephraim McDowell (1771–1830) in Danville, Kentucky. At that time, there was no general anesthesia (a strong medicine that causes unconsciousness and, thus, a lack of sensation). So the painful operation was performed with Polk conscious, strapped to a table, and holding his father's hand. He survived the ordeal, and his health improved.

Polk's formal education began the following year at a local church. He had barely learned to read and write up to that point, but he quickly excelled and moved on to a school in Murfreesboro, Tennessee. Continuing to progress rapidly and devoting all of his time to learning, Polk became proficient in English, Greek, and Latin. He took an entrance examination to the University of North Carolina and qualified for sophomore standing. He graduated in 1818 at the age of twenty-two with first honors in mathematics and classics. Felled by an illness, he did not return home for several months following graduation. He spent the time studying law.

Political career begins

When Polk returned home, he continued his studies in the offices of local attorney Felix Grundy. Polk's interest in politics was also taking shape. Like his father and grandfather, Polk admired the policies of **Thomas Jefferson** (1743–1826; see entry in volume 1), particularly his agrarian values (support for agriculture). Fellow Tennessean **Andrew Jackson** (1767–1845; see entry in volume 1), a war hero and a politician with enormous support among the rural population, was a family friend.

Polk's political career began when Grundy found him a position as clerk to the Tennessee General Assembly, the state congress. In 1820, Polk was admitted to the Tennessee bar (the legal profession). He quickly established himself as a lawyer in Columbia. An economic depression that began in 1819 and severely affected the South reinforced Polk's commitment to agrarian values. He became more involved in local politics and left his clerk position to run for the assembly. A powerful orator (speaker), Polk was playfully called the "Napoleon of the stump" because of his small stature and commanding presence. (Napoleon was a French general who became emperor of France. He was short and quick-tempered.) The assembly met in Murfreesboro. There Polk became acquainted with Sarah Childress (1803–1891; see entry on **Sarah Polk** in volume 2), who came from a wealthy family. They became engaged and were married on New Year's Day, 1824.

 James K. Polk Timeline

1795: Born in North Carolina

1818: Graduates from the University of North Carolina

1823–25: Serves in the Tennessee House of Representatives

1825–39: Serves in the U.S. House of Representatives

1835–39: Serves as Speaker of the House

1839: Elected governor of Tennessee

1841: Fails to win reelection as governor and loses 1843 gubernatorial election as well

1844: Emerges during the Democratic national convention as the first "dark-horse" candidate for president; wins the election, primarily for his support of the annexation of Texas and expansionist sentiments

1845–49: Serves as eleventh U.S. president

1846–48: Mexican war

1849: Dies in Tennessee

Words to Know

Agrarian: One who believes in and supports issues beneficial to agriculture.

Annex: To add on to an existing thing.

Bar: A term that encompasses all certified lawyers—those who have passed all official requirements to be certified as lawyers.

Compromise of 1850: A group of bills that included allowing Texas to enter the Union as a slave state and California as a free state.

Dark horse: A little-known person given a slight chance to win a race or election.

Expansionism: A policy where a nation plans to enlarge its size or possessions.

General assembly: A state congressional system made up only of representatives from districts within that particular state.

Independent Treasury: Several banks that stored the nation's money supply and regulated currency. The treasury had been established in 1840 after the charter for the Second National Bank had been vetoed by President Andrew Jackson. The Whig Party terminated the system in 1841. The Democratic Party in Congress reestablished the treasury in 1846. It continued as the nation's banking system until 1913.

Manifest Destiny: A term that described America's right to claim and settle the western frontier.

Missouri Compromise: Legislation passed in 1820 that designated which areas could enter the Union as free states and which could enter as slave states. It was repealed in 1854.

Monroe Doctrine: A policy statement issued during the presidency of James Monroe (1817–25) that explained the position of the United States on the activities of European powers in the western hemisphere; of major significance was the United States' stand against European intervention in the affairs of the Americas.

Presidential veto: When a president declines to sign into law a bill passed by Congress.

Protectorate: A relationship where an independent nation comes under the protection and power of another nation.

Tariff: A tax a nation places on imported goods to increase their price, making imported goods as expensive or more expensive than similar products produced in the home nation.

Polk was elected to the Tennessee legislature in November of 1823. He aligned himself closely with Andrew Jackson, who was a presidential candidate in 1824. Jackson led a strong faction (subgroup)—called the Jacksonian Democrats—of the Democratic-Republican Party. The previous three presidents—Jefferson, **James Madison** (1751–1836; see entry in volume 1), and **James Monroe** (1758–1831; see entry in volume 1)—had been Democratic-Republicans, but the party grew increasingly split among the regional lines of North and South. The northern region of the country was mostly urban (city environment), while the southern region was mostly rural (country environment). The North was represented by **John Quincy Adams** (1767–1848; see entry in volume 1). The South was represented by Jackson. In the election of 1824, Jackson received more popular and electoral votes than Adams (and two other candidates), but did not receive a majority. As the Constitution mandates (commands) in such an event, the election was decided in the House of Representatives, where Adams was elected president.

Polk's support for Jackson's policies and his presidential bid in 1824 made him a popular Tennessee politician. He was elected to the House of Representatives in 1825. Bitterness over the controversial presidential election of 1824 remained. John Quincy Adams was made ineffective as president by a hostile Congress and by Jackson, who immediately began campaigning for the 1828 election.

Polk quickly emerged as a leader among Jacksonian Democrats in Congress. He advocated (supported) the limiting of federal power in favor of states' rights. He reformed the banking system to reduce the influence of financial establishments of the Northeast. He worked with other Democratic-Republicans to lower tariffs. He introduced legislation to disband the Electoral College system in favor of the popular vote, but the bill was not successful. (For more information on the Electoral College, see boxes in **George W. Bush** entry in volume 5.) On slavery, Polk supported the right of individual states to decide whether or not to allow it.

Polk's political affiliation with Jackson paid off when Jackson won the presidency in 1828. As chairman of the powerful House Ways and Means Committee, a group of legislators who determine the costs and methods for enacting a

Descriptions of the events of James K. Polk's inauguration ceremony in 1845 were telegraphed to Baltimore by Samuel Morse on his new communication device. A year earlier, former first lady Dolley Madison was chosen to send the first personal message using Morse's telegraph.

James K. Polk became a leader among Jacksonian Democrats and distinguished himself in Congress. The Democrats chose him as their candidate for president in 1844.
Engraving by J. Sartrain; painting by T. Sully Jr. Courtesy of the Library of Congress.

piece of legislation, Polk led Jackson's opposition to legislation that would renew the charter of the Second Bank of the United States. The Bank had a government charter to regulate the flow of currency, control credit, and perform essential banking services for the Department of the Treasury. Jacksonian Democrats argued that the bank had a powerful voice in national affairs but was not responsive to the will of the people. They noted that of the bank's twenty-five directors, only

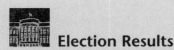

Election Results

1844

Presidential / Vice presidential candidates	Popular votes	Presidential electoral votes
James K. Polk / George M. Dallas (Democratic)	1,337,243	170
Henry Clay / Theodore Frelinghuysen (Whig)	1,299,062	105

A two-thirds majority was required by the Democrats to secure the nomination. Former president Martin Van Buren and former secretary of war Lewis Cass were the early leaders in the first seven ballots, but neither received two-thirds of the votes. Polk's name was introduced in the eighth ballot, and he won the nomination on the ninth ballot.

five were appointed by the government. Polk's congressional stand against renewing the Bank's charter helped make Jackson's presidential veto (rejection) of the eventual legislation a popular political move. The election of 1832, in fact, centered around the bank issue. Jackson won a second term easily.

Polk's influence in Congress continued to grow during Jackson's second term. He was elected Speaker of the House in 1835. He was successful in broadening the administrative powers of the Speaker, but the opposing Whig Party congressional delegation grew stronger following the elections of 1836. **Martin Van Buren** (1782–1862; see entry in volume 1), Jackson's vice president and chosen successor, won the presidential election that year, but Whigs added many congressional seats. Part of the Whig success can be traced to Jackson's banking policies, which had an unstable effect on the economy. As a Democrat—"Democrat" became the official name for the party following the 1832 convention that renominated Jackson—Polk faced increasing hostility over issues relating to banking and slavery. He worked hard and was an effective administrator during a period of waning political fortunes. Faced with growing opposition and an economic downturn called the Panic of 1837, Polk chose to return to state politics.

Polk successfully ran for governor of Tennessee in 1839. Campaigning vigorously throughout the state, he helped reenergize the downtrodden (oppressed) Democratic Party and made a national impression, which lasted even though he was defeated for reelection in 1841 and lost again in 1843.

GRAND DEMOCRATIC BANNER.

At the Democratic national convention in 1844 in Baltimore, Maryland, Martin Van Buren was expected to be voted in as the party's nominee for president. However, Van Buren failed to gain the necessary majority of delegates, principally because he was not in favor of annexing the Republic of Texas, which had ceded from Mexico. He failed to win a majority through seven ballots, lacking support from Southern states. On the eighth ballot, Polk was nominated as a compromise candidate who supported the annexation of Texas. He won unanimous approval on the convention's ninth ballot and became known as the nation's first "dark-horse" presidential candidate—a term that describes a little-known candidate who shows marginal promise.

The Whig Party nominated well-known politician Henry Clay (1777–1852; see box in **John Quincy Adams** entry in volume 1) and immediately seized on the dark-horse theme, presenting voters with the question, "Who is James K. Polk?" Democratic supporters answered by calling Polk "Young Hickory," a play on Andrew Jackson's nickname, "Old Hickory." This new nickname was used to imply that Polk was carrying on the fighting spirit of Jackson. The election centered on the issue of American expansionism (plans for territorial growth)—involving not only Texas but the Oregon Territory as well.

Polk came out clearly for annexing (adding) Texas, while Clay was less forceful. On the issue of the Oregon Territory, which the United States shared with Great Britain, Clay favored a diplomatic solution. Polk took a more vigorous stance. His viewpoint suggested that the United States would be willing to go to war with Great Britain over the Oregon Territory and beyond—including the modern-day area of the Canadian province of British Columbia, all the way north to the Alaskan border, where Russian territory began. On this issue, Democrats rallied around a popular slogan, "54°40' or Fight!" The numbers refer to the latitude parallel at fifty-four degrees, forty minutes, that is, at the southern border of Alaska ("parallel" means the imaginary line that is marked on globes to show latitude).

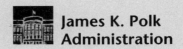 **James K. Polk Administration**

Administration Dates
March 4, 1845–March 4, 1849

Vice President
George Mifflin Dallas (1845–49)

Cabinet

Secretary of State
James Buchanan (1845–49)

Secretary of the Treasury
Robert J. Walker (1845–49)

Secretary of War
William L. Marcy (1845–49)

Attorney General
John Y. Mason (1845–46)
Nathan Clifford (1846–48)
Isaac Toucey (1848–49)

Secretary of the Navy
George Bancroft (1845–46)
John Y. Mason (1846–49)

Postmaster General
Cave Johnson (1845–49)

Polk's proexpansion policies won him solid support of the South and West, except Ohio and his home state of Tennessee. But the state of New York proved most crucial. There, a third candidate, James G. Birney (1792–1857) of the Liberty Party (which was based on an antislavery platform) took enough votes from Clay to make Polk the winner. Believing he could help reduce partisanship (blind allegiance to one's own political party), Polk announced that he would not seek a second term if elected.

Expansionist agenda

In his inaugural address (first speech as president), Polk presented four basic goals for his administration: (1) reestablish an independent treasury system, (2) lower tariffs, (3) settle the Oregon issue with Great Britain, and (4) acquire the California territory from Mexico. He succeeded on all four counts. Polk also improved White House recordkeeping to eliminate waste. He was successful in invoking (putting to use) the Monroe Doctrine (see **James Monroe** primary source entry in volume 1) in 1848. The Monroe Doctrine, a policy statement issued in 1823 during the presidency of James Monroe, explained the position of the United States against European intervention in the affairs of the Americas. Polk used the doctrine to stop what he viewed as an increasing French influence in Mexico, including the possibility that the Yucatan Peninsula would become a French protectorate (a country partially controlled by and protected by another country). All these successes should have made for a triumphant administration, but the success was overshadowed by a conflict with Mexico. This conflict dominated political, popular, and journalistic attention. Public opinion turned progressively unfavorable for Polk.

Polk's first two goals were accomplished without much difficulty. The Independent Treasury had been established in 1840 after the charter for the Second National Bank had been vetoed by Jackson. The Independent Treasury consisted of several banks that stored the nation's money supply and regulated currency. In 1841, the Whig Party terminated the Independent Treasury system, but the party could not gather enough support to charter a replacement after the vetoes of President **John Tyler** (1790–1862; see entry in volume 2). Polk and the Democratic majority in Congress that emerged on his coattails (that is, that came to power because of Polk's success) reestablished the Independent Treasury system in 1846. It would continue to be the nation's banking system through 1913.

Polk was also successful in lowering tariffs (a tax a nation places on imported goods to increase their price, making imported goods as expensive or more expensive than similar products produced in the home nation). Many tariffs at that time protected northern manufacturing interests. The administration, through the Walker Tariff Act, reduced all tariffs except for those on luxury items. The lower tariffs helped western states sell excess grain abroad. Polk had promised the sale of grain as an inducement (encouragement) for Western support of his tariff policy.

Expansionism issues created controversy. Since 1843, Americans had arrived and settled in droves in the Oregon Territory, assuming that it would become an American possession. The territory had been claimed and administered both by the United States and by Great Britain. Polk tried a diplomatic solution by staking the American claim as far north as the forty-ninth parallel, just above the Columbia River in what is now the state of Washington. Great Britain would continue to have possession of land in between that boundary and Alaska. However, Great Britain maintained important trading posts on the Columbia River and refused the offer.

Polk revived the "54°40' or Fight!" slogan, suggesting that the United States was prepared to go to war over the entire territory. Meanwhile, Great Britain was able to establish new trading posts north of the forty-ninth parallel, in the area around what is now Vancouver, British Columbia. In 1846, Great Britain agreed to setting the boundary at the forty-ninth parallel. Polk, with pressure from the U.S. Senate, agreed. The settlement extended the northern border of the United States along the forty-ninth parallel from what is now Minnesota all the way to the Pacific Ocean.

The acquisition of California from Mexico proved more difficult, and complex. Texas had been officially annexed during the final days of the administration of Polk's

Gaslights were installed in the White House while Polk was president.

Although the war with Mexico was dubbed "Mr. Polk's War" by its critics, the successful capture of substantial Mexican territory made the war popular with most Americans.
Reproduced by permission of Archive Photos.

predecessor, John Tyler. A border dispute still lingered in Texas. The United States recognized the Rio Grande as the extent of the Republic of Texas, while Mexico recognized a more northern point—the Nueces River. Emissaries failed to negotiate a treaty. Polk's plan for financing the return to power of former Mexican dictator Antonio López de Santa Anna (1794–1876), who would negotiate a treaty as a return favor, failed when Santa Anna immediately seized control of Mexico's army. When John Slidell (1793–1871), the U.S. minister to Mexico, was expelled, tensions grew worse. The forces of General **Zachary Taylor** (1784–1850; see entry in volume 2) were ordered by Polk to camp along the Rio Grande in January 1846.

An American patrol suffered casualties in April 1846 when attacked by forces of Mexican general Mariano Arista (1802–1855). On May 11, Polk spoke before Congress and demanded a declaration of war, claiming "Mexico invaded American territory and shed American blood."

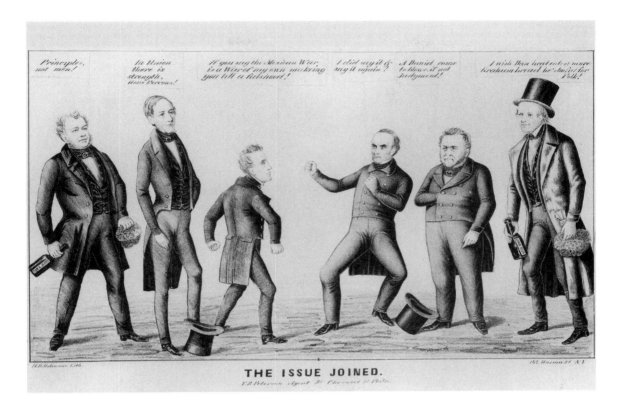

THE ISSUE JOINED.

The resulting war was hotly debated among Americans, but was popular in western states. Northerners viewed it as a pretext for expanding areas for slavery. U.S. senator and former secretary of state Daniel Webster (1782–1852; see box in **John Tyler** entry in volume 2) criticized Polk, claiming that the war was of Polk's making. First-term Illinois congressman **Abraham Lincoln** (1809–1865; see entry in volume 2) even questioned the truth of the report of a Mexican attack. He challenged Polk to show him the spot where American blood had been shed.

Nevertheless, the war moved quickly. General Taylor attacked from Texas straight through central Mexico. General Winfield Scott (1786–1866; see box in **Martin Van Buren** entry in volume 1) invaded Mexico through the port of Veracruz, east of Mexico City. Meanwhile, by August of 1846, the New Mexico area was under the command of General Stephen Watts Kearny (1794–1848). California was conquered from the sea by the forces of Commodore Robert Stockton

An editorial cartoon depicts Democratic president James K. Polk (third from left) and Whig senator Daniel Webster (third from right) fighting over U.S. involvement in the Mexican War. Polk: "If you say the Mexican War is a War of my own making you tell a fals[e]hood!" Webster: "I did say it & say it again!" Two newspaper editors supporting each party stand by their politician of choice. *Lithograph by H. R. Robinson. Courtesy of the Library of Congress.*

John C. Frémont

The first presidential candidate of the Republican Party, John Charles Frémont was an explorer, politician, and soldier. Born on January 31, 1813, in Savannah, Georgia, Frémont was the son of John Charles Frémon and Anne Whiting Pryor. (The family added a "t" to its last name after Frémon's death.) Raised in Charleston, South Carolina, Frémont showed early talent in mathematics and the natural sciences. After attending Charleston College (1829–31), he taught mathematics on a ship and sailed to South America in 1833. In 1836, he helped survey a railroad route between Charleston and Cincinnati, Ohio, and in 1836–37 he worked on a survey of Cherokee lands in Georgia.

In 1838, Frémont obtained a commission as second lieutenant in the Corps of Topographical Engineers of the U.S. Army. Assigned to an expedition that explored Minnesota and the Dakotas, he learned more about natural science and topographical engineering, as well as life on the frontier. He met Thomas Hart Benton (1782–1858), a powerful senator from Missouri, and fell in love with Benton's daughter Jessie. Benton secured an appointment for Frémont to explore the Des Moines River, which was accomplished in 1841. That fall, Frémont married Jessie Benton.

In 1842, Frémont was sent to explore the Wind River chain of the Rocky Mountains and to make a scientific exploration of the Oregon Trail. His report was filled with tales of adventure and contained an excellent map. Frémont was on his way to becoming a popular hero with a reputation as the "Great Pathfinder," but, in reality, he had been following trails established by mountain men. In 1843, Frémont headed another expedition to Oregon territory and returned by way of Mexican California. Ten thousand copies of his report were printed just as James K. Polk became president, a time when hopes were high for American expansionism.

In 1845, Polk sent Frémont and soldiers to California, which was still a province of Mexico. Expelled from California by its governor, Frémont wintered in Oregon. After the Mexican War (1846–48) broke out, Frémont returned to California under Polk's orders and assumed command of the American settlers' Bear Flag Revolt. Aided by commodores J. D. Sloat (1781–1867) and Robert F. Stockton (1795–1866), his forces were victorious, and he received the surrender of California on January 13, 1847. Frémont became embroiled immediately in a fight for the governorship of California with General Stephen W. Kearny (1794–1848), who had

John C. Frémont.
Courtesy of the Library of Congress.

marched from Missouri. Frémont was arrested, taken to Washington, D.C., and
tried for mutiny, insubordination, and conduct prejudicial to good order. Found
guilty, he was dismissed from the Army.
Polk set aside the penalty, but Frémont resigned in anger.

Frémont moved to California, on
the way conducting a private survey for a
railroad route. In California, he acquired
land in the Sierra foothills, formed the Mari-
posa estate, and grew wealthy from min-
ing. He bought real estate in San Francisco
and lived lavishly, winning election as a U.S.
senator from California. In 1853–54, he

conducted another private expedition surveying a railroad route. In 1856, the newly
formed Republican Party named Frémont
its first presidential candidate because of his
strong stand on free soil (antislavery) in
Kansas and his attitude against enforcement of the Fugitive Slave Law that returned escaped slaves to their slaveowners.
He lost the election to **James Buchanan**
(1791–1868; see entry in volume 2).

Early in the Civil War (1861–65),
Frémont performed disastrously as a major
general in St. Louis and in western Virginia.
In 1864, Radical Republicans approached
Frémont about running for president in opposition to Abraham Lincoln; Frémont first
accepted, then declined. After the war, he
was involved in promoting the Kansas and
Pacific Railroad and the Memphis and Little
Rock Railroads. Both lines went bankrupt in
1870, leaving Frémont almost penniless as
he approached the age of sixty. In 1878, he
won an appointment as governor of the
Arizona territory and held the position until
1881, when angry protests from that territory led to his removal.

Frémont's old age was filled with
frustrating schemes to recoup his fortune.
In 1890, he was pensioned at $6,000 per
year as a major general, but he died shortly
thereafter, on July 13, 1890, in New York.

(1795–1866) and by land by the forces of Captain John C. Frémont (1813–1890; see box), head of the Bear Flag army. Mexico City fell in September of 1847.

Polk carefully executed his authority as commander in chief during the war and in the ensuing (following) peace process. He was motivated in part to offset (balance) the growing heroics of Taylor, who was actively courted as a presidential candidate by the Whigs. Polk approached all the issues before him as president with the same diligence (long, steady effort and careful attention).

Treaty negotiations dragged on for several months, until February of 1848. In the resulting Treaty of Guadelupe Hildago, Mexico gave up claims to California, New Mexico, and Texas. In return, Mexico received $15 million. Additionally, all claims made by Americans for reparations (compensation) against Mexico would become the responsibility of the U.S. government. Some Americans wanted to annex all of conquered Mexico, but Polk accepted the Rio Grande as the southern U.S. border of Texas. Acquisitions of Texas, New Mexico, California, and the Oregon Territory rounded out the Southwest and Pacific Northwest of the United States to nearly its present, continental shape (except for areas in southern New Mexico and Arizona).

Triumphs overshadowed

Polk had hoped that the expansionism, the fulfillment of "Manifest Destiny"—a popular term of the time that described America's right to claim and settle the western frontier—would unite the nation. However, expansionism only further fueled the most divisive of unresolved issues affecting the nation—slavery. In August 1846, Congressman David Wilmot (1814–1868) had introduced the Wilmot Proviso, a legislative bill that would bar slavery in all states acquired through war. The bill twice passed the House of Representatives but was defeated both times in the Senate. Nevertheless, a strong abolitionist (antislavery) faction in the Northeast demanded that the new territories should be free states. This group continued to press for an end to all slavery.

Polk's attempt to deal with the issue was a frustrating failure. He himself was a slaveowner and protective of the rights of states to determine their own laws, but he was not ardently proslavery. He opposed abolitionists as well as proslavery apologists (people who argue in support of a cause), but his solution—invoking the Missouri Compromise of 1820—was not acceptable to Northern or Southern groups. The Missouri Compromise (see box in **James Monroe** entry in volume 1), legislation passed in 1820 and repealed in 1854, designated which areas could enter the Union as free states and which could enter as slave states. By trying to remain neutral on the issue, Polk angered Whigs and members of his own Democratic Party, who were splitting along regional lines. The Democratic Party's antislavery faction was led by former president Martin Van Buren. Polk had already lost a measure of popular support for the Mexican conflict, which some called "Mr. Polk's War." Polk's administration concluded with a sense of failure over the slavery issue. Only later, with the Compromise of 1850, was the issue of slavery in the new territories settled. Texas became a slave state, California would be a free state, and other states would decide individually by themselves. The issue of slavery that had slowly but surely divided the nation since its inception (beginning) had become more complicated and heated during Polk's term.

Keeping his word, Polk stepped aside from participating in the presidential election of 1848 and did not seek a second term. By that time, the president who had accomplished all his goals was not very popular. Polk returned home to Tennessee in 1849, succeeded in office by Zachary Taylor.

Polk was exhausted and in poor health. He had rarely vacationed during his term and had been extremely active in all issues. As he noted in an 1847 diary entry, "though I occupy a very high position, I am the hardest working man in this country." He died at age fifty-three in August of that year and was buried in the garden of his Nashville home, Polk Place. His wife, Sarah, lived on until 1891, always keeping the doors of their estate open to visitors from the North or South, even during the days of the Civil War.

The first annual White House Thanksgiving dinner was hosted by the Polks.

A Selection of Polk Landmarks

James K. Polk Ancestral Home. 301 West Seventh St., Columbia, TN 38401. (615) 388-2354. President Polk lived in this home, built by his father, until his marriage to Sarah Childress in 1824. Museum also on grounds. See http://www.jameskpolk.com/ (accessed on July 6, 2000).

James K. Polk Memorial. Box 475, Pineville, NC 28134. (704) 889-7145. Twenty-one acres of replicated farm buildings and exhibits highlight the life of James Polk. Site is on land near where Polk was born. See http://www.ah.dcr.state.nc.us/sections/hs/polk/polk.htm (accessed on July 6, 2000).

Tennessee State Capitol. Charlotte Ave., Nashville, TN 37243. (615) 741-2692. President and Mrs. Polk are buried on the grounds of Tennessee's state capitol.

Legacy

James K. Polk was the last of the Jacksonian Democrats, who held the White House from 1828 to 1849 (except for the ineffective Harrison-Tyler administration of 1841–45). The legacy of Jacksonian Democrats lies in promoting states' rights over federal influence. Polk's economic policies—which centered on low tariffs and the reestablishment of the Independent Treasury—departed somewhat from Jacksonian ideals. Both policies were effective. The newly reestablished Independent Treasury survived into the twentieth century before being enlarged and reformed.

During Polk's term, the nation expanded greatly and fulfilled the concept of Manifest Destiny. California became a state just two years after Polk left office. The areas of present-day Texas, New Mexico, and Arizona, as well as of Oregon and Washington, were all eventually added to the Union after being secured during Polk's administration.

The expansionism, however, brought to the forefront the most divisive issue facing the Republic: slavery. Polk's attempt to remain neutral or to rely on past compromises on the issue of slavery made him the target of ill will from abolitionists as well as those who were proslavery. Every president following him through the Civil War (1861–65) would also be challenged and overshadowed by the divisiveness.

Where to Learn More

Bergeron, Paul H. *The Presidency of James K. Polk*. Lawrence: University Press of Kansas, 1987.

Lillegard, Dee. *James K. Polk*. Chicago: Children's Press, 1988.

Lindop, Edmund. *James K. Polk, Abraham Lincoln, Theodore Roosevelt: Presidents Who Dare*. New York: Twenty First Century Books, 1995.

Polk, James K. *The Diary of James K. Polk During His Presidency, 1845–1849*. Chicago: A. C. McClurg, 1910. Reprint, New York: Longmans, Green, 1952.

Schroeder, John H. *Mr. Polk's War: American Opposition and Dissent, 1846–1848*. Madison: University of Wisconsin Press, 1973.

Sellers, Charles Grier, Jr. *James K. Polk: Continentalist, 1843–1846*. Princeton, NJ: Princeton University Press, 1966.

Sellers, Charles Grier, Jr. *James K. Polk: Jacksonian, 1795–1843*. Princeton, NJ: Princeton University Press, 1957.

Tibbitts, Alison. *James K. Polk*. Springfield, NJ: Enslow, 1999.

Sarah Polk

**Born September 4, 1803
Murfreesboro, Tennessee
Died August 14, 1891
Nashville, Tennessee**

**Was involved politically with her husband's
career; helped prioritize his papers**

Sarah Polk.
*Currier & Ives daguerreotype by
John Plumbe. Courtesy of the
Library of Congress.*

Most wives of politicians during the 1800s remained out of the public eye. Not Sarah Polk. She was an independent woman who shared in her husband's political career publicly and was a key adviser, helping him with speeches and letters. She was an avid reader and made many friends in Washington, D.C., where her husband, **James K. Polk** (1795–1849; see entry in volume 2), served for fourteen years in Congress and for four years as president. The respect she had earned for her intellect is reflected in the official visits politicians continually made to Polk Place, their estate in Tennessee. She managed Polk Place for forty years following her husband's death five months after leaving the White House.

Sarah Childress was born to a wealthy family in Murfreesboro, Tennessee, on September 3, 1803. Her father, Captain Joel Childress, and mother, Elizabeth, were planters and innkeepers. Sarah was indulged with elegance as a child and was also encouraged to be self-confident through good schooling. She was tutored at home and sent to a private Nashville school for girls before being accepted at age thirteen into the Salem Female Academy in North Carolina, con-

"It is only the hope that you [James Polk] can live through the campaign that gives me a prospect [anticipation] of enjoyment."

Sarah Polk

sidered the finest school for girls in the area. The school was founded by Moravians, a Protestant religious sect that emphasizes missionary work. Sarah and her sister attended the school, but they returned to Murfreesboro after a year following their father's death.

The family's wealth allowed Sarah to avoid doing most chores. She spent much of her time reading and studying the Bible. She became acquainted with James K. Polk when he came to Murfreesboro to serve as a clerk for the Tennessee legislature in the early 1820s. Reportedly, their romance was encouraged by **Andrew Jackson** (1767–1845; see entry in volume 1), a war hero and politician familiar with both the Polk and the Childress families. Polk and Sarah were married on New Year's Day in 1824, shortly after Polk had been elected to the Tennessee legislature. He was twenty-eight and she was twenty.

Polk was a strong supporter of Jackson, who lost the presidential election in 1824 to **John Quincy Adams** (1767–1848; see entry in volume 1). Polk was elected to the House of Representatives in 1825 and quickly established himself as an influential congressman. Sarah Polk had remained in Tennessee during Polk's first term in Congress, but she joined him in 1827, helping him with his political career. His career blossomed when Jackson won the presidency in 1828 and served two terms.

Sarah helped her husband privately, reading up on issues of the day and discussing his speeches and political maneuvers with him. Publicly, she proved to be an excellent hostess and conversationalist, even as she refused as a strict Presbyterian to attend theaters or sporting events and forbade alcohol at gatherings she hosted. She freely expressed her views while winning over with charm and good humor those critics who felt that the wives of politicians should remain in the background. Occasionally, she was accused of controlling her husband, but Polk freely sought her advice and assistance.

Polk's health was frail throughout his life. Early in his political career, he kept late hours reading over documents. When Sarah asked him to cut down on his work for the sake of his health, he responded by suggesting that she read through some of the stack of papers. She did. Thus began a common practice of the Polks. Sarah would go through her husband's political papers and mark those she felt most needed immediate attention.

During her time in Washington, Sarah Polk was admired by progressive (reform-minded) thinkers, including Supreme Court justice Joseph Story (1779–1845) and such outspoken women as Marcia Van Ness, a social activist, Floride Calhoun, wife of Senator John C. Calhoun (see box in **Andrew Jackson** entry in volume 1), and Josephine Seaton, a writer and newspaper editor. They did not share all of the Polks' political views, but they valued Sarah Polk for her own opinions and judgment. Sarah Polk's political involvement, though mostly private, was of a kind rarely seen in first ladies up to that point. The exception is **Abigail Adams** (1774–1818; see entry in volume 1), with whom Sarah Polk has been favorably compared.

Polk left Congress in 1839 and was elected governor of Tennessee. He served one term, then was defeated twice before emerging as the dark-horse (little-known) Democratic presidential candidate in 1844. He won the election, and the Polks moved into the White House. Sarah received guidance from former first lady **Dolley Madison** (1768–1849; see entry in volume 1), who helped the new first lady create her own style. Sarah also continued to assist her husband in preparation and decisionmaking. Polk was not a particularly popular president, largely because of the war with Mexico. However, he is viewed as having been successful in achieving the goals he set for his administration.

Sarah Polk was popular as first lady, even as some sources continued to wonder about how great an influence she had on her husband and the nation's affairs. Nevertheless, after Polk left office in 1849, Sarah was cited by *Peterson's Magazine,* a national journal, as among the most admirable women and role models. Polk presidential historian Charles Sellers called Sarah "increasingly indispensable" to her husband "as secretary, political counselor, nurse, and emotional resource."

Even after her husband's death five months after he left office, Polk Place in Tennessee remained an important national site, visited by state legislators, national politicians, and the general public. Polk Place housed the collection of a local historical society during the Civil War for safekeeping, and it remained open as a neutral site during the Civil War. Sarah Polk wore black for the remainder of her life after her husband's death. She lived until 1891; she was buried next to her husband at Polk Place.

Where to Learn More

Bumgarner, John R. *Sarah Childress Polk: A Biography of the Remarkable First Lady.* Jefferson, NC: McFarland, 1997.

Sinnott, Susan. *Sarah Childress Polk, 1803–1891.* Chicago: Children's Press, 1998.

Polk's Inaugural Address

Delivered on March 4, 1845; excerpted from
A Chronology of US Historical Documents **(Web site)**

President Polk outlines four major goals for his administration

In his inaugural address, **James K. Polk** (1795–1849; see entry in volume 2) outlined four basic goals for his administration: (1) limit the power of the federal government in favor of states; (2) stabilize the economy by cutting the federal debt; (3) pursue expansion of U.S. territory; and (4) participate forcefully and diplomatically in international relations. Even as he generally accomplished those goals, Polk lost popular support, primarily over America's aggressive approach to Mexico and westward expansion.

Just before Polk took office, President **John Tyler** (1790–1862; see entry in volume 2) offered statehood to the Republic of Texas (see **John Tyler** primary source entry in volume 1). The issue of Texas statehood was opposed by those Americans concerned that slavery would spread to new U.S. territories. The election of Polk, however, was viewed as a mandate by the people for annexation of Texas. Polk also set his aim on acquiring possession of Oregon territory (encompassing the present-day states of Oregon, Washington, and Idaho), which the United States controlled jointly at that time with Great Britain.

"Our Union is a confederation of independent States, whose policy is peace with each other and all the world. To enlarge its limits is to extend the dominions of peace over additional territories and increasing millions."

James K. Polk

Polk's aggressive approach to expansion marked a new era in American history. Previously, territorial expansion was viewed with concern about whether the nation had a right to expand further and how the Constitutional form of government would work in a more expansive nation. President **Thomas Jefferson** (1743–1826; see entry in volume 1), for example, debated on the Constitutionality and the wisdom of authorizing the Louisiana Purchase (1803). During Polk's term, questions about U.S. expansion were overcome in the minds of many by the belief that the United States had a right—indeed, a spiritual obligation—to spread the virtues of democracy and Christian values. That belief was termed "Manifest Destiny" during the 1840s. The views Polk expressed in his inaugural address reflect the ideals of Manifest Destiny.

Things to remember while reading an excerpt from President Polk's inaugural address:

- The excerpt focuses on the final portion of Polk's address, where he discussed the annexation of Texas and westward expansion. From there, Polk moved on to foreign policy, which he insisted would be based on respect and justice. During the second year of his term, however, the Mexican War (1846–48) was underway and tension was high between the United States and Great Britain, which jointly administered Oregon territory.

- Polk repeatedly referred to the annexation of Texas as a reunification of the territory and the United States. By portraying that relationship, Polk argued that Mexico had interfered in U.S. concerns by warring with Americans in Texas and posed a threat to the nation in general. Many Americans had settled in Texas during the 1820s and turned it into a thriving region, but the United States never controlled the area. Americans had formed the Republic of Texas, but it was viewed internationally as an independent republic. Mexico, which had inherited the former Spanish province of Texas after winning independence from Spain, continued to claim the area.

- The boldness of Polk's expansionist aims are apparent in the excerpt. Virtually all previous expansion of the United States had occurred gradually and involved treaties with foreign nations (such as France in the Louisiana Purchase) or Native American tribes (though much of that territory was acquired through war). Nevertheless, concerns about American expansion persisted, as Polk noted in the paragraph beginning, "In the earlier stages of our national existence. . . ." Polk abandoned that view. He dismissed Native American claims to lands, and he called the Oregon territory "our fertile soil." Expansion was good, argued Polk, because it spread the virtues of American democracy.

Excerpt from
President Polk's inaugural address

Fellow-Citizens:

The Republic of Texas has made known her desire to come into our Union, to form a part of our Confederacy and enjoy with us the blessings of liberty secured and guaranteed by our Constitution. Texas was once a part of our country—was unwisely ceded away to a foreign power—is now independent, and possesses an undoubted right to dispose of a part or the whole of her territory and to merge her sovereignty as a separate and independent state in ours. I congratulate my country that by an act of the late Congress of the United States the assent of this Government has been given to the reunion, and it only remains for the two countries to agree upon the terms to **consummate** *an object so important to both.*

I regard the question of annexation as belonging exclusively to the United States and Texas. They are independent powers competent to contract, and foreign nations have no right to interfere with them or to take exceptions to their reunion. Foreign powers do not seem to appreciate the true character of our Government. Our Union is a confederation of independent States, whose policy is peace with each other and all the world. To enlarge its limits is to extend the dominions of peace over additional territories and increasing millions. The world has nothing to fear from military ambition in our Government.

While the **Chief Magistrate** *and the popular branch of Congress are elected for short terms by the* **suffrages** *of those millions who*

Consummate: Complete, fulfill.

Chief Magistrate: Polk is referring to the position of president. A magistrate is a judge, and Polk suggests by using this term that the president—as the nation's highest elected official—is a chief magistrate.

Suffrages: Votes.

*must in their own persons bear all the burdens and miseries of war, our Government can not be otherwise than **pacific.** Foreign powers should therefore look on the annexation of Texas to the United States not as the conquest of a nation seeking to extend her dominions by arms and violence, but as the peaceful acquisition of a territory once her own, by adding another member to our confederation, with the consent of that member, thereby diminishing the chances of war and opening to them new and ever-increasing markets for their products.*

To Texas the reunion is important, because the strong protecting arm of our Government would be extended over her, and the vast resources of her fertile soil and genial climate would be speedily developed, while the safety of New Orleans and of our whole southwestern frontier against hostile aggression, as well as the interests of the whole Union, would be promoted by it.

In the earlier stages of our national existence the opinion prevailed with some that our system of confederated States could not operate successfully over an extended territory, and serious objections have at different times been made to the enlargement of our boundaries. These objections were earnestly urged when we acquired Louisiana. Experience has shown that they were not well founded.

*The title of numerous Indian tribes to vast tracts of country has been extinguished; new States have been admitted into the Union; new Territories have been created and our jurisdiction and laws extended over them. As our population has expanded, the Union has been cemented and strengthened. As our boundaries have been enlarged and our agricultural population has been spread over a large surface, our **federative system** has acquired additional strength and security. It may well be doubted whether it would not be in greater danger of overthrow if our present population were confined to the comparatively narrow limits of the original thirteen States than it is now that they are sparsely settled over a more expanded territory. It is confidently believed that our system may be safely extended to the utmost bounds of our territorial limits, and that as it shall be extended the bonds of our Union, so far from being weakened, will become stronger.*

None can fail to see the danger to our safety and future peace if Texas remains an independent state or becomes an ally or dependency of some foreign nation more powerful than herself. Is there one among our citizens who would not prefer perpetual peace with Texas

Pacific: Peaceful.

Federative system: National (federal) government.

Complete American Presidents Sourcebook

to occasional wars, which so often occur between bordering independent nations? Is there one who would not prefer free *intercourse* with her to high duties on all our products and manufactures which enter her ports or cross her frontiers? Is there one who would not prefer an unrestricted communication with her citizens to the frontier obstructions which must occur if she remains out of the Union?

Whatever is good or evil in the local institutions of Texas will remain her own whether annexed to the United States or not. None of the present States will be responsible for them any more than they are for the local institutions of each other. They have confederated together for certain specified objects. Upon the same principle that they would refuse to form a perpetual union with Texas because of her local institutions our forefathers would have been prevented from forming our present Union.

Perceiving no valid objection to the measure and many reasons for its adoption vitally affecting the peace, the safety, and the prosperity of both countries, I shall on the broad principle which formed the basis and produced the adoption of our Constitution, and not in any narrow spirit of sectional policy, endeavor by all constitutional, honorable, and appropriate means to consummate the expressed will of the people and Government of the United States by the reannexation of Texas to our Union at the earliest practicable period.

Nor will it become in a less degree my duty to assert and maintain by all constitutional means the right of the United States to that portion of our territory which lies beyond the Rocky Mountains. Our title to the **country of the Oregon** is "clear and unquestionable," and already are our people preparing to perfect that title by occupying it with their wives and children. But eighty years ago our population was confined on the west by the ridge of the Alleghanies. Within that period—within the lifetime, I might say, of some of my hearers—our people, increasing to many millions, have filled the eastern valley of the Mississippi, adventurously ascended the Missouri to its **headsprings**, and are already engaged in establishing the blessings of self-government in valleys of which the rivers flow to the Pacific.

The world beholds the peaceful triumphs of the industry of our emigrants. To us belongs the duty of protecting them adequately wherever they may be upon our soil. The jurisdiction of our laws and the benefits of our republican institutions should be extended over them in the distant regions which they have selected for their homes. The increasing facilities of intercourse will easily bring the

Intercourse: Communication.

Country of the Oregon: Oregon Territory.

Headsprings: The sources of rivers.

States, of which the formation in that part of our territory can not be long delayed, within the sphere of our federative Union. In the meantime every obligation imposed by treaty or conventional stipulations should be sacredly respected.

*In the management of our foreign relations it will be my aim to observe a careful respect for the rights of other nations, while our own will be the subject of constant watchfulness. Equal and exact justice should characterize all our intercourse with foreign countries. All alliances having a tendency to **jeopard** the welfare and honor of our country or sacrifice any one of the national interests will be studiously avoided, and yet no opportunity will be lost to cultivate a favorable understanding with foreign governments by which our navigation and commerce may be extended and the ample products of our fertile soil, as well as the manufactures of our skillful artisans, find a ready market and remunerating prices in foreign countries. (A Chronology of US Historical Documents [Web site])*

What happened next . . .

Texas was officially admitted into the Union in 1845. The following year, a disagreement over the south border of Texas led to skirmishes with Mexico; the president asked from Congress and received a declaration of war on Mexico. Through victory in the Mexican War, the Texas border was set at the Rio Grande River, and the United States acquired former Mexican territory that encompasses much of present-day New Mexico, Arizona, and California. Meanwhile, the United States effectively pressured Great Britain to relinquish claims on the Oregon Territory; the present-day border dividing the state of Washington and the Canadian province of British Columbia was established. U.S. territory spread to the Pacific Ocean during Polk's presidency.

The controversial Mexican War and the annexation of Texas fueled the national division over the issue of expansion of slavery. Violence resulted during the 1850s and led to the Civil War (1861–65), in which Texas fought on the side of the

Jeopard: Place in danger or jeopardy.

Confederate States of America. Expansionism had magnified internal problems within the United States.

Polk had pledged to serve only one term in office. It was unlikely that he would have been reelected anyway. The hardworking president had fulfilled the goals of his administration, but he left office exhausted. He died a few months later.

Did you know . . .

• At least one of the top two presidential candidates from 1848 to 1872 either served in or protested against the Mexican War. They include the two leading American generals during the war—**Zachary Taylor** (1784–1850; see entry in volume 2), elected president in 1848, and Winfield Scott (1786–1866; see box in **Martin Van Buren** entry in volume 1), defeated in a presidential bid in 1852. Another military leader during the war, John C. Frémont (1813–1890; see box in **James K. Polk** entry in volume 2), was defeated in an 1856 presidential bid. As a congressman, **Abraham Lincoln** (1809–1865; see entry in volume 2), who won the presidential elections of 1860 and 1864, challenged President Polk's call for a declaration of war. Lincoln disputed Polk's claim that American blood was shed on American soil by Mexican soldiers, and urged Polk to show him the exact spot where the ambush occurred. **Ulysses S. Grant** (1822–1885; see entry in volume 3), elected president in 1868 and 1872, fought in the war, but he called it "one of the most unjust wars ever waged by a stronger nation against a weaker one."

Where to Learn More

Greenblatt, Miriam. *James K. Polk: 11th President of the United States*. Ada, OK: Garrett Educational Corp., 1988.

Haynes, Sam W. *James K. Polk and the Expansionist Impulse*. New York: Longman, 1997.

Leonard, Thomas M. *James K. Polk: A Clear and Unquestionable Destiny*. Wilmington, DE: Scholarly Resources, 2000.

McCoy, Charles Allan. *Polk and the Presidency*. Austin: University of Texas Press, 1960. Reprint, New York: Haskell House Publishers, 1973.

University of Oklahoma Law Center. "Inaugural Address of President James K. Polk" *A Chronology of US Historical Documents*. [Online] http://www.law.ou.edu/hist/#1825 (accessed on July 19, 2000).

Zachary Taylor
Twelfth president (1849–1850)

Zachary Taylor

Born November 24, 1784
Montebello, Virginia
Died July 9, 1850
Washington, D.C.

Twelfth president of the United States
(1849–1850)

**"Old Rough and Ready" was willing to
share physical hardship and combat with
the men he commanded; his military
popularity led to the presidency**

Zachary Taylor was a national hero when he came to the White House in 1849. His triumphs in the Mexican War (1846–48) had brought him fame after a forty-year career in the military. He assumed the presidency with a nickname—"Old Rough and Ready"—that suited him perfectly.

As president, Taylor was a member of the Whig Party, a political party made of factions (groups) from the former Democratic-Republican Party to oppose the Democratic Party of **Andrew Jackson** (1767–1845; see entry in volume 1). Taylor was very independent-minded. He was far more suited to military command than to the diplomatic duties of president. Plain of dress and blunt in his speech, "Old Rough and Ready" had strong ideas on how the United States should proceed. He stuck to his scruples to such an extent that he brought the nation to the brink of civil war. His untimely death after little more than a year in office allowed for compromises on the slavery issue. These compromises postponed the Civil War (1861–65) for another decade.

The third of nine children born to Richard and Sarah Dabney Strother Taylor, Zachary Taylor was born in Montebel-

"If elected I would not be the mere president of a party—I would endeavor to act independent of party domination and should feel bound to administer the Government untrammeled by party schemes."

Zachary Taylor

Zachary Taylor.
Daguerreotype by Mathew Brady. Courtesy of the Library of Congress.

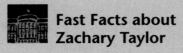

Fast Facts about Zachary Taylor

Full name: Zachary Taylor

Born: November 24, 1784

Died: July 9, 1850

Burial site: Congressional Cemetery, Washington, D.C.; moved to Zachary Taylor National Cemetery, Louisville, Kentucky

Parents: Richard and Sarah Dabney Strother Taylor

Spouse: Margaret "Peggy" Smith (1788–1852; m. 1810)

Children: Ann Margaret Mackall (1811–1875); Sarah Knox (1814–1835); Octavia Pannill (1816–1820); Margaret Smith (1819–1820); Mary Elizabeth (1824–1909); Richard (1826–1879)

Religion: Episcopalian

Education: No formal education

Occupations: Farmer; soldier

Government positions: None

Political party: Whig

Dates as president: March 5, 1849–July 9, 1850

Age upon taking office: 64

lo, Virginia, on November 24, 1784. His father had been a lieutenant colonel under **George Washington** (1732–1799; see entry in volume 1) during the Revolutionary War. As compensation for his wartime service, Richard Taylor received six thousand acres of land in Kentucky. The Taylor family moved to a large plantation near Louisville, Kentucky, when Zachary was less than a year old. Richard Taylor became a prominent citizen, a member of the state legislature, and customs collector for the port of Louisville. (A customs collector is a person who collects government taxes on goods coming into the country.)

Although Richard Taylor had a degree from William and Mary College, he showed little enthusiasm for educating his children. Zachary Taylor studied for a short time under a private tutor, but he spent far more time assisting his father with farming duties. Even with his great military success later in life, Zachary Taylor always considered himself a farmer. He enjoyed talking about raising crops, especially cotton, to the end of his life.

Drawn to the military

Taylor was groomed to run the family plantation, but in 1806 he joined the militia (civilian emergency military service) and found that he liked military life. After his first unit disbanded, Taylor was awarded a first lieutenant's commission in the Seventh Infantry by his second cousin, Secretary of State **James Madison** (1751–1836; see entry in volume 1). Taking his commission in 1810, Taylor spent the next forty years in military service, mostly on the frontier in areas of present-day Indiana, Wisconsin, Louisiana, Minnesota, and Florida. His wife, **Margaret Taylor** (1788–1853; see entry in volume 2), followed him from post to post with their six children, two of whom died very young.

Taylor first gained notice during the War of 1812 (1812–15) when his company of some fifty men held back an attack by four hundred Native Americans, led by Tecumseh (1768–1813; see box in **William Henry Harrison** entry in volume 2), on Fort Harrison in Indiana. Taylor was promoted after the victory, but at the end of the war he was returned to the rank of captain. Furious at the demotion, he resigned his commission. A short time later, in 1816, President Madison restored Taylor's rank and reassigned him to the Third Infantry in Green Bay, Wisconsin.

For the next sixteen years, Taylor moved frequently, supervising the building of forts and the recruitment of soldiers, mainly in the Louisiana Territory. Then, in 1832, he was promoted to colonel. He was sent to Fort Crawford (now Prairie du Chien, Wisconsin), where he commanded a detachment of four hundred men during the Black Hawk War of that year. During fighting with the Sauk and Fox Indians at Fort Crawford, Taylor secured the surrender of Chief Black Hawk (1767–1838; see box).

In 1837, Colonel Taylor was sent with a force of eleven hundred men to the Florida Everglades, where the Seminole nation was forcibly resisting relocation to "Indian lands" in

Zachary Taylor Timeline

1784: Born in Virginia

1806: Joins the Virginia militia at age 22

1810: Accepts a commission in the Seventh Infantry of the United States Army by his second cousin, Secretary of State James Madison

1812: Taylor's company of about fifty men holds back an attack by four hundred Native Americans led by famous warrior Tecumseh at Fort Harrison in Indiana

1832: At Fort Crawford (now Prairie du Chien, Wisconsin) during the Black Hawk War, Taylor supervises the surrender of Chief Black Hawk

1837: On Christmas Day, Taylor's forces defeat Seminoles in a battle at Lake Okeechobee in Florida

1846–48: Taylor's small army unit repulses a Mexican force three times as large at the Battle of Palo Alto during the Mexican War (1846–48); victories in Mexico at Resaca de Palma, Monterrey, and Buena Vista bring national hero status to General Taylor

1849–50: Serves as twelfth U.S. president

1850: Dies in Washington, D.C., after falling ill during a Fourth of July celebration

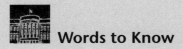

Words to Know

Armistice: An agreement to cease fire while warring parties negotiate a peace settlement.

Black Hawk War: A conflict named after Black Hawk (1767–1838), chief of the Sac, or Sauk, Native Americans. In 1804, the Sac and Fox tribes agreed to a treaty, later disputed, to give up their lands east of the Mississippi River. Suffering from hunger in their new, less fertile lands, the Sauk and Fox in 1832 returned to the disputed territory to plant crops. Skirmishes erupted into full-scale battles. The Native Americans were defeated, and Black Hawk surrendered on August 27.

"Indian lands": Lands in and around present-day Oklahoma, where Native Americans of the Southeast were forced to relocate in the 1830s.

Militia: A small military group, not affiliated with the federal government, organized for emergency service.

Secede: Formally withdraw from an existing organization.

War of 1812: A war fought from 1812 to 1815 between the United States and Great Britain. The United States wanted to protect its maritime rights as a neutral nation in a conflict between Great Britain and France.

Whig Party: A political party that existed roughly from 1836 to 1852, composed of different factions of the former Democratic-Republican Party. These factions refused to join the group that formed the Democratic Party led by President Andrew Jackson.

and around present-day Oklahoma. On Christmas Day, Taylor defeated the Seminoles in a battle at Lake Okeechobee. After that victory he was made a brigadier general. Five months later, in May of 1838, Taylor was given command of the entire Florida department. He served two years at that post, still fighting the Seminoles and making no effort to hide his dislike of the tropical climate. It was during his service in Florida that his men nicknamed him "Old Rough and Ready."

Hero of the Mexican War

The Mexican War brought Taylor to national attention after decades spent in relative obscurity. In March of

1845, the United States invited Texas (a territory recently declared independent of Mexico) to join the Union. Mexico strongly objected, since the border between Mexico and Texas was disputed. In anticipation of armed conflict, President **James K. Polk** (1795–1849; see entry in volume 2) dispatched Taylor to the disputed territory between the Nueces River and the Rio Grande. There Taylor raised an army of four thousand regulars and volunteers.

On January 13, 1846, Taylor was ordered to advance south to the Rio Grande, and his forces prepared to fight. The first major conflict occurred on May 8, 1846, when Taylor's small army drove back a Mexican force three times as large at the Battle of Palo Alto.

This victory brought Taylor a promotion to major general. "Old Rough and Ready" proved equal to the promotion in September of 1846 when he commanded another lopsided victory against the fortified city of Monterrey in northern Mexi-

The battle of Buena Vista was the decisive battle of the Mexican War. When news spread of the victory by General Zachary Taylor's troops, Whig leaders began to recruit Taylor for the presidential nomination.
Lithograph by Sarony & Major. Courtesy of the Library of Congress.

Black Hawk

Black Hawk was born into the Thunder Clan in 1767 in Sauk Sautenuk/ Saukenuk, Virginia Colony (now Rock Island, Illinois). He developed into a brave warrior and married a woman named Assheweque (Singing Bird), with whom he had three children. The chain of events that would make Black Hawk a resistance leader began in 1804, when the leaders of the southern Sauk and Fox of the Missouri signed the Treaty of St. Louis, handing over all tribal lands east of the Mississippi River to the United States. Black Hawk claimed that these tribal leaders did not speak for or represent the northern Sauk and Fox of the Mississippi River area. He refused to move to Iowa from his territory in Illinois and Wisconsin.

Black Hawk became a supporter of Shawnee tribal leader Tecumseh, who proposed a Native tribal confederacy, an alliance of tribes who would protect one another's interests. Like Tecumseh, Black Hawk sided with the British against America in the War of 1812 (1812–15), which was fought over international trading rights. The U.S. government began to hold discussions with Keokuk (1788–1848?), a younger rival chief of the Fox clan. In 1816, the U.S. Army built Fort Armstrong at Rock Island, Illinois, within Black Hawk's traditional homeland. Two years later, the Illi-

nois Territory became the twenty-first state. During the 1820s, while the state still had a small population, Black Hawk strengthened his ties with the British Empire by making frequent trading trips back and forth to Canada.

Keokuk continued to negotiate with the U.S. government for Sauk and Fox land. In 1829, he advised peace to his people. In company with two other Sauk and Fox chiefs, Keokuk gave up the Rock River land area to the United States in exchange for land west of the Mississippi in what is now Iowa and an annuity (an ongoing regular payment) for the tribe. Black Hawk's band returned from their winter hunt in the spring of 1829 to Saukenuk, their Rock River village, to find their land and homes occupied by whites. Though enraged, Black Hawk and his followers nonetheless stayed and shared their village with the newcomers for the remainder of that summer and for the next two years.

In the summer of 1831, the U.S. government invaded Saukenuk to force the two thousand dwellers of Black Hawk's village across the Mississippi River in accordance with Keokuk's agreement. Warned in advance of the attempt, however, Black Hawk and his villagers had escaped the previous night into Iowa and remained there through the following March. Black Hawk received spiritual and political support for his resistance from the Winnebago prophet White Cloud, and counted more than two thousand people, including six hundred warriors, among his followers. However, Black Hawk received no aid in the struggle from the British. On April 5, 1832, Black Hawk's band of one thousand crossed the Mississippi River back into Illinois and headed north, trying to win support from other tribes in the area. The Winnebago and Potawatomi, however, declared their neutrality and refused to support Black Hawk. Meanwhile, the U.S. Army and state militias were called up. Among the volunteers to fight were such future political notables as Zachary Taylor and Jefferson Davis. A month later, Black Hawk was ready to admit defeat and surrender.

On May 14, 1832, as his truce party approached the U.S. troops under a white flag, nervous soldiers fired on them. His warriors retaliated and won the battle, which became known as Stillman's Run, after the panicked flight of the troops of Major Isaiah Stillman (1797–1861). Happy in their victory, but cautious about reprisals, Black Hawk and White Cloud headed back north to Wisconsin. For the next two months, however, the combined U.S. forces kept Black Hawk's band on the run with minor skirmishes along the way. With no aid from other tribes, lacking food, and losing warriors to desertion, Black Hawk continued to press north into Wisconsin. On July 21, 1832, the U.S. Army and Wisconsin militia, aided by Winnebago informers, attacked Black Hawk in the Battle of Wisconsin Heights, near present-day Sauk City, northwest of Madison. Many natives were killed, but others escaped by raft across the Wisconsin River, pushing westward toward the Bad Axe River that flows into the Mississippi. On August 3, 1832, the U.S. Army attacked with cannon, artillery, and sharpshooters in what became known as the Massacre at Bad Axe River. Exhausted and demoralized, Black Hawk, White Cloud, and the remaining resistance fighters surrendered at Fort Crawford (present-day Prairie du Chien), Wisconsin, on August 27, 1832.

From Wisconsin, Black Hawk was taken to Jefferson Barracks, Missouri, and then held as a prisoner of war in Fort Monroe, Virginia. In 1833, he was taken to Washington, D.C., to meet President Andrew Jackson, and he later toured cities in the eastern United States. Black Hawk became something of a celebrity after his surrender. He died in Iowaville, Iowa, on October 3, 1838.

For religious reasons, Zachary Taylor refused to be sworn in as president on March 4, because it was a Sunday. Since President James K. Polk and Vice President George M. Dallas's terms had expired, David Rice Atchison of Missouri, president pro tem (temporary leader) of the U.S. Senate, legally served as president for twenty-four hours until Taylor was sworn in the next day.

co. Braving devastating gunfire from the enemy, Taylor and his troops invaded the city and fought hand to hand in the streets against a superior force. Mexican troops finally surrendered when Taylor agreed to an eight-week armistice (ceasefire) and allowed the Mexican soldiers to retreat with their weapons.

Victories at Palo Alto, Resaca de Palma, and Monterrey brought hero status to General Zachary Taylor, now famous for his scruffy clothing and his horse, Old Whitey. This level of success did not sit well with President Polk, who correctly perceived that Taylor might have political ambitions for a rival party. Polk expressed outrage at the armistice agreement Taylor had drawn up in Monterrey. Had the general not been so popular, the president might have relieved him of his command. As it was, Polk ordered another popular general, Winfield Scott (1786–1866; see box in **Martin Van Buren** entry in volume 1), to advance upon Mexico City—and to take the best soldiers from Taylor's force to do it.

As his most dependable troops joined Scott, Taylor was ordered to remain in Monterrey in a strictly defensive posture. He ignored the order and began to move southward with what remained of his army. On February 23, 1847, Taylor's force of five thousand met an army of fifteen thousand to twenty thousand led by famous Mexican general Antonio López de Santa Anna (1794–1876) at a hacienda (large estate) called Buena Vista. The two-day battle that followed was another resounding victory for the Americans, in no small part because Taylor showed amazing personal valor. At the end of the Battle of Buena Vista, the American force recorded 267 men killed and 456 wounded, against more than 2,000 fatalities for the Mexican army. The fighting in northern Mexico was effectively over. Some months later, Winfield Scott was able to march into Mexico City.

President Polk's plan to minimize the heroism of Taylor failed miserably. As news of the Battle of Buena Vista spread, Whig leaders across the nation began to court the popular general and to propose that he seek the presidency.

"Independent of party domination"

Although he owned a home in Louisiana and a cotton plantation with some one hundred slaves in Mississippi, Tay-

AN AVAILABLE CANDIDATE.
THE ONE QUALIFICATION FOR A WHIG PRESIDENT.

This negative campaign poster portrays a Whig candidate—it is either Zachary Taylor or Winfield Scott, both Mexican War generals—sitting atop a pyramid of skulls from the war. The Whigs nominated Taylor based on his popularity, despite the fact that he had never held public office or even voted in an election.
Courtesy of the Library of Congress.

lor had never really lived at a fixed address. He had never voted in an election and had never registered to vote. But as his popularity swept the nation, these facts hardly seemed important. Nor did it seem to matter much that no one knew how he stood on many domestic or foreign issues of the day.

In a letter made public in April of 1848, Taylor admitted that he felt ignorant of many public issues. He further

confused his supporters by declaring, "I am a Whig but not ultra Whig." He added: "If elected I would not be the mere president of a party—I would endeavor to act independent of party domination and should feel bound to administer the Government untrammeled by party schemes."

Taylor's election was helped immensely when anti-slavery Whigs defected from his platform and formed the

Election Results

1848

Presidential / Vice presidential candidates	Popular votes	Presidential electoral votes
Zachary Taylor / Millard Fillmore (Whig)	1,360,099	163
Lewis Cass / William O. Butler (Democratic)	1,220,544	127
Martin Van Buren / Charles Francis Adams (Free Soil)	291,263	0

Free Soil Party, nominating ex-president **Martin Van Buren** (1782–1862; see entry in volume 1) as its candidate. Although Van Buren finished a distant third in the popular vote, he drew enough voters away from the Democratic candidate, Lewis Cass (1782–1866; see box), to give Taylor a key victory—and thiry-six electoral votes—from the state of New York. Taylor won the presidency without a majority of the popular vote (he received 1,360,099 votes to Cass's 1,220,544 and Van Buren's 291,263). Perhaps more importantly, he won without the trust of his own party.

Taylor was inaugurated on March 5, 1849, and immediately marked himself as a controversial president. The great debate in Congress at the time concerned the extension of slavery into regions of the Southwest that had been ceded (handed over) to the United States as a result of the Mexican War. A gold rush had begun in California, and that territory expressed an interest in statehood. New Mexico and Utah had been free of slavery while in Mexican hands, but Southerners wanted to extend slavery into those areas.

A slaveowner himself, Taylor might have been expected to support the extension of slavery. He did not. He felt that the institution of slavery was based on economics and should not be used in regions where cotton could not be grown. He was also concerned that this one issue might tear the nation apart. "Old Rough and Ready" worked to prevent the breakup of the Union. For example, he invited California and New Mexico to apply for statehood, with their own local

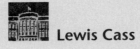

Lewis Cass

Twice a presidential nominee, Lewis Cass served as secretary of war, minister to France, and secretary of state. Born on October 2, 1782, in New Hampshire, Cass was the son of a Revolutionary War veteran, Major Jonathan Cass, and Mary Gilman Cass. He studied at Phillips Exeter Academy. In 1800, the family moved to the Ohio frontier, where Cass studied law and began a practice in 1803. In 1806, he married Elizabeth Spencer and was elected to the legislature in Ohio.

During the War of 1812 (1812–15), Cass advanced from colonel of militia to brigadier general and fought with distinction at the Battle of the Thames in present-day Ontario. In 1813, he was appointed governor of the Michigan Territory. He made a fortune by buying land in Detroit and later selling it in city lots. Promoting universal education, the establishment of libraries, road-building, and surveying tracts for settlers, Cass speeded up the American settlement of Michigan. As Indian commissioner, he conducted expeditions to the northwestern area of the territory, studied Native American languages, and supported scholarly work on Native American culture. Still, he persuaded Native Americans to cede their lands; as President Andrew Jackson's secretary of war from 1831 to 1836, he vigorously supported the forced removal of the Cherokee from the South.

Appointed minister to France in 1836, Cass used his influence against British efforts to stop the international slave trade. In 1842, he sought the Democratic nomination for president, but lost to James K. Polk. Elected to the Senate in 1845, Cass urged war against Britain, if necessary, to obtain all of the Oregon Territory. He defended American involvement in the Mexican War above protests that it was an act of aggression, and he advocated the acquisition of Cuba.

legislatures deciding whether or not to allow slavery inside their borders. Both territories had let it be known they did not want slavery. It was understood that they would be admitted as free states.

Taylor's views found favor with antislavery politicians. Not surprisingly, the vast majority of Southern slaveholders denounced the new president and began to hint that they might secede (separate) from the Union. Taylor answered the talk of secession with tough words of his own. He said he would send troops to police a disputed boundary be-

Lewis Cass.
Courtesy of the Library of Congress.

With Southern support, Cass was the Democratic nominee for president in 1848, but he lost narrowly to General Zachary Taylor. Cass returned to the Senate (1849–56) and was a candidate for president

in 1852, at age seventy, but the Democrats nominated **Franklin Pierce** (1804–1869; see entry in volume 2). Cass supported the Compromise of 1850, including the Fugitive Slave Law, which forced return of runaway slaves to their slaveowner. He supported the "popular sovereignty" doctrine of Stephen Douglas (1813–1861; see box in **Abraham Lincoln** entry in volume 2), whereby new territories could decide for themselves whether or not to permit slavery. In 1856, the Republican legislature in Michigan removed Cass from the Senate.

President **James Buchanan** (1791–1868; see entry in volume 2) made the aged Cass his secretary of state. As sectional conflicts dominated the American scene, Cass lost Southern friends by referring, in Michigan, to slavery as "a great social and political evil." He broke with Buchanan and his Southern advisers and resigned his office in 1860. He supported the Union during the Civil War. He died on June 16, 1866.

tween Texas and New Mexico, and that he would personally lead an army against any state that tried to secede.

A compromise is proposed

Moderate Whigs and Democrats viewed Taylor's hardline stand with dismay. In January of 1850, respected elder statesman Henry Clay (1777–1852; see box in **John Quincy Adams** entry in volume 1) proposed a compromise bill that would address many of the points of dissent in one piece of

A badge commemorates the inauguration of Zachary Taylor on March 5, 1849.
Courtesy of the Library of Congress.

legislation. Clay would have California admitted as a free state but would establish territorial governments for New Mexico and Utah, leaving open the issue of slavery there. He also introduced a harsh Fugitive Slave Law that would give Southern slaveowners federal assistance in retrieving fugitive (runaway) slaves. In his speech defending the bill, Clay urged his fellow lawmakers to consider the legislation a compromise that would save and strengthen the Union. The legislation became known as the Compromise of 1850.

Meanwhile, on April 19, 1850, Taylor's secretary of state, John Clayton (1796–1856), signed a treaty with Great Britain, which was represented by diplomat Sir William Bulwer. The treaty, which became known as the Clayton-Bulwer Treaty, concerned the proposed construction of a canal across the Isthmus of Panama. (An isthmus is a narrow strip of land that connects two larger pieces of land.) The frequently disputed treaty, which declared that neither nation was to "obtain or maintain for itself any exclusive control over the said ship-canal," became obsolete (no longer useful) in 1881. At that time, Secretary of State James G. Blaine (1830–1893; see box in **Chester A. Arthur** entry in volume 3), asserted that any canal built in Central America must be under the political control of the United States.

Debate on the Compromise of 1850 continued to rage in the Senate, but Taylor held to his own views and remained essentially aloof. He indicated that he would veto the legislation if it reached the executive office. This is how matters stood when fate intervened and President Taylor met an untimely death.

On July 4, 1850, Taylor attended a long ceremony to celebrate the beginning of construction on the Washington Monument. Spending hours in the hot sun listening to patriotic speeches, he drank a great quantity of cold water and ate some cherries in iced milk. That night the sixty-five-year-old president fell desperately ill and was diagnosed with "cholera morbus," or acute indigestion. Just five days after falling ill, Taylor died. After a state funeral, he was buried in Congressional Cemetery in the nation's capital. His body was later moved to the family burial grounds in Louisville, Kentucky, which later became the Zachary Taylor National Cemetery.

Legacy

Zachary Taylor's successor, **Millard Fillmore** (1800–1874; see entry in volume 2), was a moderate Whig who supported the Compromise of 1850 and signed it into law. However unpopular Taylor's stand on the Compromise had proved, Fillmore's stance (position) was just as unpopular. Fillmore was the last Whig ever to sit as president. Many Whigs moved to the Republican Party that was formed in 1854 and supported the abolition of slavery.

In the years following Taylor's sudden death, some historians declared that "Old Rough and Ready" might have been poisoned in order to clear a path for the Compromise of 1850. They interpreted the descriptions of Taylor's suffering as symptoms of arsenic poisoning. Finally, in 1991, Taylor's descendants agreed to have the distinguished general's corpse disinterred (taken out of the grave) so that tissue samples could be taken to test for the poison arsenic. Those samples proved inconsistent with any arsenic poisoning and laid to rest any arguments that Taylor was secretly assassinated.

Untutored in the arts of political diplomacy, Taylor left behind a legacy not as an effective president but as a man of principle and plain speech. His threats of an armed response to any attempt at Southern secession may have helped to stop fighting in the territories won from Mexico. The Clayton-Bulwer Treaty signed during his presidency assured that no war would break out between America and Britain over lands in Central America. The treaty declared that neither the United States nor Great Britain would be in control of the proposed Panama Canal. Seen by the common folk as a

Zachary Taylor Administration

Administration Dates
March 5, 1849–July 9, 1850

Vice President
Millard Fillmore (1849–50)

Cabinet

Secretary of State
John M. Clayton (1849–50)

Secretary of the Treasury
William Morris Meredith (1849–50)

Secretary of War
George W. Crawford (1849–50)

Attorney General
Reverdy Johnson (1849–50)

Secretary of the Navy
William Ballard Preston (1849–50)

Postmaster General
Jacob Collamer (1849–50)

Secretary of the Interior
Thomas Ewing (1849–50)

Zachary Taylor and his horse, Old Whitey. *Courtesy of the Library of Congress.*

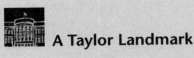

A Taylor Landmark

Zachary Taylor National Cemetery. 4701 Brownsboro Rd., Louisville, KY 40207. (502) 893-3852. Resting place of Zachary and Margaret Taylor. See http://www.findagrave.com/pictures/1023.html (accessed on July 7, 2000).

"brave old feller"—to quote one popular song of the day— Taylor was a legend in his own time, independent of his brief tenure in the White House.

Where to Learn More

Bauer, K. Jack. *Zachary Taylor: Soldier, Planter, Statesman of the Old Southwest.* Baton Rouge: Louisiana State University Press, 1985. Reprint, Newtown, CT: American Political Biography Press, 1994.

Collins, David R. *Zachary Taylor, 12th President of the United States.* Ada, OK: Garrett Educational Corp., 1989.

Kent, Zachary. *Zachary Taylor: Twelfth President of the United States.* Chicago: Children's Press, 1988.

Young, Bob, and Jan Young. *Old Rough and Ready, Zachary Taylor.* New York: J. Messner, 1970.

Margaret Taylor

Born September 21, 1788
Calvert County, Maryland
Died August 14, 1852
East Pascagoula, Mississippi

Devoted military wife followed her husband from post to post

A popular legend held that Margaret Taylor took a vow during the Mexican War (1846–48). She supposedly pledged that if her husband **Zachary Taylor** (1784–1850; see entry in volume 2) should return safely, she would withdraw from society. Her husband did return safely. His heroism in the war made him a national figure, and he was elected president in 1848. "Peggy" Taylor kept her vow. She undertook few duties as first lady, probably because her age was advanced and her health delicate after many years as a military wife.

"[Zachary Taylor's] nomination is a plot to deprive me of his society and to shorten his life by unnecessary care and responsibility."

Margaret Taylor

The life of a military wife

Peggy Taylor was born in Calvert County, Maryland, the daughter of Revolutionary War veteran Walter Smith and his wife, Ann Mackall. Peggy grew up in comfortable and genteel surroundings. She was educated in the manner of young ladies of her time. In 1809, the twenty-one-year-old Peggy traveled to Kentucky to visit her sister. There she met a handsome lieutenant named Zachary Taylor. After a brief courtship, they married on June 21, 1810.

Margaret Taylor.
Reproduced by permission of the Corbis Corporation.

At the outset of her marriage, Peggy Taylor lived on the farm her father-in-law had given the couple as a wedding gift. Her first daughter, Ann, was born there in 1811. It soon became clear, however, that Zachary Taylor's military career would not allow him to be home much. If she wanted to be with her husband, Peggy would have to travel with him from post to post, wherever his military superiors chose to send him. Thus she embarked on a decades-long pilgrimage (journey from place to place). She followed Zachary Taylor to a succession of remote outposts in the South and West.

Peggy had to educate and raise her children in sometimes harsh surroundings. In 1820, the growing Taylor family was hit with a violent and communicable fever that killed two of the youngsters—Octavia and Margaret. The fever left Peggy's own health impaired. She recovered from the tragedy sufficiently to accompany her husband on his travels. Eventually Zachary and Peggy Taylor had two more children together, Mary Elizabeth and Richard.

The surviving four Taylor children grew to adulthood. Aware of the difficulties facing military wives, Zachary Taylor strongly opposed his daughters' marrying Army men. The brunt of his irritation fell upon his daughter, Sarah Knox, who fell in love with a dashing young lieutenant named Jefferson Davis (1808–1889; see box in **Abraham Lincoln** entry in volume 2). Later in life, Davis would become president of the **Confederate States of America**, the Southern states that separated from the United States during the 1860s. Defying her parents' wishes, Sarah Knox married Davis and went to live at his Southern plantation, only to contract malaria and die three months later. The Taylors' other two daughters, Ann and Mary Elizabeth, likewise married into the military, wedding Robert C. Wood and William Bliss, respectively.

While Zachary Taylor was engaged in fighting the Mexican War, Peggy Taylor lived in a residence in Baton Rouge, Louisiana, that had been purchased in 1840. There she was a prominent member of Southern society, finding herself ever more popular as her husband's victories were reported. She was not terribly pleased to discover that his national fame might lead to a presidential nomination. At the age of sixty, she could hardly have been expected to be excited about moving to Washington, D.C. She did make the move, however.

During her husband's brief tenure (term of office) as the twelfth president, she lived in the White House by his side.

Peggy Taylor was a private first lady, rarely venturing out of her White House quarters into society except to worship at St. John's Episcopal Church. Almost all the first lady's official duties were relegated to her lively and attractive daughter, Mary Elizabeth (Betty) Bliss, whose husband served as the president's secretary. Betty Bliss proved a capable official hostess, but her career as an assistant first lady was very short. Soon after celebrating his first anniversary as chief executive, Zachary Taylor died suddenly of a gastric illness. The remaining members of his family quickly vacated the White House when **Millard Fillmore** (1800–1874; see entry in volume 2) became president, turning hostess duties over to **Abigail Fillmore** (1798–1853; see entry in volume 2).

Peggy Taylor lived only two more years after her husband's death. She passed away in 1852, survived by three of her children. Her son, Richard Taylor, served as an officer in the Confederacy during the Civil War. Her White House helper, Betty Bliss, survived into the twentieth century, dying in 1909.

Where to Learn More

Boller, Paul F. *Presidential Wives*. New York: Oxford University Press, 1998.

Klapthor, Margaret. *Maryland's Presidential First Ladies: Mrs. Zachary Taylor and Mrs. John Quincy Adams from Calvert County*. Prince Frederic, MD: Calvert County Historical Society, 1967.

Taylor's Only Annual Address to Congress

Delivered on December 4, 1849; excerpted from *The American Presidency: Selected Resources, An Informal Reference Guide* (Web site)

President Taylor presents an ill-fated plan for stopping the spread of slavery

In 1848, the year **Zachary Taylor** (1784–1850; see entry in volume 2) was elected president, the Treaty of Guadalupe Hidalgo officially ended the Mexican War (1846–48). In addition to settling the border of Texas, which was annexed to the United States in 1844 (see **John Tyler** primary source entry in volume 2), the treaty gave the United States additional territory in the Southwest (areas of present-day New Mexico, Arizona, and California). During that period of the administration of President **James K. Polk** (1795–1849; see entry in volume 2), the United States also won possession of the Oregon Territory that forms the present-day states of Oregon, Washington, and Idaho.

The large increase in territory meant that new states would soon be entering the Union. That prospect further enflamed debate over the nation's most divisive issue—slavery. Since the Missouri Compromise of 1820 (see box in **James Monroe** entry in volume 1), there had been an equal number of free and slave states in the Union, balancing federal power between the North and the South. Abolitionists and even some of those who defended the institution of slavery (like

"With a view of maintaining the harmony and tranquillity so dear to all, we should abstain from the introduction of those exciting topics of a sectional character which have hitherto produced painful apprehensions in the public mind. . . ."

Zachary Taylor

Taylor) believed that slavery should not be extended to new territories.

In his first (and only) annual address to Congress, President Zachary Taylor insisted that he could end the long debate on slavery. He recognized the Constitutional right for existing states to decide on slavery, but he would not permit slavery to spread to new territories.

Things to remember while reading an excerpt from President Taylor's address to congress:

- Early in the excerpt, President Taylor mentions that the territories of California and New Mexico were in the process of applying for statehood. The process begins when a territory holds a Constitutional convention and ratifies a Constitution. The Constitution will describe a republican form of government, where officeholders are elected. Once those conditions are met, the territory can petition the U.S. Congress for statehood. When Congress and the president approve, the territory then joins the Union and enjoys the same powers as all other states.

- The tense atmosphere of the times is reflected in President Taylor's speech. The issue of slavery divided Northern and Southern citizens and politicians. Recalling that **George Washington** (1732–1799; see entry in volume 1) had warned in his "Farewell Address" (see **George Washington** primary source entry in volume 1) about conflicts between the regions, Taylor announced his commitment to national unity. That call for unity concluded his address.

- Taylor wanted to show his respect for Congress and his interest in working with that branch of government. In the speech, he promised to respect the will of Congress by rarely, if ever, using his power to veto legislation. Taylor hoped that he could maintain national unity by working closely with Congress, respecting the rights of Southern states to continue the institution of slavery, and stopping the further spread of slavery.

- Taylor believed that slavery was necessary in the South to help that region compete against the more fertile, wealthy, and populated Northern states. Since the new territories were not as dependent on the free labor supply of slavery, Taylor did not support expanding slavery into those regions.

Excerpt from President Taylor's only annual address to Congress

No civil government having been provided by Congress for California, the people of that Territory, **impelled** by the necessities of their political condition, recently met in convention for the purpose of forming a constitution and State government, which the latest advices give me reason to suppose has been accomplished; and it is believed they will shortly apply for the admission of California into the Union as a **sovereign** State. Should such be the case, and should their constitution be conformable to the requisitions of the Constitution of the United States, I recommend their application to the favorable consideration of Congress.

The people of New Mexico will also, it is believed, at no very distant period present themselves for admission into the Union. Preparatory to the admission of California and New Mexico the people of each will have instituted for themselves a republican form of government, laying its foundation in such principles and organizing its powers in such form as to them shall seem most likely to effect their safety and happiness. By awaiting their action all causes of uneasiness may be avoided and confidence and kind feeling preserved. With a view of maintaining the harmony and tranquillity so dear to all, we should abstain from the introduction of those **exciting topics of a sectional character** which have **hitherto** produced painful apprehensions in the public mind; and I repeat the solemn warning of **the first and most illustrious of my predecessors** against furnishing "any ground for characterizing parties by geographical discriminations.". . .

Our Government is one of limited powers, and its successful administration eminently depends on the confinement of each of its coordinate branches within its own appropriate sphere. The first section of the Constitution ordains that—

> All legislative powers herein granted shall be vested in a Congress of the United States, which shall consist of a Senate and House of Representatives.

Impelled: To be convinced to act in a certain way.

Sovereign: Independent.

Exciting topics of a sectional character: Disputes between regions of the country.

Hitherto: Previously.

The first and most illustrious of my predecessors: President George Washington.

The Executive has authority to recommend (not to dictate) measures to Congress. Having performed that duty, the executive department of the Government can not rightfully control the decision of Congress on any subject of legislation until that decision shall have been officially submitted to the President for approval. The check provided by the Constitution in the clause conferring the qualified veto will never be exercised by me except in the cases contemplated by the fathers of the Republic. I view it as an extreme measure, to be resorted to only in extraordinary cases, as where it may become necessary to defend the executive against the encroachments of the legislative power or to prevent hasty and inconsiderate or unconstitutional legislation. By cautiously confining this remedy within the sphere prescribed to it in the contemporaneous expositions of the framers of the Constitution, the will of the people, legitimately expressed on all subjects of legislation through their constitutional organs, the Senators and Representatives of the United States, will have its full effect. As indispensable to the preservation of our system of self-government, the independence of the representatives of the States and the people is guaranteed by the Constitution, and they owe no responsibility to any human power but their **constituents.** *By holding the representative responsible only to the people, and exempting him from all other influences, we elevate the character of the constituent and quicken his sense of responsibility to his country. It is under these circumstances only that the elector can feel that in the choice of the lawmaker he is himself truly a component part of the sovereign power of the nation. With equal care we should study to defend the rights of the executive and judicial departments. Our Government can only be preserved in its purity by the suppression and entire elimination of every claim or tendency of one coordinate branch to encroachment upon another. With the strict observance of this rule and the other injunctions of the Constitution, with . . . respect and love for the Union of the States which our fathers cherished and enjoined upon their children, and with the aid of that overruling Providence which has so long and so kindly guarded our liberties and institutions, we may reasonably expect to transmit them, with their innumerable blessings, to the remotest posterity.*

But attachment to the Union of the States should be habitually fostered in every American heart. For more than half a century, during which kingdoms and empires have fallen, this Union has stood unshaken. The patriots who formed it have long since descended to the grave; yet still it remains, the proudest monument to their memory and the object of affection and admiration with everyone worthy

Constituents: Citizens of the district that voted in members of Congress.

to bear the American name. In my judgment its dissolution would be the greatest of calamities, and to avert that should be the study of every American.

Upon its preservation must depend our own happiness and that of countless generations to come. Whatever dangers may threaten it, I shall stand by it and maintain it in its integrity to the full extent of the obligations imposed and the powers conferred upon me by the Constitution. (The American Presidency: Selected Resources, An Informal Reference Guide (Web site).

What happened next . . .

Insisting that slavery should be prohibited to expand beyond the Southern states into new territories, President Taylor threatened to veto legislation that would give new territories the right to decide for themselves on whether to permit slavery. Nevertheless, Congress moved toward completing legislation that would grant that right to new states. Taylor died before the legislation was completed. Soon after, a series of bills called the Compromise of 1850 was submitted to President **Millard Fillmore** (1800–1874; see entry in volume 2), who signed them into law. Among other things, the Compromise allowed new territories to decide for themselves on slavery.

The Compromise was thought by some as the final answer to the issue of slavery. It was not. The Fugitive Slave Law, where runaway slaves could be pursued into the North, prosecuted, and returned to their slaveowners further enflamed abolitionists. In 1856, a civil war raged in Kansas territory between pro- and antislavery forces. Taylor was followed by three presidents—Fillmore, **Franklin Pierce** (1804–1869; see entry in volume 2), and **James Buchanan** (1791–1868; see entry in volume 2)—who permitted slavery as a means for preserving the Union. They were followed by **Abraham Lincoln** (1809–1865; see entry in volume 2), who began by taking the same position as Taylor against the expansion of slavery. When Southern states resisted Lincoln by seceding from the Union, Lincoln gained more authority and issued the Emancipation Proclamation (see **Abraham Lincoln** primary source entry in volume 2) in 1863, which began the end of slavery.

Did you know . . .

• President Taylor had been a great military leader and was thoroughly independent. He had never voted, and only became a member of the Whig Party in order to have an organization to help him run for president. He had little education, wrote little, and was not a comfortable public speaker. Most of this speech was written by his secretary of state, John M. Clayton (1796–1856).

Where to Learn More

"Annual Message: December 4, 1849." *The American Presidency: Selected Resources, An Informal Reference Guide* (Web site). [Online] http://www.interlink-cafe.com/uspresidents/1849.htm (accessed on July 19, 2000).

Smith, Elbert B. *The Presidencies of Zachary Taylor and Millard Fillmore.* Lawrence: University Press of Kansas, 1988.

Hamilton, Holman. *Zachary Taylor: Soldier in the White House.* Indianapolis, Bobbs-Merrill, 1941–51. Reprint, Hamden, CT: Archon Books, 1966.

Millard Fillmore

Thirteenth president (1850–1853)

Millard Fillmore

Born January 7, 1800
Locke (now Summerhill), New York
Died March 8, 1874
Buffalo, New York

Thirteenth president of the United States
(1850–1853)

Signed the Compromise of 1850,
which delayed the Civil War

Millard Fillmore's tenure (term of office) as the thirteenth president of the United States was brief but significant. Taking over the presidency upon the death of **Zachary Taylor** (1784–1850; see entry in volume 2) in July of 1850, Fillmore signed into law the series of five bills known as the Compromise of 1850—legislation meant to resolve issues dividing the free and slave states. While himself a Northerner who opposed slavery, Fillmore was dedicated to preserving the Union. He was willing to accept measures that many abolitionists (people against slavery) found repulsive in order to calm the Southern states. As a result, he narrowly held off a sectional crisis—between the Northern and the Southern sections of the country—and delayed the Civil War (1861–65) for another ten years.

At the time of Fillmore's presidency, the nation was expanding. New railroads were needed to move settlers into the West. A gold rush had begun in California, and that state was admitted to the Union (as a free state) while Fillmore was in the White House. New markets were needed for American goods. During Fillmore's tenure, the United States began a

"An honorable defeat is better than a dishonorable victory."

Millard Fillmore

Millard Fillmore.
Photograph by Mathew Brady.
Courtesy of the Library of Congress.

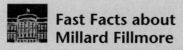

Fast Facts about Millard Fillmore

Full name: Millard Fillmore

Born: January 7, 1800

Died: March 8, 1874

Burial site: Forest Lawn Cemetery, Buffalo, New York

Parents: Nathaniel and Phoebe Millard Fillmore; Eunice Love (stepmother)

Spouse: Abigail Powers (1798–1853; m. 1826); Caroline Carmichael McIntosh (1813–1881; m. 1858)

Children: Millard Powers (1828–1889); Mary Abigail (1832–1854)

Religion: Unitarian

Education: No formal education

Occupations: Lawyer; educator

Government positions: New York state assemblyman; U.S. representative from New York; vice president under Zachary Taylor

Political party: Whig

Dates as president: July 9, 1850–March 4, 1853

Age upon taking office: 50

successful courtship of an elusive trading partner, Japan. All of these accomplishments—some of them controversial—occurred during the two-and-a-half years of Fillmore's presidency. He was the last Whig candidate to serve as a chief executive. He was the second vice president to assume the White House upon the death of a sitting president.

Imposing in stature but of modest skills as an orator (speaker), Fillmore was the perfect example of a self-made man. He did not particularly enjoy being president, but once in office he proved quite capable of making executive decisions and standing by them through immense opposition. His support of the Compromise of 1850, including its most controversial provision, the Fugitive Slave Act, however, earned him many political enemies. Those adversaries conspired to make his stay in the White House a brief one.

Ambitious and self-taught

The second child and oldest son in a family of nine, Millard Fillmore was born in Cayuga County, New York, on January 7, 1800. His ancestors had struggled in New England for several generations. His father, Nathaniel, rented a farm in what was still frontier country in western New York. Young Millard worked on the farm and was apprenticed to a textile mill in his teens. His only education came during breaks in the production schedule at the mill. He seized every opportunity to read and write and was helped in his efforts by a local schoolteacher named Abigail Powers (1798–1853; see entry on **Abigail Fillmore** in volume 2). At that time, there were no laws mandating (commanding) that children must attend school until a certain age. Fillmore attended school whenever he could. Fourteen-years-old at the time, he was one of the oldest students and just two years younger than Miss Powers.

In his late teens, Fillmore began to work for a Cayuga County attorney named Walter Wood (1815–1892). While serving as Wood's clerk and personal secretary, Fillmore began studying the law by reading the books in Wood's small personal library. When the Fillmore family moved on to East Aurora in Erie County, New York, Millard continued his legal studies and also worked as a schoolteacher.

Tall, blonde, and handsome, with a pleasing personality and high moral standards, Fillmore began slowly to win his way in the world. He was admitted to the Erie County bar (legal profession) in 1823 and opened a law office in East Aurora. Three years later, he proposed marriage to Abigail Powers, and she accepted. The couple would have two children. Fillmore moved his family and law practice to Buffalo, New York, and became active in local politics.

In 1828, Fillmore met newspaper publisher Thurlow Weed (1797–1882), an influential political boss. (A political boss is a powerful politician who can influence public policy behind the scenes.) Weed was instrumental in the formation of the Anti-Masonic Party, a new political affiliation that stood in opposition to secret fraternal organizations like the Masons. (Fraternal means brotherly; a fraternal organization is a men's

 Millard Fillmore Timeline

1800: Born in New York

1814: Begins attending school at age fourteen

1818: Begins studying law

1823: Passes New York bar

1828–31: Member of New York State Assembly

1833–35: Serves in U.S. House of Representatives as member of the Anti-Masonite Party

1836–42: Serves in U.S. House of Representatives as member of the Whig Party

1844: Fails in bid to be elected governor of New York

1849–50: Serves as vice president under Zachary Taylor

1850: Taylor dies; Fillmore becomes thirteenth president on July 10; signs Compromise of 1850

1852: Fillmore loses Whig nomination to General Winfield Scott, an antislavery advocate; Harriet Beecher Stowe's *Uncle Tom's Cabin* is published

1862: Named the first chancellor of the University of Buffalo (now State University of New York at Buffalo)

1874: Dies in New York

Words to Know

Bar: A term that encompasses all certified lawyers—those who have passed all official requirements (the bar exam) to be certified as lawyers.

Patronage: The power of appointing people to governmental or political positions.

Political boss: A politically powerful person who can direct a group of voters to support a particular candidate.

Secession: Official withdrawal from a nation.

Tariff: A tax a nation places on imported goods to increase their price, making imported goods as expensive or more than similar products produced in the home nation.

Veto: The power of one branch of government—for example, the chief executive—to reject a bill passed by a legislative body and thus prevent it from becoming law.

group that shares a common bond or interest. The Masons, also called Freemasons, are a fraternal organization noted for their secret rituals.) Weed backed Fillmore as the Anti-Masonic candidate for the state legislature. Fillmore easily won the election. He served three terms, during which he played an important role in abolishing (ending) laws that imprisoned debtors (people who cannot repay money they owe). Fillmore's success in state politics—and his friendship with Weed—prepared him for a greater role on the national level.

To Congress and beyond

Fillmore was elected to Congress as an Anti-Masonic candidate in 1832. After serving one term, he joined the Whig Party, a coalition (alliance) formed to oppose the **Andrew Jackson** (1767–1845; see entry in volume 1) administration. After refusing to run for reelection in 1834, Fillmore returned to Congress in 1836 and served three consecutive terms. Meanwhile, the Whig Party grew in prominence until it became the majority party in Congress after the 1840 election.

Immensely popular in Congress as well as back in his home state, Fillmore was given the prestigious (important) chairmanship of the House Ways and Means Committee. The committee is a group of legislators who determine the costs and methods for enacting a piece of legislation. Fillmore used this platform to promote higher tariff rates (tax rates on imports), in keeping with his belief that American businesses should be protected from foreign competition. Also, as chairman of the Ways and Means committee, Fillmore helped to secure appropriations to help Samuel Morse (1791–1872) develop the telegraph.

At the height of his popularity in 1842, Fillmore announced that he would not seek another term in Congress. However, he was not interested in leaving politics; Fillmore wanted to seek other offices. He returned to New York where he became the Whig candidate for governor in 1844. A downturn in the popularity of the Whig Party cost him the election. Fillmore and others attributed the loss to abolitionists and Catholic foreigners (immigrants of the Roman Catholic faith). At the same time, the Whig candidate for president, Henry Clay (1777–1852; see box in **John Quincy Adams** entry in volume 1), was also defeated. Fillmore returned to his law practice.

In 1847, Fillmore was elected state comptroller (a public official who oversees government accounts) by a wide margin of the popular vote. He had just completed a year in that important office when another opportunity arose, the office of vice president. This opportunity Fillmore accepted with a great deal of ambivalence (strongly contradictory feelings).

A vice president with integrity

At their presidential nominating convention in 1848, the Whigs chose as their candidate Zachary Taylor, a Southern slaveowner who opposed the extension of slavery into new territories. The Whigs needed a Northerner to balance the ticket. Their first choice was Abbot Lawrence (1792–1855), a Massachusetts cotton manufacturer and former U.S. congressman. A powerful faction led by Henry Clay opposed Lawrence. This group objected to having cotton-based moneymakers on both ends of the ticket. It was this faction that successfully pressed for Fillmore as Taylor's running mate.

The Taylor-Fillmore ticket won the presidential election in November of 1848. The victory proved very hollow for Fillmore at first. His alliance with Thurlow Weed and New York senator William H. Seward (1801–1872) came to an end when he discovered that the two men were actively undermining his political influence. Unable to dispense patronage appointments (hand out government jobs), Fillmore was left with little more than the ceremonial vice president's duty of presiding over the Senate. However, this duty became quite important in the early months of 1850, when Congress began a lengthy and heated debate on the bills collectively known as the Compromise of 1850.

The legislation known as the Compromise of 1850—much of it drafted by Henry Clay—was a desperate attempt to resolve the bitter sectional dispute that would eventually lead to the Civil War. At issue was the status of slavery in the lands acquired by the United States as a result of the Mexican War (1846–48). California was about to be admitted as a free state, but its entrance would upset the balance between fifteen free states and fifteen slave states. (California is the thirty-first state.) In addition, the slave state of Texas was laying claim to parts of what would become New Mexico and trying to extend slavery into that region.

Although he was a Southerner and a slaveholder, Zachary Taylor objected to any expansion of slavery. He threatened to send federal soldiers to enforce the boundary between Texas and New Mexico. Furthermore, he intended to veto (reject) any compromise that Congress might send to him if it held legislation supporting the expansion of slavery.

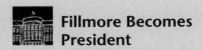

Fillmore Becomes President

Millard Fillmore became president of the United States following the death of Zachary Taylor. (See Taylor entry for election results from the Taylor/Fillmore campaign.) This marked the second time in U.S. history that a vice president became president following the death of his predecessor. Fillmore attempted unsuccessfully to be elected as president on his own. In 1852, he lost the Whig nomination to Winfield Scott; in 1856, as the American (Know-Nothing) Party nominee, he came in third place behind Democrat James Buchanan and Republican John Frémont.

From his position as president of the Senate, Vice President Fillmore listened closely. Several times he served as an arbiter (a person with the power to settle a dispute) when tempers flared. For some months, he kept his views on the matter to himself. As a vote neared, he went to the White House and told President Taylor that he would break any tie by voting in favor of the Compromise. This stand, Fillmore hastened to add, was not taken out of hostility toward Taylor. Instead, he felt he must vote out of deep conviction (belief) that the Compromise was the only way to protect the Union and avert civil war.

President Taylor had promised to veto the Compromise bills, but at an 1850 Independence Day celebration, he fell ill. Taylor died on July 9. Fillmore was immediately sworn in as the thirteenth president. His inauguration (formal ceremony installing him as president) was held the next day.

As his first official act, President Fillmore asked for and received the resignation of Taylor's entire Cabinet. The new president chose his own Cabinet, which included Daniel

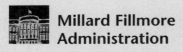

Millard Fillmore Administration

Administration Dates
July 9, 1850–March 4, 1853

Vice President
None

Cabinet

Secretary of State
John M. Clayton (1850)
Daniel Webster (1850–52)
Edward Everett (1852–53)

Secretary of the Treasury
William M. Meredith (1850)
Thomas Corwin (1850–53)

Secretary of War
George W. Crawford (1850)
Charles M. Conrad (1850–53)

Attorney General
Reverdy Johnson (1850)
John J. Crittenden (1850–53)

Secretary of the Navy
William B. Preston (1850)
William A. Graham (1850–52)
John P. Kennedy (1852–53)

Postmaster General
Jacob Collamer (1850)
Nathan K. Hall (1850–52)
Samuel D. Hubbard (1852–53)

Secretary of the Interior
Thomas Ewing (1850)
Thomas M. T. McKennan (1850)
Alexander H. H. Stuart (1850–53)

Webster (1782–1852; see box in **John Tyler** entry in volume 2) as secretary of state. His new Cabinet consisted of allies who favored the compromise measures being debated in Congress. In a statement to both houses of Congress on August 6, 1850, Fillmore recommended that Texas be paid to abandon claims to the disputed New Mexico territories—a key provision in the compromise legislation. Clearly the new president was in favor of preserving the Union at all costs. Congress quickly passed the series of bills that would come to be known as the Compromise of 1850.

A bitter compromise

The Compromise of 1850 contained five bills that produced the following results: (1) California was admitted as a free state; (2) Texas was compensated for the loss of territory in the boundary dispute with New Mexico; (3) New Mexico was granted territorial status; (4) the slave trade—but not slavery itself—was abolished in the nation's capital; and (5) most controversially, the Fugitive Slave Law was enacted, allowing slaveowners to pursue fleeing slaves and recapture them in free states. The bill even put federal troops at the disposal of slaveholders seeking fugitives. Not only did Fillmore sign the bill into law, he supervised its enactment. He felt the measure was necessary to placate the slave states, where prominent politicians were already discussing the possibility of secession (separation).

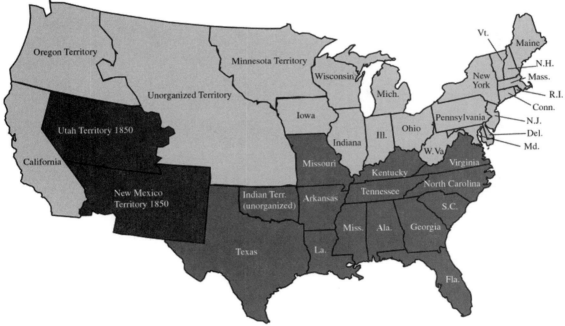

The Compromise of 1850

Free States and Territories

Slave States and Territories

Territories where voters determine status of slavery

Oregon Territory

Minnesota Territory

Wisconsin

Unorganized Territory

Mich.

Vt.

Maine

N.H.

Mass.

New York

R.I.

Conn.

Pennsylvania

N.J.

Iowa

Del.

Md.

Utah Territory 1850

Ill.

Ohio

Indiana

W. Va.

California

Missouri

Virginia

Kentucky

New Mexico Territory 1850

Indian Terr. (unorganized)

Arkansas

Tennessee

North Carolina

S.C.

Miss.

Ala.

Georgia

Texas

La.

Fla.

Not surprisingly, the Fugitive Slave Law furthered tensions between proslavery and abolitionist (antislavery) groups. The antislavery movement grew more vocal following the 1852 publication of the novel *Uncle Tom's Cabin* by Harriet Beecher Stowe (1811–1896). Stowe's book was the most sympathetic work of antislavery sentiments in popular literature up to that time. The uneasy truce won by the Compromise of 1850 did not prove to be lasting, nor did it

A map of the United States shows the status of slavery among the states and territories in 1850.
Created by Eric Wisniewski. Gale Group.

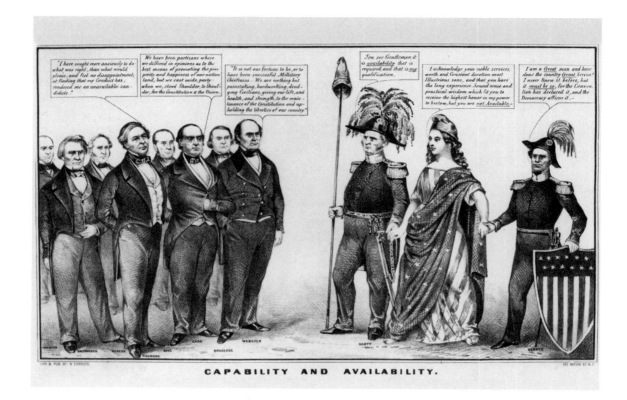

CAPABILITY AND AVAILABILITY.

This editorial cartoon laments the Whig and Democratic parties' choices of military leaders as presidential candidates—Winfield Scott (center) and Franklin Pierce (far right)—in 1852 rather than better qualified statesmen (left to right): Senator Samuel Houston, Attorney General John J. Crittendon, former senator Thomas Hart Benton, President Millard Fillmore, Senator John Bell, Senator Lewis Cass, Senator Stephen A. Douglas, and Secretary of State Daniel Webster. *Courtesy of the Library of Congress.*

heighten Fillmore's popularity as president. When the Whig Party met to nominate its ticket for the 1852 election, Fillmore lost to an antislavery candidate, General Winfield Scott (1786–1866; see box in **Martin Van Buren** entry in volume 1).

The conflict over slavery overwhelmed some important developments during Fillmore's presidency. Northern states were growing more prosperous by developing industries and investing in the expansion of the nation's railroads in the Great Plains and far West. American trade with China had opened up during the mid-1840s, and President Fillmore commissioned Commodore Matthew Perry (1794–1858; see box in **Franklin Pierce** entry in volume 2) to visit Japan and open up that nation—isolated since the seventeenth century—for trade. The nation was simultaneously experiencing exciting growth and troubling divisiveness.

This editorial cartoon shows the three candidates of the 1856 presidential campaign. American (Know-Nothing) Party nominee Millard Fillmore (center), the former president, is portrayed as the more composed "right man in the right place," breaking up a fight between Republican John C. Frémont (left) and Democrat James Buchanan (right). Fillmore, however, was soundly defeated.
Illustration by Louis Maurer. Courtesy of the Library of Congress.

Post-presidential accomplishments

Shortly after the end of his term, Fillmore returned to Buffalo as a grieving widower. Abigail Fillmore died on March 30, 1853. Fillmore never again held political office. In 1856, he was nominated as a candidate for the presidency by the American, or Know-Nothing, Party, a movement concerned with issues of national unity and curbing immigration. Fillmore felt that the American Party held the only hope of uniting the nation, still bitterly divided by the issue of slavery. He campaigned earnestly throughout the South and the North, but on election day, he was soundly defeated by Democrat **James Buchanan** (1791–1868; see entry in volume 2). Fillmore finished a distant third behind Buchanan and Republican John C. Frémont (1813–1890; see box in **James K. Polk** entry in volume 2) with only twenty-two percent of the vote. Fillmore's defeat was a decisive blow to the American Party's influence. He retired from the political arena.

Harriet Beecher Stowe

Harriet Beecher Stowe was born on June 14, 1811, in Litchfield, Connecticut. She was the seventh child of preacher Lyman Beecher and his first wife, Roxana Foote, who died when Stowe was four years old. Her father soon remarried, and Stowe had a good relationship with her stepmother, Harriet Porter Beecher. When Stowe became depressed after her mother's death she spent time with her grandmother and aunt. She soon became a good student at a girls' school and moved on to Litchfield Academy at age ten. At twelve, she won first prize for her essay "Can the Immortality of the Soul Be Proved by the Light of Nature?"

In 1824, Stowe's older sister Catherine, with whom she was very close, started a school for teenaged girls in Hartford, Connecticut. Stowe was one of her first pupils. She began writing poetry, but her sister dismissed that activity and put Stowe to work teaching girls her own age. The Stowe family moved to the Cincinnati, Ohio, area in 1832 when Stowe's father became president of Lane Theological Seminary. Having read Shakespeare, Stowe soon joined a literary society called the Semi-Colon Club. A fellow member, future Supreme Court justice Salmon P. Chase (1808–1873), introduced her to the growing antislavery movement. About the same time, Catherine Beecher started another school—Western Female Institute—where Stowe was a student and later a teacher. The sisters wrote a geography textbook that was used at the school for many years.

In 1833, Stowe wrote an article about grammar and punctuation, for which she received fifty dollars. This led her to a career of writing. The same year, she crossed the Ohio River and saw a southern plantation for the first time, an experience that provided her with the setting for *Uncle Tom's Cabin*. When a friend of hers died, Stowe began caring for the widower, Calvin Stowe, fixing his meals and mending his clothes. In January 1836, they were married and she became known as Harriet Beecher Stowe. The couple had twin daughters in September 1837.

Stowe contributed short stories, essays, and articles for the *Western Monthly* magazine. But the Fugitive Slave Law of 1850 caused Stowe to begin writing seriously. She read everything available about slavery, but did not consider writing a book until a vision of an old slave filled her mind. Convinced that God had reached out to her, she wrote down what she had seen. The first episode of *Uncle Tom's Cabin* appeared in the *National Era* in March 1851, and other episodes followed weekly. Her stories were so popular that when they were collected in a book and

Harriet Beecher Stowe.
Courtesy of the National Archives and Records Administration.

1854, Stowe wrote an average of one magazine article every two weeks.

When her husband retired in 1863, the family moved to Hartford, where they built a large home. It was here during the Civil War that Stowe wrote magazine articles advocating employment for the freed slaves and compassion toward the Confederacy once the seceded states had returned to the Union. With the coming of peace, Stowe rented a cotton plantation in Florida, installed her son, Fred, as manager, and hired former slaves to work for her. The Stowes had planned to spend their winters there, but the project proved to be unsuccessful. Stowe then bought an orange grove in Mandarin, Florida, and founded a school for former slaves. Her contributions to the state earned her the approval of General Robert E. Lee and the acceptance of the Southern people.

published for the first time in 1852, *Uncle Tom's Cabin* became a huge success. Three million copies had been sold by the time the Civil War began in 1861. The book was translated into thirty-seven languages. The book helped inspire many readers to join in efforts to abolish slavery. Its impact on society is among the greatest of any novel ever published.

To answer attacks that her novel exaggerated the harshness of the lives of slaves, Stowe compiled *A Key to Uncle Tom's Cabin,* which contains case histories to verify the scenes in her book. During 1853 and

By 1876, Stowe was wealthy, famous, and lonely. Her husband's health was deteriorating, and she felt that her life's work was completed, although there was still a demand for her writings and lectures. Her seventieth birthday, in 1881, was a national event; newspapers published editorials about her, and the school children in Hartford were given a holiday in her honor. She died on July 1, 1896, at the age of eighty-five and is buried in Andover, Massachusetts.

In his later years, Fillmore became a leading citizen of Buffalo, serving as the first chancellor (head) of the University of Buffalo (now the State University of New York at Buffalo). He was one of the founders of the Buffalo Historical Society. When the Civil War began, he supported the Union. He became increasingly concerned about the policies of **Abraham Lincoln** (1809–1865; see entry in volume 2). In the 1864 election, Fillmore labeled Lincoln a military despot (an oppressive ruler with absolute power) and supported Lincoln's opponent, George B. McClellan (1826–1885). After Lincoln's assassination, Fillmore favored **Andrew Johnson** (1808–1875; see entry in volume 2). He approved of Johnson's program for Reconstruction in the South. Reconstruction was a federal policy of assisting and policing the Southern states after the Civil War.

Fillmore's second marriage, in 1858, to Albany heiress Caroline Carmichael McIntosh (1813–1881), enabled him to undertake many philanthropic (charitable) activities, such as the creation of Buffalo General Hospital. He died quietly at his home on March 8, 1874, after suffering a stroke. Fillmore is buried beneath a commanding monument at Forest Lawn Cemetery in Buffalo.

Following the death of Abigail Fillmore in 1853, Fillmore shared his retirement with Albany heiress Caroline Carmichael McIntosh, whom he married in 1858.
Courtesy of the Library of Congress.

Legacy

The most noteworthy event of Millard Fillmore's presidency was the compromise of 1850; his support ensured that the legislation would be passed by Congress and become law. Although the compromise proved unpopular in both the North and the South, it helped delay the start of the Civil War for ten more years. During that decade, the North expanded its industrial activity immensely, giving it a distinct advantage when the war finally broke out in 1861.

A Selection of Fillmore Landmarks

Fillmore House Museum. 24 Shearer Ave., Box 472, East Aurora, NY 14052. (716) 652-8875. Home of Millard and Abigail Fillmore during the 1820s. See http://rin.buffalo.edu/c_erie/comm/cult/muse/mfh.html (accessed on July 21, 2000).

Forest Lawn Cemetery. 1411 Delaware Ave., Buffalo, NY 14209. (716) 885-1600. Final resting place of Millard Fillmore, his two wives, Abigail and Caroline, and his two children, Millard and Mary. See http://www.forest-lawn.com/fillmore.htm (accessed on July 8, 2000).

Millard Fillmore Log Cabin. Fillmore Glen State Park, 1686 State Route 38, Moravia, NY 13118. (315) 497-0130. Replica of the log cabin in which Fillmore was born sits on the site of a state park, four miles from his birthplace.

The high points of Fillmore's administration were the Compromise of 1850 and the expansion of the nation's railroads in the Great Plains and far West. President Fillmore gave America one more important legacy, however. It was Fillmore who commissioned Commodore Matthew Perry to visit Japan and open up that nation—isolated since the seventeenth century—for trade. Perry's mission was successful, producing results after Fillmore had left office.

Where to Learn More

Barre, W. L. *The Life and Public Services of Millard Fillmore.* Buffalo: Wanzer, McKim & Co., 1856. Reprint, New York: Burt Franklin, 1971.

Casey, Jane Clark. *Millard Fillmore: Thirteenth President of the United States.* Chicago: Children's Press, 1988.

Rayback, Robert J. *Millard Fillmore: Biography of a President.* Buffalo: Henry Stewart, 1959.

Smith, Elbert B. *The Presidencies of Zachary Taylor and Millard Fillmore.* Lawrence: University Press of Kansas, 1988.

Snyder, Charles M., ed. *The Lady and the President: The Letters of Dorothea Dix and Millard Fillmore.* Lexington: University Press of Kentucky, 1975.

Abigail Fillmore

Born March 13, 1798
Stillwater, New York
Died March 30, 1853
Washington, D.C.

A teacher and book lover, she petitioned Congress for funds to buy books for a White House library

A bigail Fillmore was the first of the nation's first ladies to hold a job after marriage, continuing her career as a school-teacher. In fact, it was as a teacher that she first met future president **Millard Fillmore** (1800–1874; see entry in volume 2).

The daughter of a respected Baptist minister named Lemuel Powers, Abigail Powers was born in Saratoga County, New York, in 1798. Her father died while she was still young. In order to conserve what little money remained in the family, her mother moved west, into the sparsely populated New York frontier. There, Abigail was schooled at home, using the books left behind by her father.

At age sixteen, Abigail began teaching school in the village of New Hope, New York. In those times, country schooling was somewhat informal. Students came to school when they had no farm chores to complete, and all ages crowded into one room. Thus, it was not terribly unusual that a young millworker named Millard Fillmore began coming to the school, even though he was only two years younger than the teacher. The pretty, red-headed Abigail was impressed by the young man's determination to get an education that

"I pursued much of my study with, and perhaps was unconsciously stimulated by, the companionship of a young lady whom I afterward married."

Millard Fillmore

Abigail Fillmore.
Reproduced by permission of the Corbis Corporation.

475

could improve his life. She devoted many extra hours to his schooling. Over time, a deep and lasting bond developed between them.

Abigail Powers taught school while Millard Fillmore studied law and completed his examinations. Fillmore eventually passed the test for the bar (legal profession) in Erie County and opened up a small law practice in East Aurora, New York. He and Abigail were married in 1826 while Fillmore was still a struggling young attorney.

As a newlywed, Abigail Fillmore continued to teach school for two more years while her husband's practice grew. By the time their first child, Millard Powers Fillmore, was born, the family was prosperous and Fillmore was involved in state politics.

In 1830, the Fillmore family moved to a six-room house in Buffalo, New York. A daughter, Mary Abigail, was born in 1832, the same year her father won his first Congressional election. Abigail Fillmore kept an active social calendar and was noted for her flower garden, but she still found time to read and to play music. Throughout her husband's political career, she quietly advised him, but her public role was ceremonial—standing at his side at dinners and receptions, engaging in conversation with other political wives, and doing philanthropic (charitable) work.

Abigail Fillmore moved to Washington, D.C., in 1849 when her husband was elected vice president. By that time her health was not as robust as in her youth. She began to delegate some of her official responsibilities to her daughter, Abby, who had been given a formal education and was quite up to the task of assisting her mother.

The sudden death of President **Zachary Taylor** (1784–1850; see entry in volume 2) in July of 1850 thrust the Fillmores into the White House, a mansion that they discovered to be surprisingly primitive. While Millard Fillmore ordered a cooking stove for the kitchen (where food had still been prepared over an open fire), Abigail Fillmore took the more drastic step of petitioning Congress for money to begin a White House library. She got the money and began buying books, shelving them in a charming oval room on the second floor. It was in this oval room that Abigail Fillmore spent much of her private time, reading, listening to musical concerts, and conversing with her closest friends. The room would later become the primary White House office for future presidents—the Oval Office.

A chronic sore ankle made many of Abigail Fillmore's official duties quite difficult. Often she had to stand at her husband's side shaking hands for hours at a time. She was expected to plan and preside over many dinner parties and receptions. She was an elegant dresser; she loved to wear expensive, well-made clothes. Her wit and grace made her an able first lady. Abigail Fillmore was often accompanied by her more vivacious (lively) daughter.

Millard Fillmore's tenure (time in office) as president was brief, as he failed to secure the Whig nomination in the 1852 election. Abigail Fillmore was in poor health as her husband's term ended, but she attended the inauguration (formal ceremony installing the president) of the new president, **Franklin Pierce** (1804–1869; see entry in volume 2), braving snowy conditions and a chill wind. A cold she caught at the event turned into pneumonia, and she died on March 30, 1853. Her body was returned to Buffalo for burial at Forest Lawn cemetery. Daughter Mary Abigail died the following year.

The Fillmores were sober and serious people, and they moved into the White House during a period of mourning following the death of President Taylor. Therefore, their days as president and first lady were not marked by lavish entertainment. Abigail Fillmore's lasting contribution to the White House was not a memory of spirited parties but rather a modest library of volumes that she felt would be useful to future holders of the nation's highest office.

Where to Learn More

Boller, Paul F. *Presidential Wives*. New York: Oxford University Press, 1998.

Joseph, Paul. *Millard Fillmore*. Minneapolis: Abdo Publishing Co., 1999.

Law, Kevin J. *Millard Fillmore: 13th President of the United States*. Ada, OK: Garrett Educational Corp., 1990.

Fillmore's First Annual Address to Congress

December 2, 1850; excerpted from *The American Presidency: Selected Resources, An Informal Reference Guide* (Web site)

President Fillmore announces a policy of increased international trade and relations

When **Millard Fillmore** (1800–1874; see entry in volume 2) assumed the office of president following the death of **Zachary Taylor** (1784–1850; see entry in volume 2) in July of 1850, Congress and the nation both were bitterly divided over the issue of slavery. President Taylor intended to use his power to stop the spread of slavery to new territories. Fillmore was willing to accept measures that would calm those in favor of slavery. To protect the rights of Southern states, he supported the series of bills in Congress that became known as the Compromise of 1850. President Taylor promised to veto those bills. After Fillmore became president, Congress quickly passed and Fillmore signed the bills that formed the Compromise of 1850.

Among the terms of the Compromise, California was admitted into the Union as a free state and New Mexico would be allowed to decide for itself whether to be free or to permit slavery. The most controversial part of the Compromise was the Fugitive Slave Act. Under that law, federal authorities could be enlisted to help track, prosecute, and return slaves who escape to the North. Anyone who assisted runaway slaves could be prosecuted and punished.

"All mutual concession in the nature of a compromise must necessarily be unwelcome to men of extreme opinions. And though without such concessions our Constitution could not have been formed, and can not be permanently sustained. . . ."

Millard Fillmore

At the time of his first annual address, President Fillmore had been in office less than five full months. He used the occasion to give a speech similar to an inaugural address, where a new president presents his vision for the years ahead. President Fillmore discussed foreign policy and domestic issues in his address. On the home front, he asked the American people to be patient and allow time for the legislation of the Compromise of 1850 to serve its purpose of promoting national unity.

Things to remember while reading an excerpt from President Fillmore's first annual address:

- The excerpt reflects the three main themes of President Fillmore's first annual address: he wanted to present his view of the role of the president and his vision for the nation—the common subject of a president's inaugural address (having succeeded President Taylor, who died in office, Fillmore did not give an inaugural address); he announced his foreign policy; and he discussed his domestic policy.

- The excerpt begins with Fillmore outlining his foreign policy. During this period, there were several trouble spots in the world. For example, Hungarians were attempting to form an independent country by revolting against the Austrian empire in Eastern Europe, and Cubans were threatening to revolt to free their island from Spanish authority. Fillmore pledged that the United States would not interfere in such conflicts. Just as Americans demanded that other nations not interfere with events in the United States, he argued, so, too, the United States should not interfere with events in other countries.

- In the middle portion of the excerpt, the president makes a transition to domestic issues. He promised to use the Constitution as his guide. That led into his discussion on the continued divisiveness (disagreements) in the nation even after Congress passed the Compromise of 1850 legislation and the president signed it into law. Calling for patience with the acts of the Compromise, Fillmore noted that even the Constitution was not immediately accepted. Similarly, he argued, the legislation of the Compromise should be allowed time to take effect before judging its success or failure.

Excerpt from President Fillmore's first annual address to Congress

Nations, like individuals in a state of nature, are equal and independent, possessing certain rights and owing certain duties to each other, arising from their necessary and unavoidable relations; which rights and duties there is no common human authority to protect and enforce. Still, they are rights and duties, binding in morals, in conscience, and in honor, although there is no **tribunal** to which an injured party can appeal but the disinterested judgment of mankind, and ultimately the **arbitrament** of the sword.

Among the acknowledged rights of nations is that which each possesses of establishing that form of government which it may deem most conducive to the happiness and prosperity of its own citizens, of changing that form as circumstances may require, and of managing its internal affairs according to its own will. The people of the United States claim this right for themselves, and they readily concede it to others. Hence it becomes an imperative duty not to interfere in the government or internal policy of other nations; and although we may sympathize with the unfortunate or the oppressed everywhere in their struggles for freedom, our principles forbid us from taking any part in such foreign contests. We make no wars to promote or to prevent successions to thrones, to maintain any theory of a balance of power, or to suppress the actual government which any country chooses to establish for itself. We **instigate** no revolutions, nor suffer any hostile military expeditions to be fitted out in the United States to invade the territory or provinces of a friendly nation. The great law of morality ought to have a national as well as personal and individual application. We should act toward other nations as we wish them to act toward us, and justice and conscience should force the rule of conduct between governments, instead of mere power, self-interest, or the desire of **aggrandizement**. To maintain a strict **neutrality** in foreign wars, to cultivate friendly relations, to **reciprocate** every noble and generous act, and to perform punctually and scrupulously every treaty obligation—these are the duties which we owe to other states, and by the performance of which we best entitle ourselves to like treatment from them; or, if that, in any case, be refused, we can enforce our own right with justice and a clear conscience.

Tribunal: Court of law.

Arbitrament: The act of deciding on legal claims made by opposing parties.

Instigate: Provoke.

Aggrandizement: The act of enlarging.

Neutrality: Not taking sides in a dispute.

Reciprocate: To reply in the same manner in which something was given.

*In our domestic policy the Constitution will be my guide, and in questions of doubt I shall look for its interpretation to the judicial decisions of that tribunal which was established to expound it and to the usage of the Government, sanctioned by the **acquiescence** of the country. I regard all its provisions as equally binding. In all its parts it is the will of the people expressed in the most solemn form, and the constituted authorities are but agents to carry that will into effect. Every power which it has granted is to be exercised for the public good; but no pretense of utility, no honest conviction, even, of what might be expedient, can justify the assumption of any power not granted. The powers conferred upon the Government and their distribution to the several departments are as clearly expressed in that sacred instrument as the imperfection of human language will allow, and I deem it my first duty not to question its wisdom, add to its provisions, evade its requirements, or nullify its commands. . . .*

*It was hardly to have been expected that the series of measures passed at your last session with the view of healing the sectional differences which had sprung from the slavery and territorial questions should at once have realized their beneficent purpose. All mutual concession in the nature of a compromise must necessarily be unwelcome to men of extreme opinions. And though without such concessions our Constitution could not have been formed, and can not be permanently sustained, yet we have seen them made the subject of bitter controversy in both sections of the Republic. It required many months of discussion and deliberation to secure the **concurrence** of a majority of Congress in their favor. It would be strange if they had been received with immediate **approbation** by people and States prejudiced and heated by the exciting controversies of their representatives. I believe those measures to have been required by the circumstances and condition of the country. I believe they were necessary to **allay asperities** and animosities that were rapidly alienating one section of the country from another and destroying those fraternal sentiments which are the strongest supports of the Constitution. They were adopted in the spirit of conciliation and for the purpose of conciliation. I believe that a great majority of our fellow-citizens sympathize in that spirit and that purpose, and in the main approve and are prepared in all respects to sustain **these enactments.** I can not doubt that the American people, bound together by kindred blood and common traditions, still cherish a paramount regard for the Union of their fathers, and that they are ready to **rebuke** any attempt to violate its integrity, to disturb the compromises on which it is based, or to resist the laws which have been enacted under its authority.*

Acquiescence: Quiet approval.

Concurrence: Agreement.

Approbation: Official approval.

Allay asperities: Calm fears.

These enactments: A reference to the laws associated with the Compromise of 1850.

Rebuke: Turn back.

*The series of measures to which I have alluded are regarded by me as a settlement in principle and substance—a final settlement of the dangerous and exciting subjects which they embraced. Most of these subjects, indeed, are beyond your reach, as the legislation which disposed of them was in its character final and **irrevocable**. It may be presumed from the opposition which they all encountered that none of those measures was free from imperfections, but in their mutual dependence and connection they formed a system of compromise the most conciliatory and best for the entire country that could be obtained from conflicting sectional interests and opinions.*

For this reason I recommend your adherence to the adjustment established by those measures until time and experience shall demonstrate the necessity of further legislation to guard against evasion or abuse.

*By that adjustment we have been rescued from the wide and boundless agitation that surrounded us, and have a firm, distinct, and legal ground to rest upon. And the occasion, I trust, will justify me in **exhorting** my countrymen to rally upon and maintain that ground as the best, if not the only, means of restoring peace and quiet to the country and **maintaining inviolate** the integrity of the Union.* (The American Presidency: Selected Resources, An Informal Reference Guide [*Web site*].

What happened next . . .

President Fillmore called the Compromise of 1850 "a final statement," but it did little to settle national divisiveness over slavery. Northern abolitionists only grew more determined to put an end to the institution following enforcement of the Fugitive Slave Law. Fillmore, himself, was in a bind: he did not approve of slavery, but he believed the Constitution allowed for it.

The divisiveness of the times was reflected in Fillmore's presidential career. He served only the remainder of Taylor's term and lost his nomination bid in 1852 to Winfield Scott (1786–1866; see box in **Martin Van Buren** entry in volume 1), who eventually lost the election to **Franklin Pierce**

Irrevocable: Not recoverable.

Exhorting: Strongly urging.

Maintaining inviolate: Keeping pure.

(1804–1869; see entry in volume 2). The Whig Party that he led as president dissolved over the issue of slavery; those in favor of abolition formed the Republican Party in 1854. Meanwhile, the nation grew more disunited through the 1850s after Fillmore left office. Like Fillmore, the next two presidents—Democrats Pierce and **James Buchanan** (1791–1868; see entry in volume 2)—were from the North and supported the Constitutional right for individual states to decide on slavery. They were even less effective than Fillmore.

Did you know . . .

- President Fillmore was concerned about a possible race war. He favored a plan where slaves could be emancipated and relocated to Africa or the West Indies. Fillmore considered suggesting that idea as a national policy in 1853, but he never actually pursued it.

- Fillmore ran for president once more. In 1856, he was the candidate of the American (Know-Nothing) Party, whose slogan was "Americans must rule America." (It supported limitations on foreigners.) The fading Whig Party—which was participating in what turned out to be its last presidential election—also nominated Fillmore. The former president received eight electoral votes, but came in a distant third behind Republican John C. Frémont (1813–1890; see box in **James K. Polk** entry in volume 2) and the victorious Buchanan.

Where to Learn More

"Annual Message: December 2, 1851." *The American Presidency: Selected Resources, An Informal Reference Guide* (Web site). [Online] http://www.interlink-cafe.com/uspresidents/1851.htm (accessed on July 19, 2000).

Grayson, Benson Lee. *The Unknown President: The Administration of President Millard Fillmore.* Lanham, MD: University Press of America, 1981.

Holt, Michael F. *The Political Crisis of the 1850s.* New York: Wiley, 1978. Reprint, New York: Norton, 1983.

Potter, David M. *The Impending Crisis, 1848–1861.* Edited by Don E. Fehrenbacher. Harper and Row, 1976.

Franklin Pierce

Fourteenth president (1853–1857)

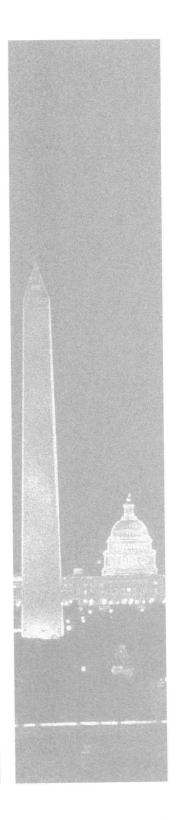

Franklin Pierce

Born November 23, 1804
Hillsborough, New Hampshire
Died October 8, 1869
Concord, New Hampshire

Fourteenth president of the United States
(1853–1857)

Reignited the debate over slavery by
making decisions that favored the South's
position on slavery

D uring the 1850s, the United States grew more bitterly divided over the issue of slavery. A compromise on the issue passed by Congress, the Compromise of 1850 was supposed to offer a balanced approach that could be acceptable to proslavery and abolitionist (antislavery) groups. But one provision of the Compromise may well have been the final cause for abolitionists to unite: the Fugitive Slave Law. This law allowed Southern slavemasters to pursue escaped slaves into the North, often resulting in violent confrontations.

When Franklin Pierce began his duties as president of the United States in March of 1853, he felt firmly that the Compromise of 1850 had settled all the differences between North and South. He was wrong. As the nation grew more divisive (divided) and frustrated over the institution of slavery, government became less effective. By the end of Pierce's term, conflicts over slavery had cost the United States an opportunity to acquire Cuba and had sparked bloody fighting in Kansas.

Other factors contributed to Pierce's dreary presidency. On the personal side, he entered the White House a heart-

"You have summoned me in my weakness. You must sustain me in your strength."

Franklin Pierce, in his inaugural address

Franklin Pierce.
Courtesy of the Library of Congress.

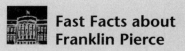

Fast Facts about Franklin Pierce

Full name: Franklin Pierce

Born: November 23, 1804

Died: October 8, 1869

Burial site: Old North Cemetery, Concord, New Hampshire

Parents: Benjamin and Anna Kendrick Pierce

Spouse: Jane Means Appleton (1806–1863; m. 1834)

Children: Franklin (1836–1836); Frank Robert (1839–1843); Benjamin (1841–1853)

Religion: Episcopalian

Education: Bowdoin College, (B.A., 1824)

Occupations: Lawyer; general

Government positions: New Hampshire state legislator; U.S. representative and senator from New Hampshire

Political party: Democratic

Dates as president: March 4, 1853–March 4, 1857

Age upon taking office: 48

broken man. His eleven-year-old son, Bennie, had died in a tragic accident just weeks before Pierce's inauguration (formal ceremony installing him as president). Pierce tended to his official duties with determination, but the death haunted both him and his frail wife throughout his single term as president.

On the political side, Pierce was more comfortable following others than serving as a leader. Only forty-eight at the time of his election—the youngest man to serve as president to that date—he was perhaps too eager to compromise for the good of his party. By the time he left office, he was widely disliked, especially in the North and the new territories west of the Mississippi River.

Groomed for politics

Franklin Pierce was born on November 23, 1804, in Hillsborough Lower Village, New Hampshire. His family roots stretched back in America to the 1630s. His father, Benjamin Pierce (1757–1839), was a decorated veteran of the Revolutionary War (1775–83) and was very active in New Hampshire politics. Young Franklin was educated at Hillsborough Center, Hancock Academy, and Bowdoin College, where he befriended noted author Nathaniel Hawthorne (1804–1864). (In addition to writing such famous short stories and novels as *The Scarlet Letter* and *The House of the Seven Gables,* Hawthorne wrote a short biography of Franklin Pierce that was used during Pierce's presidential campaign). After graduating from Bowdoin with honors, Pierce studied law and was admitted to the New Hampshire bar (legal profession) in 1827.

Pierce's real education came through his father, who served two terms as governor of New Hampshire. From him, Pierce learned a great deal about politics. He became skilled at speechmaking and consensus building. (A consensus builder is one who can convince groups of people to agree on an issue and to form a solid base of support for that issue.) Groomed for public service from the earliest age, Pierce was elected to the New Hampshire legislature in 1829. He became that body's Speaker of the House before his thirtieth birthday. In 1833, at the age of twenty-nine, Pierce was elected to Congress.

Pierce returned to Amherst in 1834 to wed Jane Means Appleton (1806–1863; see entry on **Jane Pierce** in volume 2), a shy and deeply religious woman. He had been courting her for nearly ten years. As a couple, the Pierces had opposite personalities: Pierce was comfortable mingling with people and finding ways to put aside differences; Jane Pierce was retiring and held fast to her beliefs.

Pierce's popularity as a politician led to his election to the U.S. Senate in 1837 at the age of thirty-three. He had always been willing to support party policies. The Democratic Party was organized to support states' rights during the presidency of **Andrew Jackson** (1829–1837; see entry in volume 1). Like leading members of the party, Pierce supported the rights of states to operate with minimal interference by the federal government.

Pierce's career seemed poised for greatness, but then he abruptly quit the Senate for personal reasons in 1842. His wife found life in Washington, D.C., intolerable. Jane Pierce was adamantly opposed to alcohol. She was well aware that the lifestyle of politicians in the capital often included drinking and lively parties. Out of respect to his wife—and perhaps

Franklin Pierce Timeline

1804: Born in New Hampshire

1829–33: Serves as New Hampshire state representative

1833–37: Serves as U.S. representative

1837–42: Serves in U.S. Senate

1846: Enlists to fight in the Mexican War (1846–48); rises to the rank of brigadier general

1852: Emerges as dark-horse candidate and wins election on forty-ninth ballot

1853–57: Serves as fourteenth U.S. president

1856: Loses Democratic presidential nomination to James Buchanan

1869: Dies in New Hampshire

Words to Know

Abolitionists: Those who wanted to end (abolish) slavery.

Annex: To add to an existing organization.

Bar: A term that encompasses all certified lawyers—those who have passed all official requirements (the bar exam) to be certified as lawyers.

"Bleeding Kansas:" The conflict in Kansas in 1854 between slavery advocates and abolitionists—in the form of both residents and transients, and two different governments—that led to bloodshed. It was the first indication that the issue of slavery would not be settled diplomatically.

Compromise of 1850: Legislation passed by Congress and signed into law by President Millard Fillmore consisting of five bills: (1) California was admitted as a free state; (2) Texas was compensated for the loss of territory in a boundary dispute with New Mexico; (3) New Mexico was granted territorial status; (4) the slave trade—but not slavery itself—was abolished in Washington, D.C; (5) and most controversially, the Fugitive Slave Law was enacted, allowing slaveowners to pursue fleeing slaves and recapture them in free states.

Confederate States of America: The eleven Southern states that ceded (separated) from the United States during the 1860s and fought the Union during the American Civil War.

Dark horse: A little-known candidate with modest chances for success who might emerge surprisingly strong.

Electoral College: A body officially responsible for electing the president of the United States. In presidential elections,

with a bit of concern about his own drinking habits—Pierce resigned and returned home to New Hampshire in 1842 with his spouse and two sons (another child had died in infancy).

The Mexican War

The Pierce family settled in the New Hampshire capital of Concord. Pierce opened what soon became a highly successful law firm. He continued to exert enormous political clout (power; influence) in the state, and he maintained allies in Washington, D.C.

the candidate who receives the most popular votes in a particular state wins all of that state's electoral votes. Votes are distributed among states in ratios based on population. A candidate must win a majority of electoral votes (over fifty percent) in order to win the presidency.

Fugitive Slave Law: The provision in the Compromise of 1850 that allowed Southern slaveowners to pursue and capture runaway slaves into Northern states.

Missouri Compromise of 1820: Legislation passed in 1820 intending to maintain an equal balance of slave and free states. The Compromise designated which areas could enter the Union as free states and which could enter as slave states. It was repealed in 1854.

Proviso: A clause in a document making a qualification, condition, or restriction.

Republican Party: Founded in 1854 by a coalition (an alliance) of former members of the Whig, Free-Soil, and Know-Nothing parties and of northern Democrats dissatisfied with their party's proslavery stands.

Underground railroad: A term that describes a series of routes through which escaped slaves could pass through free Northern states and into Canada. The escaped slaves were assisted by abolitionists and free African Americans in the North.

Whig Party: A political party that existed roughly from 1836 to 1852. Composed of factions of the former Democratic-Republican Party, Whigs refused to join the faction that in 1832 formed the Democratic Party led by President Andrew Jackson.

When war broke out between the United States and Mexico in 1846, Pierce raised two companies of volunteers from New Hampshire and marched south with them. He commissioned himself as a private, but the following year he was appointed a brigadier general. By May of 1847, Pierce and his troops arrived in Mexico. They marched through 150 miles of hostile territory to join the army of General Winfield Scott (1786–1866; see box in **Martin Van Buren** entry in volume 1). During the Battle of Contreras in August, Pierce fell from his horse and was injured in the leg and groin. Panic ensued among his leaderless men, some of whom deserted. His injuries were serious enough to warrant discharge, but Pierce continued to travel with the army.

Franklin Pierce. *Engraving by W. L. Ormsby. Courtesy of the Library of Congress.*

At the war's end in 1848, Pierce returned to New Hampshire, where his wife was raising the couple's surviving son (a second son had died in 1843). Pierce quickly immersed himself in state politics and turned his attention to the national Democratic Party. The issue of slavery so divided Democrats at that time that some abolitionists left to form the Free Soil Party. This new party nominated former president **Martin Van Buren** (1782–1862; see entry in volume 1), one of the founders of the Democratic Party, as its presidential candidate.

Pierce was greatly disturbed by such defections (desertions). Believing that slavery was officially approved by the U.S. Constitution, he sided with those who wanted individual states to decide on whether or not to permit slavery. Along with his Southern allies, Pierce felt that threats of federal interference on the part of Northern abolitionists was proving dangerous to the Union. Pierce so firmly held to those views that he helped to defeat a New Hampshire Democratic gubernatorial candidate (candidate for governor) who showed abolitionist sympathies.

Pierce strongly favored the Compromise of 1850, a series of laws that aimed to diffuse tensions between free and slave states. His belief in the compromise made him popular in the South. Quite suddenly he found himself back in the political limelight again.

During the Mexican War (1846–48), Pierce served under General Winfield Scott. They were on opposite sides a few years later, when Democrat Pierce defeated Whig candidate Scott in the 1852 presidential election.

Dark-horse candidate

Pierce had no presidential ambitions during the election year of 1852. His Democratic Party had several qualified candidates, including Stephen A. Douglas (1813–1861; see box in **Abraham Lincoln** entry in volume 2), **James Buchanan** (1791–1868; see entry in volume 2), and Lewis Cass (1782–1866; see box in **Zachary Taylor** entry in volume 2). However, when the nominating convention began in June of 1852, voters were hopelessly deadlocked. After forty-eight rounds of balloting (the process of voting) failed to yield a frontrunner, Pierce's name was placed into the race. He was chosen as a compromise candidate on the forty-ninth ballot—a "dark horse" (a little-known candidate) from the North who was acceptable to the South. William Rufus King (1786–1853) of Alabama was named the vice presidential candidate.

An editorial cartoon shows Whig candidate Winfield Scott pulling the "presidential chair" out from under Democratic candidate Franklin Pierce. Pierce defeated Scott in 1852.

Courtesy of the Library of Congress.

Reluctantly accepting his party's wishes, Pierce ran as "Young Hickory from the Granite State." The nickname referred back to "Old Hickory," the name supporters had given Andrew Jackson of Tennessee, who was a popular president from 1829 to 1837. The name "Young Hickory" showed that Southerners embraced Pierce as one of their own. Pierce defeated Whig candidate General Winfield Scott by a narrow margin of the popular vote but a large majority in the Electoral College, 254 votes to 42. (For more information on the Electoral College, see boxes in **George W. Bush** entry in volume 5.)

Tragedy struck as Pierce and his family traveled by train from New Hampshire to Washington, D.C. The train derailed. Pierce and his wife escaped injury, but their eleven-year-old son, Benjamin, was crushed to death before their eyes. The blow was particularly stunning to Jane Pierce, who never recovered sufficiently to undertake many of her duties as first lady.

Pierce delivered his inaugural address (his first speech as president; see **Franklin Pierce** primary source entry in vol-

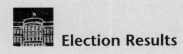

Election Results

1852

Presidential / Vice presidential candidates	Popular votes	Presidential electoral votes
Franklin Pierce / William Rufus King (Democratic)	1,601,474	254
Winfield Scott / William A. Graham (Whig)	1,386,578	42

Through fifty-two ballots, neither Scott nor incumbent president Millard Fillmore could secure enough votes to win the nomination of the Whig Party. Scott finally won on the fifty-third ballot. On the Democratic side, former secretary of state James Buchanan, Senator Lewis Cass of Michigan, Senator Stephen Douglas of Illinois, and former secretary of war William L. Marcy were early leaders, but none received a majority of electoral votes to win the nomination. Dark-horse candidate Pierce, a former senator from New Hampshire, emerged and, on the forty-ninth ballot, received a majority tally of 282 votes, securing the nomination.

ume 2) completely from memory in a March snowstorm. He advocated territorial expansion, a bold foreign policy, and strict adherence to the Constitutional rights of individual states. His Cabinet featured men with diverse opinions. Among them was Secretary of War Jefferson Davis 1808–1889; see box in **Abraham Lincoln** entry in volume 2), who would later become president of the Confederate States of America, the Southern states that seceded (separated) from the United States during the Civil War (1861–65). Pierce's vice president, William Rufus King, was sworn into office while in a hospital in Havana, Cuba, where he was receiving treatment for tuberculosis. King died one month into his term, and Pierce served without a vice president.

A rising tide

The Compromise of 1850 had achieved some positive results. It allowed California to be admitted into the Union as a free state, for example. However, the compromise also included the Fugitive Slave Law. This controversial law enabled Southern slaveholders to pursue runaway slaves across state lines into the North. By the 1850s, white abolitionists and free African Americans as well as former slaves had formed the Underground Railroad. The "railroad" was actually a se-

ries of routes through which runaway slaves were assisted in their escape to the North and into Canada, where they were free from prosecution.

The Fugitive Slave Law was very carefully enforced by Pierce, as it was by his predecessor, **Millard Fillmore** (1800–1874; see entry in volume 2). Northern abolitionists displayed contempt for the law with open hostility. Among them was Harriet Beecher Stowe (1811–1896; see box in **Millard Fillmore** entry in volume 2), whose 1852 novel *Uncle Tom's Cabin* revealed the plight of runaway slaves who sought to save their children from a life of forced labor. The novel was quickly a sensation, becoming the best-selling book of its time. Many readers inspired by the novel joined a growing movement for a repeal of the Fugitive Slave Law, but Pierce could not be moved on the subject. In fact, his administration made several fateful decisions that further deepened the rift between North and South.

Pierce's support of slavery became evident early in his presidency and contributed to a failed policy called the Ostend Manifesto. Proslavery forces feared that the Spanish colony of Cuba was about to free its slaves or be overrun by a slave revolt. They encouraged Pierce to oversee the purchase of the island for the United States. Pierce authorized his representative in Spain, Pierre Soulé (1801–1870), to begin negotiations. Soulé, along with Democrats James Buchanan, who was then minister to England, and John Y. Mason (1799–1859), minister to France, drafted a document called the Ostend Manifesto. In the manifesto (a public declaration of political intentions), the United States threatened to seize Cuba by force should Spain emancipate the slaves or allow a slave revolution. The plan was leaked to the public and caused an international uproar. Pierce disclaimed it, but the damage was done. Spain refused to sell Cuba or even to negotiate any further.

Another muddled outcome for Pierce occurred during discussions of plans for a transcontinental railroad. A route through the southern portion of the United States to California was chosen. Pierce then authorized the Gadsden Purchase,

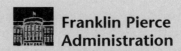 **Franklin Pierce Administration**

Administration Dates
March 4, 1853–March 4, 1857

Vice President
William Rufus De Vane King (1853)
None (1853–57)

Cabinet

Secretary of State
William L. Marcy (1853–57)

Secretary of the Treasury
James Guthrie (1853–57)

Secretary of War
Jefferson F. Davis (1853–57)

Attorney General
Caleb Cushing (1853–57)

Secretary of the Navy
James C. Dobbin (1853–57)

Postmaster General
James Campbell (1853–57)

Secretary of the Interior
Robert McClelland (1853–57)

Matthew C. Perry

Matthew Calbraith Perry was born on April 10, 1794, in Newport, Rhode Island. Entering the navy as a midshipman (a person in training to be a ship commander) in 1809, he was assigned to a vessel commanded by his elder brother, Oliver Hazard Perry. During the War of 1812 (1812–15), he served first on a large frigate (warship), then on another frigate, the *United States,* which was stranded in New London, Connecticut, during a blockade by the British navy. Venturing to New York City on leave, he courted and married Jane Slidell in 1814.

Perry enjoyed a wide variety of activities in the navy: he transported freed American slaves to Liberia, a colony established for the return of illegally captured slaves (under a recently enacted law) to Africa; he helped police African shores to rid them of slave traders and pirates; and he transported the new American minister to Russia, where the Russian Czar tried to entice him to join the Russian navy. From 1833 to the early 1840s, Perry served shore duty in the New York Navy Yard, beginning as second officer and then becoming commander. His duty there was significant: he

introduced technological and educational improvements, contributed to the development of the Naval Lyceum—a complex that includes a museum, study areas, and lecture halls, and helped start a naval magazine. For such efforts, Perry was nicknamed "chief educator of the navy."

Perry was also instrumental in transforming the U.S. navy from sailing vessels to steam-powered vessels, taking advantage of the latest development in water transportation. The superiority of steam vessels in the U.S. and British navies helped put an effective end to piracy. Perry helped design new hulls and engines and was given command of the first Navy steam warship, the *Fulton II.*

During the 1840s, Perry hunted for slave traders as commander of the Navy's African Squadron, led expeditions that captured several coastal cities during the Mexican War (1846–48), and as commander of the Gulf Squadron he backed General Winfield Scott in taking the key Mexican port city of Veracruz during the war. After the war, he supervised construction of ocean mail steamships. Meanwhile, American trade with China was expanding. Safe

a plan to buy land in what is now southern Arizona and southern New Mexico over which the railroad would run. Influential senator Stephen A. Douglas was among those with other plans. Douglas favored a railway that began in Chicago and would run across the Great Plains. By leaning toward a plan that fa-

Commodore Matthew Perry.
Courtesy of the Library of Congress.

areas for purchasing coal and supplies were needed, and American whalers in the northern Pacific Ocean needed protection. Perry was authorized by President Millard Fillmore to open trade negotiations and diplomacy with Japan. He set out from Norfolk, Virginia, on November 24, 1852, with four ships and arrived at Edo (modern Tokyo) on July 2, 1853. He had a letter requesting a treaty to present to the Japanese emperor, but upon landing in Edo he was told to go to Nagasaki, the only Japanese port open to foreigners. Perry refused, and when the Japanese saw his decks cleared for action, they relented. In an elaborate ceremony, Perry went ashore and delivered the letter to two princes representing the Emperor, promising to return in twelve months for the answer.

Perry journeyed to Hong Kong, then returned to Japan in February 1854. He received a warm welcome, especially since French and Russian naval operations in the Pacific were beginning to worry Japanese authorities. At Yokohama, representatives of the United States and Japan began negotiations; on March 31, 1854, they concluded a treaty that opened two Japanese ports, Hakodate and Shimoda, for trade and supplies and guaranteed fair treatment for shipwrecked American sailors. Japan, which had been closed to western nations, was now a trading partner with the United States. Perry returned to New York in January 1855 as a hero. After being honored with many celebratory receptions around the country, Perry prepared a report on his expedition to Japan. He finished the report in late December of 1857, and died on March 4, 1858.

vored the South, Pierce allowed the issue to become overwhelmed by debate within his own Democratic Party.

Douglas, meanwhile, introduced the Kansas-Nebraska Bill, which would create two territories between the Missouri

LIBERTY. THE FAIR MAID OF KANSAS_IN THE HANDS OF THE "BORDER RUFFIANS".

Cartoon condemning the Democratic administration under President Franklin Pierce (center) for the violence that erupted in what came to be called Bleeding Kansas. Other proslavery Democrats shown include, from left, U.S. minister to Britain James Buchanan, secretary of state William Marcy, and Senators Lewis Cass and Stephen Douglas.
Drawing by John L. Magee. Courtesy of the Library of Congress.

River and the Continental Divide (where the Rocky Mountains separate the far western states from the midwest and eastern states). Fearing that his bill would fail to gather Southern support, Douglas added the proviso (condition) that the status of any new territories—free or slave—could be settled by vote of the inhabitants. That provision opened land that had been closed to slavery by the Missouri Compromise of 1820 (see **James Monroe** primary source entry in volume 1), legislation that attempted to balance the number of slave states and free states. When the bill came to vote, Southern politicians demanded an outright repeal of the Missouri Compromise. Believing that federal restrictions on slavery were unconstitutional, Pierce agreed with them. In May of 1854, the Kansas-Nebraska bill became law and the Missouri Compromise was repealed.

Problems arose almost immediately. Wanting to ensure that Kansas would be a slave state, proslavery people from

Complete American Presidents Sourcebook

Missouri flooded into the territory, obtained the right to vote, and organized a proslavery legislature at Lecompton, Kansas. Simultaneously, abolitionists moved in, organized their own government in Topeka, and fought for free-state status. Pierce recognized only the Lecompton government and ordered the Topeka government to disband. By that time, the conflict had become violent. Known historically as "Bleeding Kansas," the conflict between residents and transients, slavery advocates and abolitionists, was the first indication that the issue of slavery would not be settled diplomatically.

Pierce did not fare much better in foreign policy. He tried to annex (add to the United States) the territories of Hawaii and Alaska, but made no progress on either initiative. The Pierce administration, following the efforts of President Fillmore, was successful in opening up trade with Japan. The ceremonial visit to Japan in 1854 of Commodore Matthew C. Perry (1794–1858; see box) was the first great highlight in relations between the two nations.

An unhappy ending

As the troubles in Kansas escalated, Pierce was depicted by hostile political cartoonists as a drunken devil trampling on liberty and condoning the worst abuses of slavery. The president hardly saw himself that way. He felt he was a champion of the Constitution and the strict stance (position) the document took on states' rights. His views alienated some Northern Democrats. Many of them left to join the newly formed Republican Party. The Republican Party was founded in 1854 by former members of the Whig, Free-Soil, and Know-Nothing parties, and some Northern Democrats unhappy with their party's proslavery stance.

Unpopular as he was, Pierce hoped to win renomination for a second term in 1856. He was replaced, instead, by James Buchanan, another Northern Democrat who supported the institution of slavery.

After leaving office, Pierce and his wife embarked for a long tour of Europe. They returned to settle in Concord, New Hampshire. From there, Pierce became a vocal critic of President **Abraham Lincoln** (1809–1865; see entry in volume

A Selection of Pierce Landmarks

Old North Cemetery. North State St., Concord, NH. Burial site of Franklin, Jane, Frank, and Bennie Pierce.

Pierce Homestead. Routes 9 and 31, Hillsborough, NH 03244. (603) 478-3168. Home of Franklin Pierce until he was thirty. The house was owned by his father, Benjamin, a two-time governor of New Hampshire. See http://www.conknet.com/~hillsboro/historic/homestead.html (accessed on July 11, 2000).

Pierce Manse. 14 Penacook St., Concord, NH 00301. (603) 224-7668. Home of Franklin Pierce before he was president. See http://www.newww.com/free/pierce/pierce.html (accessed on July 11, 2000).

2), but Pierce was by that time so widely discredited that his views were sometimes met with public scorn. After Jane Pierce's death in 1863, Franklin Pierce lived in near seclusion until his death on October 8, 1869. He was buried in a family plot in the Old North Cemetery in Concord, New Hampshire.

Legacy

Franklin Pierce was the second of three successive presidents from the North who supported the rights of states to determine whether or not to permit slavery. Like his predecessor, Millard Fillmore, and his successor, James Buchanan, Pierce felt that legislation—specifically, the Compromise of 1850—had settled the slavery issue. Instead, all three presidents were overwhelmed by national divisiveness that undermined their presidencies.

Abolitionist sentiments expanded quickly through the 1850s and led to the formation of the Republican Party in 1854 to pursue the cause nationally. A civil war erupted in Kansas in 1856 during Pierce's final year in office. More compromises and more defenses of slavery were attempted by President Buchanan, but Northern states grew more solidly abolitionist, leading to the election of Republican Abraham

Lincoln in 1860. The issue of slavery was finally settled during Lincoln's presidency through a national Civil War.

Expansion of American territory and trade were the most positive developments during Pierce's presidency. The Gadsden Purchase of 1853 expanded the territories of Arizona and New Mexico to their present-day southern borders. The United States officially began trade relations with Japan, enlarging the American presence in Asia.

The site where Franklin Pierce was born is now covered by water—Lake Franklin Pierce.

Where to Learn More

Bell, Carl Irving. *They Knew Franklin Pierce (and Others Thought They Did): A Sampling of Opinions about the 14th U.S. President Drawn from His Contemporaries.* Springfield, VT: April Hill Publishers, 1980.

Bratman, Benjamin, David Holzel, and Todd Leopold. *The Franklin Pierce Pages.* [Online] http://www.mindspring.com/~dbholzel/pierce/pierce.html (accessed on July 21, 2000).

Brown, Fern G. *Franklin Pierce: 14th President of the United States.* Ada, OK: Garrett Educational Corporation, 1989.

Hawthorne, Nathaniel. *Life of Franklin Pierce.* Boston: Ticknor, Reed and Fields, 1852. Reprint, New York: Garrett Press, 1970.

Nichols, Roy F. *Franklin Pierce: Young Hickory of the Granite Hills.* Norwalk, CT: Easton Press, 1988.

Simon, Charnan. *Franklin Pierce: Fourteenth President of the United States.* Chicago: Children's Press, 1988.

Jane Pierce

Born November 19, 1834
Hampton, New Hampshire
Died December 2, 1863
Andover, Massachusetts

Reclusive first lady disliked politics and mourned the tragic death of her son

Upon hearing that her husband, **Franklin Pierce** (1804–1869; see entry in volume 2), had received his party's nomination for president, Jane Pierce fainted. Pious, retiring, and frail, Mrs. Pierce detested Washington, D.C. She had spent much of her adult life trying to persuade her husband to retire from politics.

Perhaps no first lady in history was more reluctant to assume her post than this minister's daughter. Her distaste for official duties was made worse by the tragic death of her eleven-year-old son just weeks before Pierce's inauguration (formal ceremony installing him as president).

Raised on religion

Jane Means Appleton grew up in Brunswick, Maine, the daughter of noted Congregational minister Reverend Jesse Appleton. During much of Jane's youth, her father was president of Bowdoin College. Jane was well educated and reared in a strict and deeply religious household. After her fa-

"I have known many of the ladies of the White House, none more truly excellent than the afflicted wife of President Pierce. Her health was a bar to any great effort on her part to meet the expectations of the public in her high position but she was a refined, extremely religious and well educated lady.

Mrs. Robert E. Lee

Jane Pierce.
Engraving by John C. Buttre.
Courtesy of the Library of Congress.

ther's death in 1819 when she was thirteen, her mother moved the family to Amherst, New Hampshire. There, in 1824, Jane met Franklin Pierce, an ambitious Bowdoin graduate whose father was a high-ranking politician.

The courtship of Jane and Franklin Pierce was lengthy. Jane's family did not approve of politics as a career. Franklin was almost thirty years old and Jane was twenty-eight when they finally married in 1834. By that time, Pierce had been elected to Congress.

The marriage was not particularly happy. Three sons were born, one of them dying after only three days and another dying at the age of four from typhus, an infectious disease caused by microorganisms. A third son was healthy, but Jane Pierce did not relish the idea of bringing him up in Washington, D.C. She was appalled by the casual atmosphere and social drinking in the nation's capital. She actively encouraged her husband to retire from national office. Although he was elected to the Senate at the age of thirty-two and seemed headed for a promising career, he finally consented to her wishes in 1842. The family returned to New Hampshire, where Pierce resumed his law practice.

War and politics

The Pierce family might have lived quietly in New Hampshire thereafter, but Franklin Pierce volunteered for service in the Mexican War (1846–48). Upon his return, Pierce became active again in Democratic politics in his home state. The news that he had been nominated as the Democratic Party's candidate for president in 1852 came as an unpleasant surprise to Jane and her third son, Benjamin, to whom she was deeply devoted. Neither mother nor son wanted to move back to Washington, D.C., but Franklin Pierce was able to persuade them that his success would help to improve Benjamin's prospects in the future.

On January 6, 1853, the Pierce family was traveling by train between Concord, New Hampshire, and Boston, Massachusetts, when the train derailed (ran off the tracks). Benjamin Pierce died before his parents' eyes, while the future president and his wife escaped with minor injuries.

Jane Pierce never fully recovered from the tragedy. She interpreted it as a sign from God that her husband was not to have any distractions from his family while running the nation. Retiring by nature, she became reclusive (withdrawn). A pall (gloomy atmosphere) of sorrow lay upon the White House while the Pierces resided there. The suddenness of the tragedy—coming so soon before his inauguration—affected Franklin Pierce's ability to discharge his duties. Even the inaugural ball was canceled. The Pierce presidency was marked by a scarcity of social events.

Jane Pierce occasionally attempted to serve as her husband's official hostess. Most of the time she was not up to the task. She relied heavily upon a childhood friend, Mrs. Abigail Kent Means, to perform the duties of a first lady. Mrs. Means had married Jane's uncle. One description of Jane Pierce occurs in a letter written by Mary Anna Lee, wife of Confederate general Robert E. Lee (1807–1870; see box in **Ulysses S. Grant** entry in volume 3) and a granddaughter of **Martha Washington** (1732–1802; see entry in volume 1): "I have known many of the ladies of the White House, none more truly excellent than the afflicted [suffering] wife of President Pierce," Mrs. Lee wrote. "Her health was a bar to any great effort on her part to meet the expectations of the public in her high position but she was a refined, extremely religious and well educated lady."

When Franklin Pierce's presidential term ended, the couple toured Europe in search of treatment for Jane's ailments. Thereafter they returned to New Hampshire. Jane Pierce died there on December 2, 1863. She was buried near her son Benjamin in a family plot in Old North Cemetery, Concord in New Hampshire.

Where to Learn More

Boller, Paul F. *Presidential Wives*. New York: Oxford University Press, 1998.

Kent, Deborah. *Jane Means Appleton Pierce*. New York: Children's Press, 1998.

Pierce's Inaugural Address

Delivered on March 4, 1853; excerpted from
A Chronology of US Historical Documents **(Web site)**

*President Pierce announces his intention to
protect the principle that individual states have the
right to determine their own laws regarding slavery*

Franklin Pierce (1804–1869; see entry in volume 2) took office in troubled times. Debate over the institution of slavery had grown fierce and threatened to tear apart the Union. For Pierce, as for a majority of federally elected officials of the time, the moral crisis over slavery was of less importance than the principle that individual states had the right to determine their own laws within the framework of the U.S. Constitution, which acknowledged the existence of slavery.

The conflict between abolitionists (those against the institution of slavery) and those supporting slavery was unresolvable. The Compromise of 1850 was the most recent attempt to balance the different sides, to equalize Congressional power between the North and South, and to maintain the principle of states' rights. Pierce intended to enforce the Compromise, including the Fugitive Slave Law that enabled Southern slaveholders to pursue runaway slaves across state lines into the North.

As a Northern Democrat who was against any federal attempt to undermine the rights of states to determine for themselves the legality of slavery, Pierce was a popular candi-

"I believe that involuntary servitude [slavery], as it exists in different States of this Confederacy, is recognized by the Constitution. I believe that it stands like any other admitted right, and that the States where it exists are entitled to efficient remedies to enforce the constitutional provisions."

Franklin Pierce

date to Southern voters as well as to those in the North who did not have abolitionist sentiments. He made it clear in his inaugural address that he would continue to pursue the principles that had brought him to the presidency.

Pierce's speech consisted of fourteen sections. He began by expressing his feeling of humbleness at taking on the office of president, then he recalled that the United States had humble origins. From those origins, the nation gradually expanded to former frontier lands. Picking up present-day themes, Pierce advocated further territorial expansion and a bold foreign policy. In the final five sections, from which the following excerpt is taken, Pierce emphasized that he would strictly adhere to the Constitutional rights of individual states. He concluded by stressing that if all Americans respected that approach, there would be an end to regional differences.

Things to remember while reading an excerpt from President Pierce's inaugural address:

- Pierce viewed the institution of slavery as a political matter, rather than a moral issue. He made his position clear on this "important subject": the Constitution recognized the existence of "involuntary servitude," and as president he would uphold the Constitution. Using colorful language to praise the growth and development of the United States, Pierce made a plea for harmony through respect for laws of the land. Such respect, he asserted, would end divisiveness on the issue of slavery.

- Pierce's strong religious convictions were apparent in the speech. He asserted that Providence (divine guidance) had led the nation safely through a period of turmoil, just as it had guided the nation's founders. The speech, as a whole, reflected Pierce's belief that the nation could unite and put differences behind.

- In retrospect (looking back on an event after it happened), Pierce's speech was ironic—the events that followed were much different than the hopes he expressed. Instead of putting the issue of slavery behind, Americans grew more bitterly divided. Instead of finding harmony, Americans fought and killed each other in the territory of Kansas over the issue of slavery.

Excerpt from
Pierce's inaugural address

*The great scheme of our constitutional liberty rests upon a proper distribution of power between the State and Federal authorities, and experience has shown that the harmony and happiness of our people must depend upon a just discrimination between the separate rights and responsibilities of the States and your common rights and obligations under the General Government; and here, in my opinion, are the considerations which should form the true basis of future **concord** in regard to the questions which have most seriously disturbed public tranquillity. If the Federal Government will confine itself to the exercise of powers clearly granted by the Constitution, it can hardly happen that its action upon any question should endanger the institutions of the States or interfere with their right to manage matters strictly **domestic** according to the will of their own people.*

*In expressing briefly my views upon an **important subject** which has recently agitated the nation to almost a fearful degree, I am moved by no other impulse than a most earnest desire for the **perpetuation** of that Union which has made us what we are, showering upon us blessings and conferring a power and influence which our fathers could hardly have anticipated, even with their most **sanguine hopes** directed to a far-off future. The sentiments I now announce were not unknown before the expression of the voice which called me here. My own position upon this subject was clear and unequivocal, upon the record of my words and my acts, and it is only recurred to at this time because silence might perhaps be misconstrued. With the Union my best and dearest earthly hopes are entwined. Without it what are we individually or collectively? What becomes of the noblest field ever opened for the advancement of our race in religion, in government, in the arts, and in all that dignifies and adorns mankind? From that radiant constellation which both illumines our own way and points out to struggling nations their course, let but a single star be lost, and, if these be not utter darkness, the luster of the whole is dimmed. Do my countrymen need any assurance that such a catastrophe is not to overtake them while I possess the power to stay it? It is with me an earnest and vital belief that as the Union has been the source, under **Providence**, of our*

Concord: Harmony, agreement.

Domestic: Pertaining to one's home or country.

Important subject: Pierce is referring to slavery.

Perpetuation: Continuation.

Sanguine hopes: Heartfelt optimism.

Providence: Divine guidance. When an event is believed to have happened through an act of God, it is called providence.

*prosperity to this time, so it is the surest pledge of a continuance of the blessings we have enjoyed, and which we are sacredly bound to transmit undiminished to our children. The field of calm and free discussion in our country is open, and will always be so, but never has been and never can be **traversed** for good in a spirit of sectionalism and uncharitableness. The founders of the Republic dealt with things as they were presented to them, in a spirit of self-sacrificing patriotism, and, as time has proved, with a comprehensive wisdom which it will always be safe for us to consult. Every measure tending to strengthen the fraternal feelings of all the members of our Union has had my heartfelt **approbation**. To every theory of society or government, whether the offspring of feverish ambition or of morbid enthusiasm, calculated to dissolve the bonds of law and affection which unite us, I shall **interpose** a ready and stern resistance. I believe that **involuntary servitude**, as it exists in different States of this Confederacy, is recognized by the Constitution. I believe that it stands like any other admitted right, and that the States where it exists are entitled to efficient remedies to enforce the constitutional provisions. I hold that the laws of 1850, commonly called the "compromise measures," are strictly constitutional and to be unhesitatingly carried into effect. I believe that the constituted authorities of this Republic are bound to regard the rights of the South in this respect as they would view any other legal and constitutional right, and that the laws to enforce them should be respected and obeyed, not with a reluctance encouraged by abstract opinions as to their propriety in a different state of society, but cheerfully and according to the decisions of the **tribunal** to which their exposition belongs. Such have been, and are, my convictions, and upon them I shall act. I fervently hope that the question is at rest, and that no sectional or ambitious or fanatical excitement may again threaten the durability of our institutions or obscure the light of our prosperity.*

But let not the foundation of our hope rest upon man's wisdom. It will not be sufficient that sectional prejudices find no place in the public deliberations. It will not be sufficient that the rash counsels of human passion are rejected. It must be felt that there is no national security but in the nation's humble, acknowledged dependence upon God and His overruling providence.

*We have been carried in safety through a perilous crisis. Wise counsels, like those which gave us the Constitution, prevailed to uphold it. Let the period be remembered as an **admonition**, and not as an encouragement, in any section of the Union, to make experi-*

Traversed: Denied.

Approbation: Official approval.

Interpose: Introduce.

Involuntary servitude: Slavery.

Tribunal: Court of law.

Admonition: Warning.

*ments where experiments are fraught with such fearful hazard. Let it be impressed upon all hearts that, beautiful as our fabric is, no earthly power or wisdom could ever reunite its broken fragments. Standing, as I do, almost within view of the green slopes of **Monticello**, and, as it were, within reach of the tomb of [George] Washington, with all the cherished memories of the past gathering around me like so many eloquent voices of exhortation from heaven, I can express no better hope for my country than that the kind Providence which smiled upon our fathers may enable their children to preserve the blessings they have inherited.* (A Chronology of US Historical Documents [Web site])

What happened next . . .

Pierce's pleas for harmony were not enough to stop growing divisiveness between the North and South. The Abolitionist movement was growing stronger. Abolitionists soon overwhelmed those in the North who supported the existence of slavery based on the right of self-determination of individual states.

The Abolitionist movement gained more momentum after the 1852 publication of *Uncle Tom's Cabin,* by Harriet Beecher Stowe (1811–1896; see box in **Millard Fillmore** entry in volume 2). Her bestselling book dramatized the miserable lives of slaves who were often the victims of violence and family separations. The Fugitive Slave Law, which allowed Southern slaveowners to pursue runaway slaves into the North, also rallied Northerners against the institution of slavery. The Slave Law was part of the Compromise of 1850 that Pierce alluded to in his inaugural address. Like many politicians, Pierce expected that the Compromise would ease tensions over slavery by including some measures that would be popular in the North, and others that would be popular in the South.

As Abolitionists became a more powerful and united group, they began to disassociate themselves from the Whig and Democratic parties because each group had members

Monticello: The home of Thomas Jefferson, author of the Declaration of Independence and the nation's third president.

who were more supportive of states' rights than the abolition of slavery. Most abolitionists joined the Republican Party that was formed in 1854. It grew quickly, and in 1860 **Abraham Lincoln** (1809–1865; see entry in volume 2) became the first Republican elected president.

Meanwhile, tensions continued to escalate. The Kansas-Nebraska Act of 1854 allowed those two territories to determine whether or not they would enter the Union as free or slave states. A civil war erupted in Kansas in 1856 over the issue. Acts of violence continued on to 1861, when the full scale Civil War (1861–65) erupted. The Emancipation Proclamation, which led to the Thirteenth Amendment to the U.S. Constitution in 1865, was the beginning of the end of slavery.

Did you know . . .

- On religious grounds, Franklin Pierce chose "to affirm" rather than "to swear" the executive oath of office. He was the only president to use that choice offered by the Constitution.

Where to Learn More

Bisson, Wilfred J. *Franklin Pierce: A Bibliography.* Westport, CT: Greenwood Press, 1993.

Gara, Larry. *The Presidency of Franklin Pierce.* Lawrence: University Press of Kansas, 1991.

Stoddard, William Osborn. *Zachary Taylor, Millard Fillmore, Franklin Pierce and James Buchanan.* New York: F. A. Stokes, 1888.

University of Oklahoma Law Center. "Inaugural Address of President Franklin Pierce." *A Chronology of US Historical Documents.* [Online] http://www.law.ou.edu/hist/ (accessed on July 19, 2000).

James Buchanan

Fifteenth president (1857–1861)

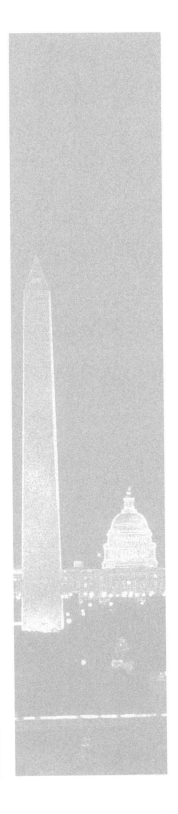

James Buchanan

Born April 23, 1791
Cove Gap, Pennsylvania
Died June 1, 1868
Lancaster, Pennsylvania

Fifteenth president of the United States
(1857–1861)

Foreign affairs expert's presidency was
marred by slavery issue; Civil War began
only weeks after he left office

"My dear sir, if you are as happy on entering the White House as I on leaving, you are a very happy man indeed."

James Buchanan, to his successor, Abraham Lincoln

James Buchanan.
Courtesy of the Library of Congress.

An incident that occurred just a month before James Buchanan left office in early 1861 would influence history's assessment of him for decades—in a negative way. On that day, a formal declaration of secession (separation) from the Union was presented to the president by seven proslavery states in the South. Buchanan's foes—Democrats and Republicans, Northerners and Southerners alike—would first blame him for action and then blame him for inaction that plunged the country into the secession crisis. The crisis would be resolved only after American blood was spilled on American soil during the Civil War (1861–65).

Buchanan was a highly skilled politician with forty years of public service before he became the fifteenth president in 1857. He possessed a solid intellectual grasp of the issues behind the secession crisis: states' rights, regional economic power, and the ability to amend the U.S. Constitution. On the slavery question, however, Buchanan was less politically adept.

Though he was a Northern Democrat, Buchanan was viewed as a Southerner in spirit. He thought that the Ameri-

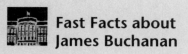

Fast Facts about James Buchanan

Full name: James Buchanan

Born: April 23, 1791

Died: June 1, 1868

Burial site: Woodward Cemetery, Lancaster, Pennsylvania

Parents: James and Elizabeth Speer Buchanan

Spouse: None

Children: None

Religion: Presbyterian

Education: Dickinson College (B.A., 1809)

Occupation: Lawyer

Government positions: Pennsylvania state representative; U.S. representative and senator from Pennsylvania; minister to Russia and England; secretary of state under James K. Polk

Political party: Democratic

Dates as president: March 4, 1857–March 4, 1861

Age upon taking office: 65

can Constitution provided adequate means of resolving such disputes as the issue over slavery. The insistence of Southern landowners on retaining their economic system and the determination of Southern politicians in Washington to allow slavery—often called their "peculiar institution"—to expand westward along with the Union had already proved unresolvable in Congress and the courts for decades. Buchanan became one of many political leaders overwhelmed by the divisiveness of the issue.

Pennsylvania lawyer

Born on April 23, 1791, James Buchanan was the last president born in the eighteenth century. He was one of eleven children of emigrants (people who leave one country to settle in another) from County Donegal, Ireland. His father, also named James Buchanan, became a storekeeper and real-estate investor in the area around Cove Gap, Pennsylvania. Young Buchanan attended school in nearby Mercersburg. At the age of sixteen, he enrolled in Dickinson College in Carlisle, Pennsylvania. After graduating with honors two years later, he studied law with an attorney in Lancaster, Pennsylvania.

Buchanan was admitted to the bar (legal profession) in Pennsylvania in 1813 and began to practice law in Lancaster. He soon earned a reputation as an astute (perceptive) trial lawyer with an impressive mastery of the law's intricacies (complexities). His practice was profitable for many years.

Buchanan's political career began when members of the local Federalist Party (those supporting a strong national government) invited him to run for a seat in the Pennsylvania assembly in 1814. He moved from the state assembly to Washington, D.C., after he was elected to the first of five terms in the U.S. House of Representatives in 1820.

Around that time, a tragedy in his personal life dimmed Buchanan's growing success. Buchanan was engaged to Anne Coleman, a young woman whose family disapproved of him. A short time after she broke off their engagement, the young woman died in what was likely a suicide. Buchanan would remain unmarried—America's only bachelor president—the rest of his life. (**Grover Cleveland** [1837–1908; see entry in volume 3] entered the White House in 1885 as a bachelor, but married fifteen months later.)

Foreign affairs expert

With the disintegration (separation into pieces or groups) of the Federalist Party in the early 1820s, Buchanan became a Jacksonian Democrat. The Democratic-Republican Party dominated the American political scene, holding the White House from 1801 to 1829. The party split into factions (groups) following the controversial presidential election of 1824. Jacksonian Democrats were a faction loyal to **Andrew Jackson** (1767–1845; see entry in volume 1), who represented the common people and favored states' rights over federal influence; another faction rallied around **John Quincy Adams** (1767–1848; see entry in volume 1), an aristocrat (person of the upper class) who favored a strong federal government. The Jackson faction dominated the party by the end of the 1820s. The party was transformed into the modern-day Democratic Party in 1832.

 James Buchanan Timeline

1791: Born in Pennsylvania

1813: Admitted to the bar of Pennsylvania and opens a law practice in Lancaster; elected to the Pennsylvania state legislature as a Federalist and re-elected in 1815

1821–30: Serves in the U.S. House of Representatives

1831: Appointed U.S. minister to Russia

1834–45: Elected to U.S. Senate as Democrat from Pennsylvania

1845–49: Serves as secretary of state under President James K. Polk

1853–56: Serves as U.S. minister to Great Britain

1857–61: Serves as fifteenth U.S. president

1859: John Brown's raid on Harpers Ferry, Virginia, furthers tension among abolitionists and supporters of slavery

1868: Dies in Pennsylvania

Words to Know

Bar: A term that encompasses all certified lawyers—those who have passed all official requirements (the bar exam) to be certified as lawyers.

Confederacy: The Southern states that ceded from the United States during the 1860s and formed the Confederate States of America (CSA).

Federalist Party: An American political party of the late eighteenth century that supported a strong national government.

Midterm elections: Congressional elections that occur halfway through a presidential term. These elections can affect the president's dealings with Congress. A president is elected every four years; representatives (members of the House of Representatives), every two years; and senators, every six years.

Missouri Compromise: Legislation passed in 1820 that designated which areas could enter the Union as free states and which could enter as slave states. Repealed in 1854.

Secession: Formal withdrawal from an existing organization.

Whig Party: A political party that existed roughly from 1836 to 1852 consisting of different groups from the former Democratic-Republican Party. The Whigs had refused to join the faction that formed the Democratic Party led by President Andrew Jackson.

Jackson, elected president in 1828, appointed Buchanan minister to Russia in 1831. Buchanan was elected to the U.S. Senate in 1834 and served over a decade there. President **James K. Polk** (1795–1849; see entry in volume 2) named Buchanan his secretary of state in 1845. Buchanan's four years in Polk's Cabinet enhanced his reputation as a solid supporter of territorial expansion. He proposed and pursued the building of a canal in Central America (realized only several decades later) and directed negotiations that settled a border dispute between America and Great Britain.

The Oregon Territory, stretching from the northern border of present-day California to the southern border of present-day Alaska, was at that time claimed both by the United States and Great Britain. As the prospect for war seemed close at hand, a compromise was reached, and the territory was divided at the forty-ninth parallel latitude (the present-day northern border that stretches from Minnesota to Washington state). In addition to helping forge that agreement, Buchanan tried to negotiate a peace with Mexico over a border dispute involving the Republic of Texas. The dispute was resolved in the two-year Mexican War (1846–48), from which America emerged victorious.

Buchanan retired from politics in 1848 at age fifty-seven when Whig Party candidate **Zachary Taylor** (1784–1850; see entry in volume 2), a hero of the Mexican War, was elected to the White House. (The Whig Party, consisting of several different groups

JAMES BUCHANAN,
DEMOCRATIC CANDIDATE FOR PRESIDENT OF THE UNITED STATES.

Democratic campaign poster of James Buchanan for president.
Courtesy of the Library of Congress.

that splintered off of the former Democratic-Republican Party, existed from about 1836 to 1852.) Buchanan returned to Pennsylvania and purchased a large estate near Lancaster. At this home, called Wheatland, Buchanan was once more able to enjoy the company of his large extended family. He had many nieces and nephews whose company he enjoyed. Buchanan was the legal guardian of one of them—**Harriet Lane** (1830–1903; see entry in volume 2), who had been orphaned at the age of eleven in 1841.

When Democrat **Franklin Pierce** (1804–1869; see entry in volume 2) won the presidential election of 1852, Buchanan was appointed minister to Great Britain. This interval of his career was notable for his involvement in the Ostend Manifesto, the declaration by the United States that it could rightfully seize Spain's enormous colony of Cuba, just off the U.S. mainland, if Spain refused to sell or relinquish (give up) the island. Proslavery forces feared that the Spanish

THE GRAND NATIONAL FIGHT 2 AGAINST 1 FOUGHT ON THE 6TH NOV. 1856

Political cartoon portraying the 1856 presidential campaign as a boxing match. Democratic candidate James Buchanan (standing, left) has knocked down American Party opponent Millard Fillmore (on the ground) and is taking on Republican Party contender John C. Frémont (standing, right).

Drawing probably by John L. Magee. Courtesy of the Library of Congress.

colony of Cuba was about to free its slaves or be overrun by a slave revolt. They encouraged President Pierce to purchase the island for the United States. The Ostend Manifesto, intended to pressure Spain, was leaked by the press and caused such an uproar at home and abroad that the United States abandoned its attempt to buy Cuba.

"Save the Union"

Pierce had lost popularity throughout his term, and antislavery forces were uniting behind the new Republican Party, founded in 1854. Buchanan, who appealed to Northern and Southern voters, won the Democratic Party nomination for president in 1856. His opponent was John C. Frémont (1813–1890; see box in **James K. Polk** entry in volume 2), the first candidate of the Republican Party. Frémont ran on an antislavery platform. Unpopular ex-president **Millard Fillmore**

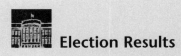

Election Results

1856

Presidential / Vice presidential candidates	Popular votes	Presidential electoral votes
James Buchanan / John C. Breckinridge (Democratic)	1,838,169	174
John C. Frémont / William L. Dayton (Republican)	1,341,264	114
Millard Fillmore / Andrew Jackson Donelson (American [Know-Nothing])	874,534	8

Buchanan received the nomination on the seventeenth ballot; incumbent president Franklin Pierce was in second place for the first fourteen ballots, before U.S. senator Stephen Douglas of Illinois overtook him. Fillmore also ran as a Whig, the last election in which the Whig Party participated.

(1800–1874; see entry in volume 2) ran as the nominee of both the Whig Party (which, as it turned out was participating in its last presidential election) and the American (Know-Nothing) Party.

Some of Frémont's more radical supporters were calling for the North to secede (separate) from the Union on grounds of their opposition to slavery. Buchanan won votes with his "Save the Union" campaign. Personally, Buchanan was opposed to slavery, but he believed that its presence in the Southern half of the United States was legal. He viewed Northern abolitionists as an increasingly dangerous element in American politics.

Buchanan won the election, receiving 1.8 million popular votes to Frémont's 1.3 million votes and winning nearly all of the Southern electoral votes. Following his victory, Buchanan named moderates and conservatives from both the North and the South to his Cabinet. His position on the slavery issue was made clear in his inaugural address (first speech as president). He stated that the federal courts should settle the question.

Just two days after his inaugural address, the U.S. Supreme Court issued a fateful ruling on the matter in the *Dred Scott v. Sandford* case. Dred Scott (1795?–1858) was a slave who sued for his freedom when his slavemaster moved

COL. FREMONT

him to a state where slavery was illegal. The High Court decided in favor of the slaveowner, arguing that a slave was not an American citizen and therefore had no right to sue in court. The ruling also negated the Missouri Compromise of 1820 (see box in **Millard Fillmore** entry in volume 2), which was Congress's master plan to keep peace by allowing one slave state to enter the Union for every free one.

The gathering storm

The *Dred Scott* decision proved controversial and strengthened popular support for the abolitionist cause. When the territory of Kansas applied to enter the Union, the issue of the expansion of slavery into the West further aroused strong emotions in the nation. The earlier Kansas-Nebraska Act of 1854 allowed prospective states to decide for themselves whether or not to permit slavery. Buchanan's efforts to engineer an agreeable compromise in 1858 failed. The majority of Kansas Territory settlers were opposed to slavery, but a proslavery government had been legitimized by the Kansas-Nebraska Act. When Kansas's application for entry into the Union as a slave state was blocked in Congress, Buchanan championed (promoted) a piece of legislation that offered a temporary resolution. His resolution: Kansas could be admitted as a slave state but with a much reduced federal land grant. Congress passed the bill, but debate in Kansas during a cooling-off period resulted three years later in Kansas being admitted into the Union as a free state.

Buchanan's faith that the Supreme Court ruling would answer critics of slavery was misguided. The slavery issue had flared into warfare during the 1850s, but Buchanan continued to believe that an acceptable solution was at hand. Meanwhile, the United States was undergoing enormous change. Railroads were stretching across the land; the invention of the steamboat improved water transportation; communication was enhanced by the telegraph; and the United States was growing into an industrial power. Cultural changes were occurring as well: advances in science challenged long-held religious beliefs, but religious revivals were happening as well. Buchanan had been a career politician who did not venture far into the land. Events were moving fast and beyond any influence he tried to exert.

Buchanan, who came to office as a foreign policy expert, saw great opportunity for expanding America's influence abroad. Trade was expanded. Latin American nations emerging from the crumbling Spanish empire were extended recog-

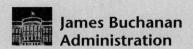 **James Buchanan Administration**

Administration Dates
March 4, 1857–March 4, 1861

Vice President
John C. Breckinridge (1857–61)

Cabinet

Secretary of State
Lewis Cass (1857–60)
Jeremiah S. Black (1860–61)

Secretary of the Treasury
Howell Cobb (1857–60)
Philip F. Thomas (1860–61)
John A. Dix (1861)

Secretary of War
John B. Floyd (1857–60)
Joseph Holt (1861)

Attorney General
Jeremiah S. Black (1857–60)
Edwin M. Stanton (1860–61)

Secretary of the Navy
Isaac Toucey (1857–61)

Postmaster General
Aaron V. Brown (1857–59)
Joseph Holt (1859–61)
Horatio King (1861)

Secretary of the Interior
Jacob Thompson (1857–61)

President James Buchanan and his Cabinet. Standing (left to right) are Secretary of State Lewis Cass, Buchanan, Secretary of the Treasury Howell Cobb, and Postmaster General Joseph Holt. Seated (left to right) are Secretary of the Interior Jacob Thompson, Secretary of War John B. Floyd, Secretary of the Navy Isaac Toucey, and Attorney General Jeremiah Black. *Reproduced by permission of the Corbis Corporation.*

nition by the United States and offered protection as well. He persuaded British officials to end attempts to control Central America. Still, divisiveness within the United States was reflected by a divided Congress. As Buchanan began losing support during the growing crisis over slavery, his ability to act decisively was compromised. He negotiated treaties with Mexico, to help protect its unstable government, and with Nicaragua, to help protect it from foreign intervention, but both treaties were rejected by the U.S. Senate.

Republicans won a plurality (largest number) of seats in the House in the midterm elections of 1858. Congressional elections occurring halfway through a presidential term can affect the president's dealings with Congress. For the final two years of Buchanan's term, all crucial legislation would be deadlocked as a result of the increasingly contentious (argumentative) political atmosphere. The controversial incident at Harpers Ferry, Virginia (later West Virginia), led by abolitionist John Brown (1800–1859; see box) in October of 1859, worsened the sectional division of the country (the division of the country into two parts, or sections, over the issue of slavery).

Abolitionist Brown had already slain five people in Kansas in a prior skirmish (short conflict during a war between small bodies of troops). He then escaped and showed up at Harpers Ferry with a plan to free the South's slave population—estimated at over 3.8 million—by seizing a federal arsenal (storage place for weapons) and dispersing the munitions (arms and ammunition) to abolitionists and slaves. Brown and his forces were caught. He was executed by hanging six weeks later.

Buchanan had a bitter attitude toward men and women like Brown, whom he believed kept the slavery question from being discussed and resolved more rationally. He enjoyed close ties to many Southern Democrats, including Jefferson Davis (1808–1889; see box in **Abraham Lincoln** entry in volume 2), the Mississippi senator who would later become president of the Confederacy (the Southern states that separated from the United States).

As tensions between North and South increased, some members of Congress began to carry weapons. With the new year of 1860, the situation further disintegrated. Buchanan was advised to send defense troops to southern ports to protect federal property. He refused on grounds that such an action would provoke Southerners to violence. The situation was so volatile (ready to erupt) that Buchanan's portrait was removed from the Capitol Building to keep his foes from vandalizing it.

Buchanan believed that a president should be limited to one term. He sat out the 1860 presidential campaign. His goal in the meantime was to maintain some appearance of political order and keep the Union intact. It was an impossible task, for even the Democratic Party split that year into North and South factions, unable to agree on a frontrunner and a platform (a formal declaration of political principles). When a former Illinois congressman and avowed (publicly declared) foe of slavery, **Abraham Lincoln** (1809–1865; see entry in volume 2), became the Republican presidential nominee, some Southern states made it clear that should he win the election they would consider secession.

John Brown

A radical abolitionist who believed that he was chosen by God to destroy slavery in the United States, John Brown led a failed raid on a federal arsenal at Harpers Ferry, Virginia (now West Virginia). He became a martyr in the eyes of antislavery Northerners. Brown was born on May 9, 1800, one of sixteen children of Owen and Ruth Brown. Brown's father taught his children that slavery was evil and Brown became a lifelong opponent of slavery.

Brown's life was frequently marked by tragedy. His mother died when he was eight; his first wife died young; and seven of his twenty children from two marriages died in childhood. He worked as a cattle driver, leather tanner, stock grower, wool merchant, and farmer, but all of his ventures ended in failure. He was forced to declare bankruptcy in 1842 and failed in subsequent efforts to recover financially.

As he grew older, Brown became fanatical on the subject of slavery. He worked on the Underground Railroad, tried to integrate the Congregational Church he attended, and grew more extreme in his views on slavery and slaveowners. He said he would be willing to die for the destruction of slavery. He told black abolitionist Frederick Douglass (1817–1895) that he planned to arm the slaves he led to freedom because violent resistance would give them a sense of their own manhood. In 1851, he urged blacks to kill any official who tried to enforce the Fugitive Slave Act, which decreed that escaped slaves must be returned to their slaveowners.

Brown was stirred to violence when Congress passed the Kansas-Nebraska Bill in 1854. This bill allowed citizens of new territories, if they so desired, to legalize slavery where it had previously been forbidden. Brown and other Northern abolitionists believed the legislation was a Southern conspiracy to introduce slavery to the territories. Five of Brown's sons joined hundreds of freesoil pioneers who set out for Kansas. They witnessed the invasion of Kansas in 1855 by Missourians who voted illegally during an election to establish Kansas as a slave state and promised to kill any abolitionist who attempted to settle in the territory. Brown's sons informed their father that a war in Kansas between freedom and slavery was imminent and implored him to join them and come armed. Brown collected an arsenal of guns and swords and hurried to Kansas.

Violence broke out in Kansas soon after Brown arrived. On the nights of May 24 and 25, 1856, Brown led four of his sons and three other men to Pottawatomie Creek where they killed five proslavery settlers. These murders and raids by proslavery Missourians helped spark an open civil war in Kansas. Brown's son Frederick was killed during the violence.

After federal forces and a new governor imposed an uneasy peace on Kansas,

John Brown.
National Archives and Records Administration.

Brown traveled to the Northeast to try to raise funds in support of his antislavery campaign. Believing that slaves would rise up and wage war to win their freedom, Brown planned to invade Virginia and march into Tennessee and northern Alabama. His attack on Virginia was delayed when one of his men revealed Brown's plans to some politicians. Returning to Kansas, Brown led a bloody raid in Missouri, freeing a number of slaves, killing one slaveholder, almost inciting another outbreak of war, and provoking President James Buchanan to put a price of $250 on his head. (Brown responded by putting a price of $2.50 on the president's head). As he had after the Pottawatomie massacre, Brown again eluded capture. He returned

east and prepared for his attack on Harpers Ferry, Virginia, the site of the federal arsenal and armory. Brown rented a farm in Maryland, seven miles from Harpers Ferry, and gathered his weapons and recruits there. On the evening of October 16, 1859, Brown and his tiny army of sixteen whites and five blacks set out for Harpers Ferry.

By the next morning, the Harpers Ferry townspeople were firing at Brown's men. Virginia and Maryland militiamen soon joined in. During the afternoon fighting, eight of the raiders (including two of Brown's sons) and three townspeople were killed. Seven of Brown's men, two of whom were later caught, escaped. During the night, troops under the command of Robert E. Lee (1807–1870) and Jeb Stuart (1833–1864) arrived. In the morning, Stuart asked Brown to surrender. When Brown refused, Stuart jumped back and gave the signal to attack. The troops quickly captured Brown.

The raid on Harpers Ferry—over barely thirty-six hours after it had begun—ended in hopeless failure. No slaves had risen up anywhere in Virginia or Maryland because they had been given no advanced warning of Brown's plans. Brown and six of his men were captured, indicted, tried, and convicted of treason, murder, and inciting slave insurrection. All were sentenced to be hanged. Brown was executed on December 2, 1859.

Crucial last weeks

A few weeks after Lincoln's victory in November of 1860, South Carolina announced its secession from the Union. Buchanan responded by asserting that a state did not have the right to secede under the Constitution. However, the Constitution offered him no remedy as chief executive in such a situation. He met with South Carolina leaders to dissuade them, but his efforts were futile. Buchanan refused to take military action to keep the Union intact.

As he finished out the last weeks of his term, Buchanan was virtually powerless. Neither side in the slavery dispute could come to an agreement or a compromise that could ease the tense situation. Buchanan urged President-elect Lincoln to call a constitutional convention to resolve the crisis, believing that the action would isolate South Carolina's secession as an extreme measure. Lincoln was not interested in pursuing compromise.

In addition to losing support, Buchanan refused to wield power when national forts were threatened in the South. Similar threats and violence against government interests were countered decisively by such presidents as **George Washington** (1732–1799; see entry in volume 1) and **Andrew Jackson** (1767–1845; see entry in volume 1). Washington had summoned several state militias to stop the Whiskey Rebellion of 1794, and Jackson had threatened federal intervention if the state of South Carolina seceded from the Union during the nullification crisis of 1832. Buchanan did not want to provoke a regional war, but his inaction did nothing to stop the growing conflict.

Many Buchanan Cabinet members resigned by New Year's Eve. Northern politicians were enraged over Buchanan's refusal to act decisively on the matter of South Carolina's secession. Southerners wanted the president to affirm their right to secede. Buchanan moved quickly to appoint new Cabinet officials—this time with many Northerners, whom Lincoln would retain. He submitted to Congress a four-point plan that he hoped might save the Union. The plan included a constitutional convention and a promise to take no action likely to provoke (possibly cause) war. Congress refused to consider the bill. Part of the resistance was led by Republican forces who wanted Lincoln to act on the crisis when he took office in March (and thus discredit—damage the reputations of—Democrats as well).

Seven Southern states formed the Confederacy—the Confederate States of America (CSA)—in February 1861. Lincoln's inaugural ceremonies the next month were tense and marred by the strong presence of federal troops to discourage potential terrorists.

Buchanan retired to Wheatland. He wrote a book on the crisis leading to the Civil War, *Mr. Buchanan's Administration on the Eve of the Rebellion,* which received little attention upon publication in 1866. He died on June 1, 1868.

Legacy

James Buchanan's attention to the slavery issue left little time for other matters. His foreign policy goals might have succeeded had Congress been able to agree on anything. Halfway through his presidency, the growing opposition in Congress refused to ratify treaties his administration negotiated. In his inaugural speech, Buchanan called for a national railroad linking the land from the Atlantic to the Pacific oceans, but Congress could not decide whether the train line should extend from the upper midwest or run through the southwest. Buchanan persisted in his aims for enacting the Ostend Manifesto by annually requesting an appropriation from Congress in the event that Spain became willing to sell Cuba. The request was rejected each year. He was successful in opening and securing American ports on the West Coast, improving trade with Asian nations.

Buchanan's presidential character was attacked during his term and for many years afterward. When he died, his *New York Times* obituary (notice of a death, usually written as a short biography) skipped over much of his presidential career. The exception was a notation that "he met the crisis of secession in a timid and vacillating [unstable] spirit, temporizing [avoiding arguments] with both parties, and studiously avoiding the adoption of a decided policy." In subsequent decades, Buchanan was ridiculed for his approach. His weak leadership was viewed as a decisive factor in the outbreak of war.

A Selection of Buchanan Landmarks

Buchanan's Birthplace State Park. Mercersburg, PA. Commemorative plaque marks the spot of James Buchanan's birthplace. See http://www.dcnr.state.pa.us/stateparks/parks/buchanan.htm (accessed on July 12, 2000). A replica of his log cabin is located on the campus of nearby Mercersburg Academy.

Harriet Lane Home. 14 N. Main St., Mercersburg, PA. Home of the niece and White House hostess of President Buchanan.

Wheatland. 1120 Marietta Ave., Lancaster, PA 17603 (717) 392-8721.James Buchanan's home from 1848 until his death in 1868. See http://www.wheatland.org/home.html and http://www.pmsd.k12.pa.us/wheatland/home.html (accessed on July 12, 2000).

Woodward Hill Cemetery. 538 East Strawberry St., Lancaster, PA. Final resting place of President James Buchanan.

More recent historical assessments have recognized that no single administration could have averted (prevented) the nation's ugliest and deadliest political dispute. Buchanan is credited by some for delaying full-scale armed conflict at a time when it seemed inevitable.

Where to Learn More

Binder, Frederick Moore. *James Buchanan and the American Empire.* Selinsgrove, PA: Susquehanna University Press, 1994.

Birkner, Michael J., ed. *James Buchanan and the Political Crisis of the 1850s.* Selinsgrove, PA: Susquehanna University Press, 1996.

Brill, Marlene. *James Buchanan: Fifteenth President of the United States.* Chicago: Childrens Press, 1988.

Collins, David R.*James Buchanan: 15th President of the United States.* Ada, OK: Garrett Educational Corp., 1990.

Curtis, George Ticknor. *The Life of James Buchanan, Fifteenth President of the United States.* New York: Harper & Brothers, 1883. Reprint, Freeport, NY: Books for Libraries Press, 1969.

Hoyt, Edwin P. *James Buchanan.* Chicago: Reilly & Lee Co., 1966.

Klein, Philip. *President James Buchanan: A Biography.* University Park, Pennsylvania State University Press, 1962. Reprint, Newtown, CT: American Political Biography Press, 1995.

Smith, Elbert B. *The Presidency of James Buchanan*. Lawrence: University Press of Kansas, 1975.

Harriet Lane

Born May 9, 1830
Mercersburg, Pennsylvania
Died July 3, 1903
Narragansett Pier, Rhode Island

Orphaned niece of bachelor president James Buchanan presided as White House hostess and became a favorite in the political world

arriet Lane, the niece of **James Buchanan** (1791–1868; see entry in volume 2), was the White House hostess for America's only bachelor president. A well-educated, well-traveled young woman, Lane became a popular Washington social figure. The term "first lady" was first used in print to describe Lane in an 1860 illustrated newspaper.

Together after tragedies

Harriet Lane was born in 1830 in Mercersburg, Pennsylvania. She grew up in the well-to-do family of Elliot Tole Lane and Jane Buchanan Lane. Her mother was the sister of James Buchanan. By the time Harriet was eleven, both her mother and father had died, and her uncle James, a U.S. senator at the time, became her guardian. Lane was sent to a private school for girls in Lancaster, Pennsylvania, and was then moved to Buchanan's home in Washington, D.C. Buchanan enrolled Lane in a convent school, the Visitation Academy in Georgetown.

"I receive so many evidences of kindnesses and good feelings and so many regrets at my leaving [the White House after Buchanan's defeat] that it makes me feel very sad."

Harriet Lane

Harriet Lane.
Reproduced by permission of the Corbis Corporation.

Buchanan's political career continued to prosper. He served as secretary of state for President **James K. Polk** (1845–1849; see entry in volume 2) and was named minister to England in 1853. Lane, then twenty-three years old, went with him. She was formally presented at court to Queen Victoria (1819–1901). Known for her vivacious (lively) personality and appreciation for the arts, Lane became a favorite of the queen, who granted her special court privileges.

Lane returned to Washington, D.C., with her uncle when he began campaigning for president in 1856. Buchanan had already begun to school her in the art of political socializing. His precise instructions included how to listen for potentially valuable clues about secret alliances, pending legislation, or other political matters. Lane was an attractive young woman with blond hair and violet eyes. A favorite type of low-cut gown she wore inspired a dress style called "the low-neck lace bertha," which became popular in her day. Lane was also a witty conversationalist and a spirited dancer.

When her uncle was elected to the White House, Lane helped make the social events of his administration a tremendous success. She introduced regal customs that had impressed her in England. She wore elaborate white dresses, decorated rooms with dozens of roses, and hired a formal White House staff that was almost entirely English. Lane redecorated the White House extensively. She was also skilled in matters of official protocol. During her uncle's administration, the country was quickly dissolving into sectional battles. Lane had to take unusual care in the seating arrangements for the weekly White House dinners, being careful not to place political foes near one another.

With her often beleaguered (hounded; harassed) uncle, whom she called "Nunc," Lane made a ritual of reading the day's papers every morning. She displayed a keen interest in and a capacity for the complexities of politics. She became the first first lady in several years to officiate at a formal event when she christened a battleship. A naval ship was named in her honor. Lane had received favorable press early in the administration, but her public approval diminished as her uncle's political woes increased.

Other causes

In England, Lane had associated with notable aristocratic (upper class) women who undertook various social reform causes. As first lady, Lane lent her support to prison reform and public education issues as well as to improved health care for Native Americans. Her health care interest made her a particular favorite among some Native American tribes.

Lane's appreciation for art ranged from the work of the European masters to far more avant-garde objects from non-Western cultures. She became the first hostess in the White House to include artists at official dinners. She also initiated evenings of musical performances. The visit of Queen Victoria's son, the Prince of Wales and future king Edward VIII (1841–1910), to the United States in the fall of 1860 was a social highlight of the Buchanan administration. Lane served as Prince Edward's official escort in Washington.

Lane was likely under great strain during the final months of the Buchanan administration, as was her uncle, who would later be blamed for a policy of inaction that led to the Civil War. Like the president, Lane felt a greater fondness for Southern manners and customs. She counted among her closest friends the women who would leave Washington, D.C., when slaveowning states began to secede (separate) from the Union in 1861. Buchanan reportedly sent Lane to ask his secretary of the treasury, Howell Cobb (1815–1868), and his wife Mary Ann, not to abandon the administration.

Ironically, the *Harriet Lane* became the first Union Navy vessel to fire a shot when Confederate forces attacked Fort Sumter in South Carolina. The ship was later captured off the coast of Galveston, Texas, and served the Southern war effort after 1863. A second vessel christened the *Harriet Lane* was used to stop contraband (smuggled) liquor shipments during the Prohibition era. (Prohibition, from 1920 to 1933, banned the manufacture and sale of alcoholic beverages.) A third *Harriet Lane* was commissioned for service in 1984.

Later life

After **Abraham Lincoln** (1809–1865; see entry in volume 2) was inaugurated in 1861, Lane returned with her

uncle to his Pennsylvania estate, Wheatland. She had rejected several offers of marriage over the years. At the age of thirty-six, she married banker Henry Elliott Johnston on January
11, 1866. Johnston was from a well-established and honored
Baltimore family. Lane moved there with her new husband
and began a family with the birth of her first son, James
Buchanan Johnston. This son and his younger brother,
Henry, died of rheumatic fever when they were in their early
teens. (Rheumatic fever is a severe infectious disease occurring mainly in children. It is characterized by fever and
painful inflammation of the joints and can cause permanent
damage to the heart.) As a result of these tragedies, the John-
stons founded the Harriet Lane Home for Invalid Children in
Baltimore. In 1972, it became part of the pediatric-care facili-
ty at Johns Hopkins University Hospital.

Buchanan died in 1868 and left to Lane his Pennsylvania home, Wheatland, at which she spent summers. In
1884, her husband died from pneumonia. Lane moved back
to Washington, where she worked to establish a national
gallery of art. Upon her death in 1903, Lane's impressive collection of paintings was donated to the Smithsonian Institution research and education center in Washington, D.C. She
also made a large endowment (gift of funds to be invested
and used as a source of income) for St. Albans, a private
school in Washington, D.C.

Where to Learn More

Boller, Paul F. *Presidential Wives*. New York: Oxford University Press,
1998.

Shelley, Mary Virginia, and Sandra Harrison Munro. *Harriet Lane, First
Lady of the White House*. Lititz, PA: Sutter House, 1980.

White House. "Harriet Lane." *The First Ladies of the United States*. [On-
line] http://www.whitehouse.gov/WH/glimpse/firstladies/html/
hl15.html (accessed on July 17, 2000).

Buchanan's Final Annual Address to Congress

Delivered on December 3, 1860; excerpted from *The American Presidency: Selected Resources, An Informal Reference Guide* (Web site)

Following the secession of South Carolina from the Union, President Buchanan makes a desperate, last-ditch plea for unity while defending the rights of states to decide on slavery

A Northerner who was against the abolition of slavery, President **James Buchanan** (1791–1868; see entry in volume 2) tried to keep peace in the United States during a period of increasing turmoil. He maintained his belief that divisiveness over slavery could be resolved without abolishing the institution. By the end of his presidency, Buchanan had little support from Northerners or Southerners.

Abraham Lincoln (1809–1865; see entry in volume 2) had already been elected president when Buchanan made his final annual address. Southern states had threatened to secede from the Union if Lincoln, an avowed opponent of slavery, was elected. Buchanan used the occasion of his final annual address as a last-ditch effort to save the Union.

Buchanan is viewed by many historians as the least effective of presidents. Even as the nation became more divided, he viewed the slavery issue in simplistic terms. He concluded his final annual address, for example, by proposing what he called an "Explanatory Amendment" to the Constitution. The proposed amendment, which would recognize the legality of slavery once and for all, was never taken seriously.

"How easy would it be for the American people to settle the slavery question forever and to restore peace and harmony to this distracted country. . . .! All that is necessary . . . and all for which the slave States have ever contended, is to be let alone and permitted to manage their domestic institutions in their own way."

James Buchanan

Things to remember while reading an excerpt from President Buchanan's final annual address:

- In the beginning of his address, President Buchanan noted that even though the country was enjoying prosperity, the nation was in the throes of a great problem. He cited the North as the cause of the problem for having interfered with the affairs of Southern states by trying to curtail and abolish slavery. Buchanan reminded Congress that **George Washington** (1732–1799; see entry in volume 1), the nation's first president, warned in his "Farewell Address" (see **George Washington** primary source entry in volume 1) against acts that promoted regional divisiveness. Agitation by the North, claimed Buchanan, had left white Southerners living in fear of a slave revolt. Earlier in the year, abolitionist John Brown (1800–1859; see box in **James Buchanan** entry in volume 2) had led a failed raid on a military arsenal. He planned to distribute weapons to abolitionists and slaves to spur a revolt.

- Buchanan continued with his theme of Northern agitation by providing a brief history of what he viewed as the dangerous abolitionist movement. He began his summary with 1835, the year the Whig Party was formed by former Democrats who disliked President **Andrew Jackson** (1767–1845; see entry in volume 1)—a Southerner who strongly supported states' rights. The abolitionist movement later gained momentum during the 1850s. The Whig Party dissolved early in that decade, and the more strongly abolitionist Republican Party emerged in 1854.

- President Buchanan made reference to president-elect Abraham Lincoln, who intended to stop the spread of slavery. Buchanan declared that such an action was not justified, and he expressed faith that normal, constitutional means could prevail. He argued that Lincoln would not have power as president to abolish slavery; that Lincoln's constitutional duty was to carry out the laws, not make them; and that Congress had the power of legislation to deny any presidential attempt to change existing laws that recognized the existence of slavery. Continuing to use the Constitution as his defense, Buchanan claimed that Northern states acted unconstitutionally when they ignored or defied the Fugitive Slave Act. Under the Act, which was part of the Compromise of 1850, federal authorities could be enlisted to help track, prosecute, and return slaves who escaped to the North. Anyone who assisted runaway slaves could be prosecuted and punished.

- To the very end of his speech, and his presidency, Buchanan believed that conciliation between the North and South could be reached. He proposed an Explanatory Amendment to the Constitution that would recognize the legality of slavery once and for all.

Excerpt from President Buchanan's final annual address to Congress

Fellow-Citizens of the Senate and House of Representatives:

*Throughout the year since our last meeting the country has been eminently prosperous in all its material interests. The general health has been excellent, our harvests have been abundant, and **plenty** smiles throughout the land. Our commerce and manufactures have been **prosecuted** with energy and industry, and have yielded fair and ample returns. In short, no nation in the tide of time has ever presented a spectacle of greater material prosperity than we have done until within a very recent period.*

*Why is it, then, that **discontent** now so extensively prevails, and the Union of the States, which is the source of all these blessings, is threatened with destruction?*

*The long-continued and **intemperate** interference of the Northern people with the question of slavery in the Southern States has at length produced its natural effects. The different sections of the Union are now arrayed against each other, and the time has arrived, so much dreaded by the **Father of his Country**, when hostile geographical parties have been formed.*

*I have long foreseen and often forewarned my countrymen of the now impending danger. This does not proceed solely from the claim on the part of Congress or the **Territorial legislatures** to exclude slavery from the Territories, nor from the efforts of different*

Plenty: Prosperity, abundance.

Prosecuted: Seen to the end.

Discontent: Dissatisfaction.

Intemperate: Emotional to the point of being out of control.

Father of his Country: George Washington.

Territorial legislatures: The governments of areas under control of the United States that have not yet become states. At the time of this speech, for example, Kansas had applied for statehood and was in the process of becoming a state.

*States to defeat the execution of the fugitive-slave law. All or any of these evils might have been endured by the South without danger to the Union (as others have been) in the hope that time and reflection might apply the remedy. The immediate peril arises not so much from these causes as from the fact that the **incessant** and violent agitation of the slavery question throughout the North for the last quarter of a century has at length produced its malign influence on the slaves and inspired them with vague notions of freedom. Hence a sense of security no longer exists around the family altar. This feeling of peace at home has given place to apprehensions of **servile insurrections**. Many a matron throughout the South retires at night in dread of what may befall herself and children before the morning. Should this apprehension of domestic danger, whether real or imaginary, extend and intensify itself until it shall pervade the masses of the Southern people, then disunion will become inevitable. Self-preservation is the first law of nature, and has been implanted in the heart of man by his Creator for the wisest purpose; and no political union, however fraught with blessings and benefits in all other respects, can long continue if the necessary consequence be to render the homes and the firesides of nearly half the parties to it habitually and hopelessly insecure. Sooner or later the bonds of such a union must be severed. It is my conviction that this fatal period has not yet arrived, and my prayer to God is that He would preserve the Constitution and the Union throughout all generations.*

*But let us take warning in time and remove the cause of danger. It can not be denied that for five and twenty years the agitation at the North against slavery has been incessant. In 1835 pictorial handbills and **inflammatory appeals** were circulated extensively throughout the South of a character to excite the passions of the slaves, and, in the language of General [Andrew] Jackson, "to stimulate them to insurrection and produce all the horrors of a servile war." This agitation has ever since been continued by the public press, by the proceedings of State and county conventions and by abolition sermons and lectures. The time of Congress has been occupied in violent speeches on this never-ending subject, and appeals, in pamphlet and other forms, endorsed by distinguished names, have been sent forth from this central point and **spreadbroadcast** over the Union.*

How easy would it be for the American people to settle the slavery question forever and to restore peace and harmony to this distracted country! They, and they alone, can do it. All that is necessary to accomplish the object, and all for which the slave States have

Incessant: Continuing without interruption.

Servile insurrections: Slave revolts.

Inflammatory appeals: Words and action intended to incite anger.

Spreadbroadcast: Widely circulated through a medium, in this case through booklets.

Complete American Presidents Sourcebook

ever contended, is to be let alone and permitted to manage their do-
*mestic institutions in their own way. As **sovereign** States, they, and*
they alone, are responsible before God and the world for the slavery
existing among them. For this the people of the North are not more
responsible and have no more right to interfere than with similar in-
stitutions in Russia or in Brazil.. . .

[The] election of any one of our fellow citizens to the office of
President does not of itself afford just cause for dissolving the Union.
This is more especially true if his election has been effected by a mere
***plurality,** and not a majority of the people, and thus resulted from*
transient and temporary causes, which may probably never again
occur. In order to justify a resort to revolutionary resistance, the Fed-
eral Government must be guilty of a deliberate, palpable, and dan-
gerous exercise of powers not granted by the Constitution. The late
Presidential election, however, has been held in strict conformity
with its express provisions. How, then, can the result justify a revolu-
tion to destroy this very Constitution? Reason, justice, a regard for
the Constitution, all require that we shall wait for some overt and
dangerous act on the part of the President elect before resorting to
*such a remedy. It is said, however, that the **antecedents** of the Presi-*
dent elect have been sufficient to justify the fears of the South that
he will attempt to invade their constitutional rights. But are such ap-
prehensions of contingent danger in the future sufficient to justify
the immediate destruction of the noblest system of government ever
devised by mortals? From the very nature of his office and its high
responsibilities he must necessarily be conservative. The stern duty
of administering the vast and complicated concerns of this Govern-
ment affords in itself a guarantee that he will not attempt any viola-
tion of a clear constitutional right. After all, he is no more than the
chief executive officer of the Government. His province is not to
make but to execute the laws. And it is a remarkable fact in our his-
tory that, notwithstanding the repeated efforts of the antislavery
party, no single act has ever passed Congress, unless we may possi-
*bly except the **Missouri compromise,** impairing in the slightest de-*
gree the rights of the South to their property in slaves; and it may
also be observed, judging from present indications, that no proba-
bility exists of the passage of such an act by a majority of both
Houses, either in the present or the next Congress. Surely under
these circumstances we ought to be restrained from present action
by the precept of Him who spake as man never spoke, that sufficient
unto the day is the evil thereof. The day of evil may never come un-
less we shall rashly bring it upon ourselves.

Sovereign: Independent.

Plurality: A greater number.
Buchanan is referring to the
fact that Abraham Lincoln
was elected by a plurality, but
not a majority—meaning that
Lincoln received the most
votes among four presidential
candidates, but he did not
receive a majority (more than
half) of all votes.

Antecedents: Previous
actions, statements, traits.

Missouri compromise:
Legislation passed in 1820
intended to maintain an equal
balance of slave and free
states.

It is alleged as one cause for immediate secession that the Southern States are denied equal rights with the other States in the common Territories. But by what authority are these denied? Not by Congress, which has never passed, and I believe never will pass, any act to exclude slavery from these Territories; and certainly not by the Supreme Court, which has solemnly decided that slaves are property, and, like all other property, their owners have a right to take them into the common Territories and hold them there under the protection of the Constitution. . . .

*The most **palpable** violations of constitutional duty which have yet been committed consist in the acts of different State legislatures to defeat the execution of the fugitive-slave law. It ought to be remembered, however, that for these acts neither Congress nor any President can justly be held responsible. Having been passed in violation of the Federal Constitution, they are therefore null and void. All the courts, both State and national, before whom the question has arisen have from the beginning declared the fugitive-slave law to be constitutional. The single exception is that of a State court in Wisconsin, and this has not only been reversed by the proper **appellate tribunal**, but has met with such universal **reprobation** that there can be no danger from it as a precedent. The validity of this law has been established over and over again by the Supreme Court of the United States with perfect unanimity. It is founded upon an express provision of the Constitution, requiring that fugitive slaves who escape from service in one State to another shall be "delivered up" to their masters. Without this provision it is a well-known historical fact that the Constitution itself could never have been adopted by the Convention. In one form or other, under **the acts of 1793 and 1850**, both being substantially the same, the fugitive-slave law has been the law of the land from the days of Washington until the present moment. Here, then a clear case is presented in which it will be the duty of the next President, as it has been my own, to act with vigor in executing this supreme law against the conflicting enactments of State legislatures. Should he fail in the performance of this high duty, he will then have manifested a disregard of the Constitution and laws, to the great injury of the people of nearly one-half of the States of the Union. But are we to presume in advance that he will thus violate his duty? This would be at war with every principle of justice and of Christian charity. Let us wait for the overt act. The Fugitive Slave Law has been carried into execution in every contested case since the commencement of the present Administration, though often, it is to be regretted, with great loss and inconvenience to the master and with considerable ex-*

Palpable: Tangible.

Appellate tribunal: An appeals court.

Reprobation: Strong condemnation.

The acts of 1793 and 1850: References to Congressional legislation that recognized and supported the existence of slavery.

Complete American Presidents Sourcebook

pense to the Government. Let us trust that the State legislatures will repeal their unconstitutional and obnoxious enactments. Unless this shall be done without unnecessary delay, it is impossible for any human power to save the Union.

The Southern States, standing on the basis of the Constitution, have a right to demand this act of justice from the States of the North. Should it be refused, then the Constitution, to which all the States are parties, will have been willfully violated by one portion of them in a provision essential to the domestic security and happiness of the remainder. In that event the injured States, after having first used all peaceful and constitutional means to obtain redress, would be justified in revolutionary resistance to the Government of the Union. . . .

But may I be permitted solemnly to invoke my countrymen to pause and deliberate before they determine to destroy this the **grandest temple** *which has ever been dedicated to human freedom since the world began? It has been* **consecrated** *by the blood of our fathers, by the glories of the past, and by the hopes of the future. The Union has already made us the most prosperous, and* **ere** *long will, if preserved, render us the most powerful nation on the face of the earth. In every foreign region of the globe the title of American citizen is held in the highest respect, and when pronounced in a foreign land it causes the hearts of our countrymen to swell with honest pride. Surely when we reach the brim of the yawning abyss we shall recoil with horror from the last fatal plunge. . . .*

Congress can contribute much to avert it by proposing and recommending to the legislatures of the several States the remedy for existing evils which the Constitution has itself provided for its own preservation. This has been tried at different critical periods of our history, and always with eminent success. It is to be found in the fifth article, providing for its own amendment. Under this article amendments have been proposed by two-thirds of both Houses of Congress, and have been "ratified by the legislatures of three-fourths of the several States" and have consequently become parts of the Constitution. To this process the country is indebted for the clause prohibiting Congress from passing any law respecting an establishment of religion or abridging the freedom of speech or of the press or of the right of petition. To this we are also indebted for the bill of rights which secures the people against any abuse of power by the Federal Government. Such were the apprehensions justly entertained by the friends of State rights at that period as to have ren-

Grandest temple: A picturesque expression describing the United States.

Consecrated: Made sacred.

Ere: Before.

dered it extremely doubtful whether the Constitution could have long survived without those amendments. . . .

This is the very course which I earnestly recommend in order to obtain an "explanatory amendment" of the Constitution on the subject of slavery. This might originate with Congress or the State legislatures, as may be deemed most advisable to attain the object. The explanatory amendment might be confined to the final settlement of the true construction of the Constitution on three special points:

An express recognition of the right of property in slaves in the States where it now exists or may hereafter exist.

The duty of protecting this right in all the common Territories throughout their Territorial existence, and until they shall be admitted as States into the Union, with or without slavery, as their constitutions may prescribe.

A like recognition of the right of the master to have his slave who has escaped from one State to another restored and delivered up to him, and of the validity of the fugitive-slave law enacted for this purpose, together with a declaration that all State laws impairing or defeating this right are violations of the Constitution, and are consequently null and void.

It may be objected that this construction of the Constitution has already been settled by the Supreme Court of the United States, and what more ought to be required? The answer is that a very large proportion of the people of the United States still contest the correctness of this decision, and never will cease from agitation and admit its binding force until clearly established by the people of the several States in their sovereign character. Such an explanatory amendment would, it is believed, forever terminate the existing dissensions, and restore peace and harmony among the States. (The American Presidency: Selected Resources, An Informal Reference Guide *[Web site]*)

What happened next . . .

Buchanan could do nothing to stop the chain of events that led to the Civil War (1861–65). Three weeks after this speech, South Carolina seceded from the Union, and within three months the Confederate States of America was founded. Within five months, the nation was at war.

President Abraham Lincoln mobilized the Union army after the Confederate military fired on a federal fort (Ft. Sumter) in South Carolina. Lincoln used his power as president to bring about the end of slavery. Because Southern states had seceded from the Union, Lincoln and Congress faced little opposition in enacting legislation and executive orders (like the Emancipation Proclamation of 1863; see **Abraham Lincoln** primary source entry in volume 2) that freed slaves. Lincoln's actions and the Civil War did not bring about a society in which all citizens enjoyed equal rights. They did achieve what Buchanan and all preceding presidents had failed to accomplish: the issue of slavery was settled, once and for all, in the United States.

Did you know . . .

- Minnesota, Oregon, and Kansas joined the Union during Buchanan's presidency. All were free states, decisively tipping the balance of power to non-slaveholding states. Southerners were losing political power steadily. A brief downturn in the economy in 1857 led Congress to enact legislation more favorable to the North; the agriculture-based Southern economy had not been hurt by the downturn, but the area was affected by legislation that increased taxes on agricultural goods. As the nation grew more industrialized and urban-based during the 1850s, many Southerners wanted to protect their traditional, rural way of life. Every issue seemed to divide the nation during Buchanan's presidency.

Where to Learn More

"Annual Message: December 3, 1860." *The American Presidency: Selected Resources, An Informal Reference Guide.* [Online] http://www.inter-link-cafe.com/uspresidents/1860.htm (accessed on July 17, 2000).

Binder, Frederick Moore. *James Buchanan and the American Empire.* Selinsgrove, PA: Susquehanna University Press, 1994.

Jaffa, Harry V. *Crisis of the House Divided.* New York: Doubleday and Co., 1959. Reprint, Chicago: University of Chicago Press, 1982.

Nichols, Roy F. *The Disruption of American Democracy.* New York: Macmillan, 1948.

Smith, Elbert B. *The Presidency of James Buchanan.* Lawrence: University Press of Kansas, 1975.

Abraham Lincoln

Sixteenth president (1860–1865)

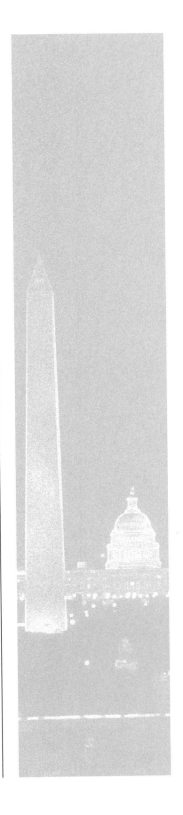

Abraham Lincoln

**Born February 12, 1809
Hodgenville, Kentucky
Died April 15, 1865
Washington, D.C.**

**Sixteenth president of the United States
(1861–1865)**

**Tremendously impacted U.S. history as he led
the country through the turmoil of the
Civil War (1861–65)**

"'A house divided against itself cannot stand.' I believe this government cannot endure permanently half-slave and half-free. . . ."

Abraham Lincoln

Abraham Lincoln.
Photograph by Mathew Brady. Courtesy of the Library of Congress.

When a president takes the oath of office, he swears to "preserve, protect and defend the Constitution." Based on that duty, Abraham Lincoln exerted more power than any previous president. He made full use of the broad Constitutional authority given to the president in case of a national uprising. He helped preserve the United States and brought about the abolition (end) of slavery.

As a self-made man leading a self-governing nation, Lincoln became a folk hero. Tales continue to be told, from stories of his humble, backwoods upbringing to examples of his leadership during the Civil War (1861–65), the nation's greatest crisis. He is the president most often written about and studied.

Ambitious and willful, Lincoln was a skilled speaker and a clever politician. He always seemed to know exactly when to be most forceful and when to wait for a better opportunity. For example, he moved more cautiously than many abolitionists (persons against slavery) who demanded to fully emancipate (free) slaves. Above all, Lincoln sought in his policies to preserve the Union. He established lenient terms

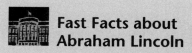
of surrender as the American Civil War ended. Then he pursued reconciliation: restoration of friendship and harmony between the states.

President Lincoln was assassinated (murdered) shortly after the war. "Now he belongs to the ages," said Secretary of War Edwin M. Stanton (1814–1869). A funeral procession witnessed by thousands and thousands of mourners traced back the route from Washington, D.C., to Springfield, Illinois. Lincoln had followed the same route to the White House fifty months earlier.

Humble origins

Abraham Lincoln was born on February 12, 1809, in a one-room, dirt-floor log cabin by Nolin Creek, near present-day Hodgenville, Kentucky. His father, Thomas (c. 1776–1851), was a skilled carpenter able to provide basic necessities for his family. Lincoln ancestors first arrived in Massachusetts from England in 1637. They spread to Pennsylvania and then to Virginia. Thomas Lincoln's father, Abraham, moved his family to Kentucky. He was killed by a Native American while clearing farmland. Lincoln's mother, Nancy (1784–1818), was illiterate (unable to read). She bore a daughter, Sarah, two years before Abraham Lincoln was born.

The family moved to a nearby farm on Knob Creek when Lincoln was two years old. As soon as he was able, Lincoln began hunting, fishing, and doing farm chores. The Lincolns crossed the Ohio River in 1816 and moved to a heavily forested area in southern Indiana. Another crude log cabin was built. The family began clearing land and establishing a farm near what is now Gentryville, Indiana.

Lincoln's mother died in 1818 from "milk sick." This illness results from drinking the milk of cows that have eaten a poisonous wild plant called white snakeroot. The following year, Thomas Lincoln married Sarah Bush Johnston (1788–1869), a widow with three children. The new family members mixed well. With his stepmother's encouragement, Lincoln learned to read, write, and do arithmetic. He worked mostly on his own. He had about one year's worth of formal schooling his entire life.

Lincoln read the Bible, the fables of Aesop (an ancient legendary Greek writer), histories, and biographies. A biography of **George Washington** (1732–1799; see entry in volume 1) deeply impressed him. Later, he enjoyed the plays of William Shakespeare (1564–1616). Most of his time was spent chopping down trees and performing the plowing, planting, and picking chores of frontier farming. He also piloted a ferryboat that transported passengers and baggage to riverboats docked along the Ohio River.

 Abraham Lincoln Timeline

1809: Born in Kentucky

1835–36: Serves in Illinois State Legislature

1847-49: Serves in to the U.S. House of Representatives

1855: Serves again in Illinois State Legislature

1858: Loses Senate race to Stephen Douglas, but achieves national recognition for the Lincoln-Douglas debates

1861–65: Serves as sixteenth U.S. president

1861: Civil War begins

1864: Reelected president

1865: Civil War ends; Lincoln assassinated; Thirteenth Amendment to the U.S. Constitution—abolishing slavery—is ratified

"Railsplitter"

By the time he was nineteen in 1828, Lincoln had reached his adult height of six feet, four inches tall. That year he was hired by a local merchant to run a flatboat down the Ohio River to the Mississippi River and south to New Orleans, Louisiana. Not long after he returned, Lincoln rejoined his family, who had moved to a frontier area about ten miles west of present-day Decatur, Illinois. In addition to working

Words to Know

Abolitionists: People who worked to end slavery.

Civil War: Conflict that took place from 1861 to 1865 between the Northern states (Union) and the Southern seceded states (Confederacy); also known in the South as the War between the States and in the North as the War of the Rebellion.

Confederate States of America: The eleven Southern states that seceded (separated) from the United States during the 1860s and fought the Union during the American Civil War.

Emancipation: The act of freeing people from slavery.

Reconstruction: A federal policy from 1865 to 1877 through which the national government took an active part in assisting and policing the former Confederate states.

Secession: The formal withdrawal of eleven Southern states from the Union in 1860–61.

Union: Northern states that remained loyal to the United States during the Civil War.

Whig Party: A political party that existed roughly from 1836 to 1854 that consisted of factions of the former Democratic-Republican Party (1796–1830). Whigs refused to join the Democratic Party led by President Andrew Jackson.

with his father, Lincoln helped local residents as a handyman. His nickname, "Railsplitter," came from his ability to split the long logs used to make fences.

Lincoln made a second trip down the Mississippi River to New Orleans in 1831. While there, he first witnessed a slave auction. Disgusted by it, he reportedly said, "If I ever get a chance to hit that thing, I'll hit it hard."

Upon returning to Illinois, Lincoln was hired as a clerk in a general store in the town of New Salem. During Lincoln's time, the general store often served as the town's informal meeting place. In addition to chatting with locals, Lincoln had plenty of time to read—his favorite form of entertainment. He was known and well liked enough to run for a seat in the Illinois House of Representatives in 1832. That summer he answered a call for volunteers to fight rebellious Native Americans led by Chief Black Hawk (1767–1838; see box in **Zachary Taylor** entry in volume 2), chief of the Sac, or Sauk, Native Americans. Lincoln was elected captain of his company, but he did not see action during his three-months' service. He returned to New Salem, lost the election for a seat in the state House of Representatives, and set up a store with a friend. The store soon went bankrupt. Neither man was a very good businessman: Lincoln spent much of his time studying law, while his friend drank steadily and piled up debts. Lincoln next served as the town postmaster.

Political career begins

Lincoln was elected to the Illinois legislature in 1834. As a member of the Whig Party (a political party that existed roughly from the mid-1830s to 1854), Lincoln supported a strong federal government and legislation favorable to business. The decade of the 1830s was dominated by Democrats on the national scene. They limited federal influence over states and pursued policies more favorable to small farmers than to urban businesses. Meanwhile, Lincoln continued to study law. He became a licensed attorney and joined a law firm in Springfield, Illinois, where the state capital had moved from Vandalia. As a leader of the Illinois legislature, Lincoln helped lead the transfer to the new political seat of Illinois.

Among other acts as a state legislator, Lincoln supported the extension of voting rights to female taxpayers (but the measure failed to win approval). He was against the expansion of slavery into new U.S. territories, but he did not support immediate national abolishment of the institution of slavery. Lincoln believed that forcing such an action would be illegal. He feared that supporting abolition would prompt reactions among slaveowners that would "increase its evil."

Lincoln had arrived in Springfield at age twenty-seven. He was so poor then that he had to borrow a horse to make the journey from New Salem. All his possessions fit into two saddlebags. He continued to read and to serve in the Illinois state congress while he wrestled with the idea of marriage. Over the years, historians have disagreed over whether Lincoln had fallen in love with a young woman named Ann Rutledge (1813–1835), whose tragic death plunged him into sadness and depression.

In 1840, he met Mary Todd (1818–1882; see entry on **Mary Lincoln** in volume 2), a Kentucky woman who was staying with her married sister in Springfield. She was educated and quite sensitive. They became engaged, but Lincoln failed to show up at the wedding ceremony on January 1, 1841. After patching things up, the couple was married in November the following year. Despite the stormy personalities of both partners and their grieving over the deaths of two sons (Eddie died at age four in 1850, Willie at age eleven in 1862), they remained devoted to each other. After Lincoln's death, a third son, Tad, died at age eighteen in 1871.

Lincoln began focusing on practicing law in 1843. He attended court in Springfield and spent six months of the year in a circuit court, a court that traveled the Illinois frontier, serving fifteen counties. Lincoln's cases were always well attended due to his reputation as a good speaker. Lincoln used the circuit court to make contacts as he pursued a national political career. After several failed attempts, he won the Whig nomination for a U.S. congressional seat in 1846 and triumphed in the general election.

Controversial congressman

Lincoln faced the challenge of most first-term congressmen. He had little opportunity to press his issues and he was an unknown in Washington, D.C., political and social circles. The Lincolns lived in a small boardinghouse with their two sons. Among their small group of friends was Georgia congressmen Alexander H. Stephens (1812–1883). Stephens would later become vice president of the Confederate States of America, the Southern states that seceded from the United States during the 1860s.

Lincoln made his mark in Congress in two areas. The United States was involved in the Mexican War (1846–48), which President **James K. Polk** (1795–1849; see entry in volume 2) asked Congress to declare after Mexican soldiers had fired on American soldiers inside the U.S. territory of Texas. In 1847, Lincoln claimed the war was unconstitutional and challenged Polk to show him the exact spot where the alleged (supposed) attack occurred. The Mexican War was generally unpopular, but not in Illinois. There, Lincoln's actions were widely denounced.

As the United States moved toward victory in the Mexican War, the expansion of slavery became a heated issue. The territories of Texas and California would soon petition for statehood. Lincoln supported the Wilmot Proviso. Congressman David Wilmot (1814–1868) had introduced a measure (the proviso) to bar slavery in all states acquired through the war. The bill twice passed the House of Representatives but was defeated both times in the Senate. Nevertheless, a strong abolitionist (antislavery) faction in the Northeast demanded that the new territories should be free states. They continued to press for an end to all slavery.

Lincoln proposed a policy on slavery: (1) all children born to slaves after January 1, 1850, would be free and apprenticed to learn a trade; (2) slaveholders could voluntarily emancipate their slaves and receive compensation (money or property given in place of something lost); and (3) voters in Washington, D.C., would be allowed to decide whether or not to abolish slavery in their district. Lincoln's moderate approach to abolition never came up for discussion.

Lincoln's term in Congress ended in 1849. He had campaigned for Whig presidential candidate **Zachary Taylor** (1784–1850; see entry in volume 2), who won the 1848 election but did not carry the state of Illinois. Lincoln had lost popularity for his stand against the Mexican War. After failing to receive a worthwhile government post from the Taylor administration, Lincoln left politics.

The Lincolns returned to Illinois. Resuming his law practice, Lincoln became a celebrated attorney. He argued cases in Chicago's federal court and in the state Supreme Court in Springfield. He made the rounds of the circuit court, through which he became reacquainted with the concerns of common people. Meanwhile, Lincoln continued to read and to form ideas about government.

Political comeback

The Kansas-Nebraska Bill of 1854 reenergized Lincoln's interest in politics. Authored by Illinois senator Stephen Douglas (1813–1861; see box), the bill allowed voters in the territories of Kansas and Nebraska to decide for themselves whether or not to permit slavery. In effect, the Kansas-Nebraska bill repealed the Missouri Compromise of 1820 (see box in **James Monroe** entry in volume 1), which set the southern border of Missouri as a demarcation (dividing) line to ensure there would remain an equal balance of slave and nonslave states. No new slave states could be formed north of that border.

Lincoln feared that slavery would be expanded further. He campaigned vigorously for fellow Whig candidates

Lincoln was an engaging speaker for several reasons. Among them was his sense of humor. During a debate, Stephen Douglas referred to him as a "two-faced man." Lincoln replied, "If I had another face, do you think I would wear this one?"

Republican Abraham Lincoln (above) lost the 1858 U.S. Senate race in Illinois to Democrat Stephen Douglas. *Photograph by Alexander Hesler. Courtesy of the Library of Congress.*

for Congress. When Douglas returned to Illinois that year to make a speech on behalf of the Kansas-Nebraska Bill, Lincoln announced that he would reply to the speech the following day. Lincoln's forceful response positioned the institution of slavery as a moral issue (that it is simply wrong and evil) rather than as a political issue. At the same time, he distanced himself from abolitionists. He wanted slavery confronted as a national issue, rather than an action (abolition) promoted by one region (the North) at the expense of another (the South). When Lincoln repeated his speech twelve days later in Peoria, Illinois, it was reported in newspapers. His speech (known as the "Peoria speech") has since become historically famous.

With his popularity expanding rapidly, Lincoln ran for the U.S. senate in 1855. He lost. Senators, in those days, were elected by the state congress. Lincoln could not attain enough votes to win the election. Lincoln then joined the recently established Republican Party. Founded in 1854, the party was made up of former Whigs as well as abolitionist Democrats.

Lincoln was nominated as a vice presidential candidate at the party's national convention in 1856. After failing to win the nomination, he campaigned hard for the party's presidential candidate, John C. Frémont (1813–1890; see box in **James K. Polk** entry in volume 2). Frémont lost to **James Buchanan** (1791–1868; see entry in volume 2), a Northern politician who had no intention of challenging the institution of slavery forcefully.

Meanwhile, the slavery issue became increasingly heated. A civil war among slavery and antislavery advocates broke out in Kansas in 1856. In the 1857 *Dred Scott v. Sandford* case, the Supreme Court ruled that Congress had no authority to restrict slavery in new American territories. Abolitionist

John Brown (1800–1859; see box in **James Buchanan** entry in volume 2) led a raid in 1859 on a federal arsenal (storage place for weapons) at Harpers Ferry, Virginia (now West Virginia). He hoped to distribute arms among abolitionists and slaves. Brown and his forces were overwhelmingly defeated. He was executed by hanging six weeks later.

Lincoln was nominated by the Illinois Republican Party as its candidate against Douglas in the 1858 Senate election. Lincoln's acceptance speech at the Republican state convention was highlighted by his use of a biblical quotation—"a house divided against itself cannot stand"—to emphasize his insistence on preserving the Union. He argued that the Union could not continue to be half slave, half free. The Union must cease to be divided, he insisted, but it would not dissolve.

During the campaign, Lincoln and Douglas engaged in a series of seven debates that are considered among the most admirable examples of American politics in action. The debates were fierce, but always respectful. As many as fifteen thousand people assembled in outdoor meeting places to hear the speakers, whose discussions were reported on nationally by newspapers.

Lincoln edged Douglas in the popular election, but once again a Democratic majority in the state legislature elected the candidate of their party. Reacting to the bitter defeat, Lincoln displayed the kind of homespun humor that often appeared in his speeches. He compared himself to a boy who stubbed his toe, adding that it hurt too much to laugh, but he was too old to cry.

Despite his loss to Douglas, Lincoln's performance in the debates made him a national figure. He was invited to speak throughout the Midwest. In the East, he greatly impressed New Yorkers with a speech on February 27, 1860. Called the "Cooper Union Speech," it offered a more moderate approach to outlawing slavery than the more firm abolitionist demands. New York senator William H. Seward (1801–1872; see box in **Andrew Johnson** entry in volume 2) was one such abolitionist and a leading contender for the Republican nomination for president in 1860. However, Seward could not gather enough support at the party convention in Chicago that year. Lincoln steadily gained ground as an alter-

Lincoln-Douglas Debates

Before the adoption of the Seventeenth Amendment to the U.S. Constitution in 1913, state legislatures elected U.S. senators. Candidates did not normally conduct a statewide campaign for the office. The times were not normal in 1858, however, when the Republicans in Illinois nominated Abraham Lincoln as their candidate for the senate seat held by Stephen Douglas. Lincoln, who had served only one term in Congress and had failed in his bid for the Senate in 1856, had nothing to lose by debating Douglas.

Speeches by the candidates and their seven debates attracted tens of thousands of listeners and received wide newspaper coverage. The debates started after Lincoln's "House Divided" speech in Springfield on June 16, 1858, at the Republican meeting endorsing him for the Senate. In that speech, Lincoln stated that the expansion of slavery into new territories had divided the nation. He used a quotation from the Bible—"A house divided against itself cannot stand"—to call for an end to the divisiveness. Douglas replied in Chicago on July 9, and Lincoln made another speech on July 10. The debates for-

mally began in Ottawa, Illinois, on August 21, 1858. The contestants then journeyed to Freeport on August 27, Jonesboro on September 15, Charleston on September 18, Galesburg on October 7, Quincy on October 13, and Alton on October 15.

The strategy of both men was set before the first formal meeting. Lincoln concentrated on the Kansas-Nebraska Act, authored by Douglas. He charged that Douglas was merely a puppet (someone used to perform unpleasant tasks for someone else) of the slave-power conspiracy, that popular sovereignty (the right of the people) had been buried by the *Dred Scott* decision, and that there was a national conspiracy to legitimatize slavery in the free states. Douglas criticized Lincoln for supporting black suffrage (voting rights) and charged him with attempted subversion of the Supreme Court. He accused Lincoln of opposing the Supreme Court's *Dred Scott* decision on the grounds that it denied citizenship to African Americans and that Lincoln would interfere with the domestic business of individual states.

Lincoln was embarrassed by Douglas' effort to associate him with abolition-

native candidate. He won the nomination on the fourth round of balloting (voting).

Lincoln's Democratic opponent was expected to be Stephen Douglas, but Douglas had lost some national support

Stephen Douglas.
Courtesy of the Library of Congress.

ism. While admitting his opposition to slavery, Lincoln acknowledged his inability to come up with a solution to the problem short of abolition. Like Douglas, Lincoln believed that blacks were basically inferior to whites; but Lincoln, unlike Douglas, held that slavery was an immoral system inconsistent with the principles and practices of democratic government. Lincoln insisted that slavery must be kept out of the new territories. Douglas countered by demand-

ing that the decision was up to settlers of a territory. Lincoln pointed out that since the *Dred Scott* decision prohibited Congress from legislating about slavery in the territories, territorial legislatures were similarly prohibited because they had been created by Congress. Douglas, seeking to salvage popular sovereignty, suggested at Freeport that regardless of the *Dred Scott* decision, the people of a territory could lawfully exclude slavery prior to the formation of a state government, for slavery could not exist without the protection of a slave code enacted by the territorial legislature. Lincoln advocated that principles of equality as set forth in the Declaration of Independence should be applied to the new territories. Douglas concluded with his belief that the nation could endure forever half slave and half free.

In the November elections, the Republicans swept Northern states, but Douglas was reelected in Illinois. The Republican state ticket in Illinois won by over four thousand votes, but the Democrats retained a majority in the legislature. In the process of losing, however, Lincoln became a national figure.

after his debates with Lincoln. Douglas, for example, had stated that a territory could outlaw slavery before it became a state—if the people refused to enact laws that would protect slaveowners. That opinion cost Douglas Southern support. After he was nominated, Southern Democrats turned to two

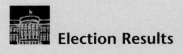

Election Results

1860

Presidential / Vice presidential candidates	Popular votes	Presidential electoral votes
Abraham Lincoln / Hannibal Hamlin (Republican)	1,866,452	180
John C. Breckinridge / Joseph Lane (Democratic [Southern])	847,953	72
John Bell / Edward Everett (Constitutional Union [American])	590,631	39
Stephen A. Douglas / Herschel V. Johnson (Democratic [Northern])	1,375,157	12

The Democratic Party divided into three sectional factions, which helped Republican Lincoln win election.

1864

Presidential / Vice presidential candidates	Popular votes	Presidential electoral votes
Abraham Lincoln / Andrew Johnson (Republican [National Union])	2,213,635	212
George B. McClellan / George H. Pendleton (Democratic)	1,805,237	21

The eleven Confederate states—comprising eighty electoral votes—did not vote in this election.

other candidates, incumbent vice president John Breckinridge (1821–1875) of Kentucky and former U.S. senator John Bell (1797–1869) of Tennessee. The divided party cost the Democrats the election. Lincoln won only forty percent of the popular vote, but he won all eighteen free states for 180 total electoral votes (152 were needed to win). Breckinridge had 72 electoral votes; Bell had 39; and Douglas had only 12.

The house divides

Even before Lincoln took office, South Carolina seceded (separated) from the Union in December 1860. By February of 1861, when Lincoln left Springfield, Illinois, for the inaugural (formal ceremony installing him as president) in Washington, D.C., seven Southern states (South Carolina, Mississippi, Florida, Alabama, Georgia, Louisiana, and Texas) had banded to form the Confederate States of America (CSA). Lincoln, meanwhile, made a triumphant tour through twelve states on his way to Washington, D.C. For security purposes, his entry into the capital occurred late at night.

The inaugural of March 4, 1861, was carried out under heavy guard. In his address, Lincoln promised not to interfere with the rights of states, pledged not to attack the South, and called the South back into the Union. The Confederacy was unmoved.

Confederate forces demanded the evacuation of Fort Sumter in South Carolina because it was within CSA territory. When basic supplies within the fort became scarce, Lincoln announced to the governor of the state that new provisions were being sent by boat. Jefferson Davis (1808–1889; see box), president of the Confederacy, ordered that Fort Sumter be taken.

On April 12, 1861, the fort was under fire and it was surrendered two days later. Under the authority of the Militia Act of 1796, President Lincoln declared that the action opposed federal laws in a manner "too powerful to be suppressed by ordinary judicial proceedings." Lincoln called for seventy-six thousand militia volunteers. Virginia, North Carolina, Tennessee, and Arkansas responded to his actions by joining the Confederacy. Many citizens of Kentucky, Maryland, and Missouri sympathized and fought with the Confederacy, but those "border states" remained in the Union.

Throughout the war, Lincoln made it clear that his main purpose was to preserve the Union. His actions were taken to suppress a rebellion and to protect free national elections. As commander in chief, he ordered a naval

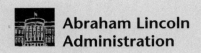

Abraham Lincoln Administration

Administration Dates
March 4, 1861–March 4, 1865
March 4, 1865–April 15, 1865

Vice President
Hannibal Hamlin (1861–65)
Andrew Johnson (1865)

Cabinet

Secretary of State
William H. Seward (1861–65)

Secretary of the Treasury
Salmon P. Chase (1861–64)
William P. Fessenden (1864–65)
Hugh McCulloch (1865)

Secretary of War
Simon Cameron (1861–62)
Edwin M. Stanton (1862–65)

Attorney General
Edward Bates (1861–64)
James Speed (1864–65)

Secretary of the Navy
Gideon Welles (1861–65)

Postmaster General
Horatio King (1861)
Montgomery Blair (1861–64)
William Dennison Jr. (1864–65)

Secretary of the Interior
Caleb B. Smith (1861–62)
John P. Usher (1863–65)

Jefferson Davis

Jefferson Davis was born on June 3, 1808, in what is now Todd County, Kentucky. Raised in Mississippi, he attended Transylvania University for three years and then entered the U.S. Military Academy at West Point, from which he graduated in 1828. He served in the infantry for seven years. While stationed at Ft. Crawford, Wisconsin, Davis fell in love with Sarah Knox Taylor, daughter of post commandant Zachary Taylor (a future U.S. president). Taylor disapproved of his daughter marrying a military man. Davis resigned his commission in 1835, married Sarah, and took her to Mississippi. However, within three months she died of malaria. Davis had also contracted a light case of the disease, and it permanently weakened his health. From 1835 to 1845, he lived in seclusion.

Davis spent much of his time reading and developed a fascination for politics. Elected to the House of Representatives in 1845, Davis and Varina Howell, his new bride, went to Washington, D.C. War with Mexico interrupted Davis's congressional service. He resigned in 1846 to command a volunteer army regiment. Distinguished service by Davis's outfit at Monterey, Mexico, was followed by real heroism at Buena Vista. A wounded Davis returned to Mississippi a hero.

In 1847, Davis was elected to the U.S. Senate. But in 1851, Mississippi Democrats called him back to run for governor, thinking that Davis's reputation might cover the party's shift from secessionist

(pro-separation) to one of cooperation. However, Davis lost the election.

President **Franklin Pierce** (1804–1869; see entry in volume 2) appointed Davis secretary of war in 1853. Davis enlarged the army, modernized military procedures, and boosted soldiers' pay (and morale). He directed important Western land surveys for future railroad construction and masterminded the Gadsden Purchase (of portions of present-day New Mexico and Arizona). Davis reentered the Senate after Pierce's presidency and became a major Southern spokesman. He worked to preserve the Compromise of 1850 as a means for maintaining peace; he argued that Congress had no power to limit slavery's extension. At the 1860 Democratic convention, Davis cautioned against secession. However, he accepted Mississippi's decision to secede. On January 21, 1861, he announced his state's secession from the Union and his own resignation from the Senate.

Davis reluctantly accepted the presidency of the Confederate States of America. He quickly grasped his problems: nine million citizens (including at least three million slaves) of sovereign Southern states pitted against twenty-two million Yankees; nine thousand miles of usable railroad track against the North's twenty-two thousand miles; no large factories, warships, or shipyards; little money; and no manufacturing arsenals to replenish military supplies. Davis built an army out of state volunteers; supplies, arms and ammunition, clothes, and

Jefferson Davis.
Courtesy of the Library of Congress.

transportation came from often reluctant governors and citizens. When supplies dwindled, Davis began confiscating private property. When military manpower shrank, a draft was authorized.

Davis made excellent choices for army commanders. He devised a strategy based on hoarding (stockpiling) supplies and repelling invaders. A series of battlefield successes led Davis to a general offensive in the summer and fall of 1862 designed to terrify Northerners not yet touched by war; to separate other, uncertain states from the Union; and to convince the outside world of Southern strength. Though it failed, the strategy had merit. Meanwhile, Virginia was secured and in spring 1863 it looked as though Vicksburg, Mississippi, would remain a stronghold.

But Union general Ulysses S. Grant's continued pressure on Vicksburg forced Davis to a gamble that resulted in the Battle of Gettysburg. It failed. Vicksburg (at a cost of over fifty thousand men) fell about the same time. Davis adopted the idea of a "theater of war" that would isolate areas into separate, large-scale operations. Undermanned, undersupplied, and underfunded, Confederate forces were fighting valiantly in a losing battle. As Confederate chances dwindled, Davis became increasingly demanding. He eventually won congressional support for most of his measures but at high personal cost. By the summer of 1864, most Southern newspapers were criticizing his administration, state governors were quarreling with him, and he had become the focus of Southern discontent. The South was losing; Davis's plan must be wrong, the rebels reasoned.

Peace sentiments arose in unaffected areas of several states, as did demands to negotiate with the enemy. Confederate money had severely declined in value. Soldiers deserted and invaders stalked the land with almost no opposition. General Robert E. Lee surrendered on April 9, 1865. Davis was captured on May 10.

Davis spent two years in prison and was treated harshly. Federal authorities decided not to try him for treason. He returned to Mississippi, wrote a book about his Confederate experiences, and died on December 6, 1889.

blockade of Southern ports, expanded the military, and directed expenditures (the cost of activities) before they were authorized by Congress. Never before had a president taken such powerful actions. By continually insisting his actions were meant to preserve the Union, Lincoln became a symbol of moral strength and inspiration to the North—a figure around whom people wanted to rally, even as the Civil War became a long and bloody conflict.

That the war would last awhile became evident early on. Union forces were defeated in July of 1861 in Virginia at the Battle of Bull Run (also called the Battle of First Manassas).

1862: Losses and triumphs

In April of 1862, thirteen thousand Union soldiers died in the Battle of Shiloh (Virginia). During the summer of 1862, Union forces suffered two more defeats (the Seven Days' Battle and the Second Battle of Bull Run, also called the Battle of Second Manassas) in Virginia. Lincoln faced other problems as well. A group of radical (extreme) Republicans in Congress viewed the Civil War as a holy crusade (a military expedition intended to spread or defend a certain belief, usually a religious faith). These radical Republicans wanted a more vigorous offensive against the South, punishment for leaders of the Confederacy, and immediate emancipation of slaves. Lincoln had already won a confrontation with his secretary of state, William H. Seward, who had begun enacting policies the radical Republicans supported without the president's permission. The radical Republicans were hoping to undermine Lincoln and gain national control in the next presidential election. In a meeting involving Lincoln's entire Cabinet and all the radical Republicans, Lincoln was able to assert his authority as president with the backing of his Cabinet. The administration and the North's conduct of the war then proceeded fully under Lincoln's direction.

Meanwhile, Lincoln was grieving over the death of his son Willie, aged eleven, in 1862. He was the second of the four Lincoln boys to die in childhood.

Lincoln was prepared to issue a proclamation (an official announcement) during the summer of 1862 that would

Abraham Lincoln (center) at Antietam, Maryland, in the fall of 1862. *Courtesy of the Library of Congress.*

free all slaves in states that had seceded from the Union. Waiting for a moment of strength to issue the proclamation, Lincoln released the Emancipation Proclamation (see **Abraham Lincoln** primary source entry in volume 2) on September 22, 1862, after a strong Union showing in the Battle of Antietam (an-TEE-tum).

The Emancipation Proclamation was scheduled to go into effect on January 1, 1863. Slave states that had not seceded were encouraged to free slaves voluntarily. Meanwhile, Lincoln pressed Congress to pass an amendment to the Constitution barring slavery throughout the land. Such amendments must be ratified by three-fourths of the states. (The Thirteenth Amendment to the Constitution—abolishing slavery—was ratified late in 1865. States that had seceded from the Union were required to ratify the amendment before they would be admitted back.)

There were other positive developments in 1862. With many new immigrants entering the United States, Lincoln signed into law the Homestead Act. Settlers in western lands could claim a lot (a "homestead") of 160 acres for a small fee, provided they remained on the land for five years. Other acts provided free federal land for states to establish agricultural and technical colleges. New railroads were being constructed to open up the West. Two new states—Nevada and West Virginia (a part of Virginia that had not seceded)—entered the Union during the Lincoln administration.

Union forces rally

Union forces continued to suffer losses on the battlefield through the spring of 1863. Two pivotal (very important) events on July 4 of that year, however, changed the momentum of the war. After several attempts, Union forces under General **Ulysses S. Grant** (1822–1885; see entry in volume 3) were victorious in the Battle of Vicksburg (Mississippi). The Union forces overtook a Confederate stronghold and gained control of the Mississippi River. Meanwhile, a steady advance into Pennsylvania by Confederate general Robert E. Lee (1807–1870; see box in **Ulysses S. Grant** entry in volume 3) was stopped at Gettysburg. After a bloody battle, Lee's forces retreated but were halted by flooding of the Potomac River.

Lincoln ordered Union general George Meade (1815–1872) to vanquish the trapped army, but Meade responded too slowly. Lee's forces escaped to Virginia.

On November 19, 1863, the battlefield at Gettysburg was consecrated (declared sacred). Lincoln made one of his most moving speeches at that ceremony (the Gettsburg Address; see **Abraham Lincoln** primary source entry in volume 2). During the same month, forces led by General Grant won a decisive battle at Chattanooga, Tennessee. By spring of 1864, Lincoln had named Grant as his supreme field commander. Lincoln had changed commanders several times during the war. George McClellan (1826–1885) was replaced in November of 1862 by Ambrose Burnside (1824–1881), who was succeeded in January of 1863 by Joseph Hooker (1814–1879). Hooker was replaced in June of 1863 by Meade, who lost Lincoln's favor by moving too slowly against Confederate general Lee.

Grant led the Union forces to victory, but not without heavy losses. In May 1864, he began the Wilderness Cam-

Actor John Wilkes Booth, who assassinated Abraham Lincoln on April 14, 1865, in Ford's Theater in Washington, D.C.
Courtesy of the National Archives and Records Administration.

paign against the forces of Robert E. Lee. Close to sixty thousand Union soldiers were killed in battles during the spring of 1864 alone. From the summer of 1864 through the winter of 1865, Union forces advanced regularly. General George H. Thomas (1816–1870) crushed Confederate forces at Nashville, Tennessee. General Philip H. Sheridan (1831–1888) systematically swept through the Shenandoah Valley of Virginia. General William Tecumseh Sherman (1820–1891) marched through Georgia and South Carolina. Finally, on April 9, 1865, General Lee surrendered at Appomattox Court House, Virginia, effectively ending the Civil War.

Reunification

Lincoln was reelected president in 1864 by four hundred thousand votes of about four million votes cast. The Thirteenth Amendment to the Constitution, the amendment barring slavery throughout the land, passed the House of Representatives in January of 1865. (It had passed the Senate in April of 1864.) Lincoln's second inaugural address (see **Abraham Lincoln** primary source entry in volume 2) was given just weeks before the end of the war. The address concluded with a soothing tone and an expression of hope for lasting peace.

The terms of surrender for the Confederacy were generous. There were to be no punitive (punishing) measures against Confederate soldiers once they pledged allegiance to the U.S. Constitution. On April 11, the president exclaimed the end of war to a large group of people gathered outside the White House. He expressed hope for a quick reunification of the United States.

Three days later, on Good Friday, April 14, 1865, the president met with his Cabinet to plan the policy of Reconstruction (restoration of the South to the Union). Afterwards, the president and Mrs. Lincoln left the White House for a carriage ride. That evening they attended a play, *Our American Cousin,* at a Washington, D.C., theater.

At around 10:00 P.M., a pro-slavery extremist, actor John Wilkes Booth (1838–1865), entered the box where the Lincolns were seated and bolted the door behind him. He shot the president in the back of the head, stabbed one of the Lincolns' guests, and leaped down upon the stage, crying "Sic semper tyrannis" (Latin for "Thus always to tyrants!"). (He was later tracked down in a Virginia barn, which was set on fire to force him out; Booth was found inside, dead of a gunshot wound.) Meanwhile, an accomplice of Booth (a partner in Booth's wrongdoing) stabbed Secretary of State William H. Seward in bed, where he was recovering from a fall. Rumors spread throughout the capital that Lincoln's entire Cabinet had been attacked. But Seward was the only other victim, and he survived. Lincoln died the morning of April 15.

Lincoln's coffin was placed in the East Room of the White House, where thousands of mourners came to pay respects. Beginning on April 19, Lincoln's body traveled in a procession that passed through many towns and cities. The procession ended on May 4 at Oak Ridge Cemetery in Springfield, Illinois, where the president was buried.

Legacy

In the year 2000, Congressional television network C-SPAN surveyed fifty-eight presidential historians, asking them to rate presidents in ten different categories. The overall ranking had Abraham Lincoln on top as the nation's greatest leader.

Using the presidency to address the issue of slavery, Lincoln held firmly to the proposition that the issue should be addressed once and for all. He held to his conviction (strong belief), and he moved gradually by focusing first on stopping the spread of slavery. He did not seek war, but when rebellion occurred Lincoln acted with more authority than any previous president. Preserving the Union was his defense.

Lincoln's example of acting as the sole authority in a time of war was repeated successfully by other presidents,

A Selection of Lincoln Landmarks

Abraham Lincoln Birthplace National Historic Site. Sinking Spring Farm, 2995 Lincoln Farm Rd., Hodgenville, KY 42748. (502) 358-3874. Marble and granite memorial to Abraham Lincoln. Within the memorial sits the log cabin in which the nation's sixteenth president was born. See http://www.nps.gov/abli/linchomj.htm (accessed on July 13, 2000).

Ford's Theatre National Historic Site. 511 Tenth St., N.W., Washington, DC 20004. (202) 426-6924. Theater where President Lincoln was shot on April 14, 1865. "The House Where Lincoln Died" sits across the street. See http://www.nps.gov/foth/index.htm (accessed on July 13, 2000).

Hildene. Historic Route 7A, Manchester, VT 05254. (802) 362-1788. Majestic summer home of Robert Todd Lincoln, son of the president. The home—located in a valley between the Taconic and Green mountains—remained in the family until 1975. See http://www.hildene.org/ (accessed on July 13, 2000).

Knob Creek Farm. U.S. 31E, Hodgenville, KY 42748. (502) 549-3741. Replica of the log cabin Lincoln lived in as a young boy. See http://www.netins.net/showcase/creative/lincoln/sites/knob.htm (accessed on July 13, 2000).

Lincoln Boyhood National Memorial. P.O. Box 1816, Highway 162, Lincoln City, IN 47552. (812) 937-4541. Lincoln family farm is replicated on this site. Lincoln lived here during his teen years. See http://www.nps.gov/libo/index.htm (accessed on July 13, 2000).

most notably **Woodrow Wilson** (1856–1924; see entry in volume 4) during World War I (1914–18) and **Franklin D. Roosevelt** (1882–1945; see entry in volume 4) during World War II (1939–45). Far greater than his conduct of war was Lincoln's struggle for peace. His forceful eloquence helped turn the institution of slavery from a political issue (the right of states to decide their own conduct) to a moral issue (slavery is wrong). At the same time, Lincoln insisted on a more gradual approach to emancipation. He wanted to make it less of an imposition of one region upon another and more a course of action that represented the highest ideals of liberty and equality that the United States stands for.

Lincoln Home National Historic Site. 413 S. Eighth St., Springfield, IL 62701-1905. (217) 492-4241. Two-story Lincoln home—the only one he owned—sits in an historic neighborhood in Illinois's capital city. See http://www.nps.gov/liho/index.htm (accessed on July 13, 2000).

Lincoln Memorial. The National Mall, 900 Ohio Dr., S.W.,Washington, DC 20242. (202) 426-6841. Dramatic memorial sits at the end of the beautiful National Mall in the nation's capital. See http://www.nps.gov/linc/index.htm (accessed on July 13, 2000).

Lincoln Museums. Numerous museums honoring Abraham Lincoln exist in the United States. The "Abraham Lincoln Online" Web site lists over twenty. See http://www.netins.net/showcase/creative/lincoln/resource/library.htm (accessed on July 13, 2000).

Lincoln Tomb. Oak Ridge Cemetery. Springfield, IL 62702. (217) 782-2717. Final resting place of President Lincoln, Mary Todd Lincoln, and three of his four children. See http://www.state.il.us/HPA/sites/lincolntombframe.htm (accessed on July 13, 2000).

Lincoln's New Salem State Historic Site. R.R. 1, Box 244A, Petersburg, IL 62675. (217) 632-4000. Recreation of village that Lincoln lived in as a young adult. See http://www.lincolnsnewsalem.com/ (accessed on July 13, 2000).

Mary Todd Lincoln House. 578 W. Main St., Lexington, KY 40205. (606) 233-9999. Childhood home of the first lady. See http://www.uky.edu/LCC/HIS/sites/todd.html (accessed on July 13, 2000).

Lincoln had other successes during his administration. The Homestead Act made it possible for people of more modest means to buy land, provided they settle and work there for at least five years. The Act helped open up the western frontier for further settlement and encouraged business growth following the Civil War. During his presidency, however, the Civil War overshadowed everything else. To the end—in his second inaugural address, in the lenient (merciful) terms of surrender offered to the Confederacy, and in his plans for Reconstruction—the war was less important than preserving the Union, and to make it more perfect.

Where to Learn More

Abraham Lincoln Online. [Online] http://showcase.netins.net/web/creative/lincoln.html (accessed on July 21, 2000).

Abraham Lincoln Research Site. [Online] http://members.aol.com/RVSNorton/Lincoln2.html (accessed on July 21, 2000).

Assassination of President Lincoln and the Trial of the Assassins. [Online] http://www.tiac.net/users/ime/famtree/burnett/lincoln.htm (accessed on July 21, 2000).

Bruns, Roger. *Abraham Lincoln.* New York: Chelsea House, 1986.

Jacobs, William Jay. *Lincoln.* New York: Scribner's, 1991.

Judson, Karen. *Abraham Lincoln.* New York: Enslow, 1998.

McPherson, James M. *Abraham Lincoln and the Second American Revolution.* New York: Oxford University Press, 1990.

Sandburg, Carl. *Abraham Lincoln: The Prairie Years and the War Years.* New York: Harcourt, Brace, 1954. Reprint, San Diego: Harcourt, Brace Jovanovich, 1982.

Mary Lincoln

Born December 13, 1818
Lexington, Kentucky
Died July 16, 1882
Springfield, Illinois

Tormented first lady was criticized for extravagance, called a traitor by her native Southerners, and depressed by tragic family deaths

"The change from this gloomy earth, to be forever reunited to my idolized husband and my darling Willie would be happiness indeed."

Mary Lincoln

Mary Lincoln.
Reproduced by permission of the Corbis Corporation.

Mary Lincoln was looking forward to life in the White House as she began the journey to Washington, D.C., from Springfield, Illinois. The Lincoln family—Abraham and Mary and their three sons—set off for the capital in February. The inaugural (formal swearing-in ceremony) of recently elected President **Abraham Lincoln** (1809–1865; see entry in volume 2) was scheduled for March 4, 1861. Lively and impulsive, witty and sarcastic, Mary Lincoln imagined herself serving as hostess to lively parties, moving within the capital's social circles, and sharing her husband's importance.

Events turned out quite different. She could not seem to please politicians or the press. Her first few parties were considered too extravagant. Her later parties were too few in number, it was said. When she attempted to celebrate the progress of Union forces during the Civil War (1861–65), she was branded as a traitor to her southern (Kentucky) heritage. Her mourning—over the death of her eleven-year-old son, Willie, in 1862, her four brothers who died fighting for the Confederate cause, and then her husband—seemed excessive to some.

Emotional, energetic, and educated, Mary Lincoln became a misunderstood and tragic figure. After the death of her devoted husband—the one person who seemed able to moderate her rapidly changing temperament—she suffered bouts of mental illness and poverty brought on by her own excesses.

Southern belle

The daughter of Eliza Parker and Robert Smith Todd, Mary Todd was born December 12, 1813, in Lexington, Kentucky. Her parents, pioneer settlers of Kentucky, were local aristocrats (wealthy landowners). While growing up, she enjoyed a spirited social life and a private education. She loved dancing, fine clothes, and riding horses. She came in contact with politicians from an early age. Her family was well-acquainted with Henry Clay (1777–1852; see box in **John Quincy Adams** entry in volume 1), a famous American statesman who ran for president in 1832, when Mary was nineteen.

Two years later she moved to Springfield, Illinois, to stay with her married sister, Ninian. Springfield soon became the state capital and had a lively social scene that Mary enjoyed. She was courted by several suitors, including Stephen Douglas (1813–1861; see box in **Abraham Lincoln** entry in volume 2)—the man her future husband, Abraham Lincoln, would later face in races for the senate (1858) and the presidency (1860).

Mary first met Abraham, a state senator and lawyer, at a dance in 1840. Lincoln approached her and said, "Miss Todd, I want to dance with you in the worst way." She was five feet, two inches, and Abe was six feet, four inches tall. According to Mary, Lincoln did dance in the worst way.

Lincoln later described himself as "a poor nobody" back then. Some members of the Todd family agreed. When Lincoln and Todd were soon engaged, some of the Todds felt Mary was marrying beneath her social level. It was Lincoln, though, who failed to show up at the wedding ceremony on January 1, 1841. But their stormy courtship was soon renewed. Although opposites in background, they were devoted to each other and married on November 4, 1842.

Robert Todd Lincoln, the first of the couple's four boys, was born in 1843. At that time, Lincoln had retired from the state senate and returned to his law practice. A second son, Edward (Eddie), was born in 1846, the year Lincoln was elected to the U.S. House of Representatives. Eddie died in 1850, the same year the couple's third son, William (Willie) Wallace was born. Thomas (Tad) was born in 1853.

The road back to D.C.

After Lincoln served one term in the House of Representatives, the Lincoln family returned to Springfield in 1849. While Lincoln worked as a lawyer and failed in two bids for the U.S. Senate, Mary raised the boys and became accustomed to a modest lifestyle. When Lincoln was elected president in 1860, Mary looked forward to being a leader in social circles. Journeying to Washington through twelve states, the Lincolns were greeted by noisy and high-spirited crowds at seemingly every stop. Mary's spirits were primed for good times ahead. However, Southern states opposed to Lincoln's antislavery views (which Mary shared) had already begun seceding (separating) from the Union. The Lincolns's entrance into the capital—under careful guard and the cover of late night—was a telling omen of things to come.

Lincoln had always been a casual man. As a lawyer in Illinois, for example, he occasionally ended a day in court by placing important documents inside his stovepipe hat for safekeeping. Mary had much more of a formal social sense, and it showed in her festive White House parties. Her years in the White House were marked by shopping sprees (she once bought over three hundred pairs of gloves in the span of four months); visits to the wounded in Civil War hospitals; and problems with her temper, occasionally brought on by headaches.

She fell into deep grief when the couple's eleven-year-old son Willie died in 1862. Her deep grieving became so pronounced that Lincoln feared he might have to have his wife hospitalized. She tried a séance (SAY-ahnss; a meeting at which participants attempt to communicate with the dead) at the White House instead, hoping to communicate with her dead son's spirit.

The couple's youngest son, Tad, was a source of joy and mischief that helped lighten White House years of tragedy and the ever bloodier Civil War (in which four of Mary's brothers were killed). Tad would often sit on his father's knee during policy discussions. He was fond of having his wagon pulled through the White House by two goats. Perhaps overhearing war talk, Tad once sentenced a doll to death for "insubordination" (not submitting to authority). Upon hearing the sentence, the President wrote down a proclamation and handed it to his son. It was an executive order pardoning the doll for its crime.

More tragedy

Mary Lincoln never quite recovered from the death of Willie. Shortly after Lincoln began his second term in office in March of 1865, however, the future seemed bright again. The Civil War was over in April. On Good Friday, April 14, 1865, the president met with his Cabinet in the early afternoon. Afterwards, the president and Mrs. Lincoln left the White House for a carriage ride. It was spring—a time of rebirth, and a time to look ahead now that the war was over. That evening the couple attended a play—one of Mary's favorite pastimes. The president shared her love for theater and literature. He often carried around a volume of Shakespeare's plays for casual reading when he had time.

At around 10:00 P.M., while they were watching the play, a proslavery extremist named John Wilkes Booth entered the box where the Lincolns were seated and bolted the door behind him. He shot the president in the back of the head. Mrs. Lincoln screamed with horror and then fainted. Lincoln died the following morning.

The assassination of her husband devastated the first lady. She was so distraught (highly disturbed) that she could not attend her husband's state funeral. Returning to Illinois, she could find no comfort for her grief and began having mental problems. She would spend lavishly and then feel miserably impoverished. She ran up debts while her husband's modest estate was settled. She suffered various physical ailments.

Robert Todd Lincoln, the only son of President Lincoln to grow to adulthood, served in the Union Army, as well as in the James Garfield, Chester Arthur, and Benjamin Harrison administrations. *Photograph by John Goldin and Co. Courtesy of the Library of Congress.*

She traveled with son Tad to Europe, hoping to improve her health. When she was granted a pension by Congress in 1870 and returned the following year to Chicago, Mary seemed to have found emotional balance. But Tad grew progressively ill in 1871 after having caught a cold. His shocking death at the age of eighteen was too much for Mary to bear. She slipped into a world of illusion.

The Lincoln's remaining son, Robert, attempted to help her, but he began to fear for her sanity. Mary Lincoln was sent to a sanitorium (an institution for rest and recuperation) in 1875, then judged mentally fit the following year. She took another trip to Europe and returned to the United States in 1880 after suffering injuries from a fall. Both her physical and mental health deteriorated (grew worse). She died in 1882 in Springfield in the same home from which she departed on her wedding day forty years before.

Robert Todd Lincoln (1843–1926) was the couple's only son to survive into adulthood. At the time of his mother's death, he was serving as secretary of war to President **Chester A. Arthur** (1829–1886; see entry in volume 3), successor to **James Garfield** (1831–1881; see entry in volume 3), who was assassinated in 1881. Robert had wanted to fight during the Civil War (he was eighteen when the war began), but his mother held him back for fear that he, too, would die young—like her other sons and her brothers. Robert Todd Lincoln eventually served on the staff of General **Ulysses S. Grant** (1822–1885; see entry in volume 3) during the war. He lived on into the twentieth century.

Where to Learn More

Baker, Jean H. *Mary Todd Lincoln: A Biography.* New York: Norton, 1987.

Collins, David R. *Shattered Dreams: The Story of Mary Todd Lincoln.* Greensboro, NC: M. Reynolds, 1994.

Mary Todd Lincoln's Research Site. [Online] http://members.aol.com/RVSNorton/Lincoln15.html (accessed on July 21, 2000).

Sandburg, Carl, and Paul M. Angle: *Mary Lincoln: Wife and Widow.* Part I, by Carl Sandburg, Part II, Letters, Documents and Appendix, by Paul M. Angle. New York: Harcourt, Brace and Company, 1932. Reprint, Bedford, MA: Applewood Books, 1995.

Santow, Dan. *Mary Todd Lincoln, 1818–1882.* New York: Children's Press, 1999.

Lincoln's Emancipation Proclamation

Delivered on September 22, 1862; excerpted from
Abraham Lincoln Online **(Web site)**

*The president presents his plan to
begin the process of abolishing slavery*

Abraham Lincoln (1809–1865; see entry in volume 2) favored gradual emancipation of slaves, a program that could keep the Union intact while moving toward ending the institution of slavery. When Southern states seceded from the Union and formed the Confederate States of America (CSA) after Lincoln's election, he was careful to focus his actions as president on preserving the Union. However, the Confederate states had united against what they felt were unfair policies of the federal government and the prospect that the expansion of slavery would be stopped and then the institution itself would be ended. When the military of the Confederacy fired upon Fort Sumter in April of 1861, President Lincoln summoned federal military power against what he considered an act of aggression. The Civil War began with these incidents.

While the war was being fought, Lincoln wanted to pursue his policy of gradual emancipation. When he met some opposition from Congress in the spring of 1862, Lincoln decided for more forceful action. On July 22, 1862, he presented his plan to make an emancipation proclamation that would begin the process of abolishing slavery. His secre-

"I do order and declare that all persons held as slaves within said designated States and parts of States are, and henceforward shall be, free. . . ."

Abraham Lincoln

Abraham Lincoln (third from left) at the first reading of the Emancipation Proclamation.
Courtesy of the Library of Congress.

tary of state, William Seward (1801–1872; see box in **Andrew Johnson** entry in volume 2), suggested that Lincoln wait for a more opportune time to issue the proclamation, since the Union was still unable to win momentum in the Civil War.

The opportunity came following the Battle of Antietam on September 17, 1862. The battle was a standoff, for the most part, but it was the most impressive Union army showing to date. Lincoln issued the Emancipation Proclamation on September 22, 1862. The Proclamation was to go into effect in one hundred days, on January 1, 1863. Lincoln said, "I never, in my life, felt more certain that I was doing right, than I do in signing this paper."

Things to remember while reading the Emancipation Proclamation:

- States of the Confederacy had seceded from the Union and, therefore, felt no obligation to comply with the

Proclamation. However, since the Proclamation ordered federal soldiers to enforce the law, any area that seceded from the Union but was later taken back would have to comply. States that allowed slavery but had not seceded were not affected by the Proclamation. Lincoln wanted to ensure that those states would remain loyal to the Union while the Civil War raged on.

• Lincoln was careful to stress his Constitutional power to issue the Proclamation. In the third paragraph, he stressed the legality of his action—"by virtue of the power in me vested as Commander-In-Chief of the Army and Navy of the United States in time of actual armed rebellion against the authority and government of the United States, and as a fit and necessary war measure for supressing said rebellion."

The Emancipation Proclamation

By the President of the United States of America: A PROCLAMA-TION

Whereas on the 22nd day of September, A.D. 1862, a proclamation was issued by the President of the United States, containing, among other things, the following, to wit:

*"That on the 1st day of January, A.D. 1863, all persons held as slaves within any State or designated part of a State the people whereof shall then be in **rebellion** against the United States shall be then, thenceforward, and forever free; and the executive government of the United States, including the military and naval authority thereof, will recognize and maintain the freedom of such persons and will do no act or acts to repress such persons, or any of them, in any efforts they may make for their actual freedom.*

"That the executive will on the 1st day of January aforesaid, by proclamation, designate the States and parts of States, if any, in which the people thereof, respectively, shall then be in rebellion against the United States; and the fact that any State or the people thereof shall on that day be in good faith represented in the Congress of the United States by members chosen thereto at elections

Rebellion: Resistance or defiance of an established government.

wherein a majority of the qualified voters of such States shall have participated shall, in the absence of strong countervailing testimony, be deemed conclusive evidence that such State and the people thereof are not then in rebellion against the United States."

*Now, therefore, I, Abraham Lincoln, President of the United States, by virtue of the power in me **vested** as Commander-In-Chief of the Army and Navy of the United States in time of actual armed rebellion against the authority and government of the United States, and as a fit and necessary war measure for **suppressing** said rebellion, do, on this 1st day of January, A.D. 1863, and in accordance with my purpose so to do, publicly proclaimed for the full period of one hundred days from the first day above mentioned, order and designate as the States and parts of States wherein the people thereof, respectively, are this day in rebellion against the United States the following, to wit:*

*Arkansas, Texas, Louisiana (except the **parishes** of St. Bernard, Plaquemines, Jefferson, St. John, St. Charles, St. James, Ascension, Assumption, Terrebonne, Lafourche, St. Mary, St. Martin, and Orleans, including the city of New Orleans), Mississippi, Alabama, Florida, Georgia, South Carolina, North Carolina, and Virginia (except the forty-eight counties designated as West Virginia, and also the counties of Berkeley, Accomac, Northhampton, Elizabeth City, York, Princess Anne, and Norfolk, including the cities of Norfolk and Portsmouth), and which excepted parts are for the present left precisely as if this **proclamation** were not issued.*

And by virtue of the power and for the purpose aforesaid, I do order and declare that all persons held as slaves within said designated States and parts of States are, and henceforward shall be, free; and that the Executive Government of the United States, including the military and naval authorities thereof, will recognize and maintain the freedom of said persons.

*And I hereby **enjoin** upon the people so declared to be free to **abstain** from all violence, unless in necessary self-defence; and I recommend to them that, in all case when allowed, they labor faithfully for reasonable wages.*

*And I further declare and make known that such persons of suitable condition will be received into the armed service of the United States to **garrison** forts, positions, stations, and other places, and to man vessels of all sorts in said service.*

Vested: Guaranteed as a legal right or privilege.

Suppressing: Subduing or putting down by force.

Parishes: Divisions of the state of Louisiana that are the equivalent of counties in other states.

Proclamation: An official public announcement.

Enjoin: Direct or command.

Abstain: Prevent oneself from taking an action.

Garrison: To occupy with troops.

*And upon this act, sincerely believed to be an act of justice, **warranted** by the Constitution upon military necessity, I invoke the considerate judgment of mankind and the gracious favor of Almighty God.* (Abraham Lincoln Online *[Web site]*)

What happened next . . .

The Emancipation Proclamation is most significant as a symbolic gesture and part of a series of events that culminated with the Thirteenth Amendment to the U.S. Constitution. That amendment, which was ratified late in 1865—after Lincoln was assassinated—outlawed slavery. The Emancipation Proclamation reflects Lincoln's approach of gradually undermining the institution of slavery in order to forcefully end it. The Emancipation did not apply to slaves in border states still in the Union; states in the Confederacy disregarded it, since they had seceded from the Union. The Proclamation is most significant for showing that the Civil War was being fought to end slavery.

The tide of battle turned in the Union army's favor in July of 1863. Still, the Civil War dragged on until April of 1865. The Thirteenth Amendment to the U.S. Constitution, outlawing slavery, was passed later that year. All of the former Confederate states had to ratify the amendment in order to be readmitted into the Union.

Did you know . . .

- The Emancipation Proclamation allowed African Americans to be recruited into the federal army. By the end of the Civil War in 1865, one in eight Union soldiers was African American.

Where to Learn More

Bennett, Lerone. *Forced into Glory: Abraham Lincoln's White Dream.* Chicago: Johnson Publishing Co., 2000.

Warranted: Authorized or supported.

Commager, Henry Steele. *The Great Proclamation, A Book for Young Americans*. Indianapolis, Bobbs-Merrill, 1960.

Donovan, Frank Robert. *Mr. Lincoln's Proclamation: The Story of the Emancipation Proclamation*. New York: Dodd, Mead, 1964.

"Emancipation Proclamation." *Abraham Lincoln Online*. [Online] http://showcase.netins.net/web/creative/lincoln/speeches/emancipate.htm (accessed on July 20, 2000).

Franklin, John Hope. *The Emancipation Proclamation*. Garden City, NY: Doubleday, 1963. Reprint, Wheeling, IL: Harlan Davidson, 1995.

Latham, Frank Brown. *Lincoln and the Emancipation Proclamation, January 1, 1863: The Document That Turned the Civil War into a Fight for Freedom*. New York: Watts, 1969.

Lincoln's Gettysburg Address

November 19, 1863; excerpted from
***The Library of Congress Exhibitions* (Web site)**

*President Lincoln's brief and powerful tribute
to the Civil War dead*

President **Abraham Lincoln** (1809–1865; see entry in volume 2) issued the Gettysburg Address at the Civil War battlefield near Gettysburg, Pennsylvania. The battlefield was being dedicated as a national cemetery. The main speaker at the dedication was Edward Everett (1794–1865), a famous American orator and statesman. Everett served in the U.S. House of Representatives for ten years, as governor of Massachusetts from 1836 to 1840, as president of Harvard University, as secretary of state under President **Millard Fillmore** (1800–1874; see entry in volume 2), and as U.S. senator from Massachusetts from 1853 to 1854.

Everett's speech lasted two hours and was widely reported in newspapers the following day. Lincoln's speech lasted less than two minutes and received much less attention at the time. After Lincoln's death, the Gettysburg Address became historically acclaimed as an example of classic oratory for its powerful phrasing. It is a tribute to the dead and a challenge to the living to continue fighting for the ideals the soldiers had defended and died for.

"We cannot dedicate—we cannot consecrate—we cannot hallow—this ground. The brave men, living and dead, who struggled here have consecrated it, far above our poor power to add or detract."

Abraham Lincoln

There were reports that Lincoln jotted down his speech on the back of an envelope on the way to the dedication. Historians generally agree, however, that he had prepared two drafts of the speech and made spontaneous changes while delivering it. The next day he wrote down his exact wording.

Things to remember while reading Lincoln's Gettysburg Address:

- From the beginning, Lincoln's speech takes on a sense of serious dignity. Instead of saying, "Eighty-seven years ago, the Founding Fathers created a new nation in North America," Lincoln chose more formal and yet colorful phrasing. From the beginning, as well, he is careful to invoke the ideals of the nation, and he maintains that the Civil War is being fought to preserve those ideals and the nation.

- The speech pays tribute to the soldiers who fought and died on the battlefield. They died, noted Lincoln, for the cause of freedom and for the ideals of the nation. In making that statement, Lincoln is insisting that the Confederacy is a threat to the American form of government, which these soldiers were defending.

- The Battle of Gettysburg was fought from July 1 through July 3, 1863. Considered by most military historians as a turning point in the Civil War, the battle ended the last major invasion of the North by the Confederate army. During the three days of battle, the Union army lost 3,070 soldiers; 14,497 were wounded, and over 5,000 were captured or missing. The Confederates lost about 3,500 soldiers; about 8,000 were wounded, and over 5,000 were captured or missing.

Four score and seven: Eighty-seven (four score equals 4 X 20).

Fathers: America's Founding Fathers, who led the country during the War of Independence in 1776 and created the U.S. Constitution.

The Gettysburg Address

Four score and seven *years ago our* ***fathers*** *brought forth upon this continent a new nation, conceived in Liberty, and dedicated to the proposition that all men are created equal.*

Now we are engaged in a great civil war, testing whether that nation or any nation so conceived and so dedicated can long endure. We are met on a great battlefield of that war. We have come to dedicate a portion of that field as a final resting place for those who here gave their lives that that nation might live. It is altogether fitting and proper that we should do this.

But, in a larger sense, we cannot dedicate—we cannot **consecrate**—we cannot **hallow**—this ground. The brave men, living and dead, who struggled here have consecrated it, far above our poor power to add or **detract**. The world will little note nor long remember what we say here, but it can never forget what they did here. It is for us the living, rather, to be dedicated here to the unfinished work which they who fought here have thus far so nobly advanced. It is rather for us to be here dedicated to the great task remaining before us—that from these honored dead we take increased devotion to that cause for which they gave the last full measure of devotion—that we here highly resolve that these dead shall not have died in vain—that this nation, under God, shall have a new birth of freedom—and that government of the people, by the people, for the people, shall not **perish** from the earth. (The Library of Congress Exhibitions [Web site]).

What happened next . . .

After the Battle of Gettysburg, the Confederate army was forced to fight a defensive war, attempting to stop the Union army from invading the South. The superior industry, transportation, supplies, and economy of the North eventually wore down the defense of the Confederacy. By the time the Gettysburg Address was made—four months after the battle—the tide of battle had shifted to the Union's favor. Days after this speech, Union general **Ulysses S. Grant** (1822–1885; see entry in volume 3) had a decisive victory at Chattanooga, Tennessee. Still, the war lasted another sixteen months. The Gettysburg Address gradually became honored as one of the greatest speeches by an American president.

Consecrate: Declare sacred.

Hallow: Make holy.

Detract: Take away.

Perish: Disappear or die.

Did you know . . .

- There are five known manuscript copies of the Gettysburg Address. President Lincoln gave one to each of his two private secretaries, John Nicolay (1832–1901) and John Hay (1838–1905). Those copies are housed in the Library of Congress. The copy that belonged to Nicolay is often called the "first draft" because it is believed to be the earliest copy that exists. However, scholars continue to debate about whether the Nicolay copy is the "reading" copy. In 1894, Nicolay wrote that Lincoln had brought with him the first part of the speech, written in ink on Executive Mansion stationery, and that he had written the second page in pencil on lined paper before the dedication on November 19, 1863. The Nicolay copy has matching folds, suggesting it could be the copy that eyewitnesses say Lincoln took from his coat pocket and read at the ceremony. However, some of the words and phrases of the Nicolay copy do not match accounts of the speech as it was recorded on paper by participants at the actual event. Lincoln would have had to depart from his written text in several instances, something he rarely did in his speeches. The "second draft," probably made by Lincoln shortly after his return to Washington from Gettysburg, was given to Hay. There are numerous variations in between the Nicolay and Hay drafts, providing readers an opportunity to examine Lincoln's process of composition.

- The other three copies of the Gettysburg Address were written by Lincoln for charitable purposes well after November 19, 1862. One copy that Lincoln wrote for Edward Everett, who spoke at the Gettysburg ceremony before Lincoln, is at the Illinois State Historical Library in Springfield; a copy written for historian George Bancroft (1800–1891) is at Cornell University; and a copy made for Colonel Alexander Bliss, Bancroft's stepson, is housed in the Lincoln Room of the White House.

Where to Learn More

Barton, William Eleazar. *Lincoln at Gettysburg: What He Intended to Say; What He Said; What He Was Reported to Have Said; What He Wished He Had Said.* New York: P. Smith, 1930. Reprint, 1950.

Handlin, Oscar. *The Road to Gettysburg*. Gettysburg: Gettysburg College, 1986.

Library of Congress. *The Library of Congress Exhibitions*. "The Gettysburg Address: Drafts." http://lcweb.loc.gov/exhibits/gadd/gadrft.html (accessed on July 20, 2000).

Murphy, Jim. *The Long Road to Gettysburg*. New York: Clarion Books, 1992.

Wills, Garry. *Lincoln at Gettysburg*. New York: Simon & Schuster, 1992.

Lincoln's Second Inaugural Address

Delivered on March 4, 1865; excerpted from
A Chronology of US Historical Documents **(Web site)**

*With the end of the Civil War in sight,
President Lincoln expresses hope for national reunification*

When **Abraham Lincoln** (1809–1865; see entry in volume 2) made his second inaugural address, the Union was close to total victory in the Civil War (1861–65). In fact, the end of the war would occur just over a month later. Thousands of spectators stood in thick mud at the Capitol to hear the president; Washington, D.C., had endured weeks of wet spring weather.

Lincoln made many memorable speeches. His second inaugural address ranks among his most significant for two reasons. The last sentence of the speech strikes a conciliatory and reverent tone in expressing hope for "a just and lasting peace." The speech took on even greater poignancy (deep effect) in history when Lincoln was assassinated just over a month later, and just days after the end of the Civil War.

Things to remember while reading President Lincoln's second inaugural address:

- Early on, Lincoln chose not to review the progress of his first administration or the war that dominated American

"With malice toward none, with charity for all, with firmness in the right as God gives us to see the right, let us strive on to finish the work we are in, to bind up the nation's wounds. . . ."

Abraham Lincoln

593

life. With Union forces nearing victory, he simply reaffirmed that those attempting to preserve the Union had hoped to avert war, but one party "would make war rather than let the nation survive." He remained firm as leader in emphasizing the justness of the Union cause. He reaffirmed his position that the war had been fought over the issue of slavery.

- Lincoln was fond of evoking Biblical references in his speeches. In his Second Inaugural Address, he equated American slavery with an offense against God, with the war as a form of punishment for that offense. All Americans were suffering for having perpetuated slavery.

- The speech had a conciliatory conclusion ("With malice toward none, with charity for all"), expressing firmness to continue the course of action—"to finish the work" of the war—and then to tend to and heal its wounds. A just and lasting peace was the goal.

President Lincoln's second inaugural address

Fellow-Countrymen:

At this second appearing to take the oath of the Presidential office there is less occasion for an extended address than there was at the first. Then a statement somewhat in detail of a course to be pursued seemed fitting and proper. Now, at the expiration of four years, during which public declarations have been constantly called forth on every point and phase of **the great contest** *which still absorbs the attention and engrosses the energies of the nation, little that is new could be presented. The progress of our arms, upon which all else chiefly depends, is as well known to the public as to myself, and it is, I trust, reasonably satisfactory and encouraging to all. With high hope for the future, no prediction in regard to it is ventured.*

On the occasion corresponding to this four years ago all thoughts were anxiously directed to an impending civil war. All dreaded it, all sought to avert it. While the inaugural address was being delivered from this place, devoted altogether to saving the Union without war, urgent **agents** *were in the city seeking to destroy*

The great contest: The Civil War.

Agents: Supporters of a divided nation who tried to convince citizens that two nations apart—the United States and the Confederate States of America—was better than one nation engaged in a civil war.

Complete American Presidents Sourcebook

it without war—seeking to dissolve the Union and divide effects by negotiation. Both parties **deprecated** war, but one of them would make war rather than let the nation survive, and the other would accept war rather than let it perish, and the war came.

One-eighth of the whole population were colored slaves, not distributed generally over the Union, but localized in the southern part of it. These slaves constituted a peculiar and powerful interest. All knew that this interest was somehow the cause of the war. To **strengthen, perpetuate, and extend** this interest was the object for which the **insurgents** would **rend** the Union even by war, while the Government claimed no right to do more than to restrict the territorial enlargement of it. Neither party expected for the war the magnitude or the duration which it has already attained. Neither anticipated that the cause of the conflict might cease with or even before the conflict itself should cease. Each looked for an easier triumph, and a result less fundamental and astounding. Both read the same Bible and pray to the same God, and each invokes His aid against the other. It may seem strange that any men should dare to ask a just God's assistance in wringing their bread from the sweat of other men's faces, but let us judge not, that we be not judged. The prayers of both could not be answered. That of neither has been answered fully. The Almighty has His own purposes. "Woe unto the world because of offenses; for it must needs be that offenses come, but woe to that man by whom the offense cometh." If we shall suppose that American slavery is one of those offenses which, in the **providence** of God, must needs come, but which, having continued through His appointed time, He now wills to remove, and that He gives to both North and South this terrible war as the woe due to those by whom the offense came, shall we discern **therein** any departure from those divine attributes which the believers in a living God always ascribe to Him? Fondly do we hope, fervently do we pray, that this mighty scourge of war may speedily pass away. Yet, if God wills that it continue until all the wealth piled by the **bondsman**'s two hundred and fifty years of unrequited toil shall be sunk, and until every drop of blood drawn with the lash shall be paid by another drawn with the sword, as was said three thousand years ago, so still it must be said "the judgments of the Lord are true and righteous altogether."

With malice toward none, with charity for all, with firmness in the right as God gives us to see the right, let us strive on to finish the work we are in, to bind up the nation's wounds, to care for him who shall have borne the battle and for his widow and his orphan, to do

Deprecated: Strongly disapproved of.

Strengthen, perpetuate, and extend: Make stronger in order to exert more lasting influence.

Insurgents: Those who undermine a recognized authority.

Rend: Tear apart.

Providence: Divine guidance.

Therein: In that respect.

Bondsman: One who assumes responsibility for an agreement. For example, a judge can allow a person charged with a crime to be free until the trial, rather than being held in jail. As part of the agreement, the accused pays "bail money"—an amount of money the judge sets that the accused must pay as part of an agreement that includes showing up on the appointed trial date. That money is held by a bondsman until the accused meets all requirements set by the judge.

*all which may achieve and cherish a just and lasting peace among ourselves and with all nations. (*A Chronology of US Historical Documents *[Web site])*

What happened next . . .

The Civil War ended on April 9, 1865, when Confederate general Robert E. Lee (1807–1870; see box in **Ulysses S. Grant** entry in volume 3) surrendered at Appomattox Court House, Virginia. Five days later, on Good Friday, April 14, 1865, President Lincoln was assassinated by a pro-slavery extremist, actor John Wilkes Booth (1838–1865). By the end of 1865, the Thirteenth Amendment to the Constitution—the abolishment of slavery—was ratified.

In his second inaugural address, Lincoln spoke "with malice toward none, with charity for all"—an ideal too often compromised in the aftermath of the war. Freed slaves faced discrimination and intimidation, and by the end of the century a new form of racism—segregation—had become commonplace. Nearly one hundred years later, in 1964, civil rights legislation was passed by Congress and signed into law by President **Lyndon B. Johnson** (1908–1973; see entry in volume 5)—a step necessary because the concept of equality was still not in practice throughout the land.

Lincoln had outlined means for reunifying the United States following the Civil War through a program called Reconstruction. Too often, however, powerful factions seeking political gain and punishment for the Southern states failed to heed the ideal "with malice toward none, with charity for all." Each act of malice made it that much more difficult to "bind up the nation's wounds."

Did you know . . .

- Abraham Lincoln made many notable speeches, but several commentators rate Lincoln's second inaugural address as perhaps his best speech. Frederick Douglass

(1817–1895), known for his book *Narrative of the Life of Frederick Douglass, An American Slave* and as a fierce abolitionist who expressed his views through his newspaper, the *North Star,* called the speech "a sacred effort." Lincoln himself thought the speech would "wear as well as—perhaps better than—anything I have produced," as he stated in a letter to Republican organizer Thurlow Weed (1797–1882). In the September 1999 issue of *Atlantic Monthly,* historian Garry Wills noted that the second inaugural address was powerful because Lincoln had learned to use phrases with many layers of meaning within a concise form, a technique Lincoln used earlier in the Gettysburg Address.

Where to Learn More

Holzer, Harold. *Lincoln Seen and Heard.* Lawrence: University Press of Kansas, 2000.

McPherson, James M. *How Lincoln Won the War with Metaphors*. Fort Wayne, IN: Louis A. Warren Lincoln Library and Museum, 1985.

University of Oklahoma Law Center. "The Second Inaugural Address of President Abraham Lincoln." *A Chronology of US Historical Documents*. [Online] http://www.law.ou.edu/hist/lincoln2.html (accessed on July 18, 2000).

Wills, Garry. "Lincoln's Greatest Speech?" *Atlantic Monthly,* September 1999, pp. 60–70.

Andrew Johnson
Seventeenth president (1865–1869)

Andrew Johnson

Born December 29, 1808
Raleigh, North Carolina
Died July 31, 1875
Carter's Station, Tennessee

Seventeenth president of the United States
(1865–1869)

Battled with Congress over the fate of the former Confederacy and was the first president impeached

Vice President Andrew Johnson was sworn into the office of president on April 15, 1865, following the assassination (murder) of President **Abraham Lincoln** (1809–1865; see entry in volume 2). The Civil War (1861–65) was over, and the task of reuniting the Northern and Southern states was ahead. Lincoln had selected Johnson as his vice president in 1864 partly as a symbolic gesture—Lincoln was a Northern Republican, Johnson a Southern Democrat. He also chose Johnson for his excellent political record.

Attempting to follow the course Lincoln set for reunifying (reuniting) the nation, Johnson was frustrated by the attitudes of Northern politicians and by discrimination against former slaves in the South. Unable to forge a strong core of support, Johnson was overwhelmed by congressmen intent on punishing the South over the war and expanding their own influence over national policies. Johnson's struggles against a mighty Congressional majority nearly led to his removal from office. This majority is referred to in history as the Radical Republicans.

"I have discharged all my official duties and discharged my pledges. And I say here tonight that if my predecessor Lincoln had lived . . . wrath would have poured out upon him."

Andrew Johnson

Andrew Johnson.
Courtesy of the Library of Congress.

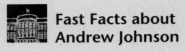

Fast Facts about Andrew Johnson

Full name: Andrew Johnson

Born: December 29, 1808

Died: July 31, 1875

Burial site: Andrew Johnson National Cemetery, Greeneville, Tennessee

Parents: Jacob and Mary McDonough Johnson

Spouse: Eliza McCardle (1810–1876; m. 1827)

Children: Martha (1828–1901); Charles (1830–1863); Mary (1832–1883); Robert (1834–1869); Andrew Jr. (1852–1879)

Religion: No formal affiliation

Education: No formal education

Occupation: Tailor

Government positions: Alderman and mayor of Greeneville, Tennessee; Tennessee state representative, senator, and governor; U.S. representative and senator from Tennessee; vice president under Abraham Lincoln

Political party: Democratic; National Union as vice president and president

Dates as president: April 15, 1865–March 4, 1869

Age upon taking office: 56

Johnson is consistently ranked among the least effective presidents. For example, in 2000, fifty-eight presidential historians were asked to rate presidents in ten different categories by the Congressional cable television network, C-SPAN. In the overall rankings, Johnson finished next-to-last. His predecessor—Abraham Lincoln—ranked first.

Johnson persevered (survived), as he had through turmoil and personal hardships his entire life. His failures as president must be understood in the context of larger problems. Congress took steps later considered unconstitutional in order to broaden its power during his administration. Former slaves were free, but not free from local and state laws enacted to limit their freedom. Political warfare between North and South continued to rage after the Civil War had ended.

A. Johnson, Tailor

Andrew Johnson, youngest of two sons of Jacob and Mary McDonough Johnson, was born in a small log house in Raleigh, North Carolina, on December 29, 1808. Jacob Johnson worked as a caretaker at a church and as a porter (a person hired to carry baggage). Already very poor, the family was made destitute (penniless; extremely poor) by Jacob's death when Andrew was three years old. Andrew Johnson never had formal schooling. At age ten he became an apprentice (one learning a trade from another) to a tailor.

Johnson moved to Greeneville, Tennessee, in his late teens. After having suffered hardships his entire life, Johnson found an opportunity at age eighteen when the best tailor left town in 1827. He set up a small shop—A. Johnson, Tailor—and began earning a living. Shortly before his twentieth birthday, Johnson married seventeen-year-old Eliza McCardle (1810–1876; see entry on **Eliza Johnson** in volume 2). They had four children over the next seven years; a fifth child was born in 1852.

Eliza helped Johnson improve his very basic reading, writing, and math skills. Johnson had become interested in education when he was an apprentice tailor; while they performed their work, the tailors were often entertained by someone reading aloud from a book. After the Johnsons joined a local debating society, the shop of A. Johnson, Tailor, became a gathering place for townspeople to discuss issues of the day. Johnson developed into a forceful speaker and a defender of small farmers and working people. He became so well known that he was elected alderman (a member of a legislative body representing a specific district) of the Greeneville town council at age twenty and went on to become the town's mayor. From 1835 to 1842, he served in the Tennessee state legislature as a congressman and senator.

Andrew Johnson Timeline

1808: Born in North Carolina

1827: Arrives in Greeneville, Tennessee, and sets up tailor shop

1828–35: Involved in Greeneville politics as alderman and mayor

1835–42: Serves in the Tennessee State Legislature as congressman and senator

1843–53 Serves in the U.S. House of Representatives

1853–56: Serves as governor of Tennessee

1857–62: Serves as U.S. senator

1862: Serves as military governor of Tennessee

1864: Elected as Abraham Lincoln's vice president

1865–69: Serves as seventeenth U.S. president following Lincoln's assassination

1868: Survives trial of impeachment by one vote

1875: Serves as U.S. senator for nearly four months before dying in Tennessee

Jacksonian Democrat

The period from 1829 to 1848 is often called the Age of Jackson. Tennessean **Andrew Jackson** (1767–1845; see entry in volume 1) served as president from 1829 to 1837.

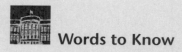

Words to Know

Alderman: A member of a city legislative body.

Army Appropriations Act: The designation of funds by Congress to support the U.S. military.

Black Codes: Laws and provisions that limited civil rights and placed economic restrictions on African Americans.

Freedmen's Bureau: An agency that provided federal help for freed slaves.

Gerrymandering: A practice whereby the political party in power changes boundaries in a voting area to include more people likely to support the party in power. This can occur when Congressional districts are rezoned (marked off into different sections) following the national census that occurs every ten years.

Impeachment: A legislative proceeding charging a public official with misconduct. Impeachment consists of the formal accusation of such an official and the trial that follows. It does not refer to removal from office of the accused.

Midterm elections: Congressional elections that occur midway through a president's term. The elections often change the balance of power in Congress, bringing in more supporters or challengers to the president.

Military governments: Government supervised or run by a military force.

Monroe Doctrine: A policy statement issued during the presidency of James Monroe (1817–25). The doctrine explained the position of the United States on the activities of European powers in the Western Hemisphere. Of major significance was the United States' stand against European intervention in the affairs of the Americas.

Reconstruction: A federal policy from 1865 to 1877 through which the national government took an active part in assisting and policing the former Confederate states.

Reconstruction Act of 1867: An act that placed military governments (governments supervised by a military force) in command of states of the South until the Fourteenth Amendment was ratified in 1868.

Secede: To withdraw from an organization.

Tenure of Office Act: A law passed by Congress to limit the powers of the presidency.

Thirteenth Amendment: An amendment to the U.S. Constitution that outlawed slavery.

Two of his key supporters served after him—**Martin Van Buren** (1782–1862; see entry in volume 1) from 1837 to 1841, and **James K. Polk** (1795–1849; see entry in volume 2) from 1845 to 1849. Like Jackson, Johnson was a Democrat whose policies favored laborers and small farmers. Johnson became a champion for those groups as a U.S. congressman. During a ten-year tenure (term in office) in Congress, Johnson fought for homestead laws that offered free public land to settlers to encourage them to build homes. His proposals never passed at the time, but Johnson became known as an independent politician who was always well prepared with facts. He consistently opposed tariffs—taxes placed on imported goods—because the higher costs hurt people of more humble means.

Johnson lost his office when the congressional district he represented was gerrymandered (divided into districts in order to give one political group more voters). He promptly ran for and was elected governor of Tennessee. During his two terms as governor, Johnson introduced taxes to help support education, mandated (formally ordered) equal pay for male and female teachers, and instituted standards for the teaching profession. He helped establish the state's first public library and first agricultural fair. On one occasion, Johnson defended his policies directed toward the less advantaged: "Whose hands built your capitol?" he asked a group of the state's wealthier citizens. "Whose toil, whose labor built your railroad and your ships?" He concluded, "I say let the mechanic and the laborer make our laws, rather than the idle and vicious aristocrat."

The summit of his ambition

U.S. senators were elected by state legislatures in those days. Upon being elected as a U.S. senator from Tennessee in 1857, Johnson stated, "I have reached the summit of my ambition." Back in Congress, he again pushed for a homestead act, but the measure was vetoed (rejected) by President **James Buchanan** (1791–1868; see entry in volume 2) in 1860. Two years later, the Homestead Act finally became law under President Abraham Lincoln.

Johnson was so well respected that he was mentioned as a possible Democratic Party presidential candidate in 1860.

The nomination went instead to Illinois senator Stephen Douglas (1813–1861; see box in **Abraham Lincoln** entry in volume 2), but Douglas was not a popular choice in the South.

The nation was deeply divided over the issue of slavery. Republican candidate Abraham Lincoln was viewed by many as a leader who would take steps to abolish the institution of slavery, an action no previous president had taken. Past presidents opposed to slavery had always approached it as a political or legal issue to be decided by individual states or by an act of Congress. Lincoln presented it to voters as an issue that had divided the nation and threatened to tear apart the Union. The prospect of his election so upset Southern political leaders that state officials began to threaten to secede (separate) from the Union. South Carolina became the first state to secede shortly after Lincoln's election in 1860.

Johnson did not take a strong stand against slavery. He generally viewed the institution as a states' rights issue, but he quickly denounced secession (separation). When his Southern colleagues (professional associates) stood up and walked out of Congress, Johnson remained in the Senate. He became a leading spokesperson for the "War Democrats"—the few members of that party left in Congress after Southern legislators departed. Johnson was branded a traitor in the South. His family was turned out of their home in Tennessee. One of Johnson's sons served in the Union army during the Civil War (1861–65).

Criticized for slurred speech

When the Union army was able to win control of a seceded state, a military government faithful to the United States was quickly established there. Johnson was named military governor of Tennessee in 1862. His mission was to restore the constitutional government of that state. Officials in the state government had to swear an allegiance (a loyalty oath) to the Constitution. Johnson replaced the mayor of Nashville and the entire city council when they refused to swear allegiance.

In 1864, the Republican Party's presidential convention met in Baltimore, Maryland. The party hoped to capitalize on the growing success of the Union army in the Civil War. The Republicans called the meeting the National Union Convention and opened the convention to all Americans interested in preserving the Union. Republicans and War Democrats united behind the presidential ticket of incumbent (current officeholder) Republican president Lincoln and War Democrat Johnson. The party hoped to show solidarity (cooperation) toward preserving the Union and to appeal to Southerners against secession. When Lincoln and Johnson won, their success marked only the second time in history that the president and the vice president were from different political parties. (Lincoln and Johnson agreed to join forces, however; in the election of 1796, Democrat-Republican **Thomas Jefferson** [1743–1826; see entry in volume 1] became vice president under Federalist **John Adams** [1735–1826; see entry in volume 1] during an era where the second-place vote-getter became vice president, regardless of party affiliation.)

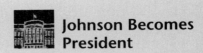

Johnson Becomes President

Andrew Johnson became president of the United States following the death of Abraham Lincoln. (See Lincoln entry for election results from the Lincoln/Johnson campaign.) This marked the third time in U.S. history that a vice president became president following the death of his predecessor. In 1868, Johnson attempted to be elected as president on his own, but lost the Democratic nomination to Horatio Seymour.

At the time of President Lincoln's second inaugural (formal ceremony installing him as president) in early March of 1865, Johnson was weak with typhoid fever. Nevertheless, he joined the inaugural festivities at Lincoln's request to project a symbol of solidarity (Northerner and Southerner, Republican and Democrat). During the festivities and speeches on a wet and windy day, Johnson sipped some brandy to help him stay alert. When his time finally came to speak, he gave a rambling speech in which he slurred (mumbled) many words, leading many in the crowd to conclude that he was drunk. Rumors that he had a drinking problem quickly spread and would follow him the rest of his life. Historians generally agree, however, that Johnson rarely drank alcohol.

The Civil War ended just over a month later with the surrender of the Confederacy on April 9, 1865. Five days later, President Lincoln was shot while watching a play at a Washington, D.C., theater. He died the next morning; later that

Thaddeus Stevens

Born April 4, 1792, in Danville, Vermont, to a poor family, Thaddeus Stevens grew up on what was then still the edge of the wilderness. His father abandoned the family when Stevens was just a boy. Stevens owed most of his future success to the virtues of industry and hard work instilled in him by his mother. Educated at Dartmouth College, Stevens became a schoolteacher in York, Pennsylvania. He went on to study law at the University of Vermont, as well as in Maryland, and became a lawyer, opening his practice in Gettysburg, Pennsylvania, in 1816.

Stevens was at first only a moderately successful lawyer. However, after defending a murderer on the grounds of insanity—an early example of the use of this plea—he suddenly became well known. Stevens was called in on most of the important cases in his area, and he argued cases before the state supreme court. As a young lawyer in Gettysburg, Stevens fought against returning runaway slaves to slaveowners and often defended them at no charge. Despite his growing reputation as an excellent lawyer, Stevens gave up his practice in 1826 to enter the iron manufacturing business. He was not particularly successful in this venture, but Stevens kept his company, Caledonia Furnace, open rather than deprive local people of their chief source of employment. It was during his years as a struggling businessman that Stevens is said to have derived his great en-

thusiasm for protective tariffs (a tax placed on imported goods) as a way to protect American manufacturers and workers. The issue of tariffs remained second to slavery as his lifelong political concern.

In 1833, he was elected to the Pennsylvania legislature as a member of the Anti-Masonic Party. He soon earned a reputation as one of the most dynamic and uncompromising politicians in the state. He began calling for free public education in Pennsylvania and became famed throughout the state for his fiery defense of taxes for education. As early as 1837, he put forth a resolution in the Pennsylvania state legislature to outlaw the slave trade and to abolish slavery in the District of Columbia. Stevens left the legislature in 1841 to return to law, opening his office in Lancaster, Pennsylvania.

In 1848, Stevens was elected to Congress as a member of the Whig Party, where he became one of the most vocal opponents of slavery. A fierce opponent of the Compromise of 1850 (which allowed for the possibility of slavery in new states), he did everything in his power to prevent the Fugitive Slave Act from being passed. That act made it legal for slaveowners to pursue runaway slaves into the North and claim their "property."

The willingness of the Whig Party to compromise with Southern states on the issue of slavery was so offensive to Stevens

Thaddeus Stevens.
Courtesy of the Library of Congress.

that he left Congress. With the formation of the antislavery Republican Party, Stevens found his political home. He played a major role in the formation of the party's Pennsylvania branch in 1855. At the Republican national convention in Philadelphia in 1856, Stevens dazzled the assembly with his speeches. Elected to Congress as a Republican in 1858, at age sixty-six, he assumed the undisputed leadership of his party. He took part in all debates that raged before the secession of the South and the beginning of the Civil War.

During the war, Stevens chaired the powerful House Ways and Means Committee. This committee had broad power over all tax legislation and almost every measure concerned with the conduct of the war. Urging a more vigorous policy against the Confederacy than did President Abraham Lincoln, Stevens denounced the South in the harshest terms and maintained that the Constitution no longer applied to the rebels. He disagreed forcefully with Lincoln's plans for Reconstruction, considering him soft on the rebels.

After the Civil War, many in the North were willing to be friendly to their former foes, but many others—Stevens among them—sought revenge. With the close of the war and the assassination of President Lincoln, Stevens took the lead in having the previously elected senators and congressman from the Southern states barred from Congress. He participated in the drafting of the Fourteenth Amendment and the Reconstruction Acts of 1867 that provided for military occupation of the Southern states. Stevens became the leader of the vengeful Northern congressmen known as the Radical Republicans. As their spokesman, Stevens fought for the rights and interests of the former slaves, called for the confiscation of (seizing of) Southern plantations to the benefit of the freedmen, and demanded the strictest terms for the admission of Southern states to the Union.

A bitter foe of Andrew Johnson, Stevens led the group of congressmen that drew up the document to impeach the president. However, as the trial began, Stevens's health began to fail. He died in Washington on August 11, 1868.

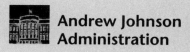

Andrew Johnson Administration

Administration Dates
April 15, 1865–March 4, 1869

Vice President
None

Cabinet

Secretary of State
William H. Seward (1865–69)

Secretary of the Treasury
Hugh McCulloch (1865–69)

Secretary of War
Edwin M. Stanton (1865–68)
Ulysses S. Grant (1867–68; interim)
John M. Schofield (1868–69)

Attorney General
James Speed (1865–66)
Henry Stanberry (1866–68)
William M. Evarts (1868–69)

Secretary of the Navy
Gideon Welles (1865–69)

Postmaster General
William Dennison Jr. (1865–66)
Alexander W. Randall (1866–69)

Secretary of the Interior
John P. Usher (1865)
James Harlan (1865–66)
Orville H. Browning (1866–69)

day, Johnson was sworn into office. Johnson faced an explosively unstable situation. Lincoln's assassination by proslavery extremist John Wilkes Booth (1838–1865) played into the plans of a group of congressmen known as the Radical Republicans. Prominent Radical Republicans included U.S. representative Thaddeus Stevens (1792–1868; see box) of Pennsylvania and Secretary of War Edwin M. Stanton (1814–1869). This group sought harsh punishment against the former Confederate states. Those who favored the more conciliatory approach of Lincoln and Johnson included moderate Republicans and almost all Democrats. Over the next two decades, the Radical Republicans pursued actions that restricted the full participation of those states in national affairs. By doing so, they maintained their own substantial base of power. Bitterness over the war remained in the South as well. Hostilities arose over issues surrounding the new status of emancipated slaves.

Foreign policy achievements

Johnson would become one of the most maligned (viciously criticized) and ineffective presidents. His combative (ready for a fight) attitude only worsened his situation. His presidency was marked by losing battles with Congress, and he was nearly removed from office. Johnson's prolonged and losing battles with Congress over Reconstruction (government policy for rebuilding the South after the Civil War) and the powers of the presidency dominated his tenure in office. The conflict overshadowed several foreign policy successes that would have greater impact in future years.

In 1867, Secretary of State William H. Seward (1801–1872; see box) negotiated the purchase of Alaska territory from Russia for just over $7 million. The purchase of the vast area far north from the continental United States (at the time Oregon, nearly one thousand miles away, was the nearest state to Alaska) was widely ridiculed at the time as "Seward's Folly."

In 1867, the Johnson administration invoked (used) the Monroe Doctrine (see **James Monroe** primary source entry in volume 1) to stop France from setting up a prince as co-emperor of Mexico. The doctrine was a policy statement issued during the presidency (from 1816 to 1824) of **James Monroe** (1758–1831; see entry in volume 1) that discouraged European intervention in American affairs. The Johnson administration also demanded Civil War reparations (payments) from Great Britain for having built a battleship, the *Alabama,* for use by the Confederacy. The reparations were later secured by the administration of Johnson's successor, President **Ulysses S. Grant** (1822–1885; see entry in volume 3).

 Thirteenth Amendment

The Thirteenth Amendment, ratified on December 6, 1865, outlawed slavery.

Section 1. Neither Slavery, nor involuntary servitude, except as a punishment for crime whereof the party shall have been duly convicted, shall exist within the United States, or any place subject to their jurisdiction.

Section 2. Congress shall have power to enforce this article by appropriate legislation.

Caught between extremes

While Congress was adjourned (not in session) from April to December of 1865, Johnson began his program of Reconstruction. He offered full membership into the Union to all seceded states, but the states had to meet certain conditions. Ten percent of their citizens had to swear an oath to uphold the constitution. State conventions were required to ratify (formally approve) the Thirteenth Amendment (see box) to the Constitution outlawing slavery. Only then were the states granted power to elect national senators and representatives.

Johnson's Reconstruction policy made headway in 1865. By May 9, he recognized the new government of Vir-

William H. Seward

Born and raised in Florida, New York, in 1801, William Henry Seward entered Union College in Schenectady, New York, in 1815. In 1818, after a disagreement with his father over money matters, Seward ran away to Georgia, where he taught school. He returned to New York in 1820 and completed his schooling. He began a law practice in Auburn, New York, in 1822. He met master politician Thurlow Weed (1797-1882), who became his political mentor and a shrewd guide to public office. Seward was elected state senator in the fall of 1830. He later served two terms as governor of New York, gaining nationwide attention for his battle with Southern governors over the return of fugitive slaves.

Seward resumed his law practice in 1842. In 1846, two African Americans, both clearly mentally ill, were brought to trial in Auburn on the charge of murder. Seward's eloquent defense of them spread his fame far: his *Argument in Defense of*

William Freeman was widely read. Seward was elected to the U.S. Senate in 1849. Sectional feelings (differences in point of view between the North and the South) had become intense. The Mexican War (1846–48) raised the issue of slavery in newly acquired territories. Seward supported the Wilmot Proviso (1848), a bill that barred slavery from any territory acquired from Mexico. Seward was reelected in 1854, the year Stephen A. Douglas introduced his Kansas-Nebraska Bill and the Republican Party was created. He spoke against Douglas's bill, which allowed the states of Kansas and Nebraska to decide for themselves whether or not to allow slavery.

When Abraham Lincoln was elected president in 1860, he chose Seward as secretary of state. Seward planned to assume a leading role for a president he considered inferior in experience and abilities to himself. But Seward soon became one of Lincoln's most loyal defenders and one of

ginia. By the end of May, he offered amnesty (political pardon for wrongdoing) to all Confederates who swore allegiance to the Union. Southern states began repealing secession and ratifying the Thirteenth Amendment, the amendment outlawing slavery. However, several local and state governments began introducing "Black Codes"—laws and provisions that limited civil rights and placed economic restrictions on African Americans. (Civil rights in the United States refer to the rights and liberty guaranteed to citizens by the Constitution.)

William Henry Seward.
Photograph by Mathew Brady. Courtesy of the Library of Congress.

the nation's greatest secretaries of state. For instance, while the North rejoiced at the seizure of two Confederate agents on board a British ship, Seward wisely accepted England's protest and returned the men. Quietly and forcefully, he lobbied against English and French recognition of the Confederacy, and neither nation took official action.

Seward urged Lincoln to run again in 1864. He was connected so closely with Lincoln that an attempt was made on his life on the same night the president was assassinated. Seward remained in the Cabinet after Lincoln's death and supported President Andrew Johnson's efforts to bring the Southern states back into the Union. He remained loyal even when impeachment proceedings were brought against Johnson. Seward completed his diplomatic career by successfully challenging French influence in Mexico's government and by negotiating the purchase of Alaska from Russia. At the time, the purchase was widely ridiculed as "Seward's Folly," or "Seward's Icebox." After leaving office, Seward traveled around the world. He died at his home in Auburn, New York, in 1872.

Already angered by Johnson's conciliatory (willingness to settle differences) Reconstruction program, Radical Republicans seized on the issue of the Black Codes when Congress reconvened (assembled again) at the end of 1865. Wanting a more punitive (punishment-oriented) approach to the South, those congressmen created the Joint Committee on Reconstruction with Radical Republican leader Thaddeus Stevens as chairman. They were able to draw wider support from Northern colleagues when the South reelected many of the same leaders who had supported secession. Through the

Fourteenth Amendment (see box) to the Constitution in 1868, Congress moved to refuse to seat any congressman who had served in the Confederate Congress.

Johnson's Reconstruction program emphasized working with states to bring about reunification of the nation, but Congress began imposing (forcing) federal acts on the former Confederate states. In 1866, Congress created the Freedmen's Bureau. The agency provided federal help for freed slaves. Congress successfully overrode Johnson's veto of a civil rights bill and the bill creating the Freedmen's Bureau. Never before did Congress override a presidential veto on such a major piece of legislation.

A political cartoon shows two political enemies: Angered by Andrew Johnson's moderate Reconstruction program, Radical Republican Thaddeus Stevens challenged Johnson whenever he could, ultimately calling for Johnson's impeachment. *Courtesy of the Library of Congress.*

Sorry spectacles

The 1866 midterm elections—Congressional elections halfway through the president's term of office that can change the balance of power in Congress—brought more difficulty for Johnson. To counter the formidable power of his opponents, Johnson tried to bring together supporters from both parties. He reconvened the National Union Convention—the assembly of Republicans and Democrats that had met in 1864 to bolster (strengthen) President Lincoln's reelection campaign and that had nominated Johnson as vice president. However, Johnson's action in 1866 came too close to election day to be effective. When Johnson campaigned for candidates who supported his moderate reconstruction policies, he was often challenged by hecklers (persons who challenge or taunt a speaker).

As a speaker, Johnson was always well prepared, but he was short-tempered and stubborn. During his campaign appearances in 1866, he often argued long and loud with hecklers, turning political rallies into sorry spectacles—events resulting in scorn and ridicule. Opponents pointed to his

Fourteenth Amendment

The Fourteenth Amendment, ratified on July 9, 1868, was intended to protect the civil rights of all citizens, particularly freedmen, and clarified some of the requirements for election to Congress. Radical Republicans also took the opportunity to include a section that barred former officers of the Confederacy from being elected to federal offices.

Section 1. All persons born or naturalized in the United States, and subject to the jurisdiction thereof, are citizens of the United States and of the State wherein they reside. No State shall make or enforce any law which shall abridge the privileges or immunities of citizens of the United States; nor shall any State deprive any person of life, liberty, or property, without due process of law; nor deny to any person within its jurisdiction the equal protection of the laws.

Section 2. Representatives shall be apportioned among the several States according to their respective numbers, counting the whole number of persons in each State, excluding Indians not taxed. But when the right to vote at any election for the choice of electors for President and Vice President of the United States, Representatives in Congress, the Executive and Judicial officers of a State, or the members of the Legislature thereof, is denied to any of the male inhabitants of such State, being twenty-one years of age, and citizens of the United States, or in any way abridged, except for participa-

tion in rebellion, or other crime, the basis of representation therein shall be reduced in the proportion which the number of such male citizens shall bear to the whole number of male citizens twenty-one years of age in such State.

Section 3. No person shall be a Senator or Representative in Congress, or elector of President and Vice President, or hold any office, civil or military, under the United States, or under any State, who, having previously taken an oath, as a member of Congress, or as an officer of the United States, or as a member of any State legislature, or as an executive or judicial officer of any State, to support the Constitution of the United States, shall have engaged in insurrection or rebellion against the same, or given aid or comfort to the enemies thereof. But Congress may by a vote of two-thirds of each House, remove such disability.

Section 4. The validity of the public debt of the United States, authorized by law, including debts incurred for payment of pensions and bounties for services in suppressing insurrection or rebellion, shall not be questioned. But neither the United States nor any State shall assume or pay any debt or obligation incurred in aid of insurrection or rebellion against the United States, or any claim for the loss or emancipation of any slave; but all such debts, obligations and claims shall be held illegal and void.

Section 5. The Congress shall have power to enforce, by appropriate legislation, the provision of this article.

often mean-spirited campaign appearances to renew the false claim that Johnson drank alcohol excessively.

Encouraged by midterm election victories of more Radical Republicans, Congress passed the Reconstruction Act

The Impeachment of Andrew Johnson

President Andrew Johnson was impeached (officially charged with misconduct) on charges of violating a federal law, the recently enacted Tenure of Office Act, and of defying the authority of Congress. The impeachment process begins with a House committee that debates whether or not the president committed impeachable offenses. If the committee agrees that the president has committed such actions, they draft articles of impeachment—items that note specific offenses of which the president is accused. The entire House of Representatives then votes on whether to impeach the president on those articles. If two-thirds of the representatives vote for impeachment, the president is placed on trial in the Senate. A two-thirds majority vote in the Senate is required to remove the president from office. The following excerpt from the U.S. Constitution (Article I, Section 3) describes the rules of impeachment.

The Senate shall have the sole Power to try all Impeachments. When sitting for that Purpose, they shall be on Oath or Affirmation. When the President of the United States is tried, the Chief Justice shall preside: And no Person shall be convicted without the Concurrence of two thirds of the Members present.

Judgment in Cases of Impeachment shall not extend further than to removal from Office, and disqualification to hold and enjoy any Office of honor, Trust or Profit under the United States: but the Party convicted shall nevertheless be liable and subject to Indictment, Trial, Judgment and Punishment, according to law.

Radical Republicans dominated the House Committee that evaluated Johnson's actions. The committee voted for eleven articles of impeachment: ten articles were violations of the Tenure of Office Act, and the eleventh article cited the president for undermining Congress.

For an impeachment trial in the Senate, the House of Representatives appoints a number of its members to act as managers in prosecuting the case against the president before the Senate. The president is defended by his lawyers. Johnson's lawyers argued that the president was testing the constitutionality of the Tenure of Office Act by dismissing Secretary of War Edwin M. Stanton. They also noted that Stanton had been appointed to his position by President Lincoln; since President Johnson had the right to appoint his own Cabinet members, the Tenure of Office Act did not apply to his dismissal of Stanton, Johnson's lawyers contended.

When the arguments were completed, the Senate voted first to determine whether each of the eleven articles were grounds for impeachment. They voted against all but three. The next step—voting on the three remaining articles—would determine whether or not the president would be removed from office.

Republican senators managed to delay the vote until they could be sure they had enough support to convict the president and have him removed from office. At

Edmund Gibson Ross, whose senate vote against impeachment saved President Andrew Johnson from being removed from office.
Reproduced by permission of the Corbis Corporation.

the time, there were 54 senators; 36 of them had to vote "guilty" in order to achieve the two-thirds majority needed to remove Johnson from office. Forty-two senators were Republican at the time. At first, twelve Republicans were planning to vote "guilty," but during the delays, that number dwindled to six. During the vote, however, a seventh Republican—Edmund Ross, a first-term senator from Kansas—voted "not guilty." That made the vote 35-19: the Senate failed to remove the president from office by one vote.

Republicans then postponed the next two votes. After ten days, however, they failed to change any minds. The 35-19 tally was repeated for the final two articles.

Edmund Ross, like the other six Republicans who voted against removing Johnson from office, failed to be reelected to the senate. Ross was shunned back home in Kansas, and eventually moved to New Mexico in 1882. He switched his political allegiance to the Democratic Party in 1872, was publisher of several newspapers for over twenty years, and served as governor of the Territory of New Mexico for four years beginning in 1885. He ended up dying in poverty. He was not forgotten, however. During the 1998 impeachment trial of President **Bill Clinton** (1946– ; see entry in volume 5), stories about the Johnson impeachment trial were published to help provide the public with information about the history of such events. Ross was often cited for his brave action. An article in *Time* magazine (December 21, 1998) noted that Ross had been "hunted like a fox" by supporters from both sides of the impeachment debate to try and win his support.

In 1955, future president **John F. Kennedy** (1917–1963; see entry in volume 5) wrote about his admiration of Ross. He included Ross in his book *Profiles in Courage,* a Pulitzer-Prize winning best-seller that presented biographies of people Kennedy considered courageous Americans. Kennedy stated that Ross's vote "may well have preserved for ourselves and posterity constitutional government in the United States."

This cartoon shows Andrew Johnson being crushed by the same Constitution he was trying to uphold. His opposition to Congress's Reconstruction plans brought about his impeachment.
Reproduced by permission of Archive Photos.

of 1867. The Act placed military governments (governments supervised by a military force) in command of states of the South until the Fourteenth Amendment was ratified in 1868. Congress went further and passed two acts that increased its authority over the executive branch. The Tenure of Office Act made it impossible for the president to remove an officeholder, including a Cabinet member, without approval from Congress. The Army Appropriations Act limited the president's command of the military. Both acts were unconstitutional, but Congress overrode Johnson's veto of the Tenure of Office Act. Meanwhile, because the Appropriations bill included the annual appropriation (money reserved for a specific purpose) for the military, Johnson signed it into law.

The success or failure of a politician often depends on how they choose to fight significant political battles. Johnson's response to the actions of Congress was not effective. He decided to test the Tenure of Office Act by suspending his secretary of war, Edwin M. Stanton (1814–1869), a Radical Republican sympathizer. Stanton responded by barricading himself in his White House office while Congress mounted vigorous criticism against the president. Johnson named Civil War hero Ulysses S. Grant as an interim (temporary) secretary of war. Grant fulfilled a mission of traveling through the South and reporting on conditions there, and then stepped down.

Johnson felt betrayed by Grant's action. Grant replied that he had planned to serve only temporarily. Grant's resignation certainly made him more appealing as a presidential candidate to Republicans. When Johnson finally dismissed Stanton, Radical Republicans reacted sternly. Because Johnson had violated the Tenure of Office Act, Republicans began impeachment hearings, legislative proceedings charging him with misconduct (see box). The impeachment trial began on March 30, 1868, and ended with the final impeachment votes on May 16.

Just say nay

"I almost literally looked down into my open grave," said first-term Kansas senator Edmund Ross (1826–1907; see box on impeachment proceedings), as he rose to announce his vote regarding Johnson's future as president. "Friendships, position, fortune, everything that makes life desirable to an ambitious man were about to be swept away by the breath of my mouth, perhaps forever." Voting his conscience over his party, Ross voted "not guilty." It proved to be the decisive vote when the conviction of President Johnson failed by one vote. Radical Republicans made sure Ross's national political career was over.

Johnson's presidency was saved. Nevertheless, he remained virtually powerless during the last few months of his administration. He continued to veto legislation, and Congress continued to override his vetoes. (Johnson's twenty-nine vetoes as president were the most ever by a president up to that time.) He was passed over for the Democratic nomination for president in 1868 in favor of New York governor Horatio Seymour (1810–1886). Ulysses S. Grant, the Republican nominee, won the election. A bitter Johnson left office criticizing Congressional Republicans in his final annual address

A Selection of Johnson Landmarks

Andrew Johnson Birthplace. Mordecai Historic Park, Raleigh, NC 27601. (919) 834-4844. The house in which President Johnson was born sits in an historic park in downtown Raleigh. See http://www.itpi.dpi.state.nc.us/vvisits/mordecai.html (accessed on July 14, 2000).

Andrew Johnson National Historic Site. P.O. Box 1088, College and Depot Streets, Greeneville, TN 37744. (423) 638-3551. Site includes the Johnson tailor shop, two Johnson homes, and the Andrew Johnson National Cemetery, where he and his wife are buried. See http://www.nps.gov/anjo/ (accessed on July 14, 2000).

President Andrew Johnson Museum and Library. Tusculum College, Greeneville, TN 37743. (423) 636-7348. The oldest building on the campus of Tusculum College includes artifacts of the late president, many of which were donated by his daughter, Margaret Johnson Patterson Bartlett. See http://www.tusculum.edu/museum/johnson.html (accessed on July 14, 2000).

(see **Andrew Johnson** primary source entry in volume 2) and in his farewell address.

Belated salute

Johnson returned to Tennessee after his presidency. He remained active politically and won back the respect he had enjoyed before his political problems in the 1860s. Remarkably, Johnson was elected U.S. senator from Tennessee in 1874, making him the only president to have later served as senator. He received a standing ovation when he first entered the senate floor in 1875, and his desk there was covered with flowers. But Johnson was not able to serve for long. He suffered a stroke that summer and died on July 31, 1875. He was buried in Greeneville, Tennessee, the town where he pulled himself up from poverty and where his early political career was launched.

Legacy

Andrew Johnson's tireless work for the Homestead Act (1862), which provided land to settlers for a small fee, showed his true political spirit—fighting for the less advantaged. He showed courage in remaining in Congress to place the Union above the concerns of individual states. His presidential administration took some controversial stands that proved historically wise (for example, a moderate approach to Reconstruction, and the purchase of Alaska).

Johnson, however, is generally regarded as one of the least effective presidents. Even if some of his stands proved wise, historically, he did not have the political savvy (practical know-how) to overcome his opponents. Johnson's actions contributed to the sorry political spectacle of his administration. Nevertheless, the failure to remove Johnson from office following his impeachment in the House may have saved the Constitution from being rewritten by Congress.

Beginning in the Johnson years, Congress dominated the national political scene through the early 1890s. A series of strong presidents—**Grover Cleveland** (1837–1908; see entry in volume 3), **William McKinley** (1843–1901; see entry in volume 3), and especially **Theodore Roosevelt** (1858–1919; see entry in volume 3) and **Woodrow Wilson** (1854–1924; see entry in volume 4)—helped restore the power and independence of the office of president decades later.

Where to Learn More

Dubowski, Cathy East. *Andrew Johnson: Rebuilding the Union*. Englewood Cliffs, NJ: Silver Burdett Press, 1991.

HarpWeek. *The Impeachment of Andrew Johnson*. [Online] http://www.impeach-andrewjohnson.com/ (accessed on July 21, 1999).

Hearn, Chester G. *The Impeachment of Andrew Johnson*. Jefferson, NC: McFarland & Co., 2000.

McKitrick, Eric L. *Andrew Johnson and Reconstruction*. Chicago: University of Chicago Press, 1960. Reprint, New York: Oxford University Press, 1988.

Simpson, Brooks D. *The Reconstruction Presidents*. Lawrence: University Press of Kansas, 1998.

Stevens, Rita. *Andrew Johnson: 17th President of the United States*. Ada, OK: Garrett Educational Corp., 1989.

Trefousse, Hans L. *Andrew Johnson: A Biography*. New York: W. W. Norton, 1989. Reprint, Newtown, CT: American Political Biography Press, 1998.

University of Missouri–Kansas City School of Law. "The Andrew Johnson Impeachment Trial." *Famous American Trials*. [Online] http://www.law.umkc.edu/faculty/projects/ftrials/impeach/impeachmt.htm (accessed on July 21, 2000).

Eliza Johnson

Born October 4, 1810
Greeneville, Tennessee
Died January 15, 1876
Carter County, Tennessee

Ill health left many of the
first lady duties to her daughter

When **Andrew Johnson** (1808–1875; see entry in volume 2) first came to Greeneville, Tennessee, at age seventeen, he caught the eye of fourteen-year-old Eliza McCardle. She must have seen something in that tired and disheveled (untidy) young man. Eliza said to one of her friends, "There goes my beau."

Johnson had just crossed the mountains between North Carolina and Tennessee and was riding on a rickety wagon pulled by a rundown horse. Eliza helped him find a place to stay that day. Within a year, Eliza and Andrew were married.

While content with a humble life, Eliza was always looking for ways to improve herself. She helped improve Andrew Johnson's meager reading, writing, and math skills. Andrew Johnson soon became a politician dedicated to improving the lives of poor and humble folk, fighting for their cause locally, then statewide, and later nationally.

"I knew he'd be acquitted; I knew it."

Eliza Johnson

Eliza Johnson.
Courtesy of the Library of Congress.

Home, shop, and meeting place

Eliza Johnson was born on October 4, 1810, in Leesburg, Tennessee. Like Andrew Johnson's father, her father, John, died when she was very young. Eliza's mother, Sarah, supported the family by sewing quilts. Eliza had some schooling at the local Rhea Academy. Johnson had no schooling. His family was very poor, and he began learning the tailor trade at age ten.

Johnson enjoyed another stroke of luck in Greeneville—besides meeting Eliza—when the local tailor left town. Johnson opened up a small shop and went into business. He and Eliza lived in the back part of the shop building after being married in 1827. Eliza helped teach Johnson to read and write and to do arithmetic. Soon, the shop of A. Johnson, Tailor, became a meeting place where townsfolk gathered to discuss politics. Johnson impressed people with his views. He was elected to the Greeneville town council at age twenty. By age twenty-six, he was the town's mayor.

Eliza, meanwhile, focused on raising the family. By 1834, the Johnsons had four children, two girls (Martha and Mary) and two boys (Charles and Robert). Johnson began serving in the Tennessee legislature in 1835. From 1843 to 1853, he served Tennessee in the U.S. House of Representatives. Eliza and the family remained in Tennesee most of the time, except for occasional visits to Washington, D.C.

After Johnson served as governor of Tennessee for four years, he returned to Washington, D.C., as a senator. He was in that position as the 1860s started, a decade that would prove more difficult for the Johnsons than their struggle to overcome poverty as young adults.

A decade of conflict

When **Abraham Lincoln** (1809–1865; see entry in volume 2) was elected president in 1860, Southern states began to secede (separate) from the Union. The Civil War (1861–65) began in April of 1861. Johnson refused to follow his fellow Southern legislators when they walked out of Congress to join the Confederate States of America. He wanted to help preserve the United States.

In 1862, he was appointed military governor of Tennessee and stationed in Nashville. The area around Greenville, where Eliza Johnson and the children stayed, was loyal to the Union. Beginning in April of 1862, all Union sympathizers were ordered out of the area by Confederate soldiers. Eliza was allowed to remain because of an illness, but by September she had to leave. She was allowed to cross Confederate lines to join her husband. With her ten-year-old son (Andrew, born in 1852), she survived cold, hunger, and the insults of Confederate sympathizers.

Johnson became vice president in 1864, but he assumed the office of president after Lincoln's assassination in April of 1865. By then, Eliza had become an invalid (a chronically ill person). She suffered from tuberculosis, a lung ailment. In those days, remaining indoors was considered the best treatment for tuberculosis. Eliza chose a room on the second floor of the White House as the center for family activities and rarely left it. She read, sewed, and spent time with her children and grandchildren.

Andrew and Eliza Johnson shared their living quarters with their sons Robert and Andrew, widowed daughter Mary and her two children, and daughter Martha and her three children. The Johnsons' son Charles had died fighting in the Civil War, as had Mary's husband.

Eliza Johnson was seen publicly at only two White House social functions. In August 1866, she attended a gathering for Queen Emma of Hawaii, and in December of 1868 she attended a Children's Ball. The White House was filled with children dancing and playing on that occasion—the date of President Johnson's sixtieth birthday.

The Johnson White House years were troubled by the president's ongoing battles with Congress. These battles began in 1865 and concluded with his impeachment trial in 1868. (An impeachment is a legislative hearing charging a public official with misconduct while in office.) After Johnson survived the impeachment trial in mid-May of 1868, the gloomy atmosphere of the White House was lightened. For the final nine months of Johnson's term, more White House festivities were held. The Johnsons' eldest daughter, Martha Johnson Patterson (1828–1901), served as hostess.

Martha was married to Tennessee senator David T.
Patterson (1818–1891). Her additional duties involved overseeing the restoration of the White House. Many furnishings
and walls had been ruined by souvenir seekers following the
assassination of President Lincoln. Martha had previously visited the White House in her late teens, when she was a guest
of President **James K. Polk** (1795–1849; see entry in volume
2) and his wife, **Sarah Polk** (1803–1891; see entry in volume
2). The Polks, like the Johnsons, were from Tennessee.

A better life

Martha and her mother were happy to leave the
White House in 1869. Both preferred a quieter life in Tennessee. For Andrew and Eliza Johnson, the tough decade of
the 1860s ended with another misfortune. Their son Robert
died in 1869 at the age of twenty-five.

The Johnsons returned to Tennessee in 1869. Their home had been restored after having been vandalized during the war. Johnson gradually returned to politics. After the turmoil of his presidency, he won a measure of vindication (freedom from being blamed) by being elected senator of Tennessee in 1874. He was received warmly back in Washington, D.C. Unfortunately, that satisfaction was short-lived. Johnson died in July of 1875.

Eliza moved in with daughter Martha at the Pattersons' home. She died there seven months after her husband passed away.

Where to Learn More

Boller, Paul F. *Presidential Wives*. New York: Oxford University Press, 1998.

Malone, Mary. *Andrew Johnson*. Berkeley Heights, NJ: Enslow Publishers, 1999.

Reece, Brazilla Carroll. *The Courageous Commoner: A Biography of Andrew Johnson*. Charleston, WV: Education Foundation, 1962.

Johnson's Final Annual Address to Congress

Delivered on December 9, 1868; excerpted from
The American Presidency: Selected Resources, An Informal Reference Guide **(Web site)**

Having survived an impeachment trial, President Johnson scolds Congress over its Reconstruction policies

Andrew Johnson (1808–1875; see entry in volume 2) delivered his last annual message to Congress in December of 1868, just six months after he had survived an impeachment trial. His administration had been marked by bitter, losing struggles with Congress.

Johnson wanted a moderate approach to the Southern states that had seceded and fought against the Union in the Civil War (1861–65). Congress, dominated by a powerful group of Republicans, wanted much harsher treatment toward the former Confederate states. The Congressional program won out.

Johnson took the opportunity of his final annual message to point out how Congressional actions had prolonged problems between the North and South and worsened the nation. He covered several other subjects—the national debt, foreign relations, and topics he hoped Congress would address the following year—but his ringing denunciation (criticism) of Congress' Reconstruction Plan stood out. It showed how testy the president's relations were with Con-

> "Congress, . . . refusing to perfect the work so nearly consummated, . . . after three years of agitation and strife, has left the country further from the attainment of union and fraternal feeling than at the inception of the Congressional plan of reconstruction."
>
> *Andrew Johnson*

gress and reflected the divisive mood that still gripped the nation more than three years after the war had ended.

Things to remember while reading an excerpt from President Johnson's final annual address to Congress:

- Johnson immediately launched into an attack on Congress. During his tenure as an elected official in Washington, D.C., for over twenty years, Johnson had always favored the rights of states to determine their own course. His policy of reconstruction was based on that approach. Early on in the speech, he argued that domestic troubles always occur when a national government imposes its will upon local governments. Moving from that general observation, Johnson began citing specific legislation enacted against his wishes by Congress that created turmoil and disorganized conditions within the country.

- Johnson accused Congress of having overstepped the bounds placed on that branch of the federal government by the Constitution. He, again, cited specific examples of congressional action that caused further strife and agitation throughout the land. Johnson claimed the country was moving smoothly toward reunification soon after the war ended in 1865. During that period, Congress was not in session and Johnson's program was introduced without interference.

- The larger part of Johnson's speech, not included in the following excerpt, was more typical of a president's annual address (or State of the Union speech, as it is called in modern times). Johnson discussed the nation's economy, focusing on the huge national debt that occurred because of the Civil War, and he discussed foreign relations issues.

- In the conclusion of the speech, Johnson offered his thoughts on four issues for Congress to consider as possible Constitutional amendments: (1) disbanding the Electoral College in favor of a straight popular vote for president (for more information on the Electoral College, see boxes in **George W. Bush** entry in volume 5); (2) instituting a clear line of succession should the president and vice president be unable to carry out their duties; (3) having senators elected by the people of a state rather than by state legislatures; and (4) limiting the terms of office for federal judges. (The second and third items later became laws.) After his stinging remarks at the opening of his address, however, Congress was not very likely to respect Johnson's ideas. Such acrimony (bitter disagreement) was typical of the state of the nation in 1868.

Excerpt from President Johnson's final annual message to Congress

Fellow-Citizens of the Senate and House of Representatives:

Upon the reassembling of Congress it again becomes my duty to call your attention to the state of the Union and to its continued disorganized condition under the various laws which have been passed upon the subject of reconstruction.

*It may be safely assumed as an **axiom** in the government of states that the greatest wrongs inflicted upon a people are caused by unjust and **arbitrary** legislation, or by the unrelenting decrees of **despotic** rulers, and that the timely **revocation** of injurious and oppressive measures is the greatest good that can be conferred upon a nation. The legislator or ruler who has the wisdom and **magnanimity** to retrace his steps when convinced of error will sooner or later be rewarded with the respect and gratitude of an intelligent and patriotic people.*

*Our own history, although embracing a period less than a century, affords abundant proof that most, if not all, of our domestic troubles are directly traceable to violations of the **organic law** and excessive legislation. The most striking illustrations of this fact are furnished by the enactments of the past three years upon the question of reconstruction. After a fair trial they have substantially failed and proved **pernicious** in their results, and there seems to be no good reason why they should longer remain upon the **statute** book. States to which the Constitution guarantees a **republican** form of government have been reduced to **military dependencies**, in each of which the people have been made subject to the arbitrary will of the commanding general. Although the Constitution requires that each State*

Axiom: A statement accepted as true.

Arbitrary: An action based on individual preference rather than necessity.

Despotic: Ruling with absolute authority and power.

Revocation: The act of taking back.

Magnanimity: The ability to deal with problems calmly and honorably.

Organic law: Laws that are changeable and adaptable, likened to natural (organic) growth in nature.

Pernicious: Destructive.

Statute: A law enacted by the legislative branch of government.

Republican: A form of government where supreme power resides with citizens who elect their leaders and have the power to change their leaders.

Military dependencies: A reference to the fact that Congress established military governments in the South to oversee the Reconstruction program.

shall be represented in Congress, Virginia, Mississippi, and Texas are yet excluded from the two Houses, and, contrary to the express provisions of that instrument, were denied participation in the recent election for a President and Vice-President of the United States. The attempt to place the white population **under the domination** of persons of color in the South has impaired, if not destroyed, the kindly relations that had previously existed between them; and mutual distrust has **engendered** a feeling of animosity which, leading in some instances to collision and bloodshed, has prevented that cooperation between the two races so essential to the success of industrial enterprise in the Southern States. Nor have the inhabitants of those States alone suffered from the disturbed condition of affairs growing out of these Congressional enactments. The entire Union has been agitated by grave apprehensions of troubles which might again involve the peace of the nation; its interests have been injuriously affected by the derangement of business and labor, and the consequent want of prosperity throughout that portion of the country.

The Federal Constitution—the **Magna charta** of American rights, under whose wise and **salutary** provisions we have successfully conducted all our domestic and foreign affairs, sustained ourselves in peace and in war, and become a great nation among the powers of the earth—must assuredly be now adequate to the settlement of questions growing out of the civil war, waged alone for its vindication. This great fact is made most manifest by the condition of the country when Congress assembled in the month of December, 1865. Civil strife had ceased, the spirit of rebellion had spent its entire force, in the Southern States the people had warmed into national life, and throughout the whole country a healthy reaction in public sentiment had taken place. By the application of the simple yet effective provisions of the Constitution the executive department, with the voluntary aid of the States, had brought the work of restoration as near completion as was within the scope of its authority, and the nation was encouraged by the prospect of an early and satisfactory adjustment of all its difficulties. Congress, however, intervened, and, refusing to perfect the work so nearly **consummated**, declined to admit members from the unrepresented States, adopted a series of measures which arrested the progress of restoration, frustrated all that had been so successfully accomplished, and, after three years of agitation and strife, has left the country further from the attainment of union and fraternal feeling than at the inception of the Congressional plan of reconstruction. It needs no argument to show that legislation which has produced such **baneful** conse-

Under the domination: Johnson is suggesting that when Congress extended voting rights to African Americans, it abruptly shifted electoral power in some Southern areas, leaving white voters at a disadvantage.

Engendered: Caused to exist.

Magna Charta: Magna Carta, the document of 1215 in Britain that guaranteed the rights of citizens.

Salutary: Beneficial.

Consummated: Brought to a favorable conclusion.

Baneful: Harmful.

quences should be **abrogated**, or else made to conform to the genuine principles of republican government.

Under the influence of party passion and sectional prejudice, other acts have been passed not warranted by the Constitution. Congress has already been made familiar with my views respecting the "tenure-of-office bill." Experience has proved that its repeal is demanded by the best interests of the country, and that while it remains in force the President can not enjoin that rigid accountability of public officers so essential to an honest and efficient execution of the laws. Its revocation would enable the executive department to exercise the power of appointment and removal in accordance with the original design of the Federal Constitution.

The act of March 2, 1867, making **appropriations** for the support of the Army for the year ending, June 30, 1868, and for other purposes, contains provisions which interfere with the President's constitutional functions as Commander in Chief of the Army and deny to States of the Union the right to protect themselves by means of their own militia. These provisions should be at once **annulled**; for while the first might, in times of great emergency, seriously embarrass the Executive in efforts to employ and direct the common strength of the nation for its protection and preservation, the other is contrary to the express declaration of the Constitution that "a well-regulated militia being necessary to the security of a free state, the right of the people to keep and bear arms shall not be infringed."

It is believed that the repeal of all such laws would be accepted by the American people as at least a partial return to the fundamental principles of the Government, and an indication that hereafter the Constitution is to be made the nation's safe and unerring guide. They can be productive of no permanent benefit to the country, and should not be permitted to stand as so many monuments of the deficient wisdom which has characterized our recent legislation. . . .

I renew the recommendation contained in my communication to Congress dated the 18th July last—a copy of which accompanies this message—that the judgment of the people should be taken on the **propriety** of so amending the Federal Constitution that it shall provide—

First. For an election of President and Vice-President by a direct vote of the people, instead of through the agency of electors, and making them ineligible for reelection to a second term.

Abrogated: Abolished by authoritative action.

Appropriations: Funds set aside for a specific purpose.

Annulled: Made legally invalid.

Propriety: The state of being proper.

Second. For a distinct designation of the person who shall discharge the duties of President in the event of a vacancy in that office by the death, resignation, or removal of both the President and Vice-president.

Third. For the election of Senator of the United States directly by the people of the several States, instead of by the legislatures; and

Fourth. For the limitation to a period of years of the terms of Federal judges.

Profoundly impressed with the propriety of making these important modifications in the Constitution, I respectfully submit them for the early and mature consideration of Congress. We should, as far as possible, remove all pretext for violations of the organic law, by remedying such imperfections as time and experience may develop, ever remembering that "the constitution which at any time exists until changed by an explicit and authentic act of the whole people is sacredly obligatory upon all."

*In the performance of a duty imposed upon me by the Constitution, I have thus communicated to Congress information of the state of the Union and recommended for their consideration such measures as have seemed to me necessary and expedient. If carried into effect, they will hasten the accomplishment of the great and **beneficent** purposes for which the Constitution was ordained, and which it comprehensively states were "to form a more perfect Union, establish justice, insure domestic tranquillity, provide for the common defense, promote the general welfare, and secure the blessings of liberty to ourselves and our posterity." In Congress are **vested** all legislative powers, and upon them **devolves** the responsibility as well for framing unwise and excessive laws as for neglecting to devise and adopt measures absolutely demanded by the wants of the country. Let us earnestly hope that before the expiration of our respective terms of service, now rapidly drawing to a close, an all-wise **Providence** will so guide our counsels as to strengthen and preserve the Federal Union, inspire reverence for the Constitution, restore prosperity and happiness to our whole people, and promote "on earth peace, good will toward men."* (The American Presidency: Selected Resources, An Informal Reference Guide [Web site]).

Beneficent: Beneficial.

Vested: Unconditionally guaranteed a legal right.

Devolves: Pass power on from one person or entity to another.

Providence: Divine guidance.

What happened next . . .

At the time of the speech, Johnson was a lame duck—a term that describes an official finishing a term before a successor takes over. Johnson returned home to Tennessee after his failed presidency. However, he returned to Congress when he was elected to the U.S. Senate in 1874. Upon reentering Congress in 1875, he was greeted with a standing ovation, but he died less than four months later.

The Congressional form of Reconstruction prevailed until being disbanded in 1877. The program was largely a failure and accomplished little in healing the wounds of the Civil War and reuniting the nation. Whether Johnson's program would have worked better is debatable: there were hopeful signs that a peaceful reunification would occur shortly after the war; on the other hand, such local and state legislation as the "Black Codes," which placed voting and economic restrictions on African Americans, showed that fundamental issues remained.

Did you know . . .

- Johnson was targeted for assassination on the same night that President **Abraham Lincoln** (1809–1865; see entry in volume 2) was murdered. John Wilkes Booth (1838–1865) killed the president, but his accomplice, George Atzerodt (1835–1865), was given the assignment of killing the vice president. Although Atzerodt rented a room directly above Johnson in the boarding house in which Johnson was staying, Atzerodt made no attempt on the vice president's life. Lincoln's secretary of state, William Seward (1801–1872; see box in **Andrew Johnson** entry in volume 2), who would continue to serve under Johnson, was stabbed by a would-be assassin that same night; Seward recovered from his wounds.

Where to Learn More

"Annual Message: December 9, 1868." *The American Presidency: Selected Resources, An Informal Reference Guide* (Web site). [Online] http://www.interlink-cafe.com/uspresidents/1868.htm (accessed on July 18, 2000).

Baker, Gary G. *Andrew Johnson and the Struggle for Presidential Reconstruction, 1865–1868*. Boston: Heath, 1966.

Chadsey, Charles E. *The Struggle between President Johnson and Congress over Reconstruction*. New York: Columbia University, 1896.

Mantell, Martin E. *Johnson, Grant, and the Politics of Reconstruction*. New York, Columbia University Press, 1973.

Sefton, James E. *Andrew Johnson and the Uses of Constitutional Power*. Boston: Little, Brown, 1980.

Where to Learn More

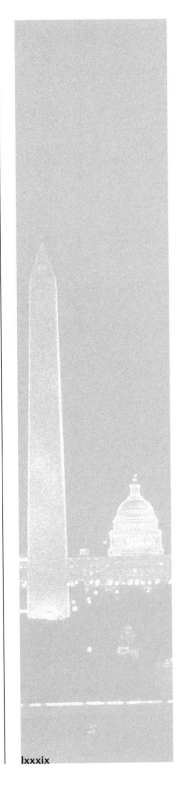

The following list of resources focuses on material appropriate for middle school or high school students. Please note that the web site addresses were verified prior to publication, but are subject to change.

Books

Bailey, Thomas A. *The Pugnacious Presidents: White House Warriors on Parade.* New York: Free Press, 1980.

Barber, James David. *The Presidential Character: Predicting Performance in the White House.* 4th ed. Englewood Cliffs, NJ: Prentice-Hall, 1992.

Barzman, Sol. *Madmen and Geniuses: The Vice-Presidents of the United States.* Chicago: Follett, 1974.

Berube, Maurice. *American Presidents and Education.* Westport, CT: Greenwood Press, 1991.

Boller, Paul F., Jr. *Presidential Anecdotes.* Rev. ed. New York: Oxford, 1996.

Boller, Paul F., Jr. *Presidential Campaigns.* Rev. ed. New York: Oxford, 1996.

Boller, Paul F. Jr. *Presidential Wives: An Anecdotal History.* Rev. ed. New York: Oxford, 1998.

Brace, Paul, Christine B. Harrington, and Gary King, eds. *The Presidency in American Politics.* New York: New York University Press, 1989.

Brallier, Jess, and Sally Chabert. *Presidential Wit and Wisdom.* New York: Penguin, 1996.

Brinkley, Alan, and Davis Dyer, eds. *The Reader's Companion to the American Presidency*. New York: Houghton Mifflin, 2000.

Brogan, Hugh, and Charles Mosley. *American Presidential Families*. New York: Macmillan Publishing Co., 1993.

Bumann, Joan. *Our American Presidents: From Washington through Clinton*. St. Petersburg, FL: Willowisp Press, 1993.

Campbell, Colin. *The U.S. Presidency in Crisis: A Comparative Perspective*. New York: Oxford University Press, 1998.

Clotworthy, William G. *Presidential Sites*. Blacksburg, VA: McDonald & Woodward, 1998.

Cook, Carolyn. *Imagine You Are the . . . President*. Edina, MN: Imaginarium, 1999.

Cooke, Donald Ewin. *Atlas of the Presidents*. Maplewood, NJ: Hammond, 1985.

Cronin, Thomas, ed. *Inventing the American Presidency*. Lawrence: University of Kansas Press, 1989.

Cunliffe, Marcus. *American Presidents and the Presidency*. New York: Houghton Mifflin, 1986.

Dallek, Robert. *Hail to the Chief: The Making and Unmaking of American Presidents*. New York: Hyperion, 1996.

Davis, James W. *The American Presidency*. 2nd ed. Westport, CT: Praeger, 1995.

DeGregorio, William. *The Complete Book of U.S. Presidents*. 4th ed. New York: Barricade Books, 1993.

Fields, Wayne. *Union of Words: A History of Presidential Eloquence*. New York: The Free Press, 1996.

Fisher, Louis. *Presidential War Power*. Lawrence: University of Kansas Press, 1995.

Frank, Sid, and Arden Davis Melick. *Presidents: Tidbits and Trivia*. Maplewood, NJ: Hammond, 1986.

Frost, Elizabeth, ed. *The Bully Pulpit: Quotations from America's Presidents*. New York: Facts On File, 1988.

Genovese, Michael. *The Power of the American Presidency, 1789–2000*. New York: Oxford, 2001.

Gerhardt, Michael J. *The Federal Impeachment Process: A Constitutional and Historical Analysis*. 2nd ed. Chicago: University of Chicago Press, 2000.

Goehlert, Robert U., and Fenton S. Martin. *The Presidency: A Research Guide*. Santa Barbara, CA: ABC-Clio Information Services, 1985.

Havel, James T. *U.S. Presidential Candidates and the Elections: A Biographical and Historical Guide*. New York: Macmillan Library Reference USA, 1996.

Henry, Christopher E. *The Electoral College*. New York: Franklin Watts, 1996.

Henry, Christopher E. *Presidential Elections*. New York: Franklin Watts, 1996.

Hess, Stephen. *Presidents and the Presidency: Essays*. Washington, DC: The Brookings Institution, 1996.

Israel, Fred L., ed. *The Presidents*. Danbury, CT: Grolier Educational, 1996.

Jackson, John S. III, and William Crotty. *The Politics of Presidential Selection*. 2nd ed. New York: Longman, 2001.

Jamieson, Kathleen Hall. *Packaging the Presidency: A History and Criticism of Presidential Campaign Advertising*. 3rd ed. New York: Oxford, 1996.

Kessler, Paula N., and Justin Segal. *The Presidents Almanac*. Rev. ed. Los Angeles: Lowell House Juvenile, 1998.

Kruh, David, and Louis Kruh. *Presidential Landmarks*. New York: Hippocrene Books, 1992.

Kunhardt, Philip B. Jr., Philip B. Kunhardt III, and Peter W. Kunhardt. *The American President*. New York: Penguin, 1999.

Laird, Archibald. *The Near Great—Chronicle of the Vice Presidents*. North Quincy, MA: Christopher Publishing House, 1980.

Mayer, William G., ed. *In Pursuit of the White House: How We Choose Our Presidential Nominees*. Chatham, NJ: Chatham House, 1996.

Murray, Robert K., and Tim H. Blessing. *Greatness in the White House: Rating the Presidents*. 2nd ed. University Park: Pennsylvania State University Press, 1994.

Neustadt, Richard E. *Presidential Power and the Modern Presidents: The Politics of Leadership from Roosevelt to Reagan*. New York: The Free Press, 1990.

Patrick, Diane. *The Executive Branch*. New York: Franklin Watts, 1994.

Presidents of the United States. A World Book Encyclopedia. Chicago: Field Enterprises Educational Corp., 1973.

Riccards, Michael, and James MacGregor Burns. *The Ferocious Engine of Democracy: A History of the American Presidency. Vol I: From the Origins through William McKinley. Vol. II: Theodore Roosevelt through George Bush*. Lanham, MD: Madison Books, 1996.

Robb, Don. *Hail to the Chief: The American Presidency*. Watertown, MA: Charlesbridge, 2000.

Rose, Gary L. *The American Presidency Under Siege*. Albany: State University of New York Press, 1997.

Sanders, Mark C. *The Presidency*. Austin, TX: Steadwell Books, 2000.

Shenkman, Richard. *Presidential Ambition: How the Presidents Gained Power, Kept Power, and Got Things Done*. New York: HarperCollins, 1999.

Shogan, Robert. *The Double-Edged Sword: How Character Makes and Ruins Presidents, from Washington to Clinton*. Boulder, CO: Westview Press, 2000.

Sisung, Kelle S., ed. *Presidential Administration Profiles for Students*. Detroit: Gale Group, 2000.

Smith, Nancy Kegan, and Mary C. Ryan, eds. *Modern First Ladies: Their Documentary Legacy*. Washington, DC: National Archives and Records Administration, 1989.

Stier, Catherine. *If I Were President*. Morton Grove, IL: Albert Whitman, 1999.

Suid, Murray I. *How to Be President of the U.S.A*. Palo Alto, CA: Monday Morning Books, 1992.

Truman, Margaret. *First Ladies: An Intimate Group Portrait of White House Wives*. New York: Ballantine, 1995.

Vidal, Gore. *The American Presidency*. Monroe, ME: Odonian Press, 1998.

Wheeless, Carl. *Landmarks of American Presidents*. Detroit: Gale, 1995.

Video

The American President. Written, produced, and directed by Philip B. Kunhardt Jr., Philip B. Kunhardt III, and Peter W. Kunhardt. Co-production of Kunhardt Productions and Thirteen/WNET in New York. 10 programs.

Web Sites

The American Presidency: Selected Resources, An Informal Reference Guide (Web site). [Online] http://www.interlink-cafe.com/uspresidents/ (accessed on December 11, 2000).

C-Span. *American Presidents: Life Portraits.* [Online] http://www.american presidents.org/ (accessed on December 11, 2000).

Grolier, Inc. *Grolier Presents: The American Presidency.* [Online] http://gi.grolier.com/presidents/ea/prescont.html (accessed on December 11, 2000).

Internet Public Library. *POTUS: Presidents of the United States.* [Online] http://www.ipl.org/ref/POTUS/index.html (accessed on December 11, 2000).

Public Broadcasting System. "The American President." *The American Experience.* [Online] http://www.pbs.org/wgbh/amex/presidents/nf/intro/intro.html (accessed on December 11, 2000).

University of Oklahoma Law Center. *A Chronology of US Historical Documents.* [Online] http://www.law.ou.edu/hist/ (accessed on December 11, 2000).

White House. *Welcome to the White House.* [Online] http://www.whitehouse.gov/ (accessed on December 11, 2000).

The White House Historical Association. [Online] http://www.whitehousehistory.org/whha/default.asp (accessed on December 11, 2000).

Yale Law School. *The Avalon at the Yale Law School: Documents in Law, History and Diplomacy.* [Online] http://www.yale.edu/lawweb/avalon/avalon.htm (accessed on December 11, 2000).

Index

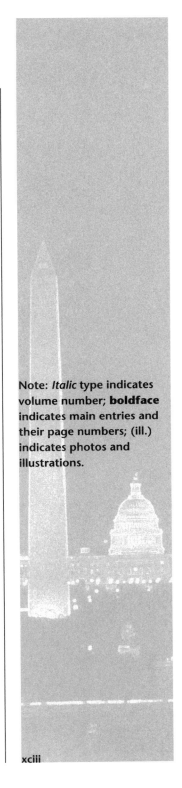

retirement, *1:* 71–72
"Thoughts on Government," *1:* 59, **81–89**
Adams, John II, *1:* 243
Adams, John Quincy, *1:* 67, 211 (ill.), **217–37,** 219 (ill.); *5:* 1279, 1618
abolitionist, *1:* 234–35, 246
Amistad case, *1:* 235, **245–53**
ancestry, *1:* 221
Calhoun, John C., *1:* 270
Clay, Henry, *1:* 226–27, 266
contested election, *1:* 226–27
daily routine, *1:* 232
death, *1:* 235
diplomatic career, *1:* 220, 224–25, 241–42
early years, *1:* 221–23
election of 1820, *1:* 193
election of 1824, *1:* 227, 266, 298; *2:* 399; *5:* 1612
election of 1828, *1:* 232, 266, 267, 298
European travels, *1:* 223–25
Harrison, William Henry, *2:* 334–35
Jackson, Andrew, *1:* 219–20, 226–27, 236, 265; *2:* 519
legal and writing careers, *1:* 224
marriage and family, *1:* 224, 225–26, 233, 240
Monroe years, *1:* 203
"Old Man Eloquent," *1:* 233–35
presidency, *1:* 227–32
Van Buren, Martin, *1:* 246, 297
Adams, Louisa, *1:* **239–44,** 239 (ill.), 243 (ill.)
British heritage, *1:* 239, 240
diplomatic travel, *1:* 241–44
family tragedies, *1:* 243
London years, *1:* 240–41
marriage and family, *1:* 240–41, 242
writer, *1:* 240, 244
Adams, Nabby, *1:* 80
Adams, Samuel Hopkins, *3:* 924
Address to Congress on the Crisis in Kuwait (George Bush), *5:* **1537–44**
Adenauer, Konrad, *4:* 994 (ill.)
Advisory Committee on Government Organization, *5:* 1412
AEF. *See* American Expeditionary Force (AEF) (World War I)
Aerial surveillance, of Soviet Union by United States, *4:* 1245, 1250–51
Afghanistan, *5:* 1467
African Americans. *See also* Civil rights

Brown v. Board of Education of Topeka, *2:* 561; *4:* 1249; *5:* 1292
Carter, Jimmy, *5:* 1444
cavalry unit, *4:* 970
Jim Crow laws, *3:* 871
Kennedy, John F., *5:* 1290–91
Missouri Compromise, *1:* 199
Populists, *3:* 823
Reconstruction, *3:* 655–56
Roosevelt, Eleanor, *4:* 1164
segregation, *2:* 596; *4:* 1045
World War II, *4:* 1232
African Game Trails (Theodore Roosevelt), *3:* 899
Africans, slave trade cases, *1:* 246
"Age of Jackson," *1:* 257; *2:* 603
The Age of Reason (Paine), *1:* 191
Agnew, Spiro T., *5:* 1380, 1406, 1408
election of 1968, *5:* 1366
election of 1972, *5:* 1366
Agrarian movement. *See* Populism
Agricultural Adjustment Administration (AAA), *4:* 1172
Agricultural Marketing Act, *4:* 1097–98
Agriculture, Populism, *3:* 823
Air Commerce Act, *4:* 1067
Air Force One, *4:* 1251
Air strikes, North Vietnam, *5:* 1334
Air traffic controllers strike, *5:* 1481
Airplane, *3:* 901
Alabama, *2:* 562
King, Martin Luther, Jr., *5:* 1293
Wallace, George, *5:* 1291
Alabama, *2:* 611; *3:* 654–55, 656
Alaska, *2:* 611, 613
Gold Rush, *3:* 849, 860
Harding tour, *4:* 1030
Albanians, in Serbia, *5:* 1564
Albany Regency, *1:* 297, 312
Albright, Madeleine, *5:* 1561, 1562–63, 1563 (ill.), 1564, 1565
Alcoa (Aluminum Company of America), *4:* 1022
Alcoholic beverages. *See also* Prohibition; Temperance movement
Coolidge, Calvin, *4:* 1059–60
Grant, Ulysses S., *3:* 643
Harding, Warren G., *4:* 1020
Harrison, William Henry, *2:* 335, 337
Johnson, Andrew, *2:* 607
Pierce, Franklin, *2:* 489–90
Alden, John and Priscilla, *1:* 221
Algiers Treaty, *1:* 26, 29
Alien Acts, *1:* 67, 68–69, 108
Alien and Sedition Acts, *1:* 66–70, 68–69, 108–9, 154
Alien Act, *1:* 68–69

Alien Enemies Act, *1:* 67, 68
Naturalization Act, *1:* 67
Sedition Act, *1:* 69
Alien Enemies Act, *1:* 67, 68
Alliance for Progress, *5:* 1284
Allied Powers (World War I), *4:* 973–76, 1004, 1005, 1010, 1046
Allied Powers (World War II), *4:* 1147, 1150, 1181, 1221, 1235, 1241, 1242
Alternative energy sources, *5:* 1448
Aluminum Company of America (Alcoa), *4:* 1022
Alzheimer's disease, *5:* 1489, 1493–94, 1499
Amendment(s). *See* Bill of Rights; Constitution; specific amendment, e.g., Twelfth Amendment
"America First," *4:* 1025
American Ballet Theater, *5:* 1329–30
American Colonization Society, *1:* 198
American Expeditionary Force (AEF) (World War I), *4:* 971, 1002–3
American imperialism. *See* Imperialism
American Indians. *See* Native Americans
American Individualism (Hoover), *4:* 1116
American (Know Nothing) Party, *2:* 469, 484
An American Life (Reagan), *5:* 1489
American military, World War I, *4:* 971, 976, 1002–3
"American Prince of Wales." *See* Adams, John Quincy
American Relief Administration (ARA), *4:* 1092, 1093 (ill.), 1111
American Revolution, *1:* 10–16, 11 (ill.), 82
Adams, John and Abigail, *1:* 76
Adams, John Quincy, *1:* 223
Anti-British sentiment, *1:* 9
Declaration of Independence, *1:* 125–34
Franklin, Benjamin, *1:* 17
Jackson, Andrew, *1:* 260–61
Jefferson, Thomas, *1:* 98–99, 101–2
Lafayette, Marquis de, *1:* 33 (ill.), 186–87, 187 (ill.)
Marshall, John, *1:* 64–65
Monroe, James, *1:* 182–83, 205–6
Paine, Thomas, *1:* 190
privateers, *1:* 205
Randolph, Edmund Jennings, *2:* 362

Washington, George, *1:* 10–16, 11 (ill.)
Washington, Martha, *1:* 32–34
"American System" (Clay), *1:* 228, 230–31
Americans, Reagan's view, *5:* 1502
Americans with Disabilities Act, *5:* 1521
Americas, Monroe Doctrine, *1:* 200
Ames, Oakes, *3:* 657
Amistad case, *1:* 234, 245–46
    closing argument (John Quincy Adams), *1:* **245–53**
Anderson, John, election of 1980, *5:* 1477, 1478
Anderson, Marian, *4:* 994 (ill.), 1164
Andropov, Yuri, *5:* 1484
Angola, *5:* 1415
Annexation, Texas, *1:* 308
Annual Address to Congress. *See also* State of the Union Address
Arthur, Chester A., *3:* **769–74**
Buchanan, James, *2:* **539–48**
Fillmore, Millard, *2:* **479–84**
Grant, Ulysses S., *3:* 659
Johnson, Andrew, *2:* **629–36**
Roosevelt, Theodore, *3:* **909–16**
Taft, William Howard, *3:* **949–56**
Taylor, Zachary, *2:* **451–56**
Antelope case, *1:* 246
Anthony, Susan B., *3:* 785, 786–87, 787 (ill.)
Anti-American sentiment, Iran, *5:* 1450–51
Anti-Communism, *4:* 1143
Antidrug campaign, *5:* 1493
Antietam, Battle of, *2:* 568, 582
Anti-Federalist(s), *1:* 45, 60, 135–36, 141, 153. *See also* Democratic-Republican Party; Federalist(s) vs. Anti-Federalist(s)
Anti-Imperialism League, *3:* 791
Anti-Jacksonians, *1:* 51; *2:* 364
Anti-Masonic Party, *1:* 300; *2:* 461–62, 608
Antislavery. *See* Abolition
Antitrust laws, *3:* 915
Anti-union legislation, *4:* 1203
Antiwar (Vietnam War) protests, *5:* 1334, 1335, 1337, 1366, 1391–92, 1396–97
Reagan, Ronald, *5:* 1475–76
"Silent Majority" Speech (Nixon), *5:* **1391–97**
Apaches, *4:* 970
Apartheid, *5:* 1522
Appleton, Jane Means. *See* Pierce, Jane
Appleton, Jesse, *2:* 505

Stimson, Henry L., *4:* 1101
Truman, Harry S., *4:* 1196, 1197–99, 1212, 1221
Atomic Energy Commission, *4:* 1226
"Atoms for Peace" campaign, *4:* 1245; *5:* 1412
Attlee, Clement, *4:* 1196, 1221
Attorney general. *See also* administration of specific president
    first, *1:* 20
Atzerodt, George, *2:* 635
Audiotapes, Watergate, *5:* 1360, 1376, 1379 (ill.), 1379–80, 1407, 1432
Austria, *1:* 194–95
    World War I, *4:* 1025
    World War II, *4:* 1147
Austria-Hungary, World War I, *4:* 972–73
Aviation
    commercial, *4:* 1067
    Lindbergh, Charles A., *4:* 1064–65
    Truman-Austin bill, *4:* 1194
Axis Powers, World War II, *4:* 1147
Axson, Ellen Louise. *See* Wilson, Ellen

B

Babbitt, Bruce, *5:* 1487
Babcock, Orville E., *3:* 657, 658
Bacall, Lauren, *4:* 1203 (ill.)
Bache, Benjamin Franklin, *1:* 67
Bad Axe River Massacre, *2:* 435
Baker, Howard H., *5:* 1376–77
Baker, Newton D., *3:* 901
Baldwin, Roger S., *1:* 234
Ballots, election of 2000, *5:* 1614, 1615
The Ballpark in Arlington (Texas Rangers), *5:* 1602, 1623
Bancroft, George, *2:* 590
Bank notes, Civil War, *3:* 695. *See also* Greenbacks
Bank of the United States
    First, *1:* 21, 25, 141
    Second, *1:* 269, 273, 276, 300; *2:* 367, 400
Bank of the United States, Veto Message Regarding (Jackson), *1:* **285–90**
"Bank War," *1:* 286, 289
Banking, New Deal legislation, *4:* 1138–39, 1175–80
Banking and Currency committee, *3:* 717
Banking houses, *3:* 793

Banning Segregation in the Military: Executive Order (Truman), *4:* **1229–32**
Baptists (Southern Convention), *5:* 1453–54
Barbara Bush: A Memoir (Barbara Bush), *5:* 1533
Barbara Bush Foundation for Family Literacy, *5:* 1531
Barbary Coast pirates, *1:* 26, 29, 111, 154
Barkley, Alben W., election of 1948, *4:* 1205
Barnett, Ross R., *5:* 1291
Baseball, *3:* 935
Battle(s)
    Battle of Antietam, *2:* 568, 582
    Battle of Bloody Angle, *3:* 645
    Battle of Brandywine Creek, *1:* 13, 14
    Battle of Buena Vista, *2:* 433 (ill.), 436, 564
    Battle of Bull Run, First (Battle of First Manassas), *2:* 566
    Battle of Bull Run, Second (Battle of Second Manassas), *2:* 566
    Battle of Bunker Hill, *1:* 223
    Battle of Chancellorsville, *3:* 649
    Battle of Chattanooga, *2:* 589; *3:* 645
    Battle of Chickamauga, *3:* 717
    Battle of Cold Harbor, *3:* 645
    Battle of Concord, *1:* 10, 12
    Battle of Contreras, *2:* 491
    Battle of Fallen Timbers, *2:* 328, 332
    Battle of First Manassas), *2:* 566
    Battle of Five Forks, *3:* 650
    Battle of Fredericksburg, *3:* 649
    Battle of Gettysburg, *2:* 565, 568, 588, 589; *3:* 650
    Battle of Little Big Horn, *3:* 770
    Battle of Monterrey, *2:* 433–34, 436
    Battle of New Orleans, *1:* 263–64, 265 (ill.)
    Battle of Palo Alto, *2:* 433
    Battle of San Jacinto, *2:* 385
    Battle of Saratoga, *1:* 13
    Battle of Second Manassas (Second Battle of Bull Run), *2:* 566
    Battle of Shiloh, *2:* 566; *3:* 644, 647, 650
    Battle of South Mountain, *3:* 686
    Battle of Thames, *1:* 157; *2:* 331, 333
    Battle of the Bulge, *4:* 1241
    Battle of Tippecanoe, *1:* 306; *2:* 330 (ill.), 330–31
    Battle of Trenton, *1:* 11, 13
    Battle of Veracruz, *4:* 969

Congregationalism, *1:* 56
Congress, *2:* 621, 629. *See also* Annual Address; Confederate Congress; Continental Congress; House of Representatives; Senate; State of the Union Address
    Articles of Confederation, *1:* 38
    Budget Office, *5:* 1411
    declarations of war, *4:* 997
    declares war on Axis powers, *4:* 1150–51
    declares war on Japan, *4:* 1181–82, 1184
    election of 1876, *3:* 693
    Emergency Banking Act, *4:* 1178
    Fourteen Points (Wilson), *4:* **1005–11**
    gag rule on slavery, *1:* 234–35
    Great Depression, *4:* 1103
    Hayes, Rutherford B., *3:* 696, 719
    impeachment of Andrew Johnson, *2:* 616–17
    impeachment of Bill Clinton, *5:* 1548
    Jackson censure, *1:* 273, 300–301; *2:* 364
    legislation freeing slaves, *2:* 547
    Message Opposing the Annexation of Hawaii (Cleveland), *3:* **803–8**
    Missouri Compromise, *1:* 198
    Native Americans, *3:* 753–54
    New Deal legislation (The Hundred Days), *4:* 1137, 1138–41, 1172
    president's relationship, *1:* 298; *2:* 354
    Reconstruction, *2:* 610, 629–30
    relationship to president (1970s), *5:* 1419
    riders (legislative), *3:* 736
    Speech to a Special Session (Harding), *4:* **1013–32**
    Tariff of Abominations, *1:* 232
    War Message to Congress (Wilson), *4:* **997–1004**
    Watergate babies, *5:* 1411–12
    Watergate scandal, *5:* 1406–7
Congressional Government (Wilson), *4:* 959, 968
Conkling, Roscoe, *3:* 721, 722, 751, 752, 752 (ill.), 753, 758, 781–82
Connally, John C., *5:* 1291
Connecticut Plan, *1:* 150
Conner, Fox, *4:* 1239
Conscription, *1:* 297
Conservation
    Carter, Jimmy (fuel), *5:* 1445–48
    Johnson, Lady Bird, *5:* 1346

Roosevelt, Theodore, *3:* 896–99
Conservatives, Republican, *5:* 1419, 1474, 1476–77, 1483, 1507, 1511, 1521, 1525
Constitution, *1:* 18, 43, 88, 106
    Bill of Rights, *1:* 106, 151, 152, 169–71
    central ideas, *1:* 82
    commander in chief, *4:* 997
    Congress and Andrew Johnson, *2:* 630–31
    constructionists, *1:* 136
    Electoral College, *5:* 1610, 1612–13
    federal government, *1:* 135–37
    Fifteenth Amendment, *3:* 652, 655–56, 687
    Fourteenth Amendment, *2:* 609, 615; *3:* 787
    Great Depression, *4:* 1027
    "high crimes and misdemeanors," *5:* 1572
    Lee, Richard Henry, *1:* 100
    Madison, James, *1:* 170–71
    Marshall, John, *1:* 65
    Nineteenth Amendment, *3:* 787
    presidential succession, *2:* 338, 357–58
    ratification, *1:* 18, 150–54, 169–70, 178, 188
    removal of a chief executive, *5:* 1383
    "Revolution Against" speech (Garfield), *3:* **735–43**
    slavery issue, *2:* 452, 510, 518, 540–41
    Thirteenth Amendment, *2:* 568, 570, 596, 611, 612; *3:* 677
    treaties, *2:* 386
    Twelfth Amendment, *1:* 73, 115
    Twentieth Amendment, *4:* 1145
    Twenty-third Amendment, *5:* 1613
    vs. Articles of Confederation, *1:* 37, 43
Constitutional Conventions, *1:* 18, 43, 149, 151; *2:* 362
    Madison's role, *1:* 169–71, 177–78
    Washington's role, *1:* 52, 169
Constitutionality
    appropriations riders, *3:* 736
    Constitutionality of a National Bank (Jefferson), *1:* **135–42**
    Emancipation Proclamation, *2:* 583
    New Deal legislation, *4:* 1139, 1141, 1144
Constitutionality of a National Bank (Jefferson), *1:* **135–42**
Constructionists, *1:* 107, 112, 136, 137; *2:* 357
Continental Army, *1:* 11, 12

Curtis, Charles
   election of 1928, *4:* 1096
   election of 1932, *4:* 1134
"Custer's Last Stand," *3:* 770
Custis, Daniel Park, *1:* 32
Custis, Martha Dandridge. *See*
   Washington, Martha
Custis, Mary Anne Randolph, *3:*
   648
Czechoslovakia, democratization, *5:*
   1482, 1522
Czolgosz, Leon F., *3:* 859, 859 (ill.),
   860 (ill.), 866

D

Dade County, Florida, election of
   2000, *5:* 1610, 1614
Dakota Territory, *3:* 884
Dallas, George M., *2:* 402 (ill.)
   election of 1844, *2:* 401
Dana, Francis, *1:* 223
Darrow, Clarence, *3:* 857
Darwin, Charles, *3:* 892
"A date which will live in infamy"
   speech (Franklin D. Roosevelt),
   4: 1150, 1181, 1182
Daugherty, Harry M., *4:* 1019, 1020,
   1021, 1024, 1025 (ill.),
   1025–26
Daughters of the American Revolu-
   tion, *3:* 827, 829; *4:* 1164
Davie, William Richardson, *1:* 260
Davies, Dale, *3:* 693
Davis, Henry G., *3:* 894–95
   election of 1904, *3:* 895
Davis, Jefferson, *2:* 448, 495, 527,
   563, 564–65, 565 (ill.); *3:* 649
Davis, John W., election of 1924, *4:*
   1056, 1060
Davis, Manvel H., *4:* 1194
Davis, Nancy. *See* Reagan, Nancy
Dawes Act (General Allotment Act),
   3: 773–74, 784
Dawes, Charles G., election of 1924,
   4: 1060
Dawes Plan (German reparations),
   4: 1027, 1063
Dayton, William L., election of
   1856, *2:* 523
D-Day, World War II, *4:* 1153, 1241
De Priest, Mrs. Oscar, *4:* 1113
De Reus Metallica (Hoover, Herbert
   and Lou), *4:* 1111
De Wolfe, Henry, *4:* 1034
Deaf, education, *3:* 724–25
Dean, John, *5:* 1376, 1377 (ill.),
   1378
Death of presidents

by assassination. *See* Assassina-
   tions
on July 4, *1:* 71–72, 119, 201
Debt, national, *1:* 21–22
*Decision—The Conflicts of Harry S.
   Truman* (TV series), *4:* 1211
Declaration of Independence, *1:*
   81, 88, 98–99, **125–34**
central ideas, *1:* 82
charges against George III, *1:*
   127–28
Committee of Five, *1:* 126, 133
   (ill.)
introduction, *1:* 127
Jefferson, Thomas, *1:* 125–34
preamble, *1:* 127
signers, *1:* 133–34
Declaration of Independence Com-
   mittee, *1:* 13, 133 (ill.)
Declaration of the Rights of Man
   and the Citizen (initiative of
   Lafayette), *1:* 186
*Defence of the Constitutions of Gov-
   ernment of the United States of
   America* (John Adams), *1:* 59
"The Defense of Fort McHenry"
   (Key), *1:* 159
"Defense of the Constitutionality of
   the Bank" (Hamilton), *1:* 140
Defense spending
   post–World War II, *4:* 1264, 1270
   Reagan era, *5:* 1481–82
   World War II, *4:* 1147
Deism, *1:* 191
Delahanty, Thomas, *5:* 1479 (ill.)
Delaware, *1:* 169
Delaware River, *1:* 10, 11
Democratic Advisory Council, *4:*
   1247
Democratic Leadership Council, *5:*
   1554
Democratic National Convention
   (1968), *5:* 1335, 1337, 1367
Democratic National Headquarters
   committee offices (Watergate
   burglary), *5:* 1375, 1405, 1516
Democratic Party, *1:* 272; *2:* 489; *3:*
   661–62
Bryan, William Jennings, *3:*
   856–57
Hayes, Rutherford B., *3:* 696, 719
post–Civil War, *3:* 735
Van Buren, Martin, *1:* 300, 309
Democratic-Republican Party, *1:* 46,
   51, 67, 71, 107, 272, 296, 297.
   See also Anti-Federalist(s)
Adams, John Quincy, *1:* 225
election of 1800, *1:* 109–10
Jacksonian Democrats, *1:* 272,
   297–98, 300–301, 309; *2:* 399,
   519, 603–4

adoptive family, *1:* 281, 282
death, *1:* 266–67
frontier girl, *1:* 280–81
slandered, *1:* 279–80
Jacksonian Democrats, *1:* 272,
297–98, 300–301, 309; *2:* 399,
519, 603–4
Japan
attack on Pearl Harbor, *4:* 1150,
1185
cherry trees for Nellie Taft, *3:* 947
MacArthur, Douglas, *4:* 1209
Manchurian invasion, *4:* 1100,
1102, 1147, 1181
Perry opens trade, *2:* 468, 473,
499, 501
Russo-Japanese War, *3:* 895–96,
903; *4:* 970
World War I, *4:* 978
World War II, *4:* 1150, 1152,
1153, 1184, 1185, 1197–98,
1199, 1199 (ill.), 1221–22,
1226–27
Japanese internment camps (World
War II), *4:* 1101
Jaworski, Leon, *5:* 1379
Jay, John, *1:* 20, 23, 27, 27 (ill.), 152
election of 1789, *1:* 19
election of 1800, *1:* 109
Jay's Treaty, *1:* 26, 27, 28
Jay Cooke & Company, *3:* 658–59
Jay's Treaty, *1:* 26, 27, 28, 224, 240
"The Jazz Age," *4:* 1049
The Jazz Singer, *4:* 1063
Jefferson, Martha, *1:* 97, 103, 104,
121–24, 122
courtship duet, *1:* 122
marriage and family, *1:* 123–24
Jefferson, Peter, *1:* 94
Jefferson, Thomas, *1:* 20, 22 (ill.),
71 (ill.), **91–120,** 93 (ill.), 133
(ill.); *5:* 1618
Adams, John, *1:* 108–9, 110, 119
Alien and Sedition Acts, *1:* 70
anti-Federalists, *1:* 60
Committee of Five, *1:* 126
constructionist, *1:* 136, 137
death and epitaph, *1:* 119
Declaration of Independence, *1:*
98, 126–28, 147
early life, *1:* 94–95
election of 1796, *1:* 61; *5:* 1612
election of 1800, *1:* 109–10; *5:*
1612
election of 1804, *1:* 109
Hamilton, Alexander, *1:* 106–7
Hemings, Sally, *1:* 104–5
Madison, James, *1:* 109
marriage and family, *1:* 97, 103,
121–24
Monroe, James, *1:* 183

**Opinion on the Constitutional-
ity of a National Bank,** *1:*
135–42
presidency, *1:* 110–18
retirement, *1:* 118–19
Virginia's new government, *1:*
99–106
Washington, George, *1:* 107
writer and politician, *1:* 95–98,
123, 126
Jennings, Lizzie, *3:* 750
Jim Crow laws, *3:* 871; *4:* 1204
John F. Kennedy Center for the Performing Arts, *5:* 1313
Johns Hopkins University, *3:* 829
Johnson, Andrew, *2:* **599–621,** 601
(ill.), 614 (ill.), 618 (ill.)
administration, *2:* 610
early years, *2:* 602–3, 624
effectiveness as president, *2:* 602
election of 1864, *2:* 562, 606–7
**Final Annual Message to Con-
gress,** *2:* 619, **629–36**
foreign policy, *2:* 610–11
impeachment, *2:* 616–17; *3:* 639
marriage and family, *2:* 603, 624,
625
negative political rallies, *2:*
614–15
political career, *2:* 603–7, 624
presidency, *2:* 607–19, 625
succeeds Lincoln, *2:* 610, 635
Johnson, Eliza, *2:* **623–27,** 623 (ill.)
ill first lady, *2:* 625
marriage and family, *2:* 624
Johnson, Herschel V., election of
1860, *2:* 562
Johnson, Hiram W., election of
1912, *4:* 966
Johnson, Joshua, *1:* 224, 240
Johnson, Lady Bird, *5:* 1308 (ill.),
1323 (ill.), 1324 (ill.), **1341–47,**
1341 (ill.), 1345 (ill.)
campaign of 1964, *5:* 1344
Head Start, *5:* 1343–44
highway beautification project, *5:*
1344
marriage and family, *5:* 1342
"Mrs. Johnson at Work," *5:* 1346
Johnson, Louisa Catherine. *See*
Adams, Louisa
Johnson, Lyndon B., *5:* 1308 (ill.),
1315–40, 1317 (ill.), 1323 (ill.),
1325 (ill.), 1329 (ill.)
administration, *5:* 1327
civil rights, *5:* 1274, 1280,
1325–26, 1327
domestic program: The Great Society, *5:* 1326–30
early years, *5:* 1318–19
education policy, *5:* 1328

Meade, George, *2:* 569

Means, Abigail Kent, *2:* 507

Meat-packing industry, *3:* 895

Media coverage, *4:* 968. *See also*
 Journalism; Radio; Television;
 Yellow Journalism
   Clinton, Hillary Rodham, *5:*
 1583–85
   Ford, Gerald R., *5:* 1414, 1415
   news agencies call election 2000,
 5: 1608, 1609

Medicaid, *5:* 1328

Medicare, *5:* 1328, 1561

Meiji, emperor of Japan, *3:* 660, 668

Mellon, Andrew W., *4:* 1022–23,
 1023 (ill.), 1024, 1098

Mellon National Bank, *4:* 1022,
 1023

Memoirs, Year of Decisions (Truman),
 4: 1211

Mencken, H. L., on Coolidge,
 Calvin, *4:* 1068–69

Mercenaries, *1:* 10

Merchant marine, *4:* 1061

Meredith, James, *5:* 1291

Merit system, *3:* 784

Merry Mount (Adams), *1:* 223

**Message to Congress Opposing
 the Annexation of Hawaii**
 (Cleveland), *3:* 803–8

**Message to the Senate Supporting
 the Annexation of Hawaii**
 (Benjamin Harrison), *3:*
 831–35

Metal detector, *3:* 722, 725

Methodist Woman's Home Missionary Society, *3:* 703

Mexican Americans, *5:* 1319, 1328

Mexican War, *1:* 229; *2:* 371, 391,
 406 (ill.), 406–10, 424, 520, 612
   Adams, John Quincy, *1:* 235
   Calhoun, John C., *1:* 271
   Frémont, John C., *2:* 408, 410
   Grant, Ulysses S., *2:* 425; *3:* 640
   Kearny, Stephen, *2:* 407, 408
   Lee, Robert E., *3:* 648
   Lincoln, Abraham, *2:* 425, 556
   Perry, Matthew C., *2:* 498
   Pierce, Franklin, *2:* 490–93
   Polk, James K., *2:* 406, 410
   Scott, Winfield, *1:* 305; *2:* 407
   Stockton, Robert, *2:* 407
   Taylor, Zachary, *2:* 425, 432–36
   Van Buren, Martin, *2:* 425

Mexico
   Clinton, Bill, *5:* 1565
   Grant, Ulysses S., *3:* 660
   leased oil lands seized, *4:* 1061
   North American Free Trade
 Agreement (NAFTA), *5:* 1525,
 1560

Pershing, John J. "Black Jack," *4:*
 971

Polk, James K., *2:* 404

Revolution of 1920, *3:* 937

Rockefeller, Nelson, *5:* 1412

Wilson, Woodrow, *4:* 969–72

Zimmerman note, *4:* 1006

Miami tribe, *2:* 332

Michigan
   Ford, Gerald, *5:* 1403–4
   Michigan Territory, *2:* 440

Michner, H. T., *3:* 818

Middle class, *4:* 1057

Middle East, *5:* 1370, 1371, 1525

Midnight appointments, *1:* 71, 73

Military, "Don't ask, don't tell" policy, *5:* 1558

Military draft, World War II, *4:* 1152

Military leaders, as presidential candidates, *2:* 468 (ill.)

Military spending. *See* Defense
 spending

Militia
   Massachusetts, *1:* 10
   Tennessee, *1:* 262
   Virginia (American Revolution),
 1: 6

Militia Act of 1796, *2:* 563

Miller, William E., election of 1964,
 5: 1326

Millie's Book (Barbara Bush), *5:* 1533

Milligan, Lambdin, *3:* 816

Milosevic, Slobodan, *5:* 1564

Milton, John, *1:* 88

Minimum wage, failed New Deal
 legislation, *4:* 1141

Minnesota, free state, *2:* 547

Minutemen (Massachusetts militia),
 1: 10, 12

"Misdemeanors," *5:* 1572

"Missile gap," *4:* 1248, 1250–51

Missile reduction (Bush-Gorbachev,
 1991), *5:* 1522, 1523

Mississippi, *2:* 562
   Davis, Jefferson, *2:* 564
   Meredith, James, *5:* 1291

Mississippi River, *1:* 113–14
   flood of 1927, *4:* 1060, 1093–96

Mississippi River Commission, *3:*
 817–18

Missouri
   remains in Union, *2:* 563
   statehood debate, *1:* 228

Missouri
   Japanese surrender, *4:* 1199 (ill.)
   Truman, Harry S., *4:* 1191, 1194

Missouri Compromise of 1820, *1:*
 197, 198–99, 202–3; *2:* 411,
 451, 524, 557

Missouri River, *1:* 112

Mitchell, John, *5:* 1378, 1380

Nasser, Gamal Abdel, *5:* 1446, 1447
Nast, Thomas, *3:* 690
National Aeronautics and Space
  Agency (NASA), *4:* 1250; *5:*
  1290, 1322
National American Women Suffrage
  Association, *3:* 787
National Association for the Ad-
  vancement of Colored People
  (NAACP), *4:* 1164; *5:* 1332
National bank. *See also* Bank of the
  United States
  charter, *1:* 289
  Federalists' view, *1:* 21, 24–25,
    135–37
  Federalists vs. anti-Federalists, *1:*
    105–6, 135–37
  First Bank of the United States, *1:*
    21, 25, 140–41, 285
  Second Bank of the United States,
    1: 141, 159, 269, 273, 276,
    285–86, 289, 300; *2:* 367
National Bank, Constitutionality
  of (Jefferson), *1:* **135–42**
National Civil Service Reform
  League, *3:* 760
National Consumers' League, *4:*
  1142
National Cultural Center, *5:*
  1312–13
National debt, *1:* 21–22
  Hayes, Rutherford B., *3:* 695
  Jackson, Andrew, *1:* 273–74
  Reagan, Ronald, *5:* 1481–82, 1490
National Defense Education Act, *4:*
  1250
National Democratic Party, *2:* 372
National Endowment for the Arts,
  5: 1329, 1425
National First Ladies' Library, *3:* 863
National Foundation for the Arts
  and Humanities, *5:* 1329
National Gallery of Art, *4:* 1023
National health insurance
  failed Clinton health plan, *5:*
    1559–60
  failed New Deal legislation, *4:*
    1141
National Industrial Recovery Act
  (NIRA), *4:* 1027, 1139, 1172
National Labor Relations Act, *4:*
  1141
National Labor Relations Board
  (NLRB), *4:* 1141
National League of Families of
  American Prisoners and Miss-
  ing in Action in Southeast
  Asia, *5:* 1496
National Liberation Front. *See* Viet-
  cong (Vietnamese commu-
  nists)

National monuments, *3:* 899
National park(s), *3:* 899
National Progressive Republican
  League, *3:* 937
National Public Radio, *5:* 1330
National Recovery Administration
  (NRA), *4:* 1139
National Republican Party, *1:* 272,
  300, 301
National Security Council, *5:* 1370,
  1417
National Socialist Party (Nazis), *4:*
  1102
  Lindbergh, Charles A., *4:* 1065
National Union Convention, *2:* 614
National Union Party, Republican
  Party, *1:* 62
National Women Suffrage Associa-
  tion, *3:* 787
National Youth Administration, *4:*
  1139, 1164; *5:* 1321
Native Americans. *See also* specific
  tribe or nation, e.g. Seminole
  nation
  Adams, John Quincy, *1:* 231–32
  Arthur, Chester A., *3:* 769–74
  Battle of Toledo, *1:* 26
  Black Hawk, *2:* 434–35
  Cass, Lewis, *2:* 440
  Cleveland, Grover, *3:* 784–85
  Coolidge, Calvin, *4:* 1066
  Curtis, Charles, *4:* 1096, 1097
  Grant, Ulysses S., *3:* 656
  Harrison, William Henry, *2:* 330
  Indian Appropriation Act, *3:* 656
  Jackson, Andrew, *1:* 258, 274–75
  Jefferson, Thomas, *3:* 769–70,
    771
  Lane, Harriet, *2:* 537
  Monroe, James, *1:* 199
  Polk, James K., *2:* 421
  Taylor, Zachary, *2:* 431–32
  Tecumseh and the Prophet, *2:*
    332–33, 434
  U.S. citizenship, *3:* 774
  Van Buren, Martin, *1:* 306
NATO. *See* North Atlantic Treaty Or-
  ganization (NATO)
Natural resources, *3:* 896–99
Naturalization Act, *1:* 67, 68, 108
Naval disarmament conferences, *4:*
  1027, 1046, 1100
Naval Lyceum, *2:* 498
Navy
  Arthur, Chester A., *3:* 761, 762
  Perry, Matthew C., *2:* 498–99
  Roosevelt, Theodore, *3:* 886, 887
Nazis (National Socialist Party), *4:*
  1065, 1102, 1195, 1223
Nessen, Ron, *5:* 1425
Neutrality

Washington, George, *1:* 23
World War I, *4:* 973, 998
Nevada, *2:* 568
New Deal, *4:* 984, 1135, 1138–41, 1151, 1154, 1167, 1172. *See also* e.g., Social Security Act; individual acts
Johnson, Lyndon B., *5:* 1321
Roosevelt, Eleanor, *4:* 1163–64
Roosevelt, Franklin D., *4:* 1167, 1172, 1179
New Democrats, *5:* 1554
New Freedom agenda, *4:* 959, 967, 974, 984
New Frontier program, *5:* 1273, 1290
New Hampshire, *1:* 169
Pierce, Franklin, *2:* 489, 490–91
New Jersey
Cleveland, Grover, *3:* 142
Wilson, Woodrow, *4:* 965
New Jersey Plan, *1:* 150
New Mexico, *2:* 503
free state, *2:* 439–40, 452, 466
New Nationalism, *4:* 967
New Orleans, Battle of, *1:* 263–64, 265 (ill.)
New Orleans, Louisiana, *1:* 111–12, 189, 263
"New South," *5:* 1515
"New world order," *5:* 1537, 1538, 1543
New York
Arthur, Chester A., *3:* 749, 762, 766
Cleveland, Grover, *3:* 779–82, 783
Conkling, Roscoe, *3:* 752–53
Fillmore, Millard, *2:* 460–62
Perkins, Frances, *4:* 1137, 1142–43
Roosevelt, Franklin D., *4:* 1131–33
Roosevelt, Theodore, *3:* 883, 884, 885, 888
Van Buren, Martin, *1:* 294, 297, 315
New York Customs House, *3:* 695, 752, 753
New York Evening Journal, 3: 854
New York Journal, 3: 850
New York Public Library, *3:* 691
New York State Industrial Commission, *4:* 1142
New York Stock Exchange, *4:* 1098
New York Times, 5: 1396
New York World, 3: 852–53
News conference, *4:* 968
News reporting, *3:* 923
Newsweek, 5: 1575
Ngo Dinh Diem, *5:* 1287

Nicaragua, *3:* 936–37, 950; *4:* 1061, 1100
Marxist revolution (1979), *5:* 1482
Nicolay, John, *2:* 590
Nineteenth Amendment, *3:* 787
Ninety-ninth Pursuit Squadron, *4:* 1232
Nixon, Julie, *5:* 1388 (ill.)
Nixon, Pat, *5:* 1301,**1385–90,** 1385 (ill.), 1388 (ill.)
marriage and family, *5:* 1387
political life, *5:* 1387–89
role as first lady, *5:* 1389
shy of public spotlight, *5:* 1385, 1388, 1389
Nixon, Richard, *5:* 1281 (ill.), **1357–84,** 1359 (ill.), 1369 (ill.), 1379 (ill.), 1388 (ill.)
administration, *5:* 1368
audiotapes, *5:* 1360, 1376, 1379 (ill.), 1379–80, 1432
Bush, George, *5:* 1516
"Checkers" speech, *5:* 1364
early years, *5:* 1360
economic policy, *5:* 1368–69
Eisenhower, Dwight D., *5:* 1364
election of 1952, *4:* 1243, 1244; *5:* 1364
election of 1956, *4:* 1244
election of 1960, *5:* 1281–82, 1365
election of 1968, *5:* 1366–67
election of 1972, *5:* 1366, 1372
Environmental Protection Agency, *5:* 1367
Ford, Gerald R., *5:* 1404, 1406, 1407
foreign relations, *5:* 1369–73
Hiss case, *5:* 1363
House Committee on Un-American Activities, *4:* 1206
impeachment process, *5:* 1377, 1380–81, 1428
Kennedy-Nixon debates, *5:* 1282
Khrushchev, Nikita, *5:* 1364, 1372
marriage and family, *5:* 1361, 1387
military service, *5:* 1361, 1387
Pardon of Richard Nixon (Ford), *5:* 1381, 1408–11, **1427–33**
People's Republic of China, *5:* 1273 (ill.), 1369, 1372–73
political career, *5:* 1361–67, 1387–89
presidency, *5:* 1364–81, 1389
public opinion, *5:* 1428
resignation and retirement, *5:* 1381–82, 1389, 1408
"Silent Majority" Speech, *5:* **1391–97**

O

Old Whitey (Taylor's horse), *2:* 436, 444 (ill.)
Olympic Games (1980), boycott, *5:* 1467
On the Wings of Eagles (Perot), *5:* 1526
Onassis, Aristotle Socrates, *5:* 1305
Onassis, Jacqueline Kennedy. *See* Kennedy, Jacqueline
O'Neill, Tip, *5:* 1488 (ill.)
"The only thing we have to fear is fear itself" (Franklin D. Roosevelt), *4:* 1135, 1168
"The Open Door" (Grace Coolidge), *4:* 1075
Open Door Policy, *3:* 851
Operation Desert Shield, *5:* 1523
Operation Desert Storm, *5:* 1523–23
Opinion on the Constitutionality of a National Bank (Jefferson), *1:* **135–42**
Opposing parties, presidency and vice presidency, *1:* 61
Orchestra Association (Cincinnati), *3:* 944
Oregon, free state, *2:* 547
Oregon Territory, *1:* 113, 197; *2:* 403, 404, 405, 424, 440, 451, 520
Oregon Trail, *2:* 408
Orlando, Vittorio, *4:* 1011
Osceola, *1:* 305
Osgood, Samuel, *1:* 20
Ostend Manifesto, *2:* 497, 521–22
Oswald, Lee Harvey, *5:* 1294, 1294 (ill.), 1324
Our American Cousin, *2:* 571, 578
Oval Office, *2:* 477

P

Pacific Rim nations, *5:* 1560
Pahlavi, Mohammad Reza, Shah of Iran, *5:* 1448–49, 1449 (ill.), 1450, 1467
Paine, Thomas, *1:* 188, 190–91, 191 (ill.)
Palestine and Palestinians, *5:* 1446, 1447
Palestinian-Israeli peace negotiations, *5:* 1563, 1568, 1578–79
Palm Beach County, Florida, election of 2000, *5:* 1609, 1616
Palo Alto, Battle of, *2:* 433
Panama, *3:* 903; *5:* 1445
Noriega, Manuel, *5:* 1522, 1607
Panama Canal, *2:* 442, 443; *3:* 696, 894, 931; *5:* 1466
Pan-American Conference, *3:* 757

Pan-American Exposition, McKinley assassination, *3:* 866–67
Panic of 1837, *1:* 276, 289, 293, 302
Panic of 1873, *3:* 658–59, 695
Panic of 1893, *3:* 790, 793
Paper money. *See* Currency; Gold standard
Pardon of Richard Nixon (Ford), *5:* 1381, 1408–11, **1427–33**
Paris Summit (1960), cancellation, *4:* 1251
Parker, Alton B., *3:* 894
election of 1904, *3:* 895
Parks, Rosa, *5:* 1292
Partisanship, *3:* 748; *5:* 1521, 1599
Party system, modern, *1:* 300
Patronage system, *3:* 663, 713, 721, 722, 748, 751, 781, 885
Patterson, Martha Johnson, *2:* 625–26, 626 (ill.)
Paul, François Joseph, *1:* 16
Payne-Aldrich Act, *3:* 932
Payne, Dolley. *See* Madison, Dolley
Peace agreements, *4:* 1046; *5:* 1282
Peace Corps, *4:* 1165; *5:* 1312, 1337
Peace movement (Vietnam War), *5:* 1334
"Peace through strength" (Reagan), *5:* 1482
Peanuts, *5:* 1441 (ill.)
Pearl Harbor, Oahu, Hawaii, *4:* 1150, 1151 (ill.), 1181, 1182, 1185, 1200, 1222, 1240
Pendleton Civil Service Reform Act, *3:* 723, 726, 760, 761–62, 784
Pendleton, George H., *3:* 760
election of 1864, *2:* 562
Pennsylvania
Buchanan, James, *2:* 518
Stevens, Thaddeus, *2:* 608
Pennsylvania Fiscal Agency, *3:* 657
Pennsylvania Gazette, *1:* 17
Pension (old-age), New Deal legislation, *4:* 1141
"Pentagon Papers," *5:* 1375–78, 1396–97
People's Party. *See* Populist Party (People's Party)
People's Republic of China, *4:* 1210; *5:* 1563. *See also* China
Bush, George, *5:* 1516
Carter, Jimmy, *5:* 1445
Clinton, Bill, *5:* 1558–59
Kissinger, Henry, *5:* 1371
Korean War, *4:* 1209
Nixon, Richard, *5:* 1273 (ill.), 1369, 1372–73
"Peoria speech" (Lincoln), *2:* 558
Perestroika ("restructuring"), *5:* 1482, 1484
"The Period of No Decision," *3:* 834

The Prophet (Tenskwatawa), *2:* 330, 331 (ill.), 332, 333
Prophet's Town, *2:* 332
Protective tariffs, *2:* 608. *See also* Tariff(s)
Protectorate, *3:* 832
Protest movement (Vietnam War, 1968), *5:* 1334, 1355, 1367, 1391–92, 1396–97, 1475–76
"Silent Majority" Speech (Nixon), *5:* **1391–97**
Prussia, *1:* 195
Adams, John Quincy, *1:* 224–25, 241
PT-109, *5:* 1277
Public Credit Act, *3:* 652
Public utilities, New Deal legislation, *4:* 1140–41
Public Works Administration (PWA), *4:* 1139
Puerto Rico, *3:* 850
Pulitzer, Joseph, *3:* 850, 852–53, 853 (ill.)
Pulitzer Prize
Kennedy, John F., *5:* 1279, 1302
Lindbergh, Charles, *4:* 1065
Pure Food and Drug Act, *3:* 895, 915, 924; *4:* 980
Puritan(s), *1:* 56–57; *4:* 1016

Q

"Quads," *4:* 964–65
Quakers (Society of Friends), *1:* 163–64; *3:* 786; *4:* 1088; *5:* 1360
Quasi-War, *1:* 66, 70
Quayle, Dan
election of 1988, *5:* 1519
election of 1992, *5:* 1555
Quezon, Manuel, *4:* 1208
Quota system, immigration, *5:* 1329

R

Rabin, Yitzhak, *5:* 1565 (ill.), 1568
Race relations
Grant, Ulysses S., *3:* 655–56, 659
Harding, Warren G., *4:* 1045
Kennedy, John F., *5:* 1290–91
Race riots (1968), *5:* 1334
Racial segregation. *See* Segregation
Wallace, George, *5:* 1367
Racial segregation. *See also* Segregation

King, Martin Luther, Jr., *5:* 1292–93
Marshall, Thurgood, *5:* 1332
Radical Republicans, *2:* 566, 601, 609, 610, 613; *3:* 752
Grant, Ulysses S., *3:* 656
impeachment of Andrew Johnson, *2:* 616, 619
Stevens, Thaddeus, *2:* 608–9, 609 (ill.), 610, 614 (ill.)
Radio, *4:* 1040, 1045, 1051, 1092
Roosevelt, Franklin D., *4:* 1137, 1150, 1175, 1182
Railroad(s), *2:* 473, 525, 564; *3:* 770, 784. *See also* Infrastructure
Morgan, J. P., *3:* 792–93
overexpansion, *3:* 790
rate reform, *3:* 895; *4:* 1026
transcontinental, *2:* 497–99
World War I, *4:* 976
Railroad Pension Act, *4:* 1172
"Railsplitter." *See* Lincoln, Abraham
Rainbow Battalion, *4:* 1208
Raleigh Tavern (Williamsburg), *1:* 9
Rand, Ayn, *5:* 1566
Randolph, Edmund Jennings, *1:* 20, 22 (ill.); *2:* 361, 362–63, 363 (ill.)
Randolph, Lucretia. *See* Garfield, Lucretia
Randolph, Patsy Jefferson, *1:* 124
Randolph, Peyton, *2:* 362
Rationing, World War II, *4:* 1152
Ray, James Earl, *5:* 1293
Reading and family literacy, *5:* 1531–32, 1533–34, 1623–24
Reagan, Nancy, *5:* 1381 (ill.), **1493–99,** 1493 (ill.), 1497 (ill.), 1498 (ill.)
acting career, *5:* 1494
California's first lady, *5:* 1496
Foster Grandparents Program, *5:* 1496
"Just Say No!" to drugs, *5:* 1497
marriage and family, *5:* 1495
role as first lady, *5:* 1496–98
tough times and retirement, *5:* 1498–99
"The Reagan Revolution," *5:* 1507
Reagan, Ronald, *5:* 1366, 1381 (ill.), **1469–92,** 1471 (ill.), 1476 (ill.), 1479 (ill.), 1485 (ill.), 1488 (ill.), 1490 (ill.), 1498 (ill.)
acting career, *5:* 1473–74, 1495
administration, *5:* 1480
Alzheimer's disease, *5:* 1489, 1493–94, 1499
assassination attempt, *5:* 1479, 1479 (ill.), 1493, 1518
Carter, Jimmy, *5:* 1502

"Revolution Against the Constitution" speech (Garfield), *3: 735–43*

Revolutionary War. *See* American Revolution

Rhode Island, *1: 178*

Richards, Ann, *5: 1603, 1623*

Richardson, Eliot, *5: 1378*

Richardson, William A., *3: 658*

Rickover, Hyman, *5: 1439*

Riders (legislative), *3: 736*

Ridgway, Matthew B., *4: 1210*

Righteous and Harmonious Fists, *3: 858; 4: 1089*

The Rights of Man (Paine), *1: 190*

Rio Grande, *2: 391, 406, 410, 424, 433*

River of Doubt (Roosevelt River), *3: 900*

Roads. *See* Infrastructure

"Roaring Twenties," *4: 979, 1016, 1045, 1049, 1115*

Robards, Lewis, *1: 261, 279*

Robards, Rachel Donelson. *See* Jackson, Rachel

Robb, Charles, *5: 1346*

Robbins, Anne Frances. *See* Reagan, Nancy

Robeson, George, *3: 652*

Robinson, Joseph T., election of 1928, *4: 1096*

Rochambeau, Jean-Baptiste, *1: 16*

Rockefeller, John D., *3: 934; 5: 1408, 1414, 1416*

Rockefeller, Nelson, *5: 1366, 1370, 1412–13, 1413 (ill.), 1417*

Rocky Mountains, *2: 408*

Rodham, Hillary. *See* Clinton, Hillary Rodham

Roe v. Wade, 5: 1477

Rolfe, John, *4: 991*

Roman Catholicism, *4: 1094, 1096; 5: 1280*

Ronald and Nancy Reagan Research Institute, *5: 1489, 1494, 1499*

Roosevelt, Alice Lee, *3: 882, 883, 884 (ill.), 906*

Roosevelt, Anna ("Bamie"), *3: 884*

Roosevelt, Corinne, *3: 906*

Roosevelt, Edith, *3: 905–8, 905 (ill.)*
active household manager, *3: 906–7*
charming first lady, *3: 905, 907*
marriage and family, *3: 906*
Republican spokesperson, *3: 908*

Roosevelt, Eleanor, *4: 1113 (ill.), 1146 (ill.), 1159–65, 1159 (ill.), 1163 (ill.), 1179 (ill.)*
columnist, *4: 1164*
husband stricken with polio, *4: 1162*

most politically active first lady, *4: 1159, 1162–65*
social causes, *4: 1161, 1162–64*
Truman, Harry S., *4: 1196*

Roosevelt, Franklin D., *4: 1123–57, 1125 (ill.), 1131 (ill.), 1144 (ill.), 1146 (ill.), 1153 (ill.)*
administration, *4: 1136*
assassination attempt, *4: 1135*
commander in chief, *4: 1155–56*
death while in office, *4: 1154, 1165, 1196*
declares war on Japan, *4: 1152 (ill.)*
early years, *4: 1126–27*
Eisenhower, Dwight D., *4: 1241*
election of 1920, *4: 1021*
election of 1932, *4: 1104–5, 1106, 1121, 1134*
election of 1936, *4: 1134, 1140–41*
election of 1940, *4: 1134, 1150, 1153–54, 1173*
election of 1944, *4: 1134*
fireside chats, *4: 1179 (ill.), 1179–80*
First Fireside Chat, *4: 1175–80*
First Inaugural Address, *4: 1167–73*
foreign policy, *4: 1145–54, 1156*
Great Depression, *4: 1125, 1162*
Hoover, Herbert, *4: 1121*
marriage and family, *4: 1127–28, 1160–61*
memorable phrases, *4: 1182*
New Deal, *4: 1125, 1135–45, 1163–64*
one hundred days, *4: 1135–37*
Perkins, Frances, *4: 1143*
physically challenged, *4: 1126, 1130–31, 1132–33, 1162*
political career, *4: 1128–33, 1161–62*
presidency, *4: 1135–54*
progressive legislation, *4: 1137–45*
Smith, Alfred E., *4: 1095*
superstitious nature, *4: 1150*
Supreme Court, *4: 1027*
War Message to the American People, *4: 1181–85*
World War II, *4: 1125–26, 1148–49, 1153, 1155–56*
Yalta Conference, *4: 1149, 1154, 1156, 1195*

Roosevelt, Sara, *4: 1179 (ill.)*

Roosevelt, Theodore, *3: 877–904, 879 (ill.), 885 (ill.), 887 (ill.), 889 (ill.), 898 (ill.), 932 (ill.)*
administration, *3: 897*

U-2 aerial surveillance incident,
4: 1250–51
United Nations, *4:* 977
Vietnam War, *5:* 1330–35, 1338,
1391–92, 1396–97
Watergate scandal, *5:* 1359,
1375–82
World War I, *4:* 973–76, 1005,
1092
World War II, *4:* 1147, 1150–52,
1221–23, 1226–27, 1240–42
United States Bank, *1:* 228
United States v. Susan B. Anthony, 3:
787
University of Virginia, *1:* 214
Upper Creek nation, *1:* 263
Urban areas, 1920s, *4:* 1115
Urban laborers, Populism, *3:* 823
U.S. citizenship, Native Americans,
4: 1066
U.S. Civil Service Commission. *See*
Civil Service Commission
U.S. Congress. *See* Congress
U.S. Constitution. *See* Bill of Rights;
Constitution; specific amend-
ments, e.g., Twenty-third
Amendment
U.S. Forest Service. *See* Forest Ser-
vice
U.S. House of Representatives. *See*
House of Representatives
U.S. Housing Authority, *4:* 1140
U.S. Navy. *See* Navy
U.S. Senate. *See* Senate
U.S. Steel Corporation, *3:* 793, 934,
935
U.S. Supreme Court. *See* Supreme
Court
U.S.S. *K–1, 5:* 1439
U.S.S. *Maddox, 5:* 1331
U.S.S. *Maine, 3:* 849, 850, 851 (ill.),
855, 887
U.S.S. *Mayaguez, 5:* 1417
U.S.S. *Missouri, 4:* 1199, 1199 (ill.),
1226
U.S.S. *Pomfret, 5:* 1439
U.S.S. *Seawolf, 5:* 1439
U.S.S. *Shaw, 4:* 1151 (ill.)
USSR. *See* Union of Soviet Socialist
Republics (USSR)
Utilities
federal regulation, *3:* 899
New Deal legislation, *4:* 1140–41

V

Valley Forge, *1:* 11 (ill.), 15
Washington, Martha, *1:* 33

Van Buren, Angelica Singleton, *1:*
167; *2:* 377
hostess for her father-in-law, *1:*
311, 312
Van Buren, Hannah, *1:* **311–13,**
311 (ill.),
marriage and family, *1:* 312
Van Buren, Martin, *1:* 266, 273
(ill.), 277, **291–310,** 293 (ill.),
303 (ill.), 308 (ill.); *3:* 690
Adams, John Quincy, *1:* 246
Calhoun, John C., *1:* 300
early years, *1:* 294–95
election of 1832, *1:* 267
election of 1836, *1:* 301; *5:*
1612–13
election of 1840, *2:* 336
election of 1844, *2:* 401, 402
election of 1848, *1:* 308–9; *2:* 439
Inaugural Address, *1:* **315–21**
Jackson, Andrew, *1:* 297–98,
300–301, 309, 315
legal career, *1:* 295–96, 312
marriage and family, *1:* 296–97,
312
Mexican War, *2:* 425
political career, *1:* 297–301
presidency, *1:* 302–8
retirement, *1:* 309
Van Devanter, Willis, *3:* 936 (ill.)
Van Ness, Marcia, *2:* 417
V-E Day (Victory-in-Europe Day), *4:*
1196
Venezuela, *3:* 791
Veracruz, Battle of, *4:* 969
Vermont
Coolidge, Calvin, *4:* 1051–52,
1055–56
Veterans
Vietnam War, *5:* 1338
World War I, *4:* 1104, 1113
**Veto Message Regarding the Bank
of the United States** (Jackson),
1: **285–90**
Veto, presidential. *See* Presidential
veto
Vice president
becomes president after death of
predecessor, *2:* 358, 364, 465,
607; *3:* 758, 890; *4:* 1056,
1196; *5:* 1323
first, *1:* 60–62
John Adams' view, *1:* 60
resignation of predecessor, *5:*
1408–9
Vicksburg, Battle of, *2:* 568; *3:* 640,
644, 650, 667
Vicksburg, Mississippi, *2:* 565
Victoria, queen of England, *2:* 536;
3: 660, 668